DARE TO BE A
DIFFERENCE
Maker
Volume 2

DIFFERENCE MAKERS WHO DARE TO LIVE
WITH PASSION, FOLLOW THEIR PURPOSE
AND COMMIT TO HELPING OTHERS!

MICHELLE PRINCE

DARE TO BE A
DIFFERENCE
Maker

Volume 2

Dedication

To all the "Difference Makers" in the world who are making
a difference by following your heart.
Thank you for letting your "light" shine!

Introduction

For many years, as I worked in "Corporate America", I would say to myself, *"I just want to make a difference!"* I was selling software and I'm sure I was making some difference for my clients but not in the way I wanted to. I wanted to help, serve, encourage and motivate people. I wanted to make a positive impact on their lives but I didn't know how…how could just one person really make a significant difference? So, I didn't…for a long time. I continued to work in an area that wasn't my passion or calling. I didn't follow my heart and God's promptings to go in the direction of my purpose and dreams. Instead, I just let year after year go by feel unfulfilled, unhappy and spiritually broken.

That is, until one day in 2008 when I had my "aha" moment. It hit me like a ton of bricks that it's my responsibility to follow my passions and purpose. No one can do that for me. I took action to write my first book, Winning In Life Now, began to speak, motivate and mentor others to live their best life and, as they say, "the rest is history."

What I found over this journey is that we all have a desire to make a difference. We all want to live with passion and follow our God-given callings; our purpose. It's through this understanding that I decided to write this series of books.

Dare To Be A Difference Maker 2, is my vision to have a unique collection of narratives, not only from inspired leaders, but also from those I see making a difference and impacting others in their everyday personal and professional life. These stories are about real people who are making a real difference even on a small scale.

My mission in creating the **"Difference Maker Movement"** and in writing the series of *Dare To Be A Difference Maker* books is that you will gain inspiration, wisdom & the courage you need in order to get through life's tough challenges and make a difference for others in the process.

So many people I speak with these days discuss their issues as though they are losing hope. It is my vision for this book to reach the masses and have a powerful effect on people in their everyday lives. It is my prayer that this book, and all the volumes, will breathe new life into your mind and spirit and that it will inspire you to take action in order to help others.

I've selected an exclusive group of difference-makers who I know can motivate, inspire and be a part of a movement to change people's lives. Everyone can do this; it just takes commitment and honoring of our unique and sacred gifts. It is to those people, I dedicate this book.

From one "Difference Maker" to another,

Michelle

P.S. Do you or anyone you know, have a story about making a difference? We are currently interviewing authors for our next book and would love to have you join us in this amazing journey. To submit an entry, please contact Info@PrincePerformance.com for more details. While one powerful story can be fascinating, many can move mountains!

Table of Contents

1

Becoming a "Difference Maker"

By Michelle Prince

I truly believe that most people want to do good in this world and make a positive impact in their communities, families and around the world. I believe we all want to be "Difference Makers."

I first heard the term "Difference Maker" when I was in my twenties working for Zig Ziglar. It was a part of the company's mission statement and it made a lasting impression on me. "To be a difference maker in the personal, family and business lives of enough people to make a positive difference in America and the World." Having seen Mr. Ziglar live that mission made me want to do the same so I made it my goal in life to become a "Difference Maker" too.

What is the secret to becoming a "Difference Maker?" It's a combination of many things such as finding your purpose, living with passion, overcoming obstacles and much more but it starts with taking action! It starts with defining specific goals for your life and making a plan to accomplish them!

Zig Ziglar is a big proponent of setting goals. He is always asking: What do you want to be? What do you want to do? What do you want to have? I have learned a lot from his leadership. In the Prince household, we have a tradition around setting goals. (I'll admit right now that I may have forced this tradition at first, since I am the one who is into personal development in our family.) Every New Year's Eve, we gather around, and each of us gets a piece of paper to write down five personal goals for the coming year—five things we want to be; five things we want to do; five things we want to have. We all do this, even my kids.

We started this tradition when my oldest son was four years old, and their goals when they were little were kind of sweet and funny sometimes. They would list things like going roller skating, making the soccer team, or going to Disney World. But throughout the year, when they would accomplish one of their goals, we would go to their room where the list was posted and check that goal off the list. It gave all of us a terrific sense of accomplishment.

We repeated the exercise as a family, too. As a family, what do we want to be? What do we want to do? What do we want to have? We worked toward our collective goals and grew as a family.

When my son was six years old, he said something that completely blew me away. It was the day he realized he had met all five goals he had written down for the year.

"Mom, this is so cool!" he said. "All you have to do is write it down, and it happens!"

I got such a kick out of that. We tend to complicate things so much as adults, but this little six year old got it. It was that simple. All we have to do is figure out what we want and write it down. Then, it is much more likely to happen.

Now, leading back to the topic of goals, I have a question for you. Why do some people accomplish their goals and others don't?

I am asked this question all the time, and there are many answers.

There are some people who just refuse to take the time to set goals. They think they already know what they want in life, so they shouldn't have to write it down. I can tell you from my years of coaching experience, those are typically the people who don't accomplish any of their goals.

Other people create goals, but their goals are not really tied to their passion or purpose in life. That is exactly why I think it is so important to first discover your passions before you do anything else. If you're not setting goals around something you are truly passionate about, what are the chances you will achieve those goals? You have to tie that in and make sure you look at it very closely before you set your goals.

Another reason people do not accomplish their goals is that they set a goal and never look at it again. I have been guilty of this—I set a goal, put it in the drawer, and then forget about it for months. The goal has to be in a place where you will see it every day, so that you can maintain your focus on achieving it.

There are many, many reasons why people do not achieve their goals, but one reason surpasses all the rest: procrastination.

Procrastination is such a prevalent barrier to reaching your goals. When I speak to groups, I often ask, "How many of you are procrastinators?"

You wouldn't believe the response! People are practically climbing over their chairs to claim this ailment—as if they're proud of it. It's nothing to be proud of, though.

We act like procrastination is some sort of disease that we cannot fight, but think about other aspects of your life. Did you procrastinate checking your email this morning? Did you procrastinate going on Twitter or Facebook? Probably not.

But are you procrastinating getting your work done? What about taking that trip you have always wanted to take? Procrastination is a choice, and we tend to reserve it for the big things. We procrastinate on the things that matter the most; the things that will bring the most joy and satisfaction. It's really silly when you think about it, but that's what we do. We put the important things on the back burner.

Let me tell you, your days of procrastinating are numbered. You are no longer going to wait for someday. I will walk you through a plan right now that will help you overcome procrastination and start making a difference NOW!

Step 1: Identify what's holding you back.

There are legitimate reasons why some people procrastinate.

They may have difficulty concentrating or other physical or mental hurdles to overcome. But for most of us, that's not the case.

You might be procrastinating because of fear. Fear of failure, of course, but also fear of succeeding. If you accomplish this goal, then what?

Think about why you are procrastinating. Is it fear? Anxiety? What is holding you back? You have to identify it before you can remove it. Ask yourself: Why am I procrastinating on this? Do I not believe in myself? Do I think I'm not worth it? What is the negative jabber in my head around this? Am I getting anything positive out of putting this off?

Step 2: Practice discipline and motivation.

The simple truth is achieving anything worthwhile in your life takes practice. If someone comes up to you and tells you they have an easy way for you to make a million dollars with almost no effort, run! You can achieve anything you want, but it's going to take some work.

That doesn't mean it has to be hard, though.

When you are following your goals and working on something you're passionate about, it doesn't feel like work. It's not hard, because you're right where you want to be.

When I wrote my book, *Winning in Life Now*, I got the inspiration for the book at a live event. I'm a big believer in live events, because being around other people is inspiring. I made the decision at that event to write my book.

So I went home, got out my laptop, and started cranking out that book. In three weeks, I had the entire thing written. Now, it took eight months to get all of the final pieces in place, but the big push only took three weeks. During that time, I stayed up later than I've ever stayed up; I got up earlier than I ever have before; I worked harder than I have ever worked in my life—and I had a full-time job on top of all this! And of course, motherhood never takes a break, either, so I was one busy woman.

It didn't matter. I was working very, very hard, but it wasn't difficult, because the project was pulling me, rather than me pushing the project. It was exhilarating.

If you choose a goal that is aligned with your passion, you will have the same experience. You will have to practice and develop a strong discipline and motivation, but it will not be hard, because your heart will be in it.

Step 3: Dust off your dreams.

What do you think would happen if I stood in front of a classroom of kindergarten students and asked them, "What do you want to be when you grow up? What are your dreams?"

They wouldn't hesitate to give their answers. Kids have dreams—big dreams—and they have every intension of making those dreams come true.

Do you remember your dreams? Have you thought about them lately? Dust off those old dreams, if they haven't been out in the light for awhile. Take a second look at them. They will rekindle your passion and help you to move forward in achieving your goals.

I caught a glimpse of my dream when I went to that Zig Ziglar seminar at age eighteen. I didn't even know what passion was back then, but something fired up inside of me when I was around people, successful people, who wanted more out of life. I am just as enthusiastic about this dream today as I was at eighteen.

So remind yourself of your passions. Dust off those dreams, and set goals to achieve them. Nothing strikes procrastination down faster than a passionate person with goals and plans to achieve their dreams.

Step 4: Start living now.

This one is deceptively simple, but procrastination really boils down to one thing: inaction. If you start living now, you launch into action and thwart evil procrastination. You have to make a conscious decision that you are worth it and then just do it. No waiting.

No putting it off. Start living now! Why would you want to wait to realize your dreams and live your passion every day?

I would like to tell you a story about my friend Tom. I also included this story in my book *Winning in Life Now*, because I feel it is such an important illustration.

* * * *

Tom was in his early forties. He had it all: a wonderful family, young kids in elementary school, a beautiful wife. He was one of those guys who just seemed to do everything right. He ate right, worked out, took good care of himself. He did it all.

So Tom went to his annual doctor's appointment, and his doctor discovered a little lump. They did a bunch of tests, and everything was just a bit off.

"Don't worry about it," the doctor assured him. "I'm sure it's fine. But let's just do a few more tests to be certain."

About a week later, Tom and his wife received a phone call from the doctor asking them to come back into the office. It didn't sound like he would be giving them terrific news, but nothing could have prepared them for what they heard that day. Not only did Tom have cancer, but it was in Stage IV, and he had six months to live. Six months.

What do you do with that diagnosis?

At first, Tom was mad. He flew through all of the stages of grief.

"This isn't fair!" he ranted. "How could this be happening to me? I did everything right!"

Then the sadness kicked in. "I have kids and a wife. What will happen to my beautiful family when I'm no longer here? I will miss seeing my children grow up. I will not get to grow old with my wife."

And finally, he came to acceptance. He realized that no matter what he did in that moment, he could not avoid the fact that there was a very good chance he would not be around in a few months.

That's when Tom made a decision. He said, "I'm only going to do the things I really, really love to do, and I'm going to spend whatever days I have left with the people I love the most."

That's exactly what he did. He spent time with his family, enjoying every minute with them. Another thing he loved to do was write. He had put it aside when life got busy with work and family, but in these final months, he started writing at night after his kids went to bed. He wrote letters and stories about what he did with them when they were young. He collected all of those wonderful memories in his words, so that his family could cherish them. It was a legacy that would become very valuable to them in years to come.

Tom died six-and-a-half months after that doctor's appointment. His family was understandably devastated to lose him, but Tom's wife said something to me at the funeral that has stuck with me ever since. It is something that still inspires me to keep going after my goals and do what I love to do.

She said, "Tom came to me about a week before he died and said that he was grateful for the prognosis, because without it he never would have experienced what it really feels like to live."

That hit me right between the eyes. Why do we need a prognosis of death to get over whatever is holding us back? Why do we need somebody to tell us we're sick before we decide that it's okay to follow our dreams and goals?

Don't wait until you receive a fatal prognosis before you decide to get busy and live. You have an opportunity right now to launch into action, and that is exactly my point when it comes to overcoming procrastination. There is nothing in the world that is more important than your dreams and your goals. But you do have to take action and make it happen. At the end of the day, all you have to do is get started. Take one step.

What works for you may not work for someone else, so you have to find your own path. For me personally, I had to get away from it all. I took a day off of work and got away from distractions of family and business and everything else. That's when I sat down and asked myself, "What do I really want out of life?" In the stillness, I was able to answer.

Start journaling; write down your ideas. Find out what it is you want, and then make a commitment to go after it.

There is one thing that many of us never fully realize: you are in control. You make choices every moment that put you exactly where you are today. If you want to be somewhere else, make different choices. You may not particularly like that statement, but the point is, no matter what is going on in your life, you have control over your attitude and your actions. What do you want to accomplish? Find out, and then get busy!

Make a commitment to follow your dreams. If you feel held back by responsibilities at work or at home, I urge you to make the commitment anyway—on behalf of your family and your business. You are much more valuable to everyone around you if you are leading a life that inspires them. So if you can't do it for yourself, do it for your family. When you inspire them, they will find the courage to follow your lead.

That's what happened to me when I wrote my first book. Sure, I was proud of the achievement of publishing a book, but there was so much more. I actually changed my kids' lives and so many others who were around me when I accomplished this goal. It had nothing to do with the content of the book. It was because I took action. I put one foot in front of the other and achieved a significant goal in my life. That inspired them to do the same.

You can do this, too. You can inspire others. You can be a "Difference Maker." Just make a commitment to yourself. If you can't do that, make a commitment to somebody else. Decide that you are done waiting; you will go after your goals today.

I'm not special. I'm no different than you. I'm a wife, a mom, a friend, a sister; I have a company; I'm busy; I work. So if I can do it, you can do it. And I really truly believe that.

Life is so short. We all have an opportunity to be extraordinary. Don't wait until it's too late to grab on to your opportunity. Don't be ordinary. Take action. Overcome your procrastination, and make this year the best of your life. Be the "Difference Maker" you were born to be. ∎

Michelle Prince

As a best-selling author, Zig Ziglar Motivational Speaker, business owner of multiple companies, wife of 15 years and mother of two young boys, Michelle Prince had to learn the art of juggling her personal and professional life successfully. Most people are juggling too many things, procrastinating and not getting as much done as they want, which leads to a life of frustration and unfulfilled goals. Michelle is passionate about helping people live with purpose, follow their passion and take action in big ways!

Michelle's passion ignited at the tender age of 18 when she met her mentor, Zig Ziglar. She completely embraced personal development and goal setting techniques helping her to realize her BIG goal of working for Zig Ziglar in 1994. Since that time, Michelle has journeyed through the ups and downs of life all the while holding on to her passion of inspiring, motivating and encouraging others to be the best that they can be.

*Michelle has learned the secret to living a happier, more abundant life and she's on a mission to show you how to stop juggling, overcome procrastination and get more done in your business, leadership and life! It's time for "America's Productivity Coach" to give you the tools to STOP being busy **being** busy and start being a "Difference Maker."*

Michelle Prince
CEO, Prince Performance Group & Performance Publishing
Best-Selling Author
Zig Ziglar Motivational Speaker
6841 Virginia Pkwy, Suite 103#124
McKinney, TX 75071
469-443-8768
Info@PrincePerformance.com
http://www.MichellePrince.com

2

⚜

From Reluctant Reader to Passionate Reader

By Danny Brassell, Ph.D.

My name is Danny Brassell, and I was a reluctant reader. Sound like an introduction to a 12-step program?

It is ironic and fitting that folks have deemed me "America's Leading Reading Ambassador," as I did not grow up an avid reader. Perhaps my own struggles are what shaped my interest in helping today's parents and educators inspire children to love reading.

When I was younger, I absolutely despised reading. My parents say that when I was a toddler I used to wander into their bedroom library, tear pages from their books, and eat the pages. They'd smack me on the hands and say, "Stay away from the books, Danny! Stay away from the books!" So for years I used those episodes as the excuse for my lack of interest in all things book-related, much to the chagrin of my parents and teachers.

My father was a librarian, and public libraries always had a way of putting me off. In fact, growing up, public libraries terrified me. The furniture was uncomfortable. Public libraries smelled funny. Cranky elderly women would constantly "shush" me to be quiet. And then there were the ever-present perverts, street urchins, and freaks who thought they were vampires hanging out among the book stacks.

My mom and dad were concerned that I was not a reader, but they never panicked since I performed well in school. They'd try to peak my interest by subscribing to magazines like *Boys' Life* and *Sports Illustrated*, and they'd allow me to stay up past my bedtime if I was reading in bed. However, perhaps out of the spite only a defiant child can show a parent, I never allowed my parents' admirable efforts to take hold.

It was in the seventh grade that I discovered an interest in reading. Will Hobbs taught my reading class. Yes, the same Will Hobbs who is now a best-selling author of young adult outdoor adventures like *Jason's Gold* and *Down the Yukon*. He taught at my middle school in Colorado. I am sure his teaching experiences provided him with plenty of background research to know how to pique the reading interests of incorrigible adolescents like me.

Mr. Hobbs had over five thousand books in his classroom library. Every day at the beginning of class, he told us what he was reading, we told him what we were reading, and for the rest of the class— we read! Whenever I finished a book I would go up to Mr. Hobbs and he'd put down the book he was reading and ask me three or four questions about what I'd read. If my answers satisfied him, I earned a point. Any book up to two hundred pages was worth one point. Every extra hundred pages garnered another point. Students needed twenty-five points to earn an "A" for the class, and the top five point earners had their names written on the chalkboard in the classroom. And—I—wanted—my—name—on—that—board!

Jules Verne's *Twenty Thousand Leagues Under the Sea* was a five-hundred-page book worth four points! It also happened to be an excellent Disney film starring James Mason and Kirk Douglas, and I didn't have much interest in reading a five-hundred-page book. So I approached Mr. Hobbs, he asked me four questions, and I learned a valuable lesson that day: movies aren't always like the books. And guess what Mr. Hobbs did? He gave me the four points. That's when I learned a terrific teaching strategy: guilt works. From that point on, I read every word of every page of every book. By the end of the semester I had earned forty-four points, well above and beyond what Mr. Hobbs challenged us to read.

Mr. Hobbs also used the greatest single strategy I've ever seen a teacher use to get a kid interested in reading: he found out what I was interested in. I loved football, and hardly a week went by when Mr. Hobbs didn't hand me a book about football and quip something like, "Here's a book about John Elway. I know how much you like football, and I know you'll love this book." What are the odds that I would open up that book? A hundred percent. I learned that there's nothing more powerful than someone significant in your life—a teacher, coach, pastor, parent, friend, or sibling—handing you something to read and telling you they were thinking of you. It is such a simple strategy and yet so powerful.

Of course, after taking Mr. Hobbs's class, I suffered teacher after teacher who assigned Classics about ancient subjects of little interest that usually had really depressing endings. I'm convinced that the definition of a Classic is a book that no one enjoys but everyone is pressured to read. My interest in reading waned.

Then I studied in Madrid during a semester abroad program my junior year of college. Spain overwhelmed me, as I quickly learned that it's not easy living among people who speak a different language. I suffered headaches from constantly trying to think and read in Spanish. For the first time since middle school, I yearned to read something—anything—in English. A girl in my program handed me a copy of John Grisham's *The Pelican Brief*, and I devoured it in a day. Then I repeated the process with Grisham's *A Time to Kill*. I wound up spending over thirty dollars for a battered paperback copy of The Firm, and that's when I knew I had an addiction. Gradually, I advanced to read Sydney Sheldon and Mary Higgins Clark and Jeffrey Archer. My passion for reading was back!

Upon graduation from college I could have done many things. I had worked for a homeless shelter, a United States Congressman, and for the American Society of Newspaper Editors. I could have worked for any newspaper in the country, but the dismal salaries in journalism prompted me to look elsewhere. Ironically, a school district in South Central Los Angeles offered me a teaching position on an emergency credential that paid significantly more than any reporting job. So I became a teacher for the most noble of reasons: the high pay.

Teaching in an inner-city school with low-income African-American and Latino students forever changed the way I view the world. For the first time I saw children denied the resources that were fully at my disposal as a child. While books surrounded me as a child, my students had inadequate resources in their schools and even fewer in their homes. There were no bookstores nearby and a public library that had restricted hours. Most of my students—especially the boys—had little interest in books, and most read several grade levels below their own. Most lived in single-mother households and their moms were so busy working they had little time to read to their children. The school showed little interest in inspiring students to read or even teaching students how to read. Rather, the school where I taught emphasized test scores so it could maintain its funding.

I became angry.

My entire school district reported having fifty-six thousand books in all of its K-12 school libraries. As over twenty-nine thousand students attended classes, that amounted to an average of less than two books per student. Some of the books on the shelves were well over fifty years old, for example, prophesying the possibility that man may one day walk on the moon. Recent titles were sparse, and some of the encyclopedia sets were older than similar ones I used as a child. Can you imagine a library with so few titles you'd be lucky to get "a" book, let alone one that you actually wanted? No wonder none of my students had any interest in reading. They had no exposure to reading. Becoming a reader without access to books is like becoming a surfer without an ocean—it's not going to happen.

I created my own non-profit organization, and in a little over three years we donated over eighty-four thousand books to ten different schools in the district. To obtain reading materials, I employed a two-step strategy. Step one: I asked businesses, organizations, and individuals to donate reading resources for students in my school district. Step two: I always wrote a thank-you card, which did wonders in a society that's becoming more devoid of manners and common courtesy by the day. Working with classroom teachers, I created classroom libraries that captivated children by building on their interests. We'd decorate "library corners" with cool posters, provide comfortable reading cushions and stuffed animals and, most importantly, flood the classroom with an abundance of cool books. I thought we were doing great until I met Brandon.

When I met him, Brandon Keefe was an eight-year-old boy who created (with his mother) a non-profit organization called BookEnds that had a similar mission to provide access to reading materials for students in under-resourced areas. His organization did what mine did, but he did it a lot better (and Brandon never ceased to inspire me). He mobilized kids to help other kids by leading book drives and increasing public awareness about the dearth of reading materials in many schools. I joined the Board of Directors of Book-Ends and shared my resources. Since its inception, over two hundred and fifty thousand student volunteers have helped BookEnds donate over two million books to distressed schools, group homes, and juvenile detention facilities. There are incredible organizations like BookEnds that fight everyday to ensure all children have access to quality reading materials.

Meanwhile, even though I was rolling in the bucks as a public school teacher, I decided to take a tutoring job after school to work with "underachieving geniuses." (I've always referred to all of my students as underachieving geniuses.) Working with reluctant and struggling readers became my passion, and I was blessed to have a knack for helping students become better readers and passionate readers. Four out of five struggling readers I worked with were boys, as boys tend to be a lot pickier about the types of books they'll read (joke books, nonfiction, dinosaurs, and bodily functions are among their preferred topics). I let student interests guide their reading lists, and I quickly became interested in the fact that the way students became better readers had little to do with what they read and everything to do with how much they read. I decided to do whatever I could to better understand the phenomenon.

Taking night courses to earn graduate and doctorate degrees in literacy, I worked with some extraordinary minds dedicated to helping children become better readers. I learned that there are two types of students: illiterate and alliterate. An "illiterate" person cannot read, while an "alliterate" person is someone who chooses not to read. Based on my experience, I've determined there's no such thing as "illiteracy," just different degrees of literacy. Some folks are better at reading Shakespeare, while others read road signs, while still others have mastered reading the instructions accompanying a recently-purchased item from IKEA. There is one thing all great readers have in common, though: they read a lot.

I began writing articles and books about how to encourage children to read more, and then I took my show on the road preaching my vision across North America. I created one of Google's top-ranked websites for book club recommendations, www.lazyreaders.com, in order to attract non-readers to reading books for all ages that are less than two hundred and fifty pages. I've interviewed some of the leading researchers and teachers in education, and my personal speaking website, www.dannybrassell.com, receives hundreds of weekly queries from educators, parents, and business leaders seeking ways to improve their children's reading attitudes and aptitudes. Most importantly, I've become the husband of a beautiful wife and a father who cherishes reading aloud to my three young children throughout the day and especially before bedtime. My journey has taken me from reluctant reader to teacher to philanthropist to reading advocate.

My name is Danny Brassell, and I am an avid reader. ∎

Danny Brassell, Ph.D.

America's leading reading ambassador, DANNY BRASSELL (www.dannybrassell.com) is a professor in the Teacher Education Department at California State University-Dominguez Hills, highly sought national speaker and founder of The Lazy Readers' Book Club (www.lazyreaders.com), Google's #1-ranked site for cool "short book recommendations." He is the author of over 50 journal and newspaper articles and nine books, including "A Baker's Dozen of Lessons Learned from the Teaching Trenches." *His television show* "People Make a Difference" *airs throughout Greater Los Angeles and on YouTube. Danny helps parents and educators inspire kids to love reading and achieve more.*

Danny Brassell, Ph.D.
www.dannybrassell.com
"America's Leading Reading Ambassador"
Get FREE cool, short book recommendations at: www.lazyreaders.com

3

At My Father's Knee

By Sheila Johnson

My early life seemed just ordinary. I grew up surrounded by three older brothers, one older sister and a mother and father who adored each other to the end. I loved being the youngest child and especially relished the constant affection from my precious mother. Many times I wished time would just stand still as I ran about our farm and dairy, mostly playing and dreaming—too young to work. We had chickens, pigs, cows, and horses. In the fields we grew cotton, corn, and wheat. My mother always had a delicious vegetable garden along with her beautiful flower garden. How could life be better!

I especially admired my father—six feet tall and handsome. There was just something about him that made me want to follow him around as much as he would allow. Sometimes he would say, "This is not a place for little girls." This was usually in the barn. Of course I loved to sneak to the barn as often as I could to observe all the activities. I focused on how Daddy took control, making all the major decisions and giving directions to my older brothers regarding their chores. My brothers never questioned him. From an early age my mother taught us to respect Daddy and his time. She would also threaten to tell him when we misbehaved and that we would surely receive his wrath—which rarely occurred. You see, he was a quiet, gentle man. My father was my hero!

Being the youngest of five children, I spent my childhood looking up to and observing, questioning, and learning from my siblings. I loved them, but did not always agree with their behavior. I quickly adjusted my actions so that I would stay out of trouble as I wanted attention and recognition for doing the right things. When I was unsure I just watched Daddy.

Watching Mom cooking, ironing, and sewing, I promised myself this would not be a part of my world. Daddy's world was full of adventure—this was the life for me! Wearing my red cowboy boots and overalls (like Daddy) and going off to town with him in his pick-up truck was thrilling! He also paid the bills and gave my mom a weekly allowance for the household. She was a full-time mom.

One day I told my mom I was not interested in cooking and sewing and when I got "big" I would buy my clothes and hire a cook. She just shook her head.

Lying on the ground, watching the clouds drift by with my dog was a favorite pastime. Occasionally an airplane way up high would pass over with a stream of white smoke behind interrupting my day dreams. How big is that airplane? How does it take off, land, and fly? No, I would probably never know—but then again, maybe someday I would. Would I be afraid? Then back to the clouds I turned. Why would I ever want to leave this perfect place and time?

When my brothers and sister left for school I was sad to be left behind. I found solace with my dog. And as Mom settled down in the afternoon for a nap after her chores, she took the time to teach me to read. Wow! I could travel around the world with my tiny little book.

Reading, watching the clouds, and long walks with my puppy became a routine. I dreamed of what could be—maybe a new home for my mom, a new pick-up for my dad. I began to yearn for what I did not know.

My great adventure was finally beginning as I entered first grade and was able to go to school with my sister. I had arrived! Running, playing and learning about new things and a life different from my own was so exciting. I was curious about math, science, reading, and geography. I loved it above all, and it was my own special experience. Of course, I also loved receiving recognition and praise, so I strived to achieve mostly A's on my report card. Hooray! I thought anyone could do it if he or she wanted it bad enough. I was a driven child.

The school years flew by too quickly. Sports became a very important part of my life. Competing was in my blood. It began with academics then spread to sports. I loved to win and was very willing to pay the price by practicing and studying. In retrospect, boredom was probably the biggest motivation as it was a way of entertaining myself. And always on my mind was what Daddy would think of my grades and athletic achievements.

We left the farm when I was twelve years old and moved to a small town where I graduated Number Two in my class and became the top athlete in school. How did this happen? Was it luck, courage, discipline, or a result of repeated challenges to myself to take action and trust what lies ahead? Along the way my class voted me Class Treasurer for three years. By now Daddy was Assistant City Manager in a small town about seven miles away from where we lived. His job was primarily accounting. The parallel, as I look back, is astounding. He is such a part of my soul.

Attending church and the importance of giving back to those less fortunate was a part of everyday life in our home. My parents taught me the importance of a "good name." Today I suppose it would be called "Branding." One of my favorite quotes today is, "Be the change you want to see in the world," by Gandhi.

After school and college I spent the next twenty years in the technology industry. It was during this time that I received many awards and was recognized for many "female first" achievements. As a result, the doors opened for many women in this male-dominated industry. I felt that perhaps this was my purpose in life.

Relaxing and slowing down are not something I can do for long. The financial industry seemed like a natural next step. I studied and received a Securities License. Finance came easily to me and is a gift I received from my father. After a few years I became restless again for a greater purpose. What can I do to make a difference? How can my life have more significance? Where is a niche or a need for my gifts? Where can I take my knowledge, experience, and wisdom? These were questions I asked myself.

Growing up in my father's shadow and working in the male-dominated technology and financial industries were easy for me. I asked myself, "Where can I be of service with the days I have left?" Maybe I can help women to understand and manage their finances. This was definitely out of my comfort zone. These women cook, plan parties, decorate, raise children, and go to the spa. What do I have in common with them? They are just like my sister and my mom.

My father died at age sixty-two. Mother lived to the age of eighty-seven and I was privileged to handle her finances until she passed. How very fortunate I was that my father had managed his assets in a way that money was never an issue for her. She lived for twenty-five years with no financial worries, and left a generous financial legacy to her children.

So the baton has passed to me. My mother has been gone for five years and during this time I've focused my energy on helping women achieve their financial goals so that they might leave a legacy based on their own very personal passions. Growing up in a household where love was abundant but money was not, taught me to appreciate the choices money well managed allows. And I am now more aware of my God-given talents that I alone am responsible for using to give back to others.

I believe every woman should feel smart and confident when it comes to money. Not only is it my calling, I've made it my goal and duty to continue to teach what I've learned, experienced, and what comes natural to me so that others can live a more financially secure life.

I am my Father's Daughter! ∎

Sheila Johnson

Outstanding in her community for being a devoted advocate for Financial Education and Guidance for Women, Sheila Johnson holds a 6 & 63 Security License, Insurance License, is a Registered Representative and the Managing Partner of Johnson Insurance & Financial— a Boutique Financial Service Company since 1969. She is a 2010 & 2011 recipient of the Million Dollar Round Table award for her performance and was voted one of the Top Business Women by the Chamber of Commerce in McKinney, TX the last (2) years. Sheila & her husband Bob founded a Scholarship Foundation benefiting the children of the McKinney Police & Firefighters. She created a CD, "Smart Women/Safe Money." Sheila provides one on one tutoring, Lunch & Learn Events and encourages women to identify their passion (what is in their heart). She states, "This is your Precious Life and Your Dreams Matter".

A Financial Plan will not only affect your life, but also the lives of generations to come. You can make a difference!

Shelia Johnson
Registered Representative
JOHNSON INSURANCE & FINANCIAL
www.JohnsonInsuranceandFinancial.com
7290 Virginia Pkwy, Suite 2500
McKinney, TX 75071
214.726.0000

4

❧

Black Socks and Oatmeal
A Simpler Way to True Success

Ejaz Tahir, DDS, MS

Black Socks and Oatmeal (BSOM) represents a discipline; a ritual, a life philosophy. It's a time-saving, life simplifying measure that— by already having decided the color socks you'll wear and what you'll eat for breakfast each day—allows you to focus on more important activities. You are more productive with your time.

BSOM allows leverage and autopilot by speeding up your process. While others are working out issues, you've already applied BSOM and are on to the next project.

BSOM is about going to the fundamentals. It's about sleeping and waking up at the same time each day; taking a certain percentage of money out for passive income generation; dedicating a certain amount of time to read, think and plan each day; and never wavering.

BSOM may sound boring, but I will outline how this discipline leads to freedom and provides the ultimate reward of a fulfilling life.

My story will be familiar to many of you, especially first generation immigrants to the United States. So much of the greatest guidance and advice is not new at all. If it is enduring, it's because it is based on universal truths about integrity, honesty, discipline, and focus. The real job of any teacher is to keep repeating the universal truths to those seeking to take control of their lives and increase their potential for happiness and spiritual awareness. The job of the teacher is to find ways to teach the enduring truths by retelling the lessons in ever-new ways, in a context that speaks to the current seeker. Passing the teachings on with the right energy can help the lessons 'click' and thus make the magic happen.

The teachings of one of the writers in this collection of stories and lessons will, I have absolutely no doubt, make it 'click' for many of you. I make my contribution to this collection with faith that my story and teaching will be just the right thing, at the right time, and said in just the right way for it to 'click' for some of you. The general details of my family's experience may sound so familiar to you that it may seem clichéd, but I assure you that it is a true personal testament and no less meaningful for its familiarity.

* * * * *

My father moved from Pakistan to the U.S. in 1979, when I was twelve years old, along with my mother and four siblings and only twenty-seven dollars in his pocket. He sought to find a better life in the United States and escape religious persecution. To say it was a leap of faith is a colossal understatement. My father had a PhD from a Pakistani university in veterinarian medicine, but that degree was not recognized in the U.S. He was a highly educated man who was forced to start from scratch when he and my mother decided to make life better for their family. My mother was a teacher in Pakistan, but, of course, was not able to teach when she arrived in America.

I used to think that not many people in the U.S. could relate to that experience—the complete annihilation of one's professional identity. I think that now, after the recent economic crisis, far too many may have gone through the same thing. Couple that with the abandonment of national identity/belonging and the immediate probability of utter poverty and you can get a true sense of my parents' bravery in taking that leap.

To make ends meet, my father worked at car washes and burger joints and my mother took sewing jobs and odd jobs in nursing homes. I was, of course, ridiculed for not knowing English. I assume that my parents were as well—though, they never complained in front of me. We lived in a small house and slept in the basement. It was, like many basements, damp and mildewed, but we were grateful for our safe place.

We bought groceries with food stamps until we could get on our feet. I still remember being confused by the harsh stares of others when my mother pulled out the food stamps at the checkout counter. I knew no better. I thought it was American money. The cold, weird, almost hostile stares confused me. I still remember that feeling on the back on my neck to this day.

Dad, after decades of practicing as a veterinarian, went back to school to qualify for his licensure exams in the U.S. I watched him struggle with it after so many years away, and understood that it must be important if he worked that hard at it. He would often tell me some version of, "It is not a shame to be poor in America, the land of opportunity, but it is a shame to stay poor in America." He taught me that people are paid for their know-how. The more you know about something, the more people will pay you, work with you, and help you open doors. I believed him and still keep the value of education—of all kinds—as a central theme of my life.

And he lived his talk, eventually getting his license to practice veterinary medicine. The change in our lives was almost instant, or seemed so to me at the time: more money and a better place to live; fewer hostile stares at the checkout line; and so on. Life was better. I learned that people did not have to inherit money to have a better life here. They could get it on their own if they worked diligently. The lesson stuck with me.

My dad and mom were and still are my best teachers.

* * * * *

I worked hard and graduated high school at age sixteen. Little did I know at the time what a small advantage this was, as the high school I attended was seriously below par. I graduated high school with skills equivalent to a fourth grader in math and a fifth grader in reading. To say that my first two years at the University of Illinois at Chicago were a wake-up call is like saying the Titanic's first voyage was disappointing. I thought I had excelled in high school—graduating early, doing everything I was asked, and more. How was I to know that I was being asked do to so very little? Despite being told I would be expelled from the university if my grades did not improve, I struggled on and eventually caught up and earned my degree.

All the time I was going through this, though, I wondered how it was possible for people to live in mansions and drive nice cars and take nice vacations, because I knew not everyone inherited money. I asked myself how two people given the same opportunity could end up with different results and wondered specifically how the 'lucky ones' achieved financial success. I knew by experience, that two chefs could be given the same ingredients and end up with two different dishes—one edible and one not.

Eventually, I discovered inspiring self-help literature. I read Tony Robbins. I read Jim Rohn. I read Zig Ziglar and Dale Carnegie, among others. They spoke to my desire to achieve, to make myself more than the sum of my past. I started reading everything I could get my hands on: personal growth literature, spiritual awareness literature, biographies of leaders, and business success books. My other mentors having a huge impact on my life included Ben Cummings, Dan Kennedy and Greg Stanley. I talked excitedly about what I was reading and was surprised by what I heard in response. "It's just pop psychology", "It's just fluff to sell books and seminars", or "It's all a con."

I looked at the success of those whose books and recordings I was reading and listening to and looked at the success of those who derided the messages. And the truth of it descended on me in a flash: it is fluff—until you *do it*. Those that spoke negatively of the empowering messages were usually those that did not take action, did not make a plan, or could not truly believe they were capable of the dream. My dad would call them 'talkers' not 'doers'. They, for whatever reason, were not hearing it the right way, at the right time, to take the lessons to heart. I determined that I would take it to heart. I would make the dream real in my life. I made a plan

* * * * *

All of the great teachers have wonderful advice and meaningful guidance. Read them all! But before you can put them to use, you must know what you want. That can be the hardest part of the journey: where you do you want to go? If you don't know which road to take, *any* road will take you there!

It can be difficult to weed out the noise of what everyone else tells us to think is the 'ultimate success.' The popular culture tends to focus on external measures of worth and success. You must have a house that is too big for you (as an investment, of course), a car you can practically live in (with a TV screen for each kid), and clothes so expensive that they must be spun from gold thread. Of course, that's an exaggeration, but I think you would agree that it is only slightly exaggerated. The image of success in this culture is manufactured with lots and lots of shiny things.

Add to that, the requirement to have the perfect body, the perfect family, and the most beautiful network of friends. If you take the message from the popular media too much to heart, you'll believe that you can and should have it all. It denies a very simple and unavoidable reality: success in life requires choices and priorities—and commitment to them. BSOM allows you to drill down to the fundamentals and focus on the 'big rocks' instead of lots of little pebbles.

So—throw all that imaging out of your head. It's blank slate time (the only time I advocate having a blank slate!). What do *you* want? What do you *value*? What feeds your soul? What do those that depend on you expect of you? How will you give back? What seems to come effortlessly to you where you never look at a clock to see what time it is? Ask yourself all those questions, seriously, and a hundred more like it until you are clear about exactly what 'success' means in your life.

When I went through all that questioning, I came to the conclusion that I can live without a new car (mine is now fifteen years old and paid off). I can live without the latest fashions in clothes, furniture or electronics. I can live without traveling to every corner of the world. If I fully take care of everything I already have, I already have enough. The baubles just aren't that important to me. *More of everything is not really more of anything.* Once I obtained enough money to be secure, devoting further efforts to earn even more simply robbed my time bank. In the end, you can always make more money, but never more time . More money will never replace the time I did not get to spend with my family or doing the things I'd love to do. That's my vision of success: being able to afford anything at a moment's notice became good enough for me.

I can't live without *time* with my family. I can't live without being able to take time off when I want or need a break or when my children or my wife need me. I can't live without financial security for my family (risks have to be weighed very carefully). I can't live without helping others and giving back to the community. I was lucky enough to already have a profession that I loved (orthodontics), so, what was important to me came down to—*time*. Success for me, being with my family, being a great father, and helping others, requires that I free up time. I needed a plan that would *buy me time*. Once I had that, I could truly focus on my version of true success.

One of the most meaningful things anyone has ever said to me, at the age of twenty-eight, was, "Retire now—and keep working." I thank my mentor Greg Stanley for that. For me, working to simply acquire more and more stuff is a trap. It is a different frame of mind when you've already retired and are just working because you love what you do and helping people at the same time. For me, time is the currency of happiness. What is it for you?

I strongly recommend reading about other people's lives. It helps to give you a backboard for your own ideas about what matters and, as important, what does not. Read about the people you admire. Read biographies of people that have achieved their dreams. You don't have to find one that matches exactly what you want for yourself. The basic truths are in every story. Find the ones that resonate with you. Use them as examples, good or bad, to help you refine your vision.

> *Poor people have big TVs. Rich people have big libraries.*
>
> ~ Jim Rohn

Please, if you take only one thing away from this chapter, it should be to clear your mind of all the external non-sense and diversions and truly focus on what is important to you. Nothing worthwhile can be achieved without knowing truly and honestly what is of value to you and to those you love. You might change your mind along the way and that is perfectly reasonable (as long as you are not doing it too often), but start somewhere. Create the best launching pad you can conceive.

So, I am asking you: *What do you want?* What is the target you are shooting at

* * * * *

Once you've decided what is important to you, you have created a container for your efforts. Things outside that container are just distractions and noises. It appears a paradox to most people that discipline actually *increases* your freedom (applying the fundamentals instead of looking for new outlets is the basis of BSOM), but it is an easy thing to understand—once you give it a moment.

Water boils faster when there is a lid on the pot. Ovens only work because the heat is contained. Rockets only climb into space when the explosion of fuel is directed. Electricity is only useful when it is directed and contained in a wire. A choir sounds most magnificent when in a hall or church that can reflect the voices back. Food lasts longer if we have a refrigerator to contain the cold air.

Energy without a container or something to direct it is typically wasted or expended ineffectively or at worst, it can be destructive. Energy with direction and containment achieves results.

So often, successful lives escape us because we cannot keep our energies focused. And it is very easy these days to be distracted from our main goals. Let's be realistic. Modern life offers many more options to the average person than only a hundred, or even fifty, years ago (internet, email, text, Facebook etc.). We are a blessed generation (even considering our recent economic struggles). But as in fairy tales of old, we can be easily distracted by the shiny fruits and become stagnant, forgetting who we are and where we are going.

How can you ensure your energies are contained within the most important things in your life?

You need *The Big Plan*, of course.

What are the outcomes you want? What will indicate to you that you've succeeded? How will you know you've 'made it'? You don't want to climb the proverbial ladder of success to find out it's been leaning on the wrong building! I hope you take the advice about reading other people's stories. If you do, you'll broaden your awareness of what is possible. Now, write it down.

- What do you really need to feel financially successful?
- What describes success in your family life?
- What do you aspire to spiritually?
- What comes to you effortlessly and doesn't feel like 'work' but more of a game?

Get as specific as possible. If it is not specific, it cannot be achieved. Even the gigantic sun cannot burn tissue paper without the light brought into focus. Talk it out with trusted friends, mentors, and family members. Talk to those around you that have attained what you want to achieve. Discuss it with your spiritual teachers. Use what they have to say to form your own vision, while avoiding the temptation to simply adopt their visions. In the end, you have to 'own' your path to success. By all means, don't drag the process out forever, thinking you can't proceed until you have the absolutely perfect plan. It doesn't exist and it's your plan. You can always refine the vision as you learn more about yourself and your goals. Start where you stand.

Once you've written it down keep it in front of you. Reaffirm the vision as often as you can, especially when your drive is sagging (it *will* happen to all of us). If it helps, write out your goals and affirmations on a poster for your office, a card in your wallet, or a post-it note on the bathroom mirror —whatever it takes to keep you focused in your decision-making.

Now you've got your vision of success. You've got the specifics of what that looks like in the real world—real numbers, real goals, and real desired outcomes. It's all written down. Now seek out experts.

One of the biggest mistakes we can make is to try to do it all on our own, without taking advantage of the expertise around us. Remember: we don't have to reinvent the wheel. Most truly successful people surround themselves with a bank of other people that are clear about their own path to success. To the extent that you can, consult financial planners, lawyers, business advisors, mentors, professional associations, marketers—whatever it takes to gather the information you need to make your dream real. I consulted with an expert in dental practices and he helped me find ways to cut costs and maximize return on my investments while making my patients even more satisfied with my services.

Experts have already worked out how to do more (or less) with what you have. Consulting with them can save you years of frustration. In addition to concrete strategies and tips that can make your life easier, sometimes you need someone to push you past your comfort zone. Often the thing holding us back from taking action is the uncertainty caused by a lack of real experience or information. Get recommendations and referrals from trusted advisors. Let them help you be prepared for moments of reasonable risk that you may encounter, understandably, avoided without the proper help. Often this expertise is available for the price of a book. Read every chapter in these books.

The purpose of all of this is to produce a game plan or a blueprint: steps one, two, and three—with deadlines. Now commit to the daily work. 'Overnight success' usually takes years of dedicated effort. Of course, there are true stories of instant success that are typically due to luck and they stand out because they are *rare*. Slow, steady progress can frustrate our childlike desires for fairy-tale success. We're all programmed for it. We want to win the lottery. Hit it big. It is, of course, a trap. Those stories obscure the reality of hard work, dedication, and focus behind most success stories.

> *No one sees the farmer plant seeds long in the night and early morning, but everyone sees him picking the harvest and feels jealous.*
>
> ~ Unknown

Make peace with that side of yourself. Think of it as a child version of yourself and become a wise parent. Knowing yourself is critical when times get challenging. You must discover the things that will keep you moving forward, even when you feel you have lost connection with your vision—when you're bombarded with doubts about your plan and fears of failure.

Expect it. We're all human. We get tired sometimes. Day-to-day life can distract us from our long-term goals. This is where your team of advisors, experts and mentors can provide invaluable light at the end of the tunnel. They can remind you that there is not a quitter inside of you—that your vision is solid and is completely attainable. Dark moments will pass, if you keep the faith in your plan and remain walking along your path. Singer Jeremy Camp said it best, "I will walk by faith even when I cannot see." BSOM compels you to stay on the fundamentals and keep walking.

* * * * *

Now it's down to the small plan, the day-to-day tasks that will achieve the goals leading to manifestation of the vision—and your successful life.

The following words usually make people groan until they learn the power they release in your life: discipline, focus, routine, habit, and consistency. Again, these words seem restricting, but they're actually *liberating*. The power of habit and ritual is really a short cut to success.

Have you ever watched two people work on the same project and wondered why one of them is already completing it and moving to the next one, while the other one is still planning what to do? The first person probably has a process, a method, worked out—and sticks to it (the basis of BSOM). Without finding the ways that work for us and sticking to them, we're constantly trying to reinvent the wheel. There's no need to drill a new oil well every day or sow the fields over and over. It's not usually glamorous and may lack the flash or showmanship of someone trying to reinvent him/herself all the time, but remember that often the turtle actually does win. The slight speed gains of routine and habit, over time, add up to huge leverage. Little hinges *do* open big doors.

And here we finally come to the title of this chapter: Black Socks and Oatmeal. It's something my wife said to me, with a laugh, about my habit of having oatmeal for breakfast every morning and of always wearing black socks and shoes. Ha! I know what I am eating and wearing every morning. It may seem silly to some people, but it's just an example of little things that buy me extra time each day. A little time saved here and there adds up to months and years which could be leveraged to complete high priority activities. For example, a saving of just five minutes a day is approximately equal to 2.5 extra hours at the end of the month. At the end of the year that's over 30 hrs. Think about it: what if you committed thirty hours to high priority, highly productive activities? How would that change your life? With this approach, I'm already starting my day with success!

Each habit I've established throughout the day to avoid wasting time on trivial or low priority matters buys more time for me! More importantly, it saves my creative energies for the activities that really need it. My daily habits help form the walls of my custom container for my energy. Can it be boring? Sure—sometimes. But I know that if I start obsessing about the little things in my life, it means I'm not focusing on the big things, the ones that matter.

I use a Daily Action Plan. Each night, I plan *and vision* what I need to do over the next couple of days. I make a prioritized list of activities that need my attention. It's not a new concept by any means, but it's repeated so often because it *works*. It doesn't take long at all, just a few minutes. Those few minutes, though, ensure I don't forget anything important and waste more time backtracking to complete the tasks that slipped my mind. Planning my priorities each day also allows 'me time' to evaluate how my activities do (or do not) contribute to my short and long term goals. This keeps me focused on activities that return my investments with profit— whether in time, effort, or material gain. It's a very small discipline that pays off in a very big way.

We've all known people who seem to bounce around in their own lives like ping pong balls, not using their minds to direct their actions. They're always late and they always have too many priorities—or, actually, no real priorities at all. It seems that their lives never get smoother or easier. Life gets complicated, of course, but there's no situation—none—that cannot be improved with simple planning habits. I truly believe this, as I have life experiences that prove to me that all those great teachers were absolutely right about this idea. It helps us avoid the 'blank slate' syndrome that can keep us in a state of inaction and paralysis. As I mentioned earlier in the chapter, having a blank slate is only useful in the initial process of clearing false images from your mind from which to start anew in your journey.

Think of your daily habits and routines as deposits to a bank account, accumulating interest until you reach your goal. Is it boring? Sure. Does it eventually add up to even more than you put in? Absolutely!

An activity that I absolutely make a habit of is something I call PTS: Planning, Thinking and Study Time. I thank my mentor Chuck Lewis, a professional photographer, for that. In today's world, the cross-discipline approach is becoming more and more important. Fresh ideas and approaches can come from anywhere. Physics, biology, social sciences, biographies, and poetry—anything could be the catalyst for innovation. With the abundance of information available today it's insane not to take advantage of as much of it as possible. For example, in deciding on what color to paint my new clinic, I researched how colors affect people (relaxing, energizing, cheering, etc.). This part of our routine keeps the creative side of us alive and well.

PTS gives you a moment to slow down, pace yourself, and create a space where insight is more likely to come to you. It loads your mind with new, stimulating information that can bubble up as ideas while you're showering or driving. It also provides leverage to support your better behaviors. When you learn that brushing every day actually results in fewer cavities, you're more likely to do it. When you learn that a particular type of gas will help your car (and you can afford it), you're more likely to use it. When you learn that maintaining a habit for three weeks or more rewires the brain to actually make maintaining the behavior easier, it is less of a struggle to continue on for six weeks. You will be amazed at how ideas come from nowhere and how in this frame of mind, you're doing less but achieving more.

"When you know better, you do better."
~Maya Angelou

Read the stories and works of John Boaz, Mike Crow, Howard Partridge (authors in Volume 1 of *Dare to Be a Difference Maker*), and Henry Ford. Read collections of success stories and investigate your local success stories.

* * * * *

I come from a family that risked everything for a better life, lost everything for an opportunity to start over in a better pace, and had to rely on food stamps to stay fed. I watched my parents work hard to improve our family's situation and I took that to heart. I studied the wise men and women of our time, learning that hard work pays off.

There's no denying that some people have more control over their environments than others. People start from better or worse situations. But I truly believe that *all* of us can improve our lives by using the enduring techniques that are repeated by the teachers in this book and taking their stories as inspiration to recreate ourselves. The stories of the great men and women of history have inspired me. They were born with the same twenty-four hours in a day that you and I have. We, like them, are gifted with this amazing human brain, full of unlimited potential.

So, this is my advice to you, backed by my experience. Gather the wisdom of others to form your vision of success. Personalize it to your family. Devise a plan to achieve it and adopt techniques to support you as you do the day-to-day work to make it real. Consult with experts and those that went before you. Find and adopt ways to encourage the habits, routines, and practices that make your efforts as efficient as possible. Leverage what's already been successfully done!

Commit to the values that are truly important to you. How much stuff (a larger home, more money, expensive clothes and cars and toys) do you really need to feel fulfilled? Can you be satisfied once you've reached the point of having a sufficient amount of what you need to take care of yourself and your family? Pursuing "more" just for the sake of having it won't contribute to your state of happiness. The BSOM philosophy halts the endless urge for the new and improved before you've even fully used up, enjoyed or exhausted what you already have.

I have all that I want and need. I have no urgent necessity for money; I have enough to support my family comfortably. I am no longer on the treadmill. I can now take time off if I need to without financial hardship for my family. I work in a career I love, helping people reveal their fantastic smiles. It's like what they say about delivering flowers: who tires of making people smile all day long? I just skip the flowers and go straight to the smiles! I go to work every day because I want to, not because I feel I must. I think of myself as a successful 'loafer' living a 'turbulence free' life focused on my family, health, relationships, and profession. I try to make a difference in the lives of the people I meet. I encourage and mentor the clients that visit my dental office for help in maximizing their smiles, whether they are adults or children. I've freed myself from the unrelenting rat race, the hamster-wheel of pay-check-to-paycheck living. Understanding and embracing the BSOM on a daily basis is one of the most fundamental keys to achieving this level of success for me (and can be for you too!)

BSOM is about fundamentals. It does away with the belief that successful people are somehow born with a mysterious power that rest of us don't have. BSOM has redefined my vision of success and brought peace of mind to my life. I can take the time I need to be the best dad and husband I can be. Every smile I get from my wife, son, daughters, and patients is gold to me. Every time I see someone use my mentoring to manifest his or her dream is gold to me too. I love my career, my family—my life. I am content and loved, and I try to make a difference. That is success in almost any book.

I hope my story and musings inspire you to seek more learning, more information, and more inspiration to begin manifesting your version of success. The teachers in this book give you a good place to start, but venture further—frequently. Please do not confuse the universality and familiarity of what I have shared here to mean that the information is clichéd pop-psychology or self-help silliness. It is repeated in so many places in so many ways because it is real and true. Every new generation needs to hear it. Pass it on. Learn more. It works *if and when* you are ready to start your journey. ∎

Ejaz Tahir, DDS, MS

Starting out with a life full of struggles, obstacles, and roadblocks (growing up on food stamps and even nearly being kicked out of college), Dr. Tahir began to change his life's direction with the application of fundamental self-discipline and perseverance. He credits his parents for setting a great example of working hard, working smart, and working with honor. For bringing the example more alive in him, he credits the great teachers' books he found—such as Napoleon Hills' classic "Think and Grow Rich", Richard Koch's "80/20 Principle" and multiple books on time and mind management by Dan Kennedy. They, with a host of coaches and mentors he was blessed to find, showed him how prosperity is intertwined with personal growth and that this is one of the secrets of true wealth and freedom. He now aspires to be a coach and mentor for others, to pass on the blessings he has received.

Dr. Tahir attended University of Illinois Orthodontic Specialty Graduate Program and worked with several orthodontists before establishing his own dental practice in 1995. He currently has two offices, Berwyn and Oak Lawn, IL, and serves a large local clientele. His nearly 20 years in practice has not been spent only straightening teeth (though he is still in love with revealing the beautiful smile in everyone!) He also tries to spend the time with his patients inspiring them to turn the adversity in their lives to their advantage, showing he believes in them before they believe in themselves. He loves to see the transformation in their smiles and their lives!

A lover of fables, origami (the Japanese art of paper-folding) and reading, he spends most of his time now seeking the sweet spot of life with a 'retire now, keep working' philosophy. Though being a husband and father of three keeps him busy, he remains committed to teaching others about the Black Socks and Oat Meal Discipline (BSOM) and helping others to realize their own greatness.

For more information visit www.CoolBraces.com or contact Dr. Tahir at j.tahir@comcast.net, or phone at 630-687-3393 or 708-484-8686.

5

❧

Never Give Up

By Michelle Adams

One day after eighteen years of trudging through the ditches of addiction, my mind woke up and began to think. The only problem was that when my mind finally woke up, I was in prison for first degree felony drug charges. I found myself in a place where all freedoms and luxuries were lost to me. After being awakened at 4:00 AM for breakfast, I went to work in the prison laundry as a seamstress and then, later, in the library as a librarian. This was not the freedom I sought all those years I used drugs and drank alcohol.

After completing thirteen months in prison and two months in a halfway house I was allowed to find my own place to live. It was at this time that I began to realize life would be more difficult than I expected. I went to several apartment complexes only to be turned down. They didn't want a drug dealer living on their property. I couldn't blame them. I wouldn't want a drug dealer living on my property either.

I didn't want much from life other than to just exist in this world. I had the belief that no one would want to be my friend or even ask me on a date because I had been in prison. Little did I know that I was selling myself short with that small belief. God had *big* plans for me! And those plans would come to fruition as long as I did His work and did it well.

Small, good things began to happen. I found a job at Whataburger and became the best drive through employee I could be. I went to twelve-step meetings, got a sponsor, and began working through my life with a caring woman, my sponsor. And most importantly, I joined the Cowboy Church in Brazoria, Texas where I found acceptance, love, and a gracious God that had a plan for my life.

I discovered a new-found power that had been within me all the time—God. I was able to walk through a lifetime of pain, abandonment, confusion, domestic violence, and a drug addiction that nearly took my life. I had no idea that writing about my life and reviewing it with another human being would give me the freedom I so desired.

When I did sit down to write my story and discuss it with my sponsor, I wrote about growing up poor with parents who did the best they knew how, but who I felt thought I was never good enough. I grew up believing what I was told—that I was an idiot and stupid. I don't remember much physical affection like hugs or being told that I was important. That's not to say it wasn't there, I just don't remember it.

My mom has been the only constant in my life. Everyone else has either gone away or come into my life at some point. So it's only reasonable to say that some of my struggles have been around trying to be my mom's caregiver. I always wanted to protect her from the emotional abuse we lived with. I didn't know how to fix my own pain inside so I focused on trying to make my mom better. I thought, "If I can make my mom okay and have her feel happy then I'll be happy." I have felt this way most of my life about my mom. But I was never able to control her feelings or make them better. Because of the enmeshment every attempt failed and the self-hate and self-harm became worse. This helped feed my addiction and negative sense of self for many years. Today, I know that my mom's life and her feelings are not my problem. Only she can make them better for herself. I felt like I didn't give my mom enough credit before for who she is today!

Both my mom and step-dad who raised me drank, and it was not uncommon for me to take sips of their alcoholic drinks. I was drunk for the first time by age seven at my grandfather's Potentate Ball for the Shriners. There were several men at the event who thought it was "cute" to give me glasses of champagne. Keep in mind this was in the 1970's and it was not as taboo as it is today. This was the first time that I didn't have to feel the effects of being who I truly was, a little girl in a family where I felt like I didn't exist.

I went to two junior high schools and six high schools, and had a hard time fitting in. Also, I always chose the wrong crowd to be with. I was unable to understand many of the classes that I had to take because every time I moved the classes were different. I have a six grade education in math, yet I was able to complete high school.

At age 14 my biological father and I were reunited and I was asked to go and live with him, my step mom and two sisters, one of which I had never met before. I'd soon come to find that my dad was a man of integrity and that he had always loved me. I felt sad that he wasn't in my life but very glad I was given the chance to get to know him. My dad didn't always agree with my decisions but one thing I knew was that he loved me.

After high school I went to college to be a Court Reporter. I completed Court Reporting school after three attempts at it. I then went on to take the state board exams. I passed the written exam but could not complete the machine portion of the exam because I was too high on drugs to transcribe my notes. Feeling defeated, I left the exam and never looked back. The downward spiral of drug addiction went to an all new level after this.

During my recovery, I worked through issues of no self-worth and feeling not good enough. The biggest question was—what am I to do now? I and two others started a new twelve-step meeting in Freeport, Texas called the Freedom Group and this is where my life really began to change. I was finally serving other people and it felt good. I was making a difference for good, for the first time.

After being down on the coast for one year I came home to Plano, Texas and continued my journey of helping others. I attended my local twelve-step meetings and sponsored many women through a 12-step program. I had this desire to help women even more and open a house where they recover together as a community. And after being back home for two years I made my dreams a reality. In January 2008, I founded a non-profit organization to help women in recovery from substance use disorders, Recovery Inn.

We now have six homes in the Dallas metroplex and have helped over four hundred women on their journey to freedom from addiction and alcoholism. I can't even imagine how many ripples in the water we've created that have now touched thousands. We help them with life skills and coping skills, which is what they lack the most. We also help them with spirituality, budgeting, cooking, gardening, and many other skills where they need help.

Recovery Inn has given mothers, grandmothers, sisters, and daughters back to their families. Our goal is to reignite and fuel the passion inside each woman suffering from substance use disorders. We're not successful with all women who come through our doors because some are not ready. Our current success rate is in the 70% range. The hardest part for me is knowing that they can choose to change if they become willing and honest, because I know it's possible. If I can do it so can they.

It's amazing to look at the progress I've made personally and professionally. I understand who I am as a child of God today. With worth that comes from within that shines outward. I've taken responsibility for my actions and my past addiction. I've learned that serving others takes the focus off myself and no longer allows me to live in self-pity. I will spend the rest of my days assisting others find the way out of self-pity, self-harm and into a perfect love of Christ that casts out all fear.

Last year I was able to attend SMU for a non-profit leadership program where I learned how to grow and sustain a non-profit organization. I am eight years free from any mind or mood altering substances and continue my personal journey as a person in long-term in recovery.

In 2010, I founded another non-profit organization called Texas Association of Recovery Residences. Its sole purpose is to set a standard for recovery residences and certify the recovery residence as an approved home. Also in 2010, I was asked to serve on the board of the National Association of Recovery Residences a national association that was in the start-up phase and being set up for the same purpose. My belief is that if you care about one, then you care about them all. I will continue to dedicate my life to those in recovery from substance use disorders.

I've learned through this journey called life that we all have struggles and we all have joys. They come at all stages of life and come in many different packages. Peace comes when I accept that all things are exactly as they're meant to be. I no longer fight with this world as I know I'm only passing through. I know that everything happens for a reason and I am thankful for everything I've experienced. I honor the part of me that chose to use drugs and alcohol as a way to cope because I made it out alive. I also honor the choices I continue to make that allow me to live a life that is beyond my expectations.

I am free, free at last!

May God's grace abound in your life today as it has so much in mine! ■

Michelle Adams

Michelle Adams is the Founder and Executive Director of Recovery Inn, a women's recovery program that is a non-profit 501(c)3 organization and the owner of Bentley Place, a men's recovery program in Plano, TX. She is 39 years old and resides in Texas.

She has served on the Board of Directors at City House, a shelter for children, currently serves on the Board of Directors for the National Association of Recovery Residences, and is the Founder and President of Texas Association of Recovery Residences. Her passion is helping others in recovery reach their full potential and stop the battle with drugs and alcohol.

Michelle has been featured in "Plano Profile Magazine", "Advocate Magazine", "Dallas Morning News—Neighbors Go", "Plano Star Courier", featured in several blogs, and was the Texan with Character for Channel 11 News.

Michelle Adams
Recovery Inn
www.RecoveryInn.org
Bentley Place
www.BentleyPlace.us

6

Divorce to Destiny

By Tilde Guajardo

While divorce seems to be commonplace now, it still leaves a multitude of destruction in its wake. It destroys the dreams of forever love, of a happy and united family, and of a beautiful life of growing old with someone. We run the gamut of emotions, both highs and lows, at times feeling like we may never be able to lift ourselves up again due to the pain we feel. I'm sharing my story with all of you in the hope that if you ever experience divorce, or any traumatic event, you will allow it to lead you to your destiny.

I was married at the young age of twenty-three and my husband was a baby at age twenty. Some might have called me a cougar. In reality I was a kitten. We dated for eighteen months before we were married in November of 1991. We met while we were in the Army and stationed in Maryland. He had the most beautiful eyes I'd ever seen. He was truly sweet and, at times, very cocky.

He didn't win me over right away, as I was having fun dating and going out with friends. He didn't mind, though. He waited for me to come back after a night out and left notes and flowers on my door asking me to come by if I wanted to say good night. He was the most thoughtful and romantic person I'd ever met, and he made me feel very special.

After dating for about six months or so, he gave me an ultimatum. He wanted us to be exclusive and I could tell he had very deep feelings for me by then. I'd been hurt and lied to by so many people in the past, I was hesitant to believe anyone who used those three words, "I love you." Somehow I felt differently when I heard it coming from him. It was heartfelt. So we began dating exclusively. We had our ups and downs getting to know each other, but we became the best of friends. He drove us everywhere in his little sports car, and on any given night we could be found in Annapolis, the Inner Harbor in Baltimore, or our favorite place at the Capitol steps overlooking the Mall in Washington D.C.

As I grew to trust him, I shared some of my deepest secrets and traumatic events from my childhood, which he handled as well as any twenty-year-old could. He was always gentle and willing to listen and simply hold me. I felt safer with him than anyone else I'd ever known. It was easy to say yes when he asked me to marry him.

We had a small wedding on the patio of my parents' home in south Texas. I remember the fifty- to sixty-five-mph winds and tumbleweeds flying across the patio that entire day! My friends joke now about "signs," and I have to laugh with them. I was terrified. I'd never seen winds or tumbleweeds shooting across the yard like that. Then, like a miracle, an hour before the ceremony began the winds completely stopped, the sunset was spectacular, and the moon lit up the sky making it a perfect evening. We were happily married.

The first ten to eleven years of our marriage were the best. We went through rough times that would break most marriages, but from early on we put Christ in the center of our lives. We both grew spiritually together and loved God with all our hearts. We loved each other deeply. Strangers often approached us in airports or restaurants and complimented us on how "in love and happy" we looked. Others told us how they'd noticed us "saying grace" in a public restaurant and were reminded to give thanks no matter where they were. Our biggest compliments were from other couples coming to us for advice on marriage.

From the time we met we had always worked in close proximity and had enjoyed it. We were fortunate in November of 1999 to be the first married couple to be hired as Aircraft Dispatchers for a major airline. We considered ourselves blessed as we received significant salary increases that improved our quality of life and allowed us the time and money to start a small business on the side and to pursue our passions.

I can't be certain of the date, but I can say that by our eleventh year of marriage things had changed. I don't know what happened but there was certainly a shift in our relationship. Intimacy was fading, we were building a home, and we were drifting apart. We both felt it and discussed divorce in 2003. We decided we wanted to work on our marriage because we loved each other and promised we would never bring up divorce again.

In March of 2005 we opened a small side business—a motorcycle tire and accessory store. He loved motorcycles and I loved business. In July of 2005, we bought land in our favorite small town in Colorado where we planned to build our dream home and retire. We'd been vacationing there yearly since 1999 and had fallen in love with the place and people.

In August of 2005, a week after my birthday, he shocked me to my core, telling me he no longer wanted to be married to me and had been planning to leave since March of that year. Really? We'd opened a motorcycle store and bought land to build a retirement home, and now he was telling me he didn't even see a future with me? I was stunned with disbelief! He denied there being someone else, but the truth always finds its way to the surface. What made the truth of his being involved with someone else so hurtful was that she was someone I called my friend. All three of us worked in the same office as Aircraft Dispatchers.

I'm sharing my story to give you a clear picture of the devastation and trauma of such an enormous betrayal by a man who was not only my husband, but someone I considered my best friend. Imagine having to go to work and face your ex-husband and his new girlfriend. He moved out of the house shortly after my birthday and we were officially divorced by December of 2005.

It was a whirlwind from the time he left in August 2005 to the time the divorce was final in December 2005. Immediately after he left I didn't know if I could get out of bed or even wanted to. Thanks to the support of my family and friends, I was able to survive one day at a time. They either called or came by to make sure I was okay, or they'd help take my mind off of my troubles with plenty of laughter. Still, I was now running a home, trying to sell a business, and working full time. I was overwhelmed!

Do you ever feel like you just want to go away for at least a week and sit on a beach and do nothing but spend time with God in peace? That was me.

Then, in October of 2005 I received a phone call from a friend asking if I wanted to go to Mexico for a week. She was going to a luxury resort to teach yoga and wanted me to accompany her on the trip. I was so excited to get away and this place sounded perfect. All expenses would be paid by the resort. We just had to get there. Once again, God answered my prayers.

I grabbed a book and set out on an adventure to find God in Mexico and in the process found myself. The book I brought with me was *I Married Adventure* by Lucy Swindoll. It motivated me to think of all the things I enjoyed and was passionate about. The two things that came to mind were traveling and helping women overcome past hurts.

I recalled one of my favorite gifts from my parents—a world globe. The first place I'd pinned at the age of twelve was Italy. I'd read many non-fiction mafia books and was intrigued by the culture and sites mentioned throughout those books. Back in June of 2005, I'd taken my first trip to Europe with three other women and spent fourteen memorable days traveling through Italy. When I'd stepped off the airplane in Rome tears had welled up as I remembered putting that pin on that globe as a young girl. It had been beautiful to see God giving me the desires of my heart.

Now, while in Mexico, I recalled how fulfilling it was for me to lead and teach bible studies, encouraging women and helping them understand how truly powerful they can be by allowing God to work through them. I feel very strongly about the importance of giving back to others because it takes the focus off of ourselves and forces us to realize how truly blessed we are.

I returned home from Mexico full of faith that God was with me, with hope of new beginnings, and a love of life to experience it to the fullest. This was merely the beginning of my road to healing, and I was eager to set out on my journey.

I've always had a competitive spirit about life. I've been through enough to learn I can be knocked down, but I won't stay down. I began training for my first half marathon, and the accountability with friends in the group is what got me out of bed in the mornings. I vividly remember that there were days when I was running and thinking every step I took was making me stronger. I lived day by day. At times, I ran and cried at the same time, but I was determined I was going to finish that half marathon!

I finished my first half marathon in November of 2005 and it was exhilarating! I finished my second one the following month and then began training for my first Olympic triathlon in February of 2006. I finished the one-mile swim, twenty-five-mile bike, and six-mile run in May of 2006 and raised over two thousand dollars for the Leukemia and Lymphoma society.

The Olympic triathlon was the most memorable and meaningful of my achievements. I was so honored to be part of a team of triathletes who raised over a hundred fifty thousand dollars for the Leukemia and Lymphoma society. It was motivating and moving to see the streets of Austin lined with survivors and supporters, including my family and friends. Words can't adequately express how I felt when I finished that day. It was not just a physical endurance race for me, but it was another victory for healing my soul and renewing my self-confidence.

Since then, I have been back to Italy twice and visited Switzerland, Costa Rica, Maui, and numerous cities throughout the United States. I'm looking forward to visiting many more in the coming years.

In January of 2011, I launched a website for women called www. Womanars.com, where our goal is to empower women by educating and connecting them to others. We believe "The Power of Women" lies within each of us, and we hope to enable women to tap into their own power so that they can then empower others. I'm having the time of my life meeting other women from around the world who are as passionate as I am about helping to improve the future for women and girls.

I believe I was put on this earth to do what I love to do and to be a light and example for others who have been hurt, by reminding them not to let our pasts dictate our futures. We each have passions and a purpose to fulfill while we're on this earth. Some of mine have been with me since I was a child and others I've come to realize as an adult.

Going through a divorce can lead us to wallow in self-pity for too long if we allow it. We need to recognize the importance of allowing ourselves to experience the emotions of pain, anger, and fear. But we must also realize that at some point, it's time to rise up and move on, and to remember that faith, hope, and love are waiting for us on the other side.

I did gradually heal from my divorce. Every step I took in faith, along with the hours I spent in therapy, led me to the place of healing I find myself in today. I am able to forgive faster, love deeper, and encourage others more freely. I'm thankful for all the experiences I've had in my life, both good and bad. They've all led me to exactly where I am supposed to be now. I believe the second half of my life will be a hundred times better than the first.

I pray that you, too, will find and follow your destiny and make a difference in the lives of others! ∎

Tilde Guajardo

Tilde Guajardo is the Founder & Chief Visionary Officer of Womanars. Her passion to inspire and empower women and girls throughout the world is what drives her. Since 2010, she has produced compelling women's interviews telling how they are living their best lives, and what makes women so unique in hopes that these videos will inspire others to pursue their own passions. She is an emerging leader with a vision of creating a "virtual" global online community of women who share her passion and vision.

Tilde Guajardo
Founder & Chief Visionary Officer of Womanars.com

7

❧

Dream Restored, Refined and Realized

By Shuronda Scott

S ometimes in the pursuit of our dreams we come to a crossroads. It may be a failed business venture, a sudden layoff, a broken off relationship, or a ministry dream unrealized. You find yourself standing at a crossroads amidst the ashes of shattered dreams and discarded hopes. You ask *how will God ever bring fulfillment out of the ashes of these dreams?* This is the place where I stood as my dream crumbled around me.

Young and passionate, my dream was to serve God in full-time ministry. I was deeply stirred by the scripture found in Luke 4:18.

> *The Spirit of the Lord is upon Me, because He has anoint-
> ed Me to preach the gospel to the poor; He has sent Me to
> heal the brokenhearted, to proclaim liberty to the captives
> and recovery of sight to the blind, to set at liberty those
> who are oppressed;*

Had God called me to preach the Gospel, and to bring healing to the brokenhearted? Who were the brokenhearted? I didn't fully understand how I would accomplish this call and assignment. In fact, in my church denomination, I didn't personally know of any woman that had been called into ministry, so this was all very new to me and hugely intimidating. Would I need to quit my job? I simply didn't know.

I also could not have imagined the storm of emotional and spiritual torment over the ensuing few months that would bring me to the crossroads of what I thought was the death of my dream. I had decided to pursue the call of God in my life by attending seminary. Going to seminary was a big step. I didn't know how I would pay for it, or even how it would come about—it was a giant faith leap.

A few months went by and I wondered *did God really call me to ministry?* I struggled with confusion and doubts. Why weren't things working out the way I wanted? I had given up all to pursue doing God's work. I had quit my job. I had given up my apartment. I had moved away from my home in Dallas. My plans for seminary didn't materialize, and as I walked through the process, confronting my painful disappointment, I learned several important life lessons.

Standing at this crossroads, confused and broken by life's circumstances and the great loss of my dream I questioned, "Lord, what do I do now?" I was afraid and unsure about everything. I felt as though I was holding on by an emotional thread to the promises that God had for me and doubted that I had enough faith. What I didn't know then at the age of twenty-five (that I now know over twenty years later) was that I wasn't holding on to God and His promises, He was holding on to me, and He had a plan for all my dreams even beyond my wildest imagining.

I received encouragement to simply go back to Dallas. I had left everything and I asked myself *how I would be able to return.* But I did return. God's goodness and favor in our lives is so amazing. In an instant, God turned my crumbled hopes around and restored all that was lost. I received restoration of my job, my apartment and more.

The biggest restoration was yet to come. You see, I had stepped out boldly in faith believing that God had called me to do great things for Him. But in return I'd felt like a failure—broken and defeated. The dream in me had been crushed. Fear took hold and so gripped my life that I became very afraid to step out again to do anything. I was afraid to risk the failure. I didn't want to mess it up.

I struggled with this until one day I realized that God is so much bigger than my mess ups. God is there to direct our steps and He has a wonderful plan to move us into a flourishing and thriving place. He truly desires success for us. That began the healing process from what I thought was my biggest failure and the underlying fears within me.

I remember the encouragement of one of my dearest friends who walked through this season of emotional storm with me. She comforted me, saying, "One day, you're going to look down, and the huge gash on your leg will be all healed and you'll have only a small scar. And you're going to wonder how it happened." She was right. God's healing and restoration is so complete, so thorough, and so redeeming.

I knew that God had a purpose for me and that He had called me to do something great for Him. I surely didn't know all it would cost me. But it has been well worth the miracle of healing and restoration to see impossible dreams being made possible in my life. It was worth seeing the ministry that was birthed in and through me and the opportunity to have served Him now for over twenty years.

Perhaps in the pursuit of your dreams, you, too, have come to what seems like a dead end. Adversity and opposition have done their best to derail you, but God still has a plan. No matter where you are or what your circumstances, the power of God trumps all hardships.

It is through difficult obstacles that we discover the possibilities (within) and the opportunities (without) that unfold the glorious purpose and plan for our life.

Seeing My Path Unfold

God's doesn't forget your dreams. In fact, He has placed them within your heart and holds them close to His heart. As I discovered in my own life, our dreams are never discarded; they are only refined to bring God glory! Seven years after what I had considered my biggest failure, I transitioned from my corporate job into full-time ministry.

Now after more than twenty years in ministry, I recognize that God had a plan all along and that purpose is not merely an end result or simply the accomplishment of a goal. Purpose is lived out in every day choices. It's the possibilities you choose when you stand at the crossroads (transitions and seasons of change) of your lives. Every decision positions you for your launch into the new and yet unfolding possibilities around you.

Launch Pad Moments

The month of April has always been very special to me and very significant for many reasons. It was during the month of April, that I had the opportunity to debut and launch my very first book, *A Pocketful of Possibilities: Impossible Dreams, Made Possible.*

April has also been a month in years past when I have experienced significant transition (starting my own business), change, and challenge in my life. Over the years, it has become what I have called my "launch pad" month. Today, as I look back, I recognize that each event, each challenge, each scary step was a launch pad moment that would propel me forward and position me to soar beyond my wildest dreams!

I believe because you are reading this book right now (the powerful stories of ordinary people just like you who dare to make a difference), that this is going to become your **launch pad moment** and a point of decision that releases you to step into the fullness of all your dreams and your destiny. Today marks the beginning of walking in your possibility.

You've heard the phrase "beyond your wildest dreams." It means far more than you could have hoped for or imagined. Do you believe that the impossible can be made possible in your life? And that you can soar beyond your wildest dreams?

Pushed Out of the Nest

The old familiar image of a mother bird teaching her young to fly by gently pushing it out of the nest comes to mind when I think about my transition to starting my own business. Just as the baby bird is pushed out of the nest to fly, we sometimes need a little nudge—or in some cases, a big jolt—to step forward. This would be one of the biggest transitions that I had experienced in my life personally, professionally, and in my ministry and service to God. And although I had more than twenty years experience from my corporate and ministry background, in some ways, I felt like I was starting over—being sent back to "Go" (as in the Monopoly game) and it was a place I wasn't sure how to navigate. So what now? Start a company?

It was bit scary for me as it wasn't the transition and time I'd chosen. I felt like I was stepping away from everything that made me feel secure and comfortable—starting my own business and ministry. Hadn't I been just fine before this transition? I was experiencing success and making an impact where I was. Yet, as it often the case with change, I felt a little out of control. I knew I would have to release parts of my former experiences in order to step into new opportunities. Adding to my insecurities at the time of my transition, were the many uncertainties in the economic outlook. Would I fail as a business owner?

One of my pastors encouraged me to see this as an opportunity to be launched (there is that word again) into the greater glory that God had for me. She was right! She knew this new opportunity would allow me to grow and to expand my gifts and talents. I realized at that moment that I was being pushed out of the nest and it was time to fly in a brand new way.

I didn't know it at the time, but God was designing a whole new roadmap of possibilities for me that would launch me into all my dreams. Even the dreams that I thought were sidelined.

The most difficult of circumstances—a layoff—was the catalyst for me to begin to soar in my dreams. Dreams that God had placed in my heart for me to fulfill!

He has also placed dreams in your heart that uniquely fit the person you are and He desires no more than for you to see them fulfilled. Your dreams for your life, for your family and home, for your business and professional life, or even your ministry aren't just for dreaming—they are for fulfilling. God wants to take us from dream to reality!

Dream to Reality

It has been a few short years since that April launch date of starting my own coaching and consulting business, which opened many doors that I've walked through—unfolding my pocketful of possibilities. When it comes down to it, it was simply taking one small step forward. Did I have it all figured out? My reply is always the same, even today. Absolutely not. And even now, I can say that I'm still "taking steps big and small, building the framework for the realization of my dreams and goals."

As I build the framework, I get a bigger glimpse of the picture that God is unveiling. I must say it's looking pretty good! ■

Shuronda Scott

Shuronda Scott is known as the Possibilities Coach™. As an author, speaker and life coach, she combines over 25 years of corporate and ministry background experience in helping others recognize possibilities (within) and opportunities (without)™. Strategic and intuitive in her coaching, she is adept at taking personal and leadership development to the next level.

For over fourteen years, Shuronda served on the staff of a large multi-campus church in the Dallas/Fort Worth area in various ministry roles including Director of Biblical Counseling and Women's Leadership Development Director. She also has over fifteen years of corporate experience as a trainer and consultant.

*No matter what her role, Shuronda is passionate about helping others realize the fullness of their dreams. In her recently released book, "*A Pocketful of Possibilities: Impossible Dreams, Made Possible*," she shares how to remove the ashes that limit your potential and how to create your own roadmap of possibilities to take your dreams out of the wait today!*

She is also the founder of Healing the Brokenhearted Dreamer Conferences and Intensive Weekend Encounters. In addition to her speaking and ministry platform, she is a business owner who influences in many realms. She has been highly endorsed by pastors, business executives and community leaders alike.

For more information on her coaching or ministry or to schedule her to speak at your next event, visit her at www.walkinginpossibility.com.

Shuronda Scott
Possibilities Coach™
shuronda@walkinginpossibility.com
www.walkinginpossibility.com

8

⚜

Passion?! I Don't Got No Stinkin' Passion!

By J. L. Rybolt

When I was asked to be a part of this project I must admit I chuckled to myself. Me, a difference maker?! I don't see it. But you know what? I am. You are too, in ways you're not aware of. Many things have happened in a twelve-month period that have changed my life and this is one of them. By the time you finish these couple of pages, you, too, will be able to change your life. All that is needed is your openness to see, embrace, and go for it.

I'm a firm believer in everyone being different and that what works for one person may not work for another. For me, I've tried to be open to many avenues of self-exploration as I've gone through this journey called life. I've read self-help books, gone to therapy, and participated in weekend seminars. I've started my morning and ended my day with positive affirmations. I have a vision board. I have some of the best motivational speakers in the business at my disposal, but none of these resources have worked well for me. The reason is simple: passion.

That's been the hardest part of the self-help offerings. What's your "passion?" What's your "why?" What's your "burn?" Call it what you will, but I had no idea what would drive me to get out of bed every morning (other than an animal that needed to be walked or bills to pay) and greet the day with excitement and enthusiasm.

When I followed the suggestions of the self-help professionals, no passion, burn, or why poked its head out of the internal muck.

What was wrong with me? The answer is: nothing (there's nothing wrong with you, either). Then why did all these other people get it and I didn't? It took a few years, but I finally figured out what the block has been.

As a child I grew up in an abusive home. I got through each day by listening to and doing what others wanted me to do. I had to be adept at reading the current emotional temperature of my environment (which could change by the minute) and be able to determine what needed to happen in order to keep things as peaceful and calm as possible. It was how I survived.

So when the question of passion or dreams came up, I drew a complete and utter blank. Whatever innate purpose or dreams God had for me were squashed into the dark recesses of my mind. To discover my passion, I would have to reconnect with these dreams. I've realized this off and on, but the association began to occur again very recently. This time I paid attention.

Once again, the challenge had been raised and an edict set forth that if I follow my passion everything else would fall into place with my life. I'd be happy, financially set, work wouldn't feel like work, and so on. I did a mental head slap and hands were thrown up in the air (again, mentally). I gave up. But really, I didn't. I was determined to find my drive. With my abusers gone, it became safe to ask, "Who Am I?" It's now my turn to shine.

I contracted with a friend of mine, Tony, who is a life coach. For two hours we talked about where I was in my life currently and where I wanted to be. At the end of our time together, I must admit, I was still frustrated. I felt no further along in the discovery of what I wanted from life than when he and I initially sat down. As a motivational expert, Tony gave me a lot to think about, but I didn't discover the magic bullet. Not until the end of our session.

As is common after pouring your life out to someone, there is what I call a "return to reality" period at the end of your time together. This is where you chat about other things like the kids, the family, what you're doing this next weekend, and so forth. It was during this time that Tony laid at my feet something so simple I couldn't believe it. He mentioned that he was turning fifty that year and in honor of this he'd decided to do fifty things he'd never done before; fifty new experiences. Think about the brilliance in the simplicity of that goal. It is truly something *anyone* can do.

This one passing statement put me on a course that has changed my life. This would push me out of my comfort zone and make me look outside the box I had created for myself. I decided that doing and/or experiencing fifty new things that year was something I could easily do. The only requirement was being open to what was available to experience then doing it. Since then I've gone to a NASCAR race (I'm not a "real" NASCAR fan, but I had a blast), I've attended college basketball championship games, I've seen the Thunderbirds perform, and I've been up close to small stingrays as they swam in the ocean. I've been to a roller derby game and taken a cake decorating class. The experience that most surprised me, however, was what I did with a free plane ticket I had.

I attended a conference where Michelle Prince spoke. She and I had a chance to talk privately during this particular weekend and I was immediately drawn to her. She sent a note around about a book seminar she was presenting in Dallas. I'd never been to Dallas, I'd never been to a book writing workshop and I liked Michelle. Armed with the goal of completing fifty new things, knowing that this would count for two in one shot, I went. I had no intention of writing a book at all. This was strictly something to cross off the list.

By the time I left Dallas two days later, I had the outline of a book in hand. Three months after that the book was written and off to an editor. Three months after that the bound copy of my words found their way into my hands. This book has become part of what drives me now: spreading hope and a feeling of connection with others when you feel there is none.

The book I wrote is about my experience of having a hysterectomy, looking for answers about the surgery, menopause (my mother had passed away and my older sisters were not at that phase of life yet), and how to deal with being a single, childless woman, post-surgery and not hang on to the sadness and anger that this kind of transition can produce. I wrote the book with the intent of helping others in my shoes as well as their loved ones, and I've given speeches on the topic. I wouldn't have done any of this had I not been on a quest to do fifty new things in a year.

Do I know what my passion is? Not quite, but I'm closer to it than I've ever been and I get to help people in the process. Do I believe this is a place you can start as well? Absolutely!

A motto that I live by now is "Live like a C.H.I.L.D." What this means is that I have the power to "Create How I Live Daily." You do as well. Maybe you won't find your passion, but take the journey. Open your heart and eyes to what is available to you. Check local papers. Subscribe to online communities that share event happenings. Is there something in the back of your mind that you've toyed with trying? Find an organization in your town that focuses on that thing and try it! As I was writing my first book a dear friend passed away. Life is too short. Time to get on with living.

Here's a short list of ideas to help you get started:

1. Watched the Thunderbirds perform
2. Went to a Daytona 500 race
3. Visited Universal Studios
4. Attended a Drive-In Church
5. Ate at (insert restaurant name here—one you've never been to)
6. Been to the Schermerhorn
7. Worked with a professional stage group
8. Met an Ambassador
9. Been to the symphony
10. Took a cake decorating class
11. Attended a Stanley Cup Playoff game
12. Fixed breakfast for the people I work with
13. Cooked a dozen eggs at one time

14. Watched a live air show
15. Drove a Camaro
16. Drove a Volt (an electric car)
17. Attended a military swearing in
18. Went to a Roller Derby game
19. Attended a book writing workshop
20. Wrote a book
21. Assisted putting a workshop together for bestselling author
22. Was a Pallbearer
23. Wore a boutonniere
24. Threw dirt on a grave/coffin
25. Attended a Jewish service
26. Worked with an editor
27. Cut out puzzle pieces
28. Painted glue on a canvas
29. Had a caricature made
30. Used a staple gun
31. Had a book cover designed
32. Had a web site designed
33. Went to and toured the Franklin Theatre
34. Asked people for book testimonials
35. Autographed my own books
36. Attended a new Church
37. Saw a civil war reenactment
38. Went to OVC Semi-final game
39. Took cover in a bomb shelter for protection from a tornado
40. Visited (insert name of a local tourist-y place you've never seen)
41. Took a two-hour walk on the beach
42. Ate some fried shark (spongy)
43. Tried some fried gator (no flavor, really)
44. Found a whole sand dollar
45. Watched sting rays swimming in the ocean
46. Saw Portuguese man-o-wars

47. Attended a Titanic exhibit
48. Spent time back stage at the Opry
49. Got a picture made with Brad Paisley
50. Had my picture in the newspaper
51. Participated in judging of original musicals
52. Went to the airport observatory
53. Had make-up artist do my make-up
54. Sat for a photo shoot

What ideas can you add to this list? Start where you are and put one foot in front of another. I dare you. Now it is *your* turn to shine! Let me know how you do and what ideas you come up with! ■

J. L. Rybolt

J.L. Rybolt is the founder of Nest of Hope, an organization devoted to spreading hope throughout the world one community at a time. She grew up in the middle Tennessee area and earned Bachelor's degrees in Management and Human Relations as well Psychology, minoring in Women's Studies. She is a student of people and life and has a passion for spreading hope through donations to charitable organizations, writing, speaking, and, most importantly, listening. Ms. Rybolt coaches awesome people to find their dreams.

Her first book, "Nest of Hope: One Woman's Journey Through a Hysterectomy, The Loss of a Dream and the Quest to Hatch a New One," *was released in 2012 and has received accolades from many in the medical community including a former Surgeon General nominee as well as women and men helping them through life transitions. Her third and fourth books are currently being written.*

For additional information or to purchase her books, visit her web site at NestOfHope.com. You may also contact her at Info@NestOfHope.com.

Jennifer L. Roybolt
Info@NestOfHope.com

9

Building Your Passion "On the Side"

By Allison D. Higgins

Yes, it's just another day in your busy life. Everyone up, dressed, and fed. Lunches are packed and you're all out the door on time with minimal issues. You drop the kids at school or day care or you just head to work as usual. The weather is nice. The traffic is acceptable. Life is good. Then it happens.

That idea. It's back again. That idea that pops into your head whenever you're driving or showering or exercising or relaxing. It's a brilliant idea—one that you've thought about time and again. Yes, it's changed and morphed over time but that same concept keeps coming back into your head repeatedly. It's your side business idea. It's your passion. It brings a smile to your face and a chill to your spine as you think about how amazing it would be to bring your product or service to the world to not only earn additional money but to make a real difference in the lives of those you love and your community at large. You are full of passion and excitement as you pull into your work place parking lot..

Then back to reality: Phone calls, meetings, e-mails, reports, projects. Your morning is consumed by the busyness of your job. You really have no complaints. For the most part you enjoy your job and the people that you work with. You're comfortable. Then lunch time comes around and there it is again. Your business idea. Your passion. You take a few minutes during your lunch break to surf the web and see what similar businesses are out there. You look into some possible training you could take or a book you could read to move you closer to your dream. Then it's back to work.

Your evening is consumed with dinner and kids' activities or sporting events, or even one or two good TV shows. You spend some quality time with your spouse or partner and family and then it's off to bed. As you start to fall asleep what comes back to you as your final thought for the evening? Yes, your business idea. It's not going to go away. And guess what else? It's your obligation to your family, your community, the world, the human race, and to yourself to get out there and give it a try. Give yourself permission to live your passion. Your passion is why you were put here on this amazing Earth! I give you permission.

Here's the good news. You don't have to quit your job and completely disrupt your life and the lives of those you love. You can start your business "on the side" of both your job and your busy life, effectively and healthfully. How do I know this? Because I've done it and I meet people every day who are running successful side businesses.

Some are working toward leaving their outside jobs but some are enjoying doing both and are able to balance them quite successfully. Countless numbers of small businesses are run "on the side" and are even quite profitable. Whether your dream is to leave your current job eventually or to just have the opportunity to share your passion with the world on a part-time basis, now is your time to take the leap!

That's where I was a couple years ago, so I know exactly what you're going through. I remember thinking, "Job is good. Family is good. Life is fun, rewarding and busy. But I have something more to share. But how could I possibly fit something else in?" But, but, but . . .

Well, I did it and so can you—so must you! I'm not going to kid you and say that it's easy. As the old saying goes, if it was easy then everyone would be doing it. You've got to not be "everyone." You've got to decide to be extraordinary. There will be hard work ahead of you, new information to learn, the need to balance priorities, failures, money invested, tons of time invested, and daily habits to change, but I assure you that it will be worth it!

You picked up this book for a reason. You are already someone who can and will make a difference. You just need to get started. To help you do that I am going to share with you 16 essential principles for you to master to build your business "on the side" and share your passion with the world!

16 Principles to Building Your Business "On the Side" and Sharing Your Passion With the World

Over the last several years, I've learned some valuable lessons and worked through interesting roadblocks that I know you will face as well. To help you move forward here are 16 principles that you should master as you begin your amazing journey.

Principle 1 – Allow Yourself to Be Afraid and Embrace Your Fear

Taking a leap and putting yourself out there can be scary. In fact, it will be scary. Any big change is going to cause some stress and bring out your fears and doubts. Be ready for it, soak it up, and push through the fear. It's completely natural to be afraid and every single person who's ever stepped outside his or her comfort zone has had to face fear. Those that accept it and push through it are the ones who are successful.

Principle 2 – Pick the Right Idea

Even though you've had your amazing idea for some time now, you must step back early in the process to choose the best way to approach your idea. Two significant points to remember: One, choose something that is feasible to implement "on the side"; Two, don't choose anything that is in direct competition with your employer.

Principle 3 – Create More Time for Yourself

This principle is one of the most difficult for people to master. Your week has a fixed number of hours in it and you're going to have to set aside a portion of them to build your business. To do that, many of us have to say "No" to some activities and not volunteer for others. Take a few minutes to look at your week and your activities and make it a point to remove one or two of the extra ones.

Principle 4 – Enlist Your Supporters

The support of others is essential to your success. There is no way you'll accomplish anything truly extraordinary on your own. Period. I'm not advocating hiring employees to help run your business. I'm saying it's important to surround yourself with people who are excited and encouraging about your business. You'll need that energy as you move through different levels of growth in your business.

Principle 5 – Write Everything Down

This principle may sound like a no-brainer but it's crucial as you get busy growing your business. Carry a notebook with you everywhere. Write down your ideas, conversations you have, expenses you incur, everything. You'll be glad you wrote it down!

Principle 6 – Keep Good Financial Records

Start the habit of keeping good financial records. Each week write down your income and expenses for the week and compile them once a month. You need to know where you're going and how you're doing to ensure you move your business in the right direction.

Principle 7 – Establish Daily Habits

What you do each day will make or your break your business. We all have daily habits. You'll most likely need to add several new daily habits to your routine once you start your business. You may need to write every day, call on clients every day, post on social media every day, read every day. Decide what five daily habits are most beneficial to your growth and work them into your day. It takes 21 days to form a habit, so get busy!

Principle 8 – Fail And Fail Again

Prepare yourself for failure. Failure is key to your growth. You will not be a success until you've failed many times. You have lessons to learn and mistakes to make so get busy doing them. Remember, it's okay to fail. Get your mindset around the fact that failure is good.

Principle 9 – Recommit Every Morning

Each morning when you wake up remind yourself that you're working on something great that's going to be a gift to so many. Remind yourself that while this effort will take some sacrifice, you are an amazing person who is ready to make a big difference. Recommit to your mission and jump into your day.

Principle 10 – Invest In Yourself and Your Business

This principle is one of my personal favorites. I love to read and learn and collaborate with other like-minded people to invest in my personal growth and business building skills and to seek out advice from those that have walked the same path before me. Create a budget for training, conferences, books, masterminds, and coaches. You'll need each of these to succeed.

Principle 11 – Change Your Self Chit-Chat

What you say to yourself every day has a very powerful impact. Every minute of every day we talk to ourselves with the thoughts in our heads. They are either negative thoughts or positive thoughts. To be where you want to be, change the chit-chat in your head to positive thoughts. When you think a negative thought immediately stop and change it to a positive one.

Principle 12 – Keep It "On the Side"

As you start to build your business, be sure that you keep it "on the side." Respect your current employer and work your job during the hours that you are expected to work. Work your business in the early mornings, during lunch or in the evenings. You cannot compromise your integrity by being unfair to your employer. It will come back to haunt you later on.

Principle 13 – Be Selective In Your Activities

Since you're working your business "on the side" you'll have limited time to do what needs to get done. Be very selective in what you decide to work on. For each opportunity or task or project, examine the return on investment of your precious time and money. Don't be afraid to say "No" to activities that don't bring you much in return early on in your business.

Principle 14 – Break It Down Into 90-Day Increments

You have a lot to accomplish and sometimes the mountain feels very high. I like to break everything down into 90-day increments. Use a calendar system and set your goals based on 90-day increments then break them down to monthly, weekly and daily tasks. Being this "mechanical" with your goals and tasks is key to your success and your piece of mind.

Principle 15 – Patience Is Key

I know you want to have a million dollar business next month. I do, too! But I've learned that it takes time to learn, grow, build, and change to get where I want to be. I'm a hundred percent positive you'll get there by embracing this process with patience and understanding.

Principle 16 – Do **Not** Become Consumed

I've discovered that becoming consumed by your "side" business is a very real possibility. Don't be in a rush. Don't let it to make you crazy. Take time for yourself. Enjoy the process. It will come.

There you have it. Master these 16 principles and you're on your way to building your business and sharing your passion.

Now is your time! You picked up this book for a reason—to make a difference! Starting and building a business "on the side" is how great things happen; how new ideas are born; how great corporations are started; how economies are strengthened; how lives are changed.

Take the leap. Be extraordinary. Be a difference maker. Oh, and call me. I can't wait to hear about your idea! ∎

Allison Higgins

Allison Higgins is a motivator, encourager and lover of life. She has worked in the corporate world for over 15 years and is also an Author, Speaker and Success Coach. Allison founded Success-BookCase (www.SuccessBookCase.com) to share her passion for personal growth and business success books. She recently launched the "Your Big Success" coaching workshop to help others reach their big goals and she founded "The Side Biz Women's Network" (www.SideBizWomen. com) to provide a place for women to build businesses, share their passions and together make a difference in our world. You can find out more about Allison at www.YourBigSuccess.com and she invites you to connect with her at www.Facebook.com/AllisonDHiggins.

Allison D. Higgins,
Author, Speaker and Success Coach
www.SuccessBookCase.com
www.SideBizWomen.com
www.YourBigSuccess.com

10

What You Believe You Can Achieve
Living a Life of Unlimited Prosperity and Abundance

by Christine Ruffino

I t is one of the most basic and oldest fundamental belief systems we have. One which should dispel all of our fears, eliminate every single worry, and give us the confidence we need to live a life of unlimited prosperity and abundance. The assurance of this belief appears in one of the oldest and most respected books of all time. How many of us truly live our lives in accordance with these words:

> *Ask and it will be given to you; seek and you will find; knock and the door will be opened to you. For everyone who asks receives; the one who seeks finds; and to the one who knocks, the door will be opened.*
>
> ~ Matthew 7:7-8

Regardless of our religious affiliations or spiritual alliances, our ability to become what we think about has become known as a universal law of nature. When we truly believe we can accomplish a realistic goal, and we apply the strategies required to support that belief, we can do anything. Our beliefs are a very powerful asset but, unfortunately, they can also be an even more powerful obstacle. We all start out in life with the exact same belief systems. We are unable to cognitively recognize what we can and cannot do when we are children. Then as we develop and learn more about our limitations and our abilities, we are also persuaded to believe certain things from the people and experiences in our lives. Unfortunately, we're not always given correct guidance and we start to doubt the greatness of who we are and, even more concerning, we begin to conform to the mediocrity of the world.

While I've learned quite a few skills in the past few years to strengthen my positive belief system, I was once a very oppressed and hopeless person. This hopelessness was the result of a very misguided, learned belief system that was developed through a very abusive and dysfunctional relationship. In hindsight, I can see how I enabled this behavior that temporarily distracted me from fulfilling my desires. In the end, however, I recognize how this challenge pushed me out of my comfort zone and forced me to drastically repair my beliefs and change my life for the better.

Living through this situation also created a very powerful motivation for me to become a successful provider and role model for my beautiful and bright eight-year-old daughter and my twelve-year-old handsome and loving son. It forced me to take a good hard look at myself and my situation. I made new choices to reshape my future to be in alignment with my assets, my personality, and my values. This ultimately resulted in my having the ability to impact more lives than I ever would've thought possible.

It is on the heels of this chapter of my life that I founded the Dynamic Professional Women's Network, Inc. What was initially created as a single referral group to support the new business I was launching has rapidly developed into a very productive and successful community to which professional women all over the Chicago area desire to belong. However, this journey was not one without challenges and mistakes. As an introvert, I am not naturally comfortable meeting new people and engaging with them. It is even more uncomfortable for me to speak to a group of people and share anything about myself because I feel it could be perceived as being self-serving.

I truly enjoy helping and connecting people, so when our first single chapter multiplied into three because of its success, and we continued expanding our community into multiple chapters, I discovered my true purpose in life. Creating and maintaining a structured resource to help women achieve their success was the best way for me to tap into my God-given gifts while still forcing me to be challenged and grow in areas where I am weak. It is the lessons I learned along the way that I would like to share, to help you avoid some of the pot holes I fell into and inspire you to achieve an abundant life for yourself.

Repair and Rebuild Your Belief Systems

The very first thing I had to do was repair and rebuild myself and my belief systems so I would be strong enough to move ahead and not fall back into the dysfunctional life I was used to. My first step was to have a nice cry about the situation I was in, mourn my losses, and accept that that life is forever gone. That doesn't mean that I'll never have some version of that life back, but it will never be the same. I had to embrace this loss and take a good hard look at how and why it happened so I could learn from it.

This meant I had to ask for some honest input from friends, family, and colleagues, regardless of how difficult it might be to hear. Next, I had to forgive myself and anyone else I blamed for my situation. (Forgiveness is vital to free yourself and to allow you the golden opportunity to reinvent yourself and redefine your future to be bigger, better, and more prosperous.) Finally, I had to accept the reality of where I was and understand that it was no accident. I believe that everything happens for a purpose and a reason and that at some point in my life, I will come to understand what that reason is.

> *People are always blaming their circumstances for what they are. The people who get on in this world are the people who look for the circumstances they want and if they can't find them they make them.*
> ~ George Bernard Shaw

I also had to accept that God did not intend me to endure a negative relationship for the purpose of saving that person because I did not have that power. I am a child of God who has a lot to contribute to the world and I deserved to live a fulfilling and peaceful life. I am a strong person and a talented woman who can accomplish anything my heart desires. I just had to listen to the lessons I'd learned from my mother and that I had been teaching my daughter all her life, and that I had stopped believing myself. I had to live my life, and do what I would do if I knew I could not fail.

How Big Is Your Why?

My why was huge! I had to survive now as a single mom, I had to survive all on my own without co-parental help and without co-parental financial support. I had to finally walk away from a poisonous situation and focus on a positive new and successful life. I had to accept that I could not force someone to act a certain way nor could I force that person to fulfill obligations. When someone is determined to carry out a certain mission, he or she can sometimes find a way to "temporarily" prevail. I proceeded to live each day and each month one step at a time and I continually relied on the strength of God to keep me from giving up.

> *Seek the Kingdom of God above all else, and live righteously, and he will give you everything you need. So don't worry about tomorrow, for tomorrow will bring its own worries. Today's trouble is enough for today.*
> ~ Matthew 6:33-34

Discover Your Passion and Define Your Intended Success

The one truth I knew was that regardless of how much money I had and what other people expected of me, I was going to build a new future based on how I wanted it to be. But did I really know what that looked like? I had no idea because up into this point, I'd focused more on the happiness of others rather than on my own happiness. I went to school and earned a degree in advertising and design, but I was never able to pursue that career. A key character trait of most successful people is that they are not opposed to seeking help and wisdom from others to support their mission. Thus my first step was to obtain the assistance of a career coach, and we embarked on a journey together to discover my true passions.

I have never been motivated by money, but being in a position where money became my sole focus because of its extreme lack, it really helped to work with someone who was able to remain objective during this process. She kept me focused on finding and tapping into my true passions so I could be blessed with a financial reward rather than focusing on making money. I also found faith during this season of my life. I discovered that God blessed me with certain gifts and that I was meant to use these gifts for the good of His kingdom. And if I followed his plan for my life, He would definitely provide me with a life full of abundance. I was thirty-five and I felt like a teenager right out of college who had to "figure out what I wanted to do when I grew up." It was quite funny—scary—yet funny at the same time.

My faith was still very new and although I believed that God would provide, I also feared that I did not have the luxury of chasing my dreams while I had two kids to support and a home to maintain. And then I was blessed to be exposed to the teachings of Earl Nightingale, who said. *"Success is the progressive realization of a worthy ideal. The only people who succeed are those who are progressively realizing a worthy ideal."* He taught that you don't have to be rich to be successful and he followed that up with the following quote. *"Success is not the result of making money; making money is the result of success."* I knew I did not want to live a life struggling to make ends meet, and knowing this truth removed the burden of my having to focus on becoming rich to be successful. All I had to do was follow God's plan and I would be successful regardless of the balance in my checking account.

Plan and Execute Your Destiny With Purpose and Urgency

Now that I'd gone through the prep work to discover my gifts and didn't feel the pressure to become instantly successful, I was faced with the dilemma of finding the career that would be in true alignment with my gifts. How do I find this "dream job" and how long is it going to take? With a lot of determination and hard work, and exhibiting more faith than I ever before, I eventually found my way to what I feel is God's purpose for my life. It is not a "job" but a career that is fulfilling and makes a difference in the lives of others. It has all of the challenges associated with self-employment while it rewards me with all the many benefits.

The results we achieve in anything we do are in direct proportion to the efforts we put forth and we also must be willing to pay the price to achieve the life we desire. Below is the blue print for my plan to live a life of unlimited prosperity and abundance.

1. Understand emotionally as well intellectually that we literally become what we think about.

    A man is what he thinks about all day long.
    ~ Ralph Waldo Emerson

    We must control our thoughts and engage with people who are positive, motivated, and achieving things we aspire to achieve. When we surround ourselves with people who have succumbed to the mediocrity of life, we can still enjoy them, but we need to be aware that their lack of desire will be contagious and we should limit our interaction with them.

2. Realize that our limitations are self-imposed. God created our bodies and our minds to be amazing resources and I believe we truly have the ability to do anything we set our minds to doing. The opportunities of this world are enormous beyond belief. If we believe we deserve the very best without any doubt, and if we implement the proper strategies to manifest the very best, we will receive the very best and more.

3. Visualize what an ideal life of unlimited prosperity and abundance looks like to you. Does this picture include material possessions? Does it include time spent with your loved ones?

Does it include time to focus on your spiritual, emotional, and physical health? Let your imagination soar with endless possibilities and refuse to believe there are any circumstances strong enough to deny you of your destiny. List all the various aspects associated with this abundant life and create a visual tool like a vision board, a mind map, or index cards for you to carry with you daily to reinforce the imminent fruition of this life.

4. Create a road map to make your dreams a reality. We can have all the faith in the world, but we still have to do our part for God to do His. Take each of these aspects of your abundant life and determine exactly what needs to happen for you to achieve them. This is where you will outline your goals in specific and measurable details and then create an action plan to achieve them. Determine a timeframe that is uncomfortable and work toward making it happen by your target date.

5. Refer back to Item 2 often! Our own self-doubt is most often our biggest challenge. Re-learn this behavior and create a new habit of self-assurance to replace the self-doubt.

Stop speaking to God about how big your mountains are and start speaking to your mountains about how big your God is.

~ Joel Osteen.

Remember, we don't have to know how we are going to get there; we just need to know where we are going.

Be Comfortable With Your New Life of Unlimited Prosperity and Abundance

It's very common for people to sabotage their own success for many reasons. Most of the time it's because they feel that being rich means they're not good people or that when they have something nice and flashy, they'll be viewed as pretentious. Realize, however, that what other people think should be irrelevant to you. What you think of yourself is all that matters. If you're living in accordance to God's wishes, your abundant life will continue. No one needs to know that although you drive a fifty thousand dollar car you also contribute thirty thousand dollars every year to your church or to charity. Be content with the blessings of life and continue to strive for more, because the more you have, the more you will be able to give back.

I am happy and proud to share that I have prevailed from my previous struggles, and now have a beautiful new home and my dream car. I'm working to buy a shiny new motorcycle. I've traveled to some amazing places where I've never been before. And I am a faithful contributor to my church. I am a confident person now. I love the fact that while I'm working harder to create more wealth, I'm also creating a stronger resource for my women to allow *them* to also live a life of Unlimited Prosperity and Abundance.

> *The Lord is the everlasting God, the Creator of the ends of the earth.*
> *He will not grow tired or weary, and his understanding no one can fathom.*
> *He gives strength to the weary and increases the power of the weak.*
> *Even youths grow tired and weary, and young men stumble and fall; but those who hope in the Lord will renew their strength. They will soar on wings like eagles; they will run and not grow weary, they will walk and not be faint.*
>
> ~ Isaiah 40:28-32

■

Christie Ruffino

Christie Ruffino is the President and Founder of the Dynamic Professional Women's Network, an industry exclusive networking organization designed to help women create partnerships with each other to generate ideas, alliances, and revenues within a structured referral generating format.

In the five years since its founding, more than 1,200 members have joined DPWN in Illinois and Wisconsin, recognizing it as a driving force behind the success and profitability for many of its members' businesses. This accomplishment, along with other philanthropic efforts, inspired a nomination and following honor as one of the most Influential Women in Business of 2009 by the Business Ledger and the National Association of Women Business Owners (NAWBO), and in 2010 with an Entrepreneurial Excellence Award by the Business Ledger.

Today Christie is looking to expand her impact by working more closely with business professionals who want to build more businesses, provide more value, and manifest a more prosperous life as a John Maxwell Certified Coach.

Christie L. Ruffino
Dynamic Professional Women's Network, Inc.
1879 N. Neltnor Blvd. #316, West Chicago, IL 60185
info@dpwomen.com
www.dpwomen.com
630-336-3773 Cell

11

Finding Joy in Every Turn

By Tyler Williams

A call came over the team radio. "Caution, caution back her down." I gently rolled out of the throttle with my right foot and quickly applied pressure to the brake pedal with my left foot. I stole a glance in my rearview mirror to confirm everyone behind me had received a similar message; there was a caution on the speedway. The pace car raced onto the track and assumed its position in front of the leader. My heart pounded out of my chest.

Only a few short hours before, I was debriefing with my crew after a round of practice about the changes we needed to make to our car in an effort to cut another tenth of a second off our fastest lap time. Now here I was on a Saturday night at Lanier National Speedway, just north of metro Atlanta, driving under caution behind the leader in second place. For the last thirty laps I'd been glued to the rear bumper of the leader, Jamie Stephens, Jr.

My car had never driven so well. Prior to the caution, I flew down the straightaway and gently tapped the brake as I began to arc my car down into the corner. I kept starting my turn just a little later than Stephens in order to create a wider arc. Whenever my car rolled through to the center of the corner I stuck the nose of my car to the inside of the No. 17 of Stephens. Each time I reached the center of the corner I rolled into the throttle to try to get a run on him going down the next straightaway. My main concern was that Stephens was no rookie. I knew that if he ran a low line through the corner I'd have a hard time making the pass. If I wasn't gentle enough I'd accelerate too quickly and break traction causing the car to slide or "get loose."

Now, under caution, my spotter came on the radio and said, "You're doing a great job out there tonight, bud. Keep it up. You're faster than the 17. You know what you need to do. Clean those tires off real nice and get a good restart. Let's take this thing to Victory Lane." His reassurance bolstered my confidence. I radioed back with determination, "Ten-four, I'll see what I can do." My team and I had been working almost four years for the opportunity to take our No. 87 Chevrolet Monte Carlo to Victory Lane. I had seven laps to make my dreams come true.

* * * * *

I grew up in the suburbs of Atlanta. My father was a dentist and my mother, in addition to raising her two boys, helped him run the practice. Growing up, I was adventurous. I loved to explore, both indoors and outdoors. I needed to know how things worked and why they worked the way they did. I wanted to get lost in the woods exploring the creek for hours. My first real taste of speed came when I was seven years old. I remember it like it was yesterday. Christmas morning 1991, Santa brought my brother and me a motorcycle. From that day on I was hooked. I wanted to go fast.

Several years later I was sitting in my seventh grade homeroom class when a friend of mine approached me and asked if I wanted to go to the NASCAR race at Atlanta Motor Speedway in November. I had seen a NASCAR race on TV and enjoyed watching it so I said, "Sure." Little did I know what I was getting myself into.

We sat in race traffic for what seemed like hours, but upon reaching the track I knew I was in for a great day. Flags of all shapes, sizes, and colors were whipped around by the wind. Campers were out in full force with their charcoal grills sending smoke billowing across the parking lot. My senses were on overload. I felt like I was at the circus. There was so much to see and do. By the time the green flagged dropped and forty-three of the best drivers in the world went thundering past us, I knew then and there that I wanted to be a NASCAR race driver.

What do you do when you're twelve years old and want to go NASCAR racing? I had no idea so I asked my mom to purchase a subscription to *Stock Car Racing Magazine*. For several years I read everything I could get my hands on about NASCAR, and I learned how the top drivers in the world made it to the Cup Series. There were two common themes: They all started at an early age, and it seemed they either drove sprint cars or late models. The local track in Georgia raced late models every week. I made a plan to go racing, starting with a late model.

The only problem with my plan was that I didn't have enough money to buy all the equipment and pay for the cost of racing each week. For more than two years I talked to my mom about racing. At every opportunity, I tried to sell her on the possibilities and how if they helped me, I could become the next Jeff Gordon. Finally, after a couple of years my persistence paid off. My family agreed to help me. My grandparents had given me Walmart stock every year for my birthday growing up, so I sold every bit of it to buy my first racecar, a used late model.

I knew racing wasn't going to be easy and I was up for the challenge but, boy, was I in for a big surprise. I had unknowingly jumped into shark-infested waters. By the time my first race weekend came along I had only had a hundred laps of track experience. I was going to be up against guys who'd been racing for years, some for over two decades with thousands of laps under their belts. I was humbled that night. But I made a commitment to myself to come back and fight. I was going to be a winner.

* * * * *

With seven laps to go I knew I had to make my move early or else the No. 17 would pull away. I rolled the steering wheel back left to right, left to right, quickly, in order to clear off any dust or debris that may have stuck to the hot rubber on the Hoosier racing tires. As the pace car made its way off the track I closed in to within a foot of the bumper of the No. 17. We rolled through Turns Three and Four, and the flagman released us with his wave of the green flag.

I nailed the throttle, and as soon as my foot hit the floor I was already shifting into high gear. We roared into Turn One, and I made a look to the inside but couldn't get my car to turn under the 17. I tried again on entering Turn Three but still couldn't get my car into position. Finally, entering Turn One with six laps to go, I got my nose under the 17 and as I eased back into the throttle we made slight contact. The contact was just enough to get the 17 a bit loose, which allowed me to power beside him for a drag race into Turn Three. Once I got beside him that was all I needed. I had the preferred inside groove and coming out of Turn Four, I made the pass.

We were going to Victory Lane. Or so I thought. Just as I made the pass for the lead, the caution came out. I groaned inwardly. The last thing I needed this late in the race was a caution. The final restart is where races are won and lost. Everyone lays it on the line here. All it would take is a bump and run and my race would be over. In a split second, everything I worked for could be lost.

I wasn't about to apologize for losing this one. I calmed myself and prepared for the restart. I knew Stephens would not go down without a fight. I came over the radio and said to my crew, "Pray for sticky angels on my tires for this restart." If I didn't spin my tires I felt like I could hold him off for the final laps. As the green flagged waved I captured a great restart. My car sped off down the straightaway with the 17 square on my bumper. As we entered Turn One my car rolled effortlessly through the turn. Without another caution I knew the win would be ours.

The final four laps were nerve-racking, but as each corner passed I pulled farther and farther away from the 17. As I came out of Turn Four, I saw the flagman waving the white flag and immediately my spotter radioed, "One to go, one to go." All I had to do was hold it together for one more lap. I hit my marks and made it through the last four turns. I looked up as I made my way out of the last turn to see the checkered flag waving. I threw my left hand out the side window and pumped my fist as I crossed the start-finish line, winning my first race in the NASCAR Weekly Series.

I never imagined it would take almost four years to celebrate with my team in Victory Lane. But we finally did it. We won. I made my victory lap and drove my car to the front stretch Victory Lane to my waiting crewmembers. I was busy unhooking my HANS Device, helmet, and seatbelts as my crew reached in the car to congratulate me on a driving a great race. I climbed out of the car and stood tall on the edge of the window. I threw my fist in the air with huge smile on my face. There were hugs and high fives all around as I celebrated with my team, friends and family. I was overjoyed.

The future looked bright. The year before, I'd finished second in points in the 2006 NASCAR Weekly Series at Lanier National Speedway. And now I'd just won my first race. I didn't consider myself the next Cup Series champion, but I felt I had what it took to hang with the best.

Due to a mechanical failure we missed a race in the summer and finished third in points in 2007. While disappointed, I couldn't complain. We'd had a great year.

To top it off I'd made some connections in Charlotte, the hub of all NASCAR activity, and in October I was set to test a NASCAR East Series car. I was ecstatic. I knew it was time to progress in my development as a driver and that this was the next step. The test went well, and I had a blast. I ran over a hundred laps at the famed Hickory Motor Speedway, where many of the NASCAR greats cut their teeth.

I came back to Atlanta excited but nervous. I knew what I needed to do to keep racing. I had to find sponsors for my car. There were three divisions: a touring late model series, the NASCAR East Series, or the ARCA. The budgets ranged from a quarter of a million dollars up to a million dollars. Those amounts were staggering considering our budget for the Weekly Series was never more than twenty thousand dollars.

So, there I was getting ready to graduate from the University of Georgia in December, 2007 at the age of twenty-three, trying to sell a million dollars in sponsorship to corporate America. I had no idea what I was doing and to make matters worse, the U.S. economy had begun to crash, immediately creating a ripple effect among the minor sponsorships of short-track racing.

The 2008 season was going to be upon us in no time. I had no leads and I finally began to realize my dream of making it to the top levels of NASCAR was in serious jeopardy. I sat down with my mom one afternoon and said, "I think this is it. There's no way I'm going to find that much sponsor money this late in the year." I knew it was time for me to figure out a new plan. It didn't make financial sense for us to continue racing in the NASCAR Weekly Series.

I didn't know where to turn or what to do. I sold my car, my trailer, and the majority of our equipment. My dream of being a top NASCAR driver was over.

* * * * *

What do you do when a dream you've had for nearly a decade disappears overnight like it never existed? I certainly didn't have a clue. I didn't want to get another job. I wanted to race. I loved the thrill, the speed. I enjoyed doing promotions, meeting fans, and entertaining the crowds. It was all I knew. I felt called to race. I'd never felt so lost and I couldn't figure out why. I knew I was disappointed that I wouldn't be at the racetrack on opening day but there was something else, something deeper.

A family friend offered me a job so I took it. I made it about a year before I woke up and realized it wasn't working out. I took another job that I enjoyed, but wasn't excited about. It seemed like the right thing to do at the time—I felt like I was needed there, but it didn't fulfill me. The problem was that I didn't take the job that was meant for me.

Again, after a year and a half, I knew I needed to make a change. Slowly, I began to realize I was defining who I was by my job title and position. I was trying to find my value and worth in my position in the workplace. I was letting my job define my life.

I began attending a men's group in the fall of 2011. During the course of our meetings we discussed calling and what "calling" really meant. I remember questioning my calling in high school, and I still felt haunted by the question. I needed to know what I was supposed to do with my life. I knew I wanted to make a difference, to make an impact with my work and influence those around me, but I'd been unsuccessful at discovering what that work was. During one of our gatherings, the facilitator said, "Your calling is far too big to fit into a job." I slowly began to understand what he meant. My calling isn't something I am. My calling is a way of life, a way of living each day.

Over the past year I've looked back on the last twenty-eight years of my life and realize the most valuable moments in my life are ones where I'm helping others. And my calling doesn't require a certain a job title or position to open the door for these opportunities and interactions to take place. I listened to a friend without judgment. I celebrated an accomplishment with a family member. I spoke to high school students about character. I served those in need in a foreign country. These are the moments that brought me lasting joy. I also include racing in the moments that brought me joy, but looking back, I now see how I made racing my identity and when racing was gone, so was I, for a time.

There is a mystery to life, and until I learned to embrace the mystery I kept beating myself up over what I was going to do with my life. I thought I needed to know the twists and turns I would face in life and how I would handle them. I put myself in prison with those thoughts.

Once I gave up control I found freedom embracing where I am in the moment. I now know that I'm okay as long I remember my identity is in God, and not in anything man can credit to me. More importantly I've discovered I have a voice, and when I share my voice with the world, I am most alive. ■

Tyler Williams

Author, speaker, coach and vocalist Tyler Williams shares his journey from shy teenager struggling to be heard to becoming an inspiring entertainer in his forthcoming book, "I Have a Voice." Along the way he sang in "Joseph and the Amazing Technicolor Dreamcoat," raced NASCAR, and is now singing and speaking to encourage those who have lost their way. Finding his voice, Tyler desires to share his story of building character and discovering life's calling. Based out of Atlanta, Tyler connects with audiences across the country. To learn more about Tyler and his vision for the next generation, visit www.TylerWilliamsLive.com or www.IHaveaVoiceBook.com.

Tyler Williams
www.TylerWilliamsLive.com
www.IHaveaVoiceBook.com

12

❧

A Successful Failure

By Arsen S. Marsoobian

Is it possible to have a successful failure? Is that like winning the battle but losing the war? Maybe it is. "We didn't lose the game, we just ran out of time." Over the seven score and seven years I have lived I've had many successes and many failures, depending on who counted and how it was counted. Both "Success" and "Failure" get their power from the definition assigned to them and the reaction you have to any circumstance.

In my book *Don't Die*, I cover what I've discovered to be three main activities that will keep you feeling alive. First, keep learning. Second, keep doing. Third, keep giving. Each of these actions is covered in depth, with real life stories and facts supporting my theory. The eight point action steps from my book are included at the end of this chapter as a bonus for you.

This story starts in the year 2001, with my move back to Fresno, California after an eleven-year absence due to a job change. The feelings and range of emotions went from excitement to fear of rejection by friends and family. I had survived two five-vessel heart by-pass surgeries over a span of seventy days in late 1999. I was divorced from a seven-and-half-year marriage, was unemployed, and dealing with mild form of depression. The thought of starting over as an independent life insurance representative at age sixty-six was very scary.

I wish I could tell you it was easy and I was happy but the opposite was true. A saying I learned years earlier from The Optimist International Creed gave me encouragement to move on: "Forget the mistakes of the past and press on to great achievements of the future." It took a few years but I returned to a "normal life" of work, social activities, time with my family, a relationship with a new woman, and paying my bills.

Then just as things were getting better I started to have pains in my left arm and chest during periods of exercise. Thinking it was just fatigue I ignored the possibility of a heart problem until the pains became more regular. I told my doctor what was happening and after few heart tests, I was on my way to a Northern California heart specialist for a third open-heart by-pass surgery in March of 2004.

Around three months later, on Father's Day, my son Bryan and daughter-in-law Julie thought it was time for "Pop" to slow down and enjoy retired life. They surprised me with every retiree's dream, a membership to their golf country club. It was fun learning more about the game of golf and developing my skills and making new friends. By my third year I had set the club's record of rounds played in one year at a hundred seventy-four. My scores improved, which led to my winning tournaments. A special one was the Club's Presidents Cup with my son and me as a team. Making that last winning putt and hugging Bryan was a moment in time we'll never forget. The trophy and money paled in comparison to the joy and sense of accomplishment that came over me. Could life get any better than this? This was a success, right? Wrong! I was still feeling unfulfilled and quietly asking myself if this was how I would spend my last days.

During the next four-year period and a tough series of events, I became involved in a home-based business through a friend from another state. When the company's national convention was announced I decided to join my friend for a weekend vacation in Jacksonville, Florida. The keynote speaker was Mark Victor Hansen, author of Chicken Soup for The Soul. At the end of his presentation he made a "special offer" to anyone who purchased the Internet Marketing program he promoted. This was a free ticket to attend a three-day $497.00 Mega Speaking Seminar in Los Angeles.

A few in my group bought the program thinking it would be a good opportunity to meet again, as well as learn some tips on platform speaking. The seminar turned out to be a three-day selling fest with fifteen speakers all giving good information and then selling their seminar tapes and books. The dream of my past years of being a motivational speaker came rushing back with an unbelievable feeling of elation and hope.

The feelings were so overwhelming I found myself in the back of the room signing up for one seminar after another. My friends tried to get me to stop, but the suppressed desire to be a public speaker and make a difference was erupting inside of me. Before the dust settled I put $10,000 on my credit card and registered for four different seminars in California and Las Vegas.

One person from this event made an impact on my life, and she wasn't even one of the speakers. Her name is, Lynn Rose, and she had a booth in the lobby promoting her "WOW Factor" seminar and selling her musical CDs.

One of the programs I purchased was a week-long seminar on "Presentation and Platform Skills Training" by Chris Howard. On the last day, just before the "Certification" presentation, we had a surprise speaker by the name of Les Brown. This man would become another big influence in my newfound life. The connection with Les was one of those meant-to-be-events. After hearing Les tell his story I knew I had to study with him, so out came the credit card. I was soon registered for the two-day "Story Telling Workshop."

When I returned to a calmer state of mind and thought about why I'd signed up for the speaker training sessions, I decided I had better uses for my money. Several requests for a refund went unanswered. The event was two days away when Les Brown, himself, called to ask why I'd requested a refund. My heart stopped for a minute, I took deep breath, and told him it was too late in life for me to become a platform speaker like him. During the next forty-five-minute phone conversation with a man who is paid $35,000 for his one-hour presentation, he made me believe that at age seventy-four, I still had the potential to live my dream of helping people live a better life by sharing my experiences.

You see, I was ready to give up on my dream again because I thought I was too old. But this total stranger told me, "You have greatness within you," and he was not going to let me give up. At the end of our conversation, with tears of joy I agreed to take him up on his offer to work with me and to make sure I got back in the game of life. A total cost of $2,000 had been about to keep me from living my dream. What is keeping you from finding "The greatness within you"? You have it.

The learning process has taken me to several more seminars and speakers training workshops over the last four years. The new skills have improved my speaking and storytelling abilities. The list of my teachers in addition to Les Brown are the very best in the profession: Marshall Sylver, world's greatest hypnotist; Darren La Croix, Toastmasters International World Champion Speaker; Mark Victor Hansen, best-selling author, speaker, and trainer; international speaker, author, and trainer, Chris Howard; and the young lady mentioned earlier—singer, speaker, trainer, coach and, personal friend, Lynn Rose. Lynn has a very unique two-and-a-half-day personal development program entitled "The WOW Factor."

My first "WOW Factor" came at a time when the credit cards were screaming, "Stop!" For whatever reason, Lynn, like Les, insisted I attend, and talk to the credit cards later. There were nine strangers who started this very special process. Everyone gave freely of himself or herself with each segment and we bonded into a group of lifetime friends. In the last segment we each shared a life goal in front of the group. My goal that day is the basis for this story. The goal I committed to on Sept. 12, 2009 was to be on stage speaking with the great Les Brown and Lynn Rose, on my seventy-fifth birthday, which was Dec. 22, 2009. Author and speaker Michelle Prince was the first to volunteer to help by speaking at the event for free. Best-selling author Diana Wentworth, and Lynn Rose also agreed to help me reach my goal. This was no time for second thoughts.

My goal's challenges were:

1. Seek availability and agreement by Les Brown
2. Book a facility
3. Find sponsors

4. Publicize my event
5. Prepare my own presentation
6. Develop my program for the day
7. Have contracts signed
8. Select charities to receive proceeds
9. Hire video and audio to record the event
10. Sell tickets.

All this in a hundred days. I wish I could tell you that I met my goals in those one hundred days. I didn't.

However, on March 24, 2010 at age of seventy-five, I danced my way onto the stage and back into the game of life. The feeling was overwhelming when I received standing ovation at end of the dance. That night I shared the stage with, Les Brown, Lynn Rose, Michelle Prince, Jeff Eben, Bill Walsh, Diana Wentworth, and a local gymnastic performance group called Break the Barriers. The event was booked in a 2,300-seat theater named after world famous playwright, William Saroyan, who wrote the Pulitzer Prize play, *The Time of Your Life*.

My biggest setback came two days before the event when facilities management called to inform me they needed $7,500 in advance if the event was going to be videotaped. The local NBC-TV affiliates had agreed to do the taping as part of a sponsorship agreement so a quick decision had to be made about whether to cancel, postpone, or go forward without the taping. I made the decision to do the show without the video.

The event was a "Successful Failure." The performance and information given by all the speakers touched the lives of countless people. All three hundred in attendance had a marvelous time. My goal of speaking on stage with Les Brown and Lynn Rose in my hometown was fulfilled and lifelong relationships were built. However, from the view of my banker, creditors, and facilities management, it was a failure. It cost me all of my savings and the credit cards were at a point of serious rebellion. Financial setbacks aside, it was a day that will live with me forever because it made a difference to hundreds of lives.

The best definition of success, which has guided me since 1967, when I first learned it from Earl Nightingale's "The Strangest Secret". He said "Success is the progressive realization of a worthy ideal." I have taken this to, Success is the daily progression toward a predetermined worthwhile goal." The event was a success and I continue to learn and move forward with new goals and dreams each day. Success came at the cost of money, loss of relationships, loss of sleep, and periods of doubt but I believe it was better than the alternative. My renewed life has come from the renewing of my mind, learning a new skill, and acting on my passion by giving back through sharing my experiences with young and old alike.

Take a moment and reflect on what you've accomplished in your life. Would your successes have happened without your taking action on your ideas? Now think of all the ideas, projects, and experiences that you wanted to pursue but haven't. They're still waiting to be fulfilled, if you're willing to do a little work. It's never too late. Make today, now, "the time of your life."

> *You don't have to be great to get started but you have to get started to be great.*
>
> ~ Les Brown

Writing a book was just a dream until I started the action of capturing my life experiences on paper. The action part of life is where experience comes from. You can't gain experience without acting on any subject or idea about which you've learned. The people who give us most of the things we enjoy in life are the ones who've taken action on their ideas.

What attitude will you take into the last stage of your life? Sitting around complaining and waiting for the end to come, or suiting up and getting back in the game of life?

A process is available that will help you explore the different interests you have and to choose one or two that will add life to your years. Making sure your dream is attainable before you start will save you a lot of grief. This is a formula from one of the many motivational programs that have directed my life. I hope it will help you put the pieces together and give you courage to follow your dream. This will take work on your part, but the results will "add life to your years." This process can be applied to goals in each part of your life (mental, physical, family, social, spiritual, and financial).

In the world of Real Estate a common question when establishing the value of property is, "what is its highest and best use?" What is the highest and best use of your time, talent, and energy? What is the value of your goals? These are question to ask yourself, as you go through the process.

Here is your bonus eight-step formula. Answer each question as completely as you can before moving on.

1. What do I really want to accomplish or have for the balance of my life?
2. If my answer to the first question is true, why am I not doing it or having it?
3. Make a list all the reasons you're not doing or having what you want. (This is list of short and intermediate goals and task I need to achieve to answer the first question.)
4. Develop a realistic time line to complete each activity listed from number three.
5. List the cost in terms of your time, changes to life style, finances, and energy for each activity listed in your answer to number three.
6. Now that I have action items from answering the fourth and fifth questions, I know what I need to do to achieve the goals from the third question. Is what I listed in my answer to the first question worth the cost of those actions?
7. If your answer to the sixth question is "yes" then get started because it is all but accomplished. You know where you're going and what you want, and you have a plan of action and time line to get it done. Congratulations! You're successful. You have a predetermined worthwhile goal that you can work toward on daily basis.
8. If your answer to the sixth question is "no" then discard the list from the first question because you now know the difference between a realistic attainable goal and a wish. The dream has very little chance of becoming a reality unless you are willing to overcome the obstacles listed in your answer to the third question.

I hope this formula helps you find the goals that will bring joy and prosperity into your life.

"Dare to Be a Difference Maker" — It's never too late to make an impact in your life and in the lives of those whom your life touches. If it takes learning new skills or learning more about a subject then get started right now. Take the necessary actions to gain the knowledge and then turn that knowledge into your experience.

Someday you'll look back on your life and either say, "I'm glad I did!" or "I wish I had". What will it be for you? I hope you'll "Dare to Be a Difference Maker." ■

115

Arsen Marsoobian

Arsen S. Marsoobian, C.L.U. is owner and CEO of his umbrella company for three major areas he works in. The company is called SOOB ENTERPRISES, LLC. SOOB is acronym for Arsen's philosophy. (S) Success on daily basis; (O) Optimism as philosophy of life; (O) Over-achieve in every task; (B) Belief in the GOD of Universe .He often asks his audiences if they are A SOOB? The major areas are Life Insurance Sales, Author and Speaker, and Event Planner. With over seven decades of experience in both government service and private business world he has a wealth of knowledge to share. He has been recipient of several awards in both fields and for his community service work.

Beyond formal education Arsen became a student of personal development programs going back more than 40 years. His recent mentors have been Les Brown, Chris Howard, Lynn Rose and Michelle Prince.

As a survivor of five heart surgeries, three by pass and two with stints, Arsen's book titled "DON'T DIE - 3 Essential Laws for Your Fulfilled and Happy Life" *can be found on his website,www.ArsenSMarsoobian.com*

Arsen's goal in life now is to have a positive impact on the lives that his life touches.

He is father of three children, and has six Grandchildren. He is currently living and working from his hometown of Fresno CA.

Arsen S. Marsoobian, C.L.U. SOOB ENTERPRISES, LLC

13

With a Little Perseverance

By Simone Simon

I received my education in business and interior design, and for a while I was a commercial interior designer in New York City. I loved the city and I was intoxicated by its beauty and charm.

But, as the saying goes, there's no place like home. For me, home was Golden, Missouri, where my parents lived. My husband was retiring from the Marine Corps and since home was calling, we moved to Golden just down road about a mile from my parents' place.

Golden, Missouri is as opposite of New York City as high noon is to the stroke of midnight. It is located in the rolling hills of the Ozarks, nestled on the banks of Table Rock Lake. Prime bass fishing and the quiet life style is its main draw.

In 1998 the husband of a friend of mine committed suicide. As usual, with this sort of death, my friend was left with questions unanswered. She told me that she wanted to find a rock on top of a mountain somewhere so she could just pray. I have always been a very spiritual person and she told me, "You are the only person I know who will understand this." So when she invited me to go hiking in Arizona, I went with her.

After arriving we unpacked our backpacks and grabbed a quick salad along with the single serve dressing packets. As I applied my sunscreen an idea hit me. "Why doesn't anyone have sunscreen in a single use packet?" I asked holding up the packet of salad dressing.

This was long before single use packets were available to purchase, like they are today.

"That's great idea," My friend answered.

Now, as we climbed up the trail to the top of the mountain, with each step I took my mind was racing with this idea of the sunscreen. At the top of the mountain I gave my friend time to pray and I read the ingredients on the sunscreen container. I didn't know what half the words listed in the ingredients meant. I figured if you can't say the word, it can't be good for you. That was when it struck me: Sunscreen can be all natural, and not be harmful.

If I was obsessed with the idea on the way up the mountain, I was going mad with the idea on the way down. The idea of a natural sunscreen was reeling in my mind like an endless loop. I told my idea to my friend and she liked it. It needed a name. We began tossing out names Sunpak, Sunpal—the names kept pouring out, but nothing was right. Suddenly I turned around and threw my arms up in the air and said. "Sunbuddy loves you!" I laughed because it was so corny, but corny works in marketing.

Returning home, my obsession became my calling as if it was what I'd been put on Earth to do. I trademarked the name and spent three years doing research. I learned what the ingredients in the leading sunscreens really were, and what harm they could do to people. The ingredient that prevented users from getting skin cancer, could end up giving them cancer of another type. This made me even more determined to develop an all natural product. I continued to research different formations and ingredients. No wonder the big companies used chemicals in their sunscreens, it was much easier. I finally found the perfect formula. I researched labs that could prepare the formula.

It was in November of 2000 when the product first saw the light of day and was launched. I considered who would be best served by my product. I came to the conclusion that target marketing was the best method for me. The target—places where people go for the day and may not think to bring sunscreen, or don't want to pack a bottle—like the zoo and botanical gardens.

Like all business owners I believed in the product, but doubts ran in my mind. I worried that these places wouldn't want to buy my product. Happily that was not the case. Those venues bought my product, as did their customers. Everything seemed to be going well. I was even getting reorders.

Winter came and it was cold and people didn't think much about sunscreen during this season. But I looked forward to next summer and getting my product out to even more places. And then it happened.

On February 17, 2001 the house that I'd just moved into five weeks before burned to the ground. It was gone, I lost everything I owned. In the face of this tremendous loss, I figured I had two choices. I could just walk away and move on, or I could dust myself off and rebuild. I chose to rebuild.

Within five months there was a house standing where the rubble of burnt dreams once laid. The house wasn't finished, but we were able to move back in. At least it felt a little normal. Since summer was now here I decided to refocus on building up Sunbuddy.

There was another drawback—we were short on funds. My husband found an investment brokerage firm to help us do a private placement offering to raise capital for the company. With this in place we were able to raise a little capital and increase our inventory and improve the artwork. More orders were flowing in and business was good. I was excited!

While my professional life was growing, my personal life was on its way down. I filed for divorce. It was a hard struggle now on my own, and scary at times, but I am a strong willed woman and wouldn't let it get me down. I continued trying to build up the Sunbuddy name and get more and more of the product out there.

On February 9, 2003 it happened again. My house burned to the ground. I lost everything once again. I was devastated! Once again I rebuilt. My saving grace this time was that three days earlier my horse, JC Miracles, was born. His name came to me in a dream inspired by Jesus Christ being the Maker of Miracles. And miracles were what I needed.

More challenges set in. The investment firm was involved in some unethical behavior with my soon to be ex-husband. They tried to steal the business and trademark, and forced my company into an involuntary Chapter 7 Bankruptcy. I'd trusted them and agreed to some high-interest notes to grow the company. It was a colossal mistake. They called the notes in, so I was forced to spend the next nine months in and out of bankruptcy court. It was nerve racking.

All during this time I could not sell or be around my product or I would face criminal charges and perhaps arrest. I spent many days crying and praying for God to 'take over and drive.' My prayers were answered. I won and bought back the assets and started a brand new company. Once again I was looking for funding to get my company going.

The gentleman who did my artwork told me about another man who worked for Walmart helping small business grow and potentially become vendors for Walmart. The gentleman from Walmart began spending money on new art work and arranged meetings with buyers and production people. He also arranged a meeting with another man who was willing to invest and to give me working capital. In exchange for this they each wanted a third of the company. They would have forced me out so I said no.

I'd given the man who worked for Walmart shares of the company for the money he had put in, but he sold not one thing to his connections at Walmart, and now he was going to sue me and take over my company. He wanted the name, not the product. Well I was ready for this fight and I hired a great attorney. I was struggling to survive and worked for her as a paralegal to pay the bill. One week before the trial was to begin they dropped the case.

Adding to the stress of the trial was the fact that my dad was not well, and, sadly, he passed away. Then mother fell and broke her hip.

The irony of this was I won an award for being a top woman-owned small business from the State of Missouri.

Once my mother recovered, I knew Missouri held nothing for

me and that it was time to move on. Since I'd always liked Arizona I began researching for a place to live there. It took me a year to find the right city. I settled on Prescott Valley. I even got a job offer to help ease the pain of the move.

Early in 2011, I sold what I could and loaded up two dogs and a cat and headed to the land of the sun. It seemed the perfect place for sunscreen and for me to rebuild Sunbuddy once again. As I turned onto the road that led up to my new home, The Beatles' song, *The Long and Winding Road,* was playing. I wept tears of joy for I was home. I thought my dreams were about to come true, but again, another nightmare was about to occur.

After four months, the company I working for closed its doors. I sent out resumes but there were no offers. Luckily it was summer and I had some product left to sell to pay the bills.

In September, my doctor found lumps in my breast and scheduled an MRI. Fortunately the lumps were non-cancerous. This was also the time I reconnected with a friend from high school back in Missouri. Our emails back and forth helped me stay attached to my home town.

Just like every other year, when the summer ended, orders began to dwindle and by December I was scrambling to make ends meet. The New Year brought no relief and I was two months behind in rent and facing eviction. With the help of charities and friends I was able to avoid the eviction. But bills were still piling up, and food was scarce. I was hungry and wondering where help was going to come from.

I believe that God places friends in our lives just when we need them the most. My friend and his wife back in Missouri knew I needed help without my even asking. They offered to send me money for food, gas, and other necessities. I can honestly say my friends in Arizona and Missouri kept me alive during this difficult time.

My hopes rose in March as I learned that I was to be awarded a grant from the state of Arizona. I thought my ship had come in, but it sunk just as soon as it pulled into port. It was a reimbursable grant! I had to have the money and spend it, in order to receive the money from the state.

This roller coaster ride was about to destroy me, and my friends in Missouri were riding it with me. Again late with the rent and facing eviction, I sold a 55-gallon drum of sunscreen to an esthetician group and I was able to stay and pay some bills.

All this time I was hustling to find an investor, with no luck. April brought the toughest month. Orders were coming in, but I couldn't fill them without the funding to pay for and sell my product, to then submit the paid invoices and be reimbursed by my grant. To make matters worse, I learned I had to use the grant by the end of June or I would lose it.

Again I was facing eviction, I was scared to death that I was going to be living in my truck with my pets. They're like my kids and I could never leave them. My friends were still helping me, but I was out of luck, money, and product and had no hopes for a job. I was praying, my friends were praying, whole churches were praying. Then it happened.

Friends here in Arizona agreed to invest ten grand. It was the answer to my prayers. With that money I was able to pay the rent, the bills that were past due, and get drums ordered. This allowed me to use the grant money, which enabled me to order more drums.

I'm doing well now, but I know that at any moment dark days could appear again. However, I don't worry, for I'm inspired to remember the *Book of Job*. And I know that with the love of friends, the Light of God, and the power of prayer I can make it through anything. ■

Ms. Simon has always been fascinated with natural and holistic health & nutrition. She became obsessed with finding a healthy alternative to the chemical based sunscreen products on the market researching and working with FDA cosmetic labs. She was able to launch Sunbuddy®Sunscreen.

Experienced in product development, formulation and distribution she decided to produce and promote SunBuddy.® She has 22 years plus expertise in business development, marketing, product, and consumer research.

Simone Simon

She is recognized for her marketing and sales ability, combined with creative thinking. As a project manager in commercial interior design based in New York City, she has been recognized for her leadership abilities, including projects with The City of New York, and the Mayo Clinic of Scottsdale Arizona.

Simone Simon is President & CEO,
of SunBuddy® Sunscreen

14

The Real Secret of Success

By Mark Ehrlich

W hat if I shared a concept with you that *could change your life* as you know it, if you implemented it, internalized it? That could guarantee your success? Was created in a way that would give you *everything* you've only dreamed about?

My life story of massive successes, then huge failures, followed by redemption, has given me the insight to write, teach and explain the *real secret of success*. Because of my failures, I've had the opportunity to work with many successful people and learn their secrets. And did I mention that ninety percent of highly successful people turned their lives around after failures using the concept I'm about to share with you? From Bill Bartmann, the billionaire nobody has heard of; Rudy Ruettiger, from the movie *Rudy*; Michael Gerber, the *Thought Leader of Entrepreneurship*; John Assaraf; Ken Blanchard; Howard Partridge; John Maxwell; and the list goes on.

There is a very serious problem with American Society today, and that problem is that people are told that their feelings are more important than anything else in the world. If you don't "like" your job, quit and get one you do like. If it feels good, do it. If it doesn't feel good, don't do it. If you don't like your wife, divorce her and get another one. If you don't want to have a baby, but you want to have unprotected sex, do it, and get an abortion. If you don't feel good about something, you don't have to do it. It's a serious problem, starting with our public school system and running through the entire American society.

Feelings are the most important thing in the world. You must be very careful not to hurt the "feelings" of blacks, men, women, Asians, Hispanics, employees, coworkers, people of different faiths from yours, homosexuals, lesbians, animals, and fish.

My point is best summarized by the ex-heavyweight champion Joe Frasier, who was asked why he got up every morning and ran five miles. His reply was, "Every job has its roadwork." This means every job has its difficult, unpleasant, non-enjoyable, and bad-feeling aspects. And so does every relationship, every education, every marriage, every child, and everything. Period.

Now let me introduce you to the concept of OMA, which stands for Obsessive Mental Attitude. This concept might be better explained by Bill Bartmann's philosophy of "picking every single hair off the rabbit." This means being obsessive in doing, learning, and thinking, and acting with focus, determination, dedication, and deep thought. It's important to note that Obsessive Mental Attitude (OMA) and Positive Mental Attitude (PMA) are different concepts.

PMA, or Positive Mental Attitude, is what fostered this "feelings" idea in the first place. And so did every other positive motivation concept out there. They all have a list of rules for how to follow their exact plans to stay positive—have a positive marriage, a positive job experience, a positive child birth (or child abortion), a positive relationship with your fellow workers, and on and on. If you've tried these programs, you've no doubt learned that *you can't stay positive*, so all of these programs fail sooner or later. And guess who the scapegoat is—you, you, you. It's your fault the program didn't work because you didn't stay positive, or didn't follow their daily mantras, affirmations, or step by step programs. It is not the fault of the programs; it's your fault.

The same thinking flows over to your marriage, your work, your job, your family, and your life in general. If you can't stay positive about your job, your marriage, your education, then you can quit.

It is not your fault you can't stay positive, it is the job's fault or your wife's fault. If you keep looking long enough, sooner or later you'll find the perfect marriage, the perfect job, the perfect child, the perfect vocation.

But remember Joe Frasier, "Every job has its roadwork." Every job, every marriage, every child, every education. Every aspect of life has its positive and negative points, and often the negatives seem more prevalent than the positives. And if you are relying upon the power of positive thinking, PMA, seed faith, or any of the other "feeling" motivational ideas, you are not going to get the job done. It is only with the power of an Obsession that you will have the strength to get through the negative and the positive aspects of life and become successful. Using OMA, not only will help you "get through" the positives and negatives, you won't even notice them with any great concern.

When my son makes a mistake, I don't silently put another mark on the side of "leaving him in the street for the dogs." I am Obsessed with him. He can make mistakes, but I will spend a lifetime forgiving him and directing him so that he does less wrong, and more right. It should be that way in your marriage, your work, your education, your vocation. If you are Obsessed about your job the way you are Obsessed about your child, you will take the good with the bad. The long hours will go by like seconds, as you use every working moment to achieve your vision.

While I was researching this article I discovered to my amazement that many people didn't even know the phrase Positive Mental Attitude, and that bothered me until I remembered that everyone does know the word Positive. If you asked a hundred people the mental secrets of success they would probably say, "Staying positive."

And so I ask, "What do you think are the mental aspects of success? What are the steps that you must take mentally to assure your success?" Most people would be hard pressed to answer these questions at all, but those who have read several motivational books and attended motivational lectures, would probably give you an answer something like this:

1. You must have a written list of goals.
2. You must have a deadline for the date you will achieve your goals.
3. You must have a plan of action for achieving those goals.
4. You must stay positive and believe in yourself while you work toward your goals.
    a. To do that, we suggest, reading motivational books daily, attending motivational seminars, watching DVDs, and buying more books.
    b. To stay positive we also suggest that you write down your goals on a sheet of paper and review them daily to be sure you're taking action on your goals, and staying positive while you follow your plan of action.

This is a fine list of the mental aspects of success, and we've all probably used it dozens, hundreds, even thousands of times, and failed. Is it your fault for not following the plan of action and saying your affirmations correctly? How can you follow the "proven plans of success" so many times and keep failing? What could be wrong?

What's wrong is that when you wrote down your goals, plan of action, and daily affirmations, you forgot the most important thing— "The Obsession." All these steps would work just fine if the first piece—the written set of goals—was an Obsession rather than just a set of goals.

The most profitable scam in business today is selling "goal setting ideas." Time and time again we're asked to write a list of the things we would do if we Knew We Could Not Fail, the things we would buy if we Knew We Could Not Fail, the type of person we would be, if we Knew We Could Not Fail. Most people, with a little prodding, are capable of writing down a million dollars, fame, fortune, happy marriage, health, education, travel, and so on. And the speakers smile and say, "That's great. Now the only thing stopping you is you and your attitude as you begin your efforts to achieve these goals."

All you have to do is "believe" and you will "succeed" at any of these goals. They really believe that, and for a few days you might too. Until you actually begin working on attaining your "wish list," and realize that you just can't seem to stay positive long enough to complete all the items on your lists. You see, the problem is that these "goals" are just adventures in Creative Writing 101 for adults. They're just imagination stretchers and dream castles that you build with the speakers' help, and your eyes closed. Only when your "dream" is an Obsession will you make it your possession.

Let me ask you to fill out a better list, instead of writing a list of the things you would do, if you were sure you could not fail, or if money was no object. Make a list of the things you would not want to lose at any cost. In fact, make a list of the things for which you would sacrifice to keep, and make a list of the things you would die for. This is a real list of items that you would work to get, are working to get, and will work to get, and the amount of money or time or effort necessary won't matter.

Your list is your personal list of your Obsessions. For some it may include children, and for others it will include your work. For all, it will include air, food, water, heath, freedom, security, happiness, home, etc. The other stuff, the stuff on your "dream PMA list" is not on this list, and that's why you don't have it.

Let me ask you another question. How do you motivate your children to succeed? Most people would respond with the old PMA stuff—trying to help them stay positive about themselves, and telling them they can do anything they want, if they just stay positive and believe. That's great, but they can't stay positive, so you'd better add Obsession. Give them Obsession. Give them moral character as an Obsession. Give them courage as an Obsession. Give them hard work, the love of work, as an Obsession. Give them faith in God as an Obsession. Then, tell them whatever they want to accomplish they can, and they will *know it is true.*

Don't tell your children there is no right or wrong, there is no good or bad, there is no God. Don't tell them that the Government owes them a living. Don't tell them that if they don't like it they don't have to do it. Give them Obsession to do good, Obsession to serve their fellow man, Obsession to do something great for America, Obsession to protect those around them, and they will become great people.

Now I challenge you to look at your life, your vision, your mission, and your purpose with an Obsessive attitude. You can't afford to fail. There's too much riding on it. Just remember the struggles that Rudy faced to get into Notre Dame, to play football, to make that tackle. He didn't do it with a positive mental attitude. He accomplished it with an Obsessive Mental Attitude. Nothing was going to stop him. Rudy acted like his life depended on it. He is the exemplar of "Never, ever give up!" What could be more obsessive? More all consuming?

What about you? What are your obsessions? What do you want to accomplish as if your life depended on it? What's really important in your life? What are you going to get Obsessive about? What do you really want in your life? How important are your hopes, dreams, and aspirations? What problems are you going to solve? ■

Mark Ehrlich

I have been called The Coach to the Coaches, A Quilt Maker and Chief Negotiator. My background and experience allows me to support your workshops, seminars, keynote speaking, and coaching, aiding your personal and professional growth through study and practical application of today's proven leadership methods. Working together, I will move you and/or your team or organization in the desired direction to reach your goals.

As a highly experienced, "been there done that" business executive bringing real world experience to the table, in the last 10 years I have been a Chief Negotiator for some of the world's most recognized organizations and business leaders. My clients have included major sports agents, medical professionals, sought after inspirational lecturers, global leadership gurus and self-made billionaires. My clients have included motivational speaker Rudy Ruettiger, "Everything Counts" author Gary Ryan Blair, "The Dreaming Room," " E-myth" author and entrepreneurial thought leader, Michael Gerber, Bill Bartmann, the billionaire that nobody ever heard of and "The Secret's" John Assaraf of One Coach to mention a few. I have also had the opportunity to Coach the Coaches like Howard Partridge, Lance Edwards, Michelle Prince, Rudy Ruettiger etc.

My passion is to support, mentor and coach those companies and individuals who positively impact small business. According to Michael Gerber, this is the Age of the New Entrepreneur. I am fortunate to work with this new brand of new entrepreneur who is interested in solving many of the problems that are facing our global community today.

As a founding member of the Franchise Community Foundation. I have served on the board of the Educational Foundation of the International Franchise Association (IFA), on the advisory council of the IFA's Supplier's Council, and on the organization's Minority in Franchise Committee and Public Relations Committee. I have also worked as the national co-vice chair of the National Federation of Independent Business Association

Foundation (NFIB), was a delegate to the International Small Business Council in Toronto, and served as the president of the Oakland Raider's Lineman's Club and support the Deacon Jones Foundation.

Most recently I am a founder and director of the Fallen Heroes Family Camp. The camp is dedicated to teaching the children of the fallen soldiers how to ride horses and have a week of camp learning new skills.

I am looking forward to assisting you on your journey to becoming a successful leader. Please contact me via email at ehrlichm@msn.com or via phone at 858-354-2611 to discuss your dreams, goals, aspirations and vision.

Mark Ehrlich
858 354-2611
ehrlichm@msn.com
www.johnmaxellgroup/markehrlich

15

❦

Against the Wind

By Ruth Jaechen

This is a story for all the people who started off in life as relatively ordinary, nothing special, and certainly not a "difference maker." Then one day you walk through a door that clearly states "Do Not Enter," and everything changes.

I was brought up in Northern California by devoted Christian parents who were very involved in the Presbyterian Church. Both my parents worked full-time jobs. My dad was one of thirteen assistant attorneys in the office of the California Attorney General's Office. My mom was a full-time nurse. We had vacation home in Tahoe City (Lake Tahoe, California) where we spent most weekends, summers, and some Holidays. My parents worked a many hours and my dad traveled extensively for work. As a result, I had plenty of unsupervised time during which I picked up some very bad habits early in life.

My very first and closest friend was Beth, who lived in Tahoe City not far from where our cabin was. I was eight years old when we met. Beth and I drank alcohol and smoked marijuana and by the age of fourteen, I was an alcoholic. This pattern of drug and alcohol addiction would follow me through most of my youth and early adult life. I always felt lonely and alone growing up and I spent a lot of time trying to remedy those feelings.

In my quest to feel loved, I opened the next wrong door and

became pregnant at the age of fifteen-and-a-half by a twenty-two year old man—and found no love there. He was afraid of facing charges for statutory rape and quickly orchestrated his way out to protect himself. My family never knew who the father was and insisted on an abortion. I was too young to understand the choice I was making. My mom, who I trusted completely and who was a nurse, said it was best for me—my life would be ruined otherwise. Some wrong doors can never be closed, or the pain from their opening lessened.

I met my first husband, Mark, as part of a group of friends when I was seventeen and he was fifteen. When we met again, I was twenty-three and we began dating. The tornado in my life had landed and I walked through yet another wrong door.

Soon after Mark and I began dating my health started to decline. I was diagnosed with hypothyroidism and later diagnosed through surgery with polycystic ovarian disease. I've also been in five car accidents, suffered multiple spinal and head injuries, and developed fibromyalgia, degenerative disc disease, and pre-diabetes in my early twenties.

Mark and I were together for fourteen years. We both had the same bad habits with drug addiction and alcoholic behaviors. Things began to change a few years after we got married. Mark was diagnosed as bipolar. He chose to self-medicate rather than seek a doctor.

Mark became violent and unpredictable. I learned quickly what "walking on eggshells" meant. He had severe mood swings, combined with depression and long bouts of crying and feelings of worthlessness. Mark had been emotionally abused for years by his alcoholic father. I was determined to be a source of salvation and comfort to Mark even through the violence. But my daily stress and anxiety affected my own health conditions to the point that I could hardly move and could not work anymore.

Mark turned out to be a master manipulator and was difficult to live with, keep house for, cook for, shop for, and so on. Picture Julia

Roberts in the movie, *Sleeping with the Enemy*, and you've got the picture. Mark was always in and out of work so we lived off and on with his mother.

He separated me from my family by convincing me they were against him. He tried to separate Beth and me, but Beth was my lifeline to sanity. All my other friends were friends we shared in common. Most of them knew nothing of the tortured life I lived behind closed doors except Beth and Mike (Mark's oldest and best friend).

The illness and the pain I suffered were a very sore spot for Mark. He blamed me for getting sick and making his life tedious and boring. He began to spend more and more time away, staying with friends, sometimes for days at a time. I learned that, if I was smart, I wouldn't ask Mark where he'd been or when he was coming home.

Women hung out at his friends' houses where he played pool and partied. I was crushed when I went to my doctor with a female problem only to find out I had HPV Virus (a sexually transmitted disease). I knew I hadn't given it to myself. When I asked him about it, I was accused of cheating.

My story is filled with trials and pain, but that's not really what it's about. You see, although I had walked away from God, He had never left me. He was always there, in the background, waiting for me to finally walk through the "right door." A series of events transpired in a few short years that I know with all my soul were His protection and gentle nudging to come back to Him and He would heal my pain. But my trial by fire was not nearly over.

When I became pregnant, it was a surprise to both of us. We didn't think I could at this point. It was clear that a child could not be provided for; Mark didn't work and sat around doing drugs and playing video games. I was terrified of what he might do to a baby after the way treated he me. I suggested adoption. Mark would have none of that. At first he suggested an abortion as the most "convenient" solution. The thought horrified me. Not again!

I believed that if the baby were left in our care, it would come to a terrible end. Since adoption was not an option for Mark, I opened the last door I would ever open again on that part of my life. I didn't know that complete infertility was just around the corner.

I first fell into a pattern of drug and alcohol abuse to fit in with the crowd, and, finally just to cope and survive. I'd made many, many bad decisions while under the influence and lost two children because of these decisions. Over time, I'd become a cocaine addict, an alcoholic, a pot addict, and a psilocybin mushroom addict. My best friend Beth had become a crank addict, an alcoholic, and a prescription drug abuser due to her severe pain and debilitation from arthritis.

The Lord, in His infinite mercy and grace, had not abandoned me. I wholeheartedly believe God took these addictions from me one by one and saved my life more than once.

I woke up one morning with blood pouring from my nose and vomiting blood from the damage done to my sinuses from cocaine. I was so terrified, that I stopped that week.

Shortly after a particularly alcohol-soaked Halloween party where I drank and smoked until I passed out on the lawn, I became very ill. I had started a one-year training program after college for printing technology and graphic design to put my fine arts bachelor degree to good use. On the days I worked with the printing press and used the press cleaning chemicals, I'd have to run outside and vomit. I became so ill over the next four months, that I finally went to the doctor to find out why. I had also the same reaction when I tried to drink alcohol.

It turned out I had hepatitis. I was not able to finish the printing side of my training nor was I able to take a drink for over two years due to liver damage! I lost my taste for alcohol and it has never been a problem again. The marijuana addiction would take a little longer to kick.

I was smoking a lot while I was dating a guy between breakups with Mark. I was at my "date's" home with a few of our friends and

I had smoked way too much of some experimental pot. I passed out and my friends told me later I had stopped breathing and my heart had stopped. One of my friends knew CPR and helped bring me back, but I will never forget the sensations and feelings in my body right before I went down. I was cleared of yet another addiction. The Lord had saved my life again.

I didn't party anymore, but the pain from the illnesses in my body was becoming excruciating. I knew I'd hit rock bottom when I couldn't sleep and was so terrified of Mark that I dreaded every time he came home. I begged God to end my life and take me away, quietly in my sleep. I'd occasionally tried passive suicide with drugs and alcohol. For my last attempt I stood on a busy road and watched a Mack truck head straight for me. There's no earthly explanation for how the truck driver was able to swerve at the last minute and not tip over.

I knew at that point I was on this earth for more than just myself. But what was my purpose? I fell to my knees and begged God to explain what He was doing and give me a way out. I wanted a solid, kind Christian man to provide for me and whom I could love. "Please, Lord, I need you!" I prayed. It would be five more years before my prayer was answered.

Mark's friend Mike was separated from his wife and living in Oregon operating a contracting business. He stayed with us for two weeks and saw how bad our situation had become. Mike met a group of Christians in Coos Bay, California who brought him to the Lord and helped him reconcile with his wife. Now he was attempting to do the same with Mark. On the night before Mike left to return to Oregon, he sat up with Mark to discuss what was going on. They were behind closed doors so Mark felt safe to open up and the conversation that ensued was a revelation—and I happened to overhear it. I heard him tell Mike how he had manipulated me, emotionally tormented me, and physically abused me for years.

Mike begged Mark to come to Oregon with him for a few weeks to help him finish a large construction project. He was working very long hours and was exhausted.

Mike never made it to Oregon. Soon after Mike's visit, we learned he had been in a terrible head-on collision and was killed. Mark was devastated and more depressed than ever. I couldn't leave him. It's amazing what the mind will allow us to forget, temporarily.

I took a part-time job as a secretary for a landscape design company after being put on pain medication and anti-depressants to help with my illnesses. I was invited to a birthday party for co-workers and the events that followed would forever change my life.

I went with a friend from work who was also my chaperone and during the party, we were both drugged with Rohypnol, the date rape drug that causes memory loss and an inability to fight back. Wrong door, wrong night and one of the worst mistakes I ever made! I was dragged into a shower and then into a bedroom where I was raped by multiple men. I was taken to the hospital where I was examined and tested. After a criminal investigation that never went to trial, I was granted victim witness status by the California District Attorney and granted one year with W.E.A.V.E. counseling and three years of crisis counseling, free.

After the charges were dropped, I was given a file with all the information on everyone who was at the party. Mark and his friends demanded that I hand over the names and addresses of the perpetrators. I disposed of the files instead. God's grace was still in my life.

This ordeal opened the first "right" door I walked through. Months of counseling in a W.E.A.V.E. survivor group with other women finally opened my eyes to what is known as "the cycle of violence" I was stuck in. The main thing I learned is 'why we stay.' I learned from the crisis counselor that Mark's self-medication of drugs and alcohol combined with a bipolar personality had turned Mark clinically psychotic and very dangerous. I learned to become stronger and began my plan of escape. All the while, Mark could see my strength growing and tried everything he could to discredit my sources and undermine the path that I was now on.

We lost the duplex and moved in with Mark's mother. We had

preplanned meal nights for spaghetti, hot dogs, taco salad, and meatloaf. It was Wednesday, hot dog night. Earlier in the day my mom had given me some groceries which included the ingredients for meatloaf, which was usually a Saturday night treat when we could afford it. Mark was working again and I wanted to surprise him with the special treat. He came in after work and blew his top. How dare I make meat loaf on hot dog night and deviate from his plan! At first I was stunned, then angry.

He stormed out, went to Taco Bell and came back with that instead. He went up to "our room" and his mom followed him up. After a few minutes she came down and said, "He wants you to come up and sit with him while he eats." "Why?" I asked. "Because you're his wife. He's upset and needs comforting."

At that moment, all the events of the of the past months and years came rushing back to me: the overheard conversation with Mike; Mark's manipulation; the assault and Mark's anger at me for not giving him the perpetrators' names; the counseling; the women in W.E.A.V.E.; my parents begging me to leave him; everything.

And everything changed in the blink of an eye. I realized he wanted me to be her, his mom! I told her this and she was floored. "No, that's not right. I only loved and cared for him. His father did this!" But I knew the truth and it had finally set me free. I finally had the strength I needed to leave.

I had to leave my cat, my clothes, and everything else that night. I ran home to my parents and apologized for everything I'd put them through. I also called my brother in San Francisco and did the same.

I did get my cat back and what was left my belongings (after Mark had sold some of them off), and started a new life. I had made a commitment before God and family to love Mark my whole life and to stay married. It hurt to know that I couldn't fulfill my commitment, but my dad made it clear that the family couldn't witness any more abuse and if I insisted on staying married, I'd have to do it from a shelter. All the bills were in my name, but I had no other choice than to leave.

I know my leaving was God's work as well. He has saved my life more times than I can count and although the memories of those times still haunt me, He has given me the strength and courage to use them to help and comfort others.

The last break from that old, destructive life was with the friends that Mark and I had shared. I didn't see anyone after the separation. The only friend I had left was Beth. Beth had moved to Sacramento some time ago and had been living with a wonderful and devoted man named Tom, a few blocks from my parent's house. I desperately needed my best friend's love at that point. Mark was still calling me and begging me to come home. He could still manipulate me into tears of remorse and regret so strong that I still felt at some level it was my duty to "save" him. I was so afraid he'd commit suicide. One day, my dad had had enough and exclaimed, "Enough! Get on with your life."

I dove back into friendship with Beth and all her new friends (most of whom I did not like much). She was openly having an affair with another man and living with him part-time. Tom and I sat many evenings commiserating over our losses. We cried, we talked, we laughed, we watched movies, and one particularly bad evening for both of us, we shared the better part of two six-packs of beer and slept together. I'd never done something so completely out of character for me in my life. This mistake was devastating to me and I couldn't live with it. I told Tom I was going to tell Beth the truth when she got home. Tom begged me not to, he would lose her completely. And I knew I might lose the oldest and dearest friend I'd ever had if I did. But the lie I would have to live with was worse than the act.

I told her. She left Tom. She left me, and before she did, she called Mark. And between the two of them they called everyone I knew and made sure no one would ever talk to me again. During this time my parents were in Hawaii and I couldn't contact them. My brother was going through his own trials in San Francisco so I could not reach him either. I'd committed a terrible sin, hurt someone I dearly loved, and I couldn't talk to anyone about it. I sat for the better part of a month, alone and crying, almost beyond consolation.

And that was when I remembered Someone was still there for me—waiting. I got down on my knees and I prayed my heart out to God. I told Him everything. I railed and ranted and cried and finally—silence. In that silence I felt His presence more powerfully than I ever had felt it before. He still loved me. He would always be there for me. I could feel His great love for me. Nothing had changed, nobody called, but I was different.

Things changed around me too. Finally, the torturing phone calls from Mark stopped. On his last call he said, "Thanks to you, I finally hate you to the point that I can finally move on with my life." The new people that Beth had brought into my life were gone as well. But they were not missed. They were neither nice nor good people—and certainly they weren't Christians. I re-entered my parent's church, joined the choir, taught Sunday school, and got a new job with real possibilities for advancement. I also got myself healthy for the first time in years. God had pulled me through again.

People disagree that God had any hand in that single, terrible night. But I know the truth. God works in mysterious ways. I was moving right along toward a new career and a new life serving God, and the stress and pain slowly started to melt away. My health improved significantly throughout 1999 and I thought I'd finally settled into the life God wanted me to live.

I had taken a secretarial position a financial company. I was still lonely so my boss encouraged me to go online and find a new man. I met Stephen who lived in Santa Barbara, California and we emailed, instant messaged, and finally called each other. Our first phone conversation was three hours long! It was very obvious that this was who God wanted me to spend the rest of my life with.

We finally met a month later, got engaged, and we planned for the wedding. It truly was a match made in Heaven! I've never known someone more perfectly matched for me and I for him.

Although my health was greatly improved when I left Sacramento, it was not to remain so. I learned I was developing uterine cancer early in 2000. The doctors tried to reverse it so Stephen and I could have a child together. The condition could not be changed and 2001 brought a hysterectomy and a real feeling of new loss. My fibromyalgia came back and worsened after the medications and the surgery. For the first time in my life, I needed someone to care for me.

And now I understood that there was another reason God wanted me to be with Stephen—salvation for my eternal soul. Although I knew God and had heard all the stories of Jesus, I'd never heard of the possibility of a personal Savior. Stephen asked me that all important question, "Did I want Christ to be my personal Savior and did I know what that meant?" He received the great joy of bringing me to the saving knowledge of our Lord Jesus Christ. Stephen has watched me grow in faith ever since. My life has never been the same. I've never doubted this was God's plan all along. Life has not gotten easier, by any means, but I now have a peace that I've never known before.

In 2002, we moved from Santa Barbara to Carson City, Nevada. About four months after we moved to Carson City, I took a fall down an embankment at Lake Tahoe, California and severely injured my lower spine and needed spinal surgery immediately. At the same time, Beth became very seriously ill and needed hospitalization. I lost my dearest and oldest friend without ever getting to say goodbye or bring her to the Lord.

My fibromyalgia has become debilitating in recent years. I was recently diagnosed with an auto-immune thyroid disease called Hashimoto's disease. I struggle to manage my various conditions, but through it all, my Lord and Savior sees me through. In 2003, Stephen and I started a small carpet cleaning company in Carson City. It's a growing company that inspires hard work, loyalty, and new ideas.

My life is so different now. I now teach a Creation Science Ministry with the churches in our area. I accepted a position as Creation Ministry teacher to a Home Schooling Co-op at our home church in the fall. I plan to work with local agencies to open more women's shelters here in Nevada and help young mothers facing the choice of abortion over life for their unborn babies.

God can and does use the least likely people to accomplish His goals. Examples of this are found throughout the Bible. He uses people even when they choose to walk away, like me. There is no greater patience and love that I know of than the love of Jesus, our Lord. At any time He can take a lost and broken life that is completely without hope and turn everything around. When this happens, neither we nor our lives become perfect, but we are changed on a fundamental level. He can help us accomplish amazing things if we only open our eyes and our hearts to the Him. I am living proof that a disabled, ex-drug addict, ex-alcoholic, and ex-adulterer can be washed and healed in His love. You don't have to be "whole" to be a "difference maker." You just have to be willing. ■

Ruth Jaenchen

Ruth Jaenchen earned her Bachelor of Fine Arts Degree and Minor in Zoology at Sacramento State University of California. Ruth is an advocate for abused women and crisis pregnancy outreach and plans to develop new groups in her area. She has a passion for science and teaches Creation Science classes to various groups in Northern Nevada. She is an artist, a jewelry designer, and author of the up-coming book "Against The Wind – A Woman's Journey of Hope." *She is co-owner of Summit Cleaning Services. She and her husband, Stephen, live in Carson City, Nevada.*

For more information on Ruth, visit her website www.AgainstTheWind-AJourneyOfHope.com or email her at rajaenchen@aol.com.

Ruth Jaenchen
Summit Cleaning Services
www.AgainstTheWind-AJourneyOfHope.com
rajaenchen@aol.com

16

⚜

The Accidentally On Purpose Entrepreneur: How Uncanny Opportunities Position You to Make a Difference

By Tami Call

During the last semester of my MBA program I walked into the career center to investigate employment and internship opportunities. In the midst of the rack full of pink and blue flyers (pink for internship and blue for job) I found a posting that read something like this:

> *Student needed to attend five-day seminar in Palm Beach, Florida to create a seminar participant manual based on seminar content. All travel expenses paid. Project fee $1,500. Dates of travel, April 9-15. Deadline for completion, June 30.*

I knew that most first year students wouldn't pursue the opportunity as the seminar was smack dab in the middle of finals week. I also knew that most of my colleagues wouldn't have a clue about how to create a participant manual for a seminar. But my having been an English major with a secondary education certificate and having taught eighth and ninth grade for a year (lesson plans daily) made me the perfect candidate!

I applied for the internship and got it. I rearranged my final exams and off to Florida I went for the week.

As it turned out, the internship was being offered by a man named Bob Apgood. He had contracted with the American Management Association (AMA) to write all the course materials for this particular seminar on Mergers and Acquisitions. But like any good business person does, Bob thought, "Why should I write this myself when I can find a bright student to write it for me and still pocket a nice fee?" So Bob subcontracted the job to me while the real client was the AMA.

Fortunately for me, one of the presenters didn't show up in Florida. So I was off to AMA headquarters in New York City to sit in on the missing seminar piece and create the content we'd missed. While there, Bob introduced me to Ed Selig, then Portfolio Manager over the Finance category for the AMA. Ed had seen my work on the rest of the Mergers and Acquisitions content and sat me down for a chat.

"How much would you charge to do a three day seminar?" Ed asked. "You'd create the participant notebook, an instructor's guide telling other course leaders how to present the course, and then create the Power Point presentations for them to use."

As a former interning English teacher who had only made $9,000 for the entire school year (my first and only experience with full-time employment), I had no clue how to answer this question. Based on what Bob had paid me I said, in a voice that I'm sure sounded like I was guessing, "$1,500?"

Ed looked at me and shook his head, "No. That's not enough. Try again."

"$2,000?" I guessed again.

Seeing that this guessing game would take far longer than it would for him to just tell me what they were willing to pay for a project, Ed said, "No. You need to tell me something like $6,500."

I'm sure my eyes bugged out. At least I managed not to gasp. "Um…okay…$6,500."

"Deal!" he said. Then he went on to tell me about the next

financial seminar he wanted me to develop.

I went on to create, revise or consult on more than fifty seminars for the American Management Association over the course of eleven years. During that time I moved three times (living in Atlanta, Detroit and Phoenix) and had three children.

What started out as a free trip to Florida for fun turned into the perfect opportunity for me to work from home, keep my own schedule, and be with my kids. I couldn't have planned it any better myself!

A Painful Change of Course

After the birth of my third child, I let my friends at the AMA know that I was going on a sabbatical to enjoy my last little one. After two years "off" I called to say I was ready to go back.

"Great!" declared the Director of Design and Development. "I'll have something for you in the next three weeks."

I was thrilled. Nothing was easier than working from home and getting checks in the mail at New York City rates. Then the bottom fell out of the economy.

After six weeks with no word from the AMA, I called to follow up. They had laid off the entire Design and Development Department. Over seventy people were gone. Only two remained—one project manager and one instructional designer.

"We won't be developing or revising any products until the economy turns around," they explained. (And we're all still waiting for that to happen.)

In one day I had gone from expecting easy checks in the mail to feeling deeply depressed. Other than the AMA I had no real resume. I had never marketed myself. It had never been necessary. I had three kids at home and the idea of going to work every day, showing up early, staying late, and trying to impress my superiors literally made me sick. And the objective of going back had been to get out from under a mountain of debt we had acquired when my husband when back to school. That liberation now seemed completely unachievable.

Keeping the Faith in Troubled Times

Soon it was December. In our family this is the time of year when we review our finances and make sure we have kept our commitment to God to pay a full tithe on what we earn. The only income on which I hadn't tithed was money I'd received from my mother for helping with the sale of an apartment building after my father had died the year before. The money I had left was about $2,000—the exact amount I "owed" if I were to tithe fully and honestly.

Until that moment I never fully understood the widow's mite story from the Bible. I never knew what it felt like to give away everything I had to the Lord with no idea, plan, or even hope that I would ever have another dollar come to me. It was the hardest thing I've ever done. But I did it.

And God blessed me for my faith.

Throwing Open the Windows of Heaven

In January I attended a women's writers group. After the meeting I was at the piano playing and singing a song I had written. My friend Stephanie Fleming was standing next to me listening.

"You're going to make millions someday," she said.

"So are you," I answered. And based on her writing, I meant it.

At the time, Stephanie was a copywriter for a software company called Infusionsoft. Because Infusionsoft was preparing for their annual users conference, she asked if I could come in and help with some of the writing for the event. So I did.

After a few weeks writing banner slogans, articles and email campaigns at ten dollars an hour, I told Stephanie, "This work is very interesting to me, but at ten dollars an hour I can't even cover childcare." So I stopped going in. You can also imagine how I felt working for ten dollars an hour when I'd been accustomed to at least seventy-five dollars an hour or more.

A couple weeks later Stephanie called again.

"The founder of our company has a project he's wanted to do for a long time. He asked me if I knew anyone who could create a training program online. I mentioned you and they're wondering if you can come in and talk to them tomorrow."

"I can," I replied. "But it has to be for more than ten dollars per hour."

I went in and was hired on the spot for twenty-five dollars an hour.

Over the next nine months, I worked one on one with Infusionsoft's founder, Scott Martineau, to create *The Double Your Sales Coaching Course.* In the process I learned all about copywriting, email marketing, automating the sales process, how to use Infusionsoft, online sales, how to measure and track results, and how to figure out what the problem is when a campaign doesn't perform.

In short, I went in as an instructional seminar designer and came out as a copywriter and marketing consultant. Infusionsoft brought me in to work on in-house projects for the company and for their clients. They began sending me referrals. Suddenly I had a thriving copywriting and consulting practice.

Successful, Yet Discontent

I was successful. I felt important. *I was using my talents—improving them even—but I didn't feel "on purpose."* Something wasn't right.

The more I pondered how I'd ended up as a marketer and copywriter, the more I truly felt that this was not the end objective. I believed I'd needed to learn marketing and copywriting for a reason but I knew *God would take those talents and use them for a higher purpose.*

This feeling was confirmed when I read *Christian Life Coaching,* a book that explained a very important concept about life purpose that I had never understood before:

> *"You are prepared for your [purpose] through life experience. Your whole life to this point is the rehearsal for this ultimate performance. Until you've rehearsed, you aren't ready for the opening."*[1]

[1] Stoltzfus, Tony. Christian Life Coaching Handbook. Virginia Beach: Coach22, 2009.

That's when it happened . . .

Getting Clear and Gaining Courage

Shortly after understanding the idea of "preparatory life purpose experiences," I was attending a video shoot for a client. At the last minute, I was asked to interview one of their customers about their use of the product because the customer was too nervous to speak directly into the camera.

After the shoot was over, the customer's husband approached me and commented, "You are very good at interviewing! Do you do that often?"

"No," I answered. "This is the first time I've done this."

"Wow. You should consider interviewing people. If you were to interview people, what would you want to interview them about?"

After giving it some thought, I replied, "*You know, I'd really like to interview people about the role of faith, God and prayer in their business lives.*" As soon as I said it, I felt really good about it.

"Well, that's interesting," he said, "but I don't know how you'd monetize it."

I didn't know how to monetize it either, so I put the idea on the shelf. I tried to drop the idea altogether, but I couldn't. It sounded like so much fun!

At last, during a marketing conference I was attending I decided to mention it to a few colleagues and monitor their responses. I told them I was creating a new online community called *God and Business Today* where I would interview faith-centered entrepreneurs about the influence of God, faith and prayer in their business and personal lives.

The response was astounding.

Some people asked to be interviewed while others wanted to interview me. Friends immediately "Liked" my fan page. I knew I was on to something (if only I could muster the courage to shift into it). I knew I had found my purpose.

Just Good Luck or the Hand of God?

I have been a long-time seeker of life purpose. I used to pray and say, "Heavenly Father, just tell me what you want me to do and I'll go do it!"

But God doesn't work that way—and, frankly, neither do we. If God had told me in my twenties to go and fulfill the purpose He has for me right now, I would've either laughed in doubt or cried in despair *because I didn't have the skills and talents at that point in my life to live my purpose—yet.*

But my Father in Heaven orchestrated my life to give me just the preparation I needed. My accidental entry into the training and development field prepared me to create courses, live events, and educational products. It also gave me the ability to teach others how to do the same.

The fortuitous dip in the economy turned my path toward copywriting, online marketing and sales automation—a choice I never would have made on my own and that I fully believed was devised by God to get me on the right path.

And an observer's off-the-cuff comment about a talent I was unaware I possessed opened my mind to possibilities that never would have crossed my mind otherwise.

Some people call it luck. Others will say I was just in the right place at the right time. But I know better. I call it the hand of God in my life directing me toward a grand, bold and exciting purpose.

God prepares a willing servant. Perhaps He is preparing you?

How will you serve? What have you been prepared to do? What is your grand purpose?

Please drop by and share your story at www.Faceboook.com/GodandBusinessToday or www.GodandBusinessToday.com. ■

Tami Call

Tami Call is a copywriter, marketing strategist, business coach and author of the book "21 Ways to Build Your Business with Email Marketing." In her most recent step toward living her life purpose, Tami founded God and Business Today, a faith-centered online community. The goal of God and Business Today is to motivate entrepreneurs, professionals, and business-minded individuals around the world to involve God in their daily business practices. Tami pursues this mission by searching out and collecting inspiring stories about how God is making a difference in businesses today. You can learn more about Tami and get a free copy of her e-book "5 Simple Steps to Getting Your Prayers Heard and Answered" at www.GodandBusinessToday.com.

Tami Call, Founder
Infused Copy and God and Business Today
4904 S. Power Rd.
Suite 103--130
Mesa, AZ
480-497-6160

17

✣

Experience Over Rank

By Jason Starkey

I always knew I would make a big difference, but there was a time when it was very difficult to hold on to that belief. Living for quality and diverse life experiences have always been a pursuit of mine and for a time I thought I lacked the experience to make an impact at all. I was wrong.

As a little boy, I grew up listening to action-packed adventure stories from my father's career as a Helicopter pilot in the United States Marine Corps. We moved around quite a bit. My two brothers and I spent most of our time with our mother until my dad retired and we settled in a small town about forty-five minutes north of Indianapolis, Indiana.

As I grew older, I immensely looked forward to our family lunches when Dad would entertain us with stories about zooming between the buildings in a city. Or tales of flying just a few meters above the Atlantic, when the shadow of a giant blue whale would surface just beneath him and one huge whale eye met his before he took off on his next mission.

I loved these stories and there was a secret voice in my head telling me that I needed the exact same experiences and stories to share with my children and grandchildren one day. If I had stories to tell like these, *then* I would be significant.

It was not until my twenty-third birthday that I actually told myself that I was going to make it happen. I was *finally* going to live a life worth talking about. I was going to have my own adventures. I was going to be a Marine like my father. The only problem was that on that particular day I weighed 322 pounds. This was a big roadblock, as I was prevented from enlisting since I weighed more than 221 pounds (for my height). More than a hundred pounds was separating me from living the life I could be proud of. Dropping these excess pounds became my obsession. I was dead set on becoming a Marine and nothing was going to hold me back.

The next day I walked into the recruiter's office. From across the table, I looked him in the eye and just told him my name. I said, "I am not there yet but I am going to enlist." I then turned and left.

Just seven months later, I shipped out for Boot Camp at a spry 202 pounds. I was on cloud nine. I felt more confident than I had ever been in my entire life, and completely happy. I was going to be a Marine. I was going to have my own adventures, and I was going to be a Man that my family would be proud of. I was so happy in fact, that I refused to accept just how much physical pain my spine and back were causing me.

I was exactly where I wanted to be in life, with a marine unit getting ready to go to Afghanistan—all except for my body that is. The pain was getting worse and worse. I had x-rays taken but they went unexamined, lost somewhere in the shuffle of the rest of the military's medical responsibilities.

Two months after that, we were doing our last round of build ups before we shipped out, on a shooting range for Enhanced Mojave Viper. The pain became so intense that I couldn't even move, much less walk. When they finally got me to the hospital, the doctor discovered that I'd crushed T6 through T11 vertebrae and had repeatedly damaged them because I'd never had them looked at. That was the diagnosis and I was prescribed a medical discharge under Honorable Conditions.

Just a few days before my battery shipped overseas, they were shipping me home. This was, for me, the worst news possible. I'd worked so hard to get to where I was. I was just a few days away from living a life of valor and having the adventures I'd always dreamed of that would make my family proud.

Sitting alone in the barracks, staring at the wall, life came to a screeching halt. What now? What kind of life could I live? In the wreckage of my grief, I began to sink in a flood of depression, doubt, fear, and just about every other negative belief. The purpose of my great commitment and determination had just been taken away. I was devastated and in a state of internal depression for longer than I care to admit.

It was time to go home and face my family and friends. I was not going to be the amazing Marine my father had been and I was forced to come home early as a "failure." I went back to my old job, hung out with my friends, and I was okay. There were a few individuals who would poke fun at my "fake" military career. That was probably the worst part of it; I wanted to serve more than many people could ever understand. The emotional hurt far exceeded any physical pain in my body. And then—I had enough.

I mentally accepted the fact I wouldn't get what I wanted out of *life*, so I might as well have fun. I worked up the courage to ask this amazingly beautiful girl out on a date. Little did I know just how amazing she was—and how her *own* "screech to a halt" life experiences would affect me. We were perfect for each other, and after our first date, we were inseparable.

I remember bringing her to lunch with my parents when she announced, "I quit my job. Now I am going to make a difference." Like me, she'd been through a lot—big disappointments, opportunities just taken away—yet she had such confidence, such big plans. She talked about starting a small business where she could help create jobs and how *that* was how she wanted to serve our country and make an impact.

I began to examine my own life, and wondered how I could still serve. I wanted more! I've always known that I was destined to make an impact, and somehow I'd forgotten. I began to understand that a career in the military might have been my desire, but a career of service was my destiny.

I once had a Staff Sergeant tell me, "The Military is all about rank and rank structure, but do you know what outranks everything? Experience."

With every day that passes, that statement resonates with me more and more because it causes me to reflect on my own experiences and how they've molded me into the person that I am today. And I know that who I am today is not who I will be tomorrow or the day after. Who we are right now is a direct reflection of the accumulation of all our past experiences combined.

Here are three rules to creating and leveraging experience so you can make the difference in the world you are destined to make.

Rule # 1: Always Take Action. It's a law of physics that objects in motion stay in motion (and it's kind of a law in the military that objects at rest are in big trouble). Here's the secret. You won't always know the right or perfect move. The most important thing you can do is make a decision. You can always change your mind later. Be aware of when it's time to make a decision and pull the trigger.

It was late on a Monday night and we were sitting in my bedroom when we decided that if we were going to do this right, we needed to make a big change. We would move from my hometown of Anderson, Indiana to Texas. In Texas, we would grow our business using the unlimited resources and opportunity there.

On Tuesday morning I quit my job. On Wednesday we packed. On Thursday I said good-bye. And on Friday we were southbound to Dallas. For the first time, I felt I was having my own adventure.

I'd taken action on my twenty-third birthday when I'd decided to join the Marines, and it was the best thing I ever could've done. While things didn't turn out like I'd hoped, the experience gave me the momentum I needed to get where I am today. If I'd never taken that first step into the recruiters office, who knows where I might be today. If you don't take action, you cannot add to your experience base.

In our business, we teach a lot about the OODA loop. The OODA loop is the process a person goes through to make a decision.

OODA Loop stands for Observe, Orient, Decide, and Act. But what happens if your process takes too long and the Market changes? You have to start all over. As someone who wants to achieve, you must learn to speed this OODA Loop up.

Rule # 2: Get Comfortable with Learning on the Fly. When I arrived in Dallas, it was a completely new environment. I had zero experience in *any* kind of business. I never imagined myself as a businessman. I had this perception that business was cutthroat or underhanded. That wasn't what I wanted to be about. However, I was fortunate to sit in on some high level mastermind sessions and began to learn more about the reality of business by listening to dozens of experiences from others.

One skill I honed in the military is a heightened ability to picking up on small cues and details. I am able to get a real sense of an individual's intention very quickly.

I soaked up every little tidbit I could. I found this kind of business was good. But there was so much information; I knew I had to catch up fast so I could be ready when our first big opportunity arose. Leaving the military was a necessary step in my journey. I didn't understand it at the time, but the lessons I learned there help me serve our business better every day.

Being able to learn quickly is essential. Technology will continue to evolve exponentially faster. This is the next step in being able to adapt quickly.

I must tell you the story about one of my favorite clients—Howard Berg.

Howard is The World's Fastest Reader. Google him. He's read over thirty thousand books and has been on over eleven hundred TV shows and counting. Howard is known as a Speed-Reading Expert who teaches other people how to read faster, retain more, and be more successful. When you read thirty thousand books, you learn a thing or two. I would say with confidence that Howard is an expert in *dozens* if not *hundreds* of subjects, From Biology to Astrology to Neuro Linguistic Programming. One of my favorite lessons from Howard is: If you know more than other people do on any particular topic, you are considered an expert by them.

Once, Howard was offered a free cruise if he would teach a class on the ship as one of the extracurricular activities for the passengers. The only class that was available was Photoshop. Howard told the person on the phone booking the class, "Photoshop? Oh yes! I'm an Expert at that." When Howard got off the phone, he Googled "What is Photoshop?"

Howard ended up reading a dozen books in just under a week, and became very well versed in an extremely well-known and popular program. When he boarded the ship, seasoned photographers entered his class expressing how excited they were to finally learn from an expert.

Howard swallowed hard and taught his class. At the end, his class ranted about how amazing he was, and how it must have taken him forever to become so good.

Howard smiled knowing he'd been able to take his wife on a wonderful free cruise because he could learn on the fly. Being able to learn from other people's stories, whether it's at the kitchen table or in a book, is one of the *best* ways to bridge the gap in your experience base.

My ability to learn quickly on the fly is one of our company's most valuable assets, as I am able to create systems for our staff and for our clients that save them *hours* of time. This is one of my traits that I am most proud of.

Rule #3: Be Proud. When I ask people what their limiting beliefs are that keep them from taking action to make the difference they want to make they often say, "I don't have enough experience." or "I've never done anything that matters."

In fact, not so long ago, those were words I would tell myself. I'll tell you right now: Those beliefs are a *lie*. Everything you do matters—*especially when* the outcome doesn't turn out like you planned. It's in *those* experiences that you learn the most about yourself.

I can tell you that coming home from the military caused me to learn a lot about myself. I had to re-examine what was *truly* important to me.

You must *leverage* your successes and your failures into lessons learned that you can be proud of. *Then* you must *share them*.

Every day you wake up with a choice. You will either share your stories or you won't. You will take action or you won't. You will make a difference or you won't.

Since entering the business world, I have shared more of myself and my history than I ever thought I would. I use my experiences as a way to teach, and as a way to improve both my business and myself. What I've found is that the more I share, the more others will share in return. It's this sharing of experiences that exponentially teaches me more about business, life and people. That knowledge is invaluable to the impact I'll be able to have on the world.

I used to think that I would only be able to have pride in a successful military career modeled after my Dad. Today I write this story, proud that I'm creating my own experiences and sharing them with you. I value the experiences of my past and I value the opportunities of tomorrow.

It doesn't matter what your rank is, what your background is, how old you are, or how long you've been "in business." Being proud enough to leverage your past is one of the greatest ways to open up doors for new experiences in the future, and having enough pride in yourself to share your story is one of the biggest ways you can make a difference today.

Do you "Dare to be a Difference Maker?" I Dare you. Take Action. Learn as you Go. Be Proud. In the process you will make a bigger impact than you could ever imagine. ■

Jason Starkey

Jason Starkey is a former member of the United States Marine Corps and a Managing Partner for The Marketing Team LLC, where experts and business owners go to implement faster and grow their bottom line. Jason is committed to serving America by helping to grow successful local businesses across the country, through The Marketing Team Training Programs and their suite of done-for-you services.

Jason currently lives in Fort Worth, Texas with his giant sled-dog-turned-company-mascot, Mulligan, the Marketing Malamute. If you liked this chapter, say hello to Jason and see a picture of Mulligan at www.Facebook.com/Marketing-Fans. Visit www.TheMarketingTeam.com to find out how The Marketing Team can help you implement faster, campaign stronger and win bigger in your business today.

Jason Starkey
Managing Partner for The Marketing Team, LLC
www.TheMarketingTeam.com

18

Speaking Out Against Domestic Violence

By Desiree Duvall

I am in my early fifties and the youngest of a Mediterranean family, raised in the Puget Sound area. I survived a life-threatening disease. I was educated at the University of Puget Sound. I am the mother of three sons. I am divorced after twenty-four years of marriage. I have thirty-plus years of experience as an investor and general contractor. I am a victim of domestic violence and have authored a book about domestic violence titled *Letting Go, Surrendering My Heart to GOD*. I am also working on a documentary business with my sons.

For years I've been committed doing what I do best every day—making a difference in the world by the simple act of listening with kindness. I've listened to those in need, whether friend or stranger, helping others identify an opportunity that awaits them during a time of darkness—always taking the necessary time to be the dear friend, the sister to those in need.

After my own life took an unexpected turn, I decided to put my efforts into becoming an advocate for domestic violence victims. I knew my experience had happened for a reason and I wanted to heal the sadness of my own heart by helping others. In both my research and my own experience the main concern was hearing others speak their truths about domestic violence. All our truths varied. It was difficult to even admit it had happened to us because so many of us struggled with the humiliation of it, while trying to take care of our children.

Many fear offering true friendship because they don't know how to be a friend or are afraid to expose themselves or show weakness. Taking the "high road" is always difficult when people fight it. I continue to stress the importance of being true to yourself and of "letting go" of everything and trusting in God, as he is guiding us to our intended journeys.

When you are not true to yourself, you end up compromising your personal values and relationships and will become disheartened. For years I tried to comfort friends and family with half-truths, sparing feelings. But in the end, only telling others what they wanted to hear didn't serve anyone well. Not even me. Integrity is everything, isn't it? Making a difference requires a commitment to doing the right thing. It means taking action at the right time, paying very close attention, telling the truth, and staying disconnected to outcomes no matter what.

It is thanks to my experiences and my relationship with God that I can truly let go. Today I can honestly say I have enough courage, enthusiasm, and desire to make a difference in the world. I recognize the importance of being realistic and honest in my service to others and to not be overzealous in my attempts to make a difference.

Taking the time to understand the needs of others is key. So many people aren't ready to hear the truth, aren't ready to move forward. Even so, I am prepared to be that light for anyone who may be in need—to truly make a difference in that person's world.

The realization of what, tragically, happened to me and my sons, combined with economic pressures in the world today, have led me to never again approach life by what is best for me. Instead, I choose to serve by doing what is best for the world. This is one of the reasons for writing my book. I want to help others break through the barriers I faced. To regain hope and find trust again. I plan to direct the profits from my book to a humanitarian cause such as endowment to aid children of domestic violence victims.

As someone who believes that everything happens for a reason, my experience opened my eyes to the reality of my marriage and helped me change my life's purpose for the better. It revealed my focus in life, my circle of friends, the profound love and respect I have for my sons, and my relationship with Christ.

As the level of abuse increased with each domestic violence assault, I faced many challenges. Instead of leaving I chose to reflect on the countless options I had right in front of me. To choose the best option I needed to be honest with myself, as the true lessons for me in my situation were in the questions I shamefully avoided, because I already knew the answers.

I recognized that if I wanted to develop a new life I had to learn how to trust, and I understood that learning to trust doesn't happen overnight. It takes time to build trust. When I finally established trust, my confidence and self-esteem grew stronger and the decisions I had to make became instinctive and natural. I am very grateful for the unique bonds and sincere friendships that I formed. They validated the horrible abuse my sons and I were experiencing from this man and his family. I was given optimism and the desire to be more than I was. I was encouraged to have faith that God cared and knew my struggle.

The bond I made with these delightful and precious friends was a gift from the Divine, there's no other way to describe it. They rescued me from a loveless and unhealthy marriage. I am truly thankful and blessed that I made these connections when I did, because I couldn't have done it on my own. I can say with absolute certainty that we all need reliable and honest friends. These friends made all the difference in the world in my life and in my search for hope and happiness for the future.

It's amazing what a little reassurance can do for someone who is feeling down and lost, especially when family, community, and church are not present. I will always remember and appreciate the efforts of my friends. I encourage others to invest in the same types of quality friendships. The only treasures I will take to heaven are my closest family members and friends.

Now comes the best part of my experience. I realized that I could use my knowledge to help other victims of domestic violence, and in doing so, make a difference in the world today. I can speak openly about the dangers of domestic violence. While my community hasn't responded to the needs of the abused as it should, many other communities are responding to the needs of these victims. This is because people are speaking up and reaching out, or someone has been killed and the family has created a grant to help other victims of domestic violence.

For me, domestic violence was about emotional and physical abuse by my ex-husband. Throughout the course of the divorce he tried to make it an isolated event, but the truth about domestic violence is that it tends to intensify in cruelty over time, just like cancer. If I had not stopped the violence it would have continued, along with the feelings of fear, guilt, and shame.

My sons and I lived with terrible fear and they were at risk of being victims or, worse, being perpetrators like their father. My sons and I learned quickly that my ex-husband (and their father) was trying to socially and financially isolate us and make us dependent on him by his continued abuse. When someone shoves, slaps, punches, kicks, spits, or even hits you it is abuse. When you've been called names and put down until you feel worthless, that's abuse too. My sons and I experienced this. I never deserved to be beaten nor did my sons. I felt greatly ashamed that I stayed in this abusive relationship.

I certainly felt the constraints and isolation of my immediate family during the course of my divorce. This was common as I'd dealt with similar obstacles before, but never had I felt so alone. As a child, a teenager, and now in adulthood, never did they reach out to get to know my heart. Instead, I reached out to them—even acquainting them with their nephews. It was rare that they sought me unless they needed something. My family was continually jealous, often saying how it wasn't fair that I got everything—good looks, financial success, beautiful homes, and well-behaved handsome sons. They also "accused" me of cheating death and mastering paralysis. Their exact quote was, "If you fell into a pile of poop, you would still smell like a rose."

This was all very sad, because none of my achievements had come easily—they had taken time and exacted a price. My siblings were not very nice and were far from supportive as I struggled with domestic violence and my divorce. They repeatedly ridiculed me, saying that I could never do anything wrong until now. I was beaten along with my sons and now my family dream was shattered as I went through the breakup of my marriage. I was going through a horrible and demoralizing experience and my siblings were relishing my sadness. It broke our mother's heart.

In many abusive relationships the abuse is minimal or non-existent in the eyes of the abused. I've had friends admit to me that they honestly believed, after being shoved and pushed down several times, that they did not experience domestic violence. In some cases, there's an absence of physical abuse but emotional abuse is occurring. Emotional abuse causes mental anguish and psychological pain. In the end, it is torture.

Emotional abuse is the center of all abuse. When I ask my friends if they would tolerate this type of abuse from a stranger they say they wouldn't. Then they plead, "But it's my husband (or my wife), and what do I do about the kids?" I reply to them all that from my own experience, emotional abuse is the deliberate tactic of a perpetrator of domestic violence. I know all too well, because for twenty-four years I was a victim of emotional, mental, verbal, financial, and physical pain. I also understand what torture social isolation can be. Emotional pain is by far the worst, even more than physical pain. Blood and bruising eventually fade away, but emotional abuse is a constant reminder of your pain.

Seek out those who believe in the power and love of God, as they will support you and give you guidance and strength to take the steps to save yourself and your family. It is imperative that you have strong friends around you to bolster your courage, because the hold the perpetrator has over his or her victim is strong and limitless and has no boundaries.

My ex-husband was oblivious to what he was doing to us. From the moment he woke up until he went to bed, he never remembered a thing, except that he was always right. This is the behavior of a narcissist. He slowly pulled me in with his manipulations and then drained me by sucking the mental life out of me. He tried to change me, but it was never going to happen.

Most of the time, mental and emotional abuse are hidden from view, just as the physical injuries and pain are often invisible to others. The sadness of the pain and the overwhelming amount of hurt sometimes takes years to heal, if ever. I truly believe that emotional abuse is something that occurs every day and that we clearly don't recognize it until it's too late. Words are so easily used, without justification or reason, to cause hurt and damage self-esteem. The role of abusers is to manipulate, and most of the time they're careful and discrete in their use of hurtful words. They wait until they're behind closed doors.

So many nights I felt all alone. When my world was caving in around me he would verbally attack me only to drive me more insane. I knew he was weak, but his attempts to destroy my being only made me feel unstable and ever more distressed. He didn't want to hear my objections and tried to assure me he wouldn't treat me this way again. But I knew it was false hope as he repeated the abuse again and again. He flunked, disappointing me beyond all belief.

Domestic violence does not just involve physical violence, and people need to recognize this, especially the victims. In the end, all we can really do is try to educate our loved ones and make them aware of this fact. We can be patient and persistent and discrete with them, but it still has to be their own realization that causes them to decide to leave or stay. As a community, we can support, educate, inspire, and most importantly, we can demonstrate the right way to conduct ourselves despite religion, age, income level, sexual orientation, or education.

I'm here to remind as well as be an example—a light to any who care to listen—that domestic violence is a crime and should not be taken lightly. Don't be an enabler. There's no choice between darkness and light. Darkness is the absence of light! Gather your support group and take responsibility for your own happiness. I did, and I love the woman I have become because I'm making a difference in the lives of others. ■

Desiree Duvall

Have you ever imagined what it would be like to have your life change overnight and free from abuse? Desiree Duvall succeeded in finding it, but it came with a huge price and upset.

Desiree reminds all women and men to be aware of abuse. Her life is an example and instills us to follow our heart, and principles no matter how great the loss.

Married 24 years, she and her husband appeared to be the perfect couple, cute sons, beautiful homes, and the cool dog. The truth was it was a miserable and inadequate life. She and her sons endured emotional abuse that eventually included assault at the hands of her husband /father, who also co-managed their construction/property management business.

After escaping her marriage through divorce Desiree has rebuilt her life and is now a general contractor. She has found her niche refurbishing and selling broken and foreclosed homes, giving life and hope back to those in search as she had done with her personal life. Desiree graduated from the University of Puget Sound, and was a member of Gamma Zeta sorority. She has three adult sons and lives in Washington state.

Duvall is the author of "Letting go and Surrendering My Heart to God." *This is her memoir recounting her secret life as an abused wife and breaking through the barriers to true freedom and to find love and happiness the way it was supposed to be.*

A survivor of Domestic Violence, Desiree Duvall is like many women and men who have broken the barriers from an abused past. Seems like an unlikely victim nonetheless the truth was she grew up co-dependent and subservient, many traits of the abused victim.

Desiree Duvall
Filucy Bay Enterprises, LLC
PO BOX 2
Lake Bay, WA 98349
filucybayenterprisesllc@hotmail.com

Canada's Constitutional Revolution

Canada's
Constitutional Revolution

BARRY L. STRAYER

THE UNIVERSITY
of ALBERTA PRESS

Published by
The University of Alberta Press
Ring House 2
Edmonton, Alberta, Canada T6G 2E1
www.uap.ualberta.ca

LIBRARY AND ARCHIVES CANADA
CATALOGUING IN PUBLICATION

Strayer, Barry L. (Barry Lee), 1932–
    Canada's constitutional revolution /
Barry L. Strayer.

Includes index.
Issued also in electronic formats.
ISBN 978-0-88864-649-1

1. Constitutional history—Canada.
2. Canada. Canadian Charter of Rights
    and Freedoms.
I. Title.

KE4199.S77 2012   342.7102'9
C2012-906993-0   KF4482.S77 2012

First edition, first printing, 2013.
Printed and bound in Canada by
Houghton Boston Printers, Saskatoon,
Saskatchewan.
Copyediting by Brendan Wild.
Proofreading by Kirsten Craven.
Indexing by Judy Dunlop.

Photo, page 26.
© Library and Archives Canada.
Reproduced with the permission of Library
and Archives Canada. Source: Library
and Archives Canada / Credit: Duncan
Cameron / Duncan Cameron fonds /
Accession 1970-015, File 11202-19, frame
21-21a.

Photo, page 291.
© Her Majesty the Queen in Right of
Canada represented by the Office of the
Secretary to the Governor General (2010) /
Photo credit: Sgt Serge Grouin, Rideau
Hall / Reproduced with the permission of
the Office to the Secretary to the Governor
General.

The University of Alberta Press is committed to protecting our natural environment.
As part of our efforts, this book is printed
on Enviro Paper: it contains 100% post-
consumer recycled fibres and is acid- and
chlorine-free.

The University of Alberta Press gratefully
acknowledges the support received for
its publishing program from The Canada
Council for the Arts. The University of
Alberta Press also gratefully acknowledges
the financial support of the Government
of Canada through the Canada Book
Fund (CBF) and the Government of
Alberta through the Alberta Multimedia
Development Fund (AMDF) for its publishing activities.

This book has been published with
the help of a grant from the Canadian
Federation for the Humanities and Social
Sciences, through the Awards to Scholarly
Publications Program, using funds provid-
ed by the Social Sciences and Humanities
Research Council of Canada.

Canada   Canada Council   Conseil des Arts   Government
         for the Arts   du Canada   of Alberta ■

For Eleanor, Alison, Jonathan, and Colin

CONTENTS

PREFACE

In reflecting on aspects of my career, including severance of Canada's constitutional link with the United Kingdom, I recognize the importance of my early exposure to the institutions and history of Britain, its Empire, and Commonwealth.

Although my immigrant parents were and remained all their lives citizens of the United States, I was born a British subject (as we all were in those days) in Saskatchewan, though I also had US citizenship through my parents. I have certainly also had a lifelong connection to the United States. Most of our relatives lived in that country and we frequently visited them. I had two years of primary schooling there and had also taken a degree at an American university. Our youngest son was born in Boston. Two of my brothers have lived most of their lives in the United States. Nevertheless, the British connection was a clear reality to me while growing up. I attended for most of my first seven grades a four-room Saskatchewan village school. On its flagpole was raised every morning the Union Jack, as we had no proper Canadian flag then. Prominent at the front of every classroom was a large map of the world provided by Neilson, self-proclaimed makers of fine chocolate. The map was the standard Mercator projection of the globe, and the British Empire was coloured a bright pink. The Empire was said to occupy one-quarter of the earth's land surface, but with the projection of Canada as if the world were flat the Empire seemed to have an even greater share of that surface.

One did not speak of the British Commonwealth much in those days. Although Canada had, since the *Statute of Westminster, 1931*,[1] been included in the six self-governing former colonies (styled "Dominions") whose full autonomy was recognized in that *Statute*, we did not insist that we were in any way separate from the Empire. I attended this school through

most of World War II. Every morning we assembled in a central hall and sang patriotic songs ending with "God Save the King." There were regularly renderings of "Land of Hope and Glory," "Rule Britannia," and sentimental wartime ballads. Among the rousers was "God Bless the Empire," which included these lines: "the Empire is our country, and Canada our home..../ God bless the Empire, with heart and voice we sing/ God bless Canada, God save the King!"

This association with the Empire continued in my young adult life. In 1953, when I was in third-year Arts and first-year Law at the University of Saskatchewan, I was chosen as one of two students from the university to attend a summer seminar in India organized by World University of Canada and its Indian counterpart. This was the summer of 1953 and as it happened, because of a planned layover for our seminar group in Paris for a few days on the way to India, I was able to make a side trip to London to be there for the Coronation of Elizabeth II. My girlfriend Eleanor (later to be my wife) happened to be working in London that summer. She and I sat in covered stands in Parliament Square, just opposite Westminster Abbey, and saw the whole procession approaching and leaving it. Here was indeed the last great imperial pageant, before the process of decoloniza- tion gathered speed later in that decade. There were troops from dozens of Dominions, colonies, and dependencies. There were the scarlet-coated soldiers of the Queen's East African Rifles, Gurkhas, and all sorts of splen- didly adorned British regiments. Naturally, the Royal Canadian Mounted Police were prominently displayed. There were dozens of marching bands, with rousing imperial music: one frequently heard "Soldiers of the Queen," and even a few times "The Maple Leaf Forever." Among the great imperial and commonwealth statesmen were Churchill, Nehru, St. Laurent, and Robert Menzies of Australia, each in their respective black horse-drawn carriages. One of the crowd's favourite heads of state was Queen Sālote of Tonga, a woman some six feet three inches tall, riding in an open carriage disdainful of the London rain that was, of course, falling steadily through much of the proceedings. The Queen and Prince Phillip were resplendent in an historic gilded carriage. The whole procession took over an hour to pass, whereupon we listened to the proceedings going on inside the Abbey through a public address system. Two hours later we saw the procession leave the Abbey. I think for the first time I grasped the breadth and diversity of an Empire that was already in rapid decline.

The author as a seminar student climbing the Himalayas in Kashmir, August 1953.

This recognition was reinforced when I travelled that summer to India, until so recently the "Jewel in the Crown" of the Empire, to attend the World University Service of Canada seminar. We left Paris with a group of Canadians, as well as a few American and European students (among the latter was Olof Palme, later Prime Minister of Sweden), meeting about an equal number of students from South East Asia and Africa (including Mwai Kibaki, now President of Kenya). Among the Canadian faculty were Father Georges-Henri Lévesque, Dean of the School of Social Sciences of Laval University and later to be one of the leading influences in the Quiet Revolution; Dr Eugene Forsey, on loan for the summer from his post as Director of Research at the Canadian Congress of Labour; and Gérard Filion, publisher of *Le Devoir* and a strong critic of the Duplessis government then in power. We had seminar activities at the University of Mysore for some six weeks and then the Westerners spent another six weeks travelling around India, Pakistan, and Ceylon, as it then was. My travels that summer in India, just six years after her independence, and in Ceylon, only five years after her independence, gave me a heightened sense of the meaning of Empire and its aftermath. Of course we were made aware of some of the awful abuses of Imperial rule, but we also saw some of the positive British legacy in Indian institutions and society. At

that time there were still some British civil servants and army officers in India and Pakistan, left over from the days of the British raj, and many British traditions, including cuisine, lingered on. On occasion one could even hear from a few Indians expressions of regret that the British were gone. I was once with a small group chosen to meet with Prime Minister Nehru for an hour at his official residence. He, of course, expressed no such regrets, but he spoke English with a beautiful accent cultivated, no doubt, at Eton and Cambridge where he had studied. We were allowed to ask him questions and I asked a naive one. According to my notes the exchange was as follows:

> Q. Do you believe the people of India have accepted Mr Gandhi's principles, for example, non-violence?
>
> A. (Nehru, half-amused) The people of India are non-violent? Who told you that?...Indians are as violent as anyone else if they are stirred up...Normally they are quiet but once excited they can be as violent as anyone....Definitely people have not accepted the doctrines of Mr Gandhi into their lives. But we have his teachings as one of the factors in our national background. We may do something wrong but at least we know it is wrong....What I am opposed to are men like Hitler who glorified the use of brutality and force.

In later years, as I read more about the terrible communal rioting and bloodshed on the subcontinent at the time of partition of India in 1947 (only six years before), and reflected that Gandhi himself had been assassinated only five years before, I realized what a foolish question it was.

It seems I was destined to have a long-standing connection with the Commonwealth. As an Assistant Deputy Minister of Justice in Ottawa during the 1970s and early 1980s, I was responsible for the Department's relations with the Legal Division of the Commonwealth Secretariat in London. We had co-operative ventures of various kinds, usually to improve legal relations between member countries or to assist smaller Commonwealth jurisdictions. I was a frequent visitor to Marlborough House in London, headquarters of the Commonwealth Secretariat. This lesser palace of faded elegance, situated on the Mall a short distance from Buckingham

Palace, had been the residence of Edward VII and Queen Alexandra for some 38 years while they were the Prince and Princess of Wales, patiently awaiting his succession to his iconic mother, Queen Victoria. Among my Commonwealth activities, I attended four Commonwealth Law Ministers meetings as senior adviser to the Canadian Minister of Justice or his representative: in Lagos, Nigeria; in Barbados; in Colombo, Sri Lanka; and in Winnipeg, Manitoba (I was responsible for organizing the latter on behalf of the host country). As a member of the Commonwealth Law Association (an organization of lawyers and judges), I attended conferences of that organization in Hong Kong (where I gave a paper); Vancouver; Kuala Lumpur, Malaysia; and Melbourne, Australia. I also was loaned by the Government of Canada in 1979 as an adviser to the Indian Ocean Commonwealth state of Seychelles, to help them write a constitution, and in 1989 to the Government of Hong Kong, one of the few remaining British colonies, to advise on the drafting of a bill of rights. I have many charming memories of Commonwealth relations: countless sincere discussions of determinedly good will, albeit ever lacking much impact on the course of mankind. For example, I recall standing on a moonlit beach south of Colombo where, during a barbeque for law ministers, I successfully negotiated with Sir Michael Havers, Attorney General of England, and Hon. Mark MacGuigan, Minister of Justice of Canada, the text for the final communiqué on the subject of the Law of the Sea—a text that would not embarrass either country notwithstanding their conflicting views on the matter. One was often reminded of the diversities of culture in the Commonwealth. For example, at the Law Ministers meeting in Lagos (held in the parliamentary chamber that was available to us since, under the current military regime, there was no need for a debating facility), we had a nice discussion one morning about new developments in corrections. Two or three countries, including New Zealand and Canada, gave carefully prepared papers describing liberal pilot projects they had conducted, reducing incarceration with measures such as "diversion" of the offender into community service or fines related to the accused's income. The Attorney General of Nigeria, as chairman, often became restless to speak, so after hearing the others he said (impromptu) "We also tried a pilot project here, with execution by firing squad. After the recent civil war [in Biafra] there were many, many firearms in circulation. We became concerned about the increase in offences involving the use of firearms, so as an experiment we

made such crimes punishable by death. And as we wanted to maximize the deterrent effect, we thought that the executions should be public. So we set up some barrels on the beach here in Lagos and we executed such criminals by firing squad where everyone could see. We found that within a few weeks the incidence of this sort of crime dropped dramatically. So we are now considering extending the project to drug importation offences." No comment issued from the other ministers. At the meeting in Colombo, the Chairman, who was the Law Minister of Sri Lanka, was a rather dreamy sort who was also a well-regarded poet. On the last day, after there had been a decision the day before about where the Law Ministers would next meet (Zimbabwe), in his closing remarks he said, "And I want to thank Zambia for its invitation for the next meeting." An African voice cried out "That's Zimbabwe!" "Oh, excuse me," said the Chairman, "I guess I had Zambia in my thoughts because this is its national day." Another African voice protested "That's Gambia!" The Sri Lankan Chair obviously had some difficulty with distinguishing the nations of Africa.

In my legal studies at the University of Saskatchewan, from 1952 to 1955, we were also ever-conscious of the British connection. In constitutional law we were taught that with rare exceptions only the United Kingdom Parliament could amend the *British North America Act, 1867*,[2] Canada's constitution. We gave our greatest attention to the decisions of the Judicial Committee of the Privy Council in London which was, before 1950, the final court of appeal for Canada, with appeals going there from the Supreme Court of Canada or, on occasion, directly from provincial courts of appeal, bypassing the Supreme Court. The Privy Council was frequently engaged with Canadian constitutional appeals and its jurisprudence formed the spine of Canadian constitutional law studies, which in those days (predating the *Charter*) were largely confined to distribution of powers issues. New appeals to the Judicial Committee from any Canadian court had been abolished effective in 1950, although appeals already underway could continue. One of my clearest recollections was the anticipation, during our course in constitutional law, with which we awaited an important decision of the Judicial Committee in the appeal from the Supreme Court of Canada in *S.M.T. v Winner*.[3] This involved important issues of federal and provincial jurisdiction over intra- and interprovincial bus and truck services. It was in February 1954, I believe, when our professor, Dean F.C. Cronkite, learned from a newspaper of the decision. We were of course

anxious to see the text but that was in the days before faxes and email. It was some six weeks later that the Dean came to class triumphantly waving a mimeographed copy of the decision that he had arranged to get from London by surface mail! Just in time for the final exam!

Our constitutional studies in that epoch were also heavily laden with positivism and the supremacy of Parliament. We knew where law was to come from—from binding judicial precedents and valid legislation. Legislation was valid in Canada so long as it fit within the quantitative distribution of powers prescribed by the *BNA Act, 1867*.[4] There were no qualitative limits by way of guarantees for individual rights such as were found in the *United States Bill of Rights*. To be sure there were a few group rights protected, such as the use of both French and English in Parliament, the Quebec legislature, and in federal and Quebec courts (section 133 of the *BNA Act, 1867*); and the public funding of minority Roman Catholic or Protestant schools respectively in Ontario and Quebec (section 93) and three other provinces. But otherwise, the constitution was understood to embrace parliamentary sovereignty as summed up in Dicey's aphorism that Parliament can do anything "but make a woman a man, and a man a woman."[5] Also, in that post–Depression era judicial activism was in disrepute in liberal circles in the United States and English Canada. The dominant academic view, shared by our professor as well as many other constitutional scholars, such as Frank Scott of McGill and Bora Laskin of the University of Toronto, was that both the US Supreme Court and the Judicial Committee of the Privy Council had officiously engaged in judicial activism to strike down liberal legislative reforms that they found to violate previously unknown but implicit constitutional imperatives. Such criticisms of judicial activism of the US Supreme Court could be found in the utterances of famous American legal scholars, such as Justice Oliver Wendell Holmes and Justice Felix Frankfurter. This attitude was much closer to the British tradition of positivism, opposing as it did judicial adventurism in constitutional interpretation.

My further immersion in English jurisprudence involved two years of study at Oxford. I had majored in history at Saskatchewan and at times considered pursuing that subject further rather than the study of law. A favourite professor of history, Charles Lightbody, had instilled in me further anglophilia and he apparently saw in me some potential I had not recognized. He urged me to consider going to Oxford, his alma mater,

and arranged a place for me at Pembroke College. I arranged some financing and ultimately won a Mackenzie King Travelling Scholarship. Eleanor and I were married the summer preceding my entry at Oxford and we had a memorable two years in England, Scotland, Ireland, and on the continent. While I gained further respect for British public institutions, my mandatory studies were mostly in the private law area (including two courses in Roman Law and sometimes working from Latin texts in the Institutes of Justinian). The only public law option I could choose was Public International Law, where I took lectures from Sir Humphrey Waldock, later President of the International Court. Fortunately, all this led to an invitation from Dean Cronkite to return to Saskatoon as an Instructor for one year to teach, among other things, Constitutional Law. More on that later.

To complete this account of my formation and its potential influence on my later career, I obtained from 1961 to 1962 a Ford Foundation Fellowship in Law Teaching tenable at the Harvard Law School. There I pursued doctoral studies that also involved immersion in undergraduate courses such as American Constitutional Law. I was in a class taught by Professor Paul Freund, who had studied under Frankfurter and worked as a young lawyer in the Roosevelt New Deal Administration that had been regularly before the Supreme Court battling to defend innovative legislative reforms. From him I also came to understand the problems of judicial activism. After returning with my family to Canada, where I took up a professorship at the University of Saskatchewan, I completed my thesis and took my doctoral degree in Harvard Yard in June of 1966, sharing the occasion with hundreds of other graduands, including honorary degree recipient Averell Harriman. I later turned the thesis into a book,[6] a then unique and systematic analysis of how our courts handle constitutional adjudication. In it I urged some flexibility in the courts' treatment of old rules of standing, justiciability, and precedent: little did I foresee to what excesses this might lead.

INTRODUCTION

In 1982, with the passage at Westminster of the *Constitution Act, 1982*,[1] Canada, for the first time, achieved legal control over her constitution, thus breaking the last tie of governance with the United Kingdom, except for the purely symbolic role of the monarchy. At the same time, we also adopted a completely new constitutional device for this country, an entrenched bill of rights known as the *Canadian Charter of Rights and Freedoms*,[2] and explicit constitutional protection of Aboriginal rights.[3] Because of the profound and innovative nature of these changes, the way they were achieved, and the controversy that embroiled the country in the process, I think it is legitimate to call it a revolution—as much, say, as the Quiet Revolution in Quebec. I was involved with this process for 22 years, longer than any other official or politician. I will not undertake here to provide a complete history of the process, to which many others have contributed parts (while other parts remain to be ferreted out of government documents). Instead, around a narrative of the major issues and events, I will add some personal experiences and perspectives.

During this same period, there were other important and related legal developments that dramatically enhanced the recognition of individual and collective rights of Canadians. I had the good fortune to be involved with four of these: the establishment in Saskatchewan of the first universal public medical insurance scheme in Canada; the adoption of the *Canadian Human Rights Act*; Canada's accession to the *International Covenant on Civil and Political Rights*; and the establishment of a policy and process for the negotiation of Aboriginal land claims. All have contributed to a profound change in our society.

PART I

THE PATRIATION
PROCESS

1

ORIGINS OF THE PROBLEM

As is well known, when the *British North America Act, 1867*[1] (commonly referred to as the *BNA Act(s)*) was drafted on the basis of proposals by colonial politicians and enacted by the United Kingdom Parliament as the Constitution of Canada, it contained no provisions for the amendment within Canada of most of that constitution. The issue seems not to have been addressed seriously. This was perhaps not surprising in the context of the times: it was generally accepted that the legitimate source of a constitution for Canada was the Westminster Parliament.

This was in accord with established constitutional doctrine. It was part of the legal framework of the Empire that British laws, if in conflict with colonial laws, would prevail. That is, Westminster could legislate for the colonies.[2] After the British Conquest of Canada, the UK Parliament first exercised legislative control (as contrasted with executive control exercised by the Crown under its prerogative) by the *Quebec Act, 1774*,[3] in which it legislated a constitution for Canadian territory. The English Court of King's Bench that same year confirmed the validity of British legislation imposed on a colony in *Campbell v Hall*.[4] The power of Westminster to so legislate for Canada was consistently recognized by Canadian and English courts down to and including the adoption of the *Constitution Act, 1982*.[5] It was specifically defined and underwritten in the *Colonial Laws Validity Act, 1865*,[6] which provided that "[a]ny colonial law, which is or shall be repugnant to the provisions of any Act of Parliament extending to the colony to which such law may relate...shall be read subject to such Act...and shall, to the extent of such repugnancy, but not otherwise, be and remain absolutely void and inoperative." The British North American territories, whether before or after Confederation, were to remain colonies for the purposes of the *Colonial Laws Validity Act, 1865*: Westminster was to remain

the paramount legislative authority. It was not until the *Constitution Act, 1982*[7] that the 1865 Act ceased to apply to Canada.

From the history of the Confederation negotiation and debate in Canada, and the fact that the final product had not been specifically approved in its entirety by any colonial legislature, it seems clear that not only the legal but also the political legitimacy of a constitution adopted in London was accepted. As I will discuss later, it seems clear that Confederation would not have happened but for the wish of the Imperial government to diminish its responsibilities for its remaining North American colonies by a timely merger, and that abiding support for the project was exercised effectively through its colonial governors, who intervened to promote Confederation without serious local objection to the Imperial role. It is perhaps then not surprising that colonial statesmen of the day viewed with equanimity the possible future amendment of the constitution by the Imperial Parliament, no doubt assuming that they would be consulted about the matter. While Confederation created a viable combination of British territories and general autonomy of its governments, it did not amount to a grant of independence: there were still many vestiges of imperial control including the monarchy, powers of reservation and disallowance of federal legislation by the British government, judicial control through final appeals from Canadian courts to the Judicial Committee of the Privy Council, and the imperial conduct of foreign affairs. It was not until the founding of the Commonwealth of Australia in 1900 that Westminster conferred on a British territory a general power to amend its own constitution.[8]

During the first 40 years of Confederation, British authorities deferred to the federal government in respect of amendments of the *BNA Act, 1867*.[9] While it rejected requests and advice from provincial governments, it did not act without federal requests save in certain internal housekeeping of British statutes. The colonial relationship continued in matters of the constitution but with a fairly clear recognition that substantive change would not take place without a request from Ottawa.

In the 60 years that followed that era, the colonial relationship was seriously challenged. Canada's participation in World War I, along with that of the other senior Dominions, created strong expectations of recognition of our equality in matters of our constitution and otherwise. We signed the Treaty of Versailles separately and we came to believe that we had acquired a new international identity that was inconsistent with the imperial

custody of our constitution. As early as 1920, a Conservative administration in Ottawa unsuccessfully sought agreement with the provinces on a Canadian process to amend our constitution.[10] At an Imperial Conference in 1926 it was agreed, in a text referred to as the Balfour Declaration, that the United Kingdom and the Dominions (Canada, Australia, New Zealand, the Union of South Africa, the Irish Free State, and Newfoundland) were "autonomous communities within the British Empire, equal in status, in no way subordinate one to another in any aspect of their domestic or external affairs."[11] This clearly indicated that the United Kingdom Parliament should no longer be exercising legislative power over Canada, and certainly not in the amendment of our constitution. It was anticipated that there would be British legislation confirming this new position. Consequently, the first Dominion-Provincial Conference on the adoption of a Canadian amending procedure was convoked in Ottawa in 1927 by Prime Minister King to prepare for the advent of the new legal regime. Of course, no agreement was reached on a Canadian procedure. Therefore, when it came time for Westminster to adopt its self-denying ordinance in the form of the *Statute of Westminster, 1931*,[12] recognizing the legislative autonomy of the Dominions, Canada had to ask for an exception—section 7, which preserved Westminster's power to amend our constitution—because of our lack of ability to agree on a domestic amending formula. The wording of the *Statute* as it related to Canada was the product of dominion-provincial negotiation and an Imperial Conference in 1930. (It is said that at this Conference, Canadian Prime Minister Bennett developed an antipathy for the word *Dominion* because, in a private heads of delegation meeting, UK Prime Minister Ramsay MacDonald commented, in a manner Bennett thought condescending, that "we are all Dominions now": he thereafter took steps to eliminate the term from official Canadian use,[13] a change that has been variously blamed on, among others, Prime Ministers Pearson and Trudeau). In general that *Statute* sought to prescribe legislative autonomy for the Dominions: for example, section 2 made the *Colonial Laws Validity Act, 1865*[14] inapplicable so as no longer to invalidate laws of a colonial Parliament. Section 4 provided that thereafter no law passed by the Imperial Parliament would be deemed to apply to a Dominion unless it expressly recited that such law was passed at the request, and with the consent, of that Dominion. But all these dispositions were by section 7 made inapplicable to the amendment of the *BNA Acts*. UK power to amend

those laws remained without legal limit, subject only to the political conventions that by then required a joint resolution of the Senate and House of Commons of Canada before Westminster would so legislate.

There then followed many efforts within Canada to obtain agreement on a domestic amending formula for our constitution.[15] It was always assumed that the agents for constitutional change would have to be the federal and provincial executive governments, and possibly the legislative bodies to which they belonged. A requirement of federal consent for amendments with nationwide effect was always assumed. The main issue was always how much provincial consent should be required to amend various provisions. There was generally a consensus that certain fundamental changes, such as those concerning language and religious schools guarantees, might have to require unanimity. It was also accepted that changes affecting one or more but not all provinces would require the consent only of Parliament and the government or legislature of the province(s) affected. Studying this problem was a House of Commons committee in 1935, followed by a First Ministers' Conference that year. There were conferences of Attorneys-General in 1936, 1950, 1960, 1961, and 1964; and First Ministers' Meetings in 1950 (two of them) and a further eight between 1968 and 1981 where this subject was discussed. The context was always the "repatriation of the Constitution"—that is, finding a domestic amending procedure, thus making our constitution subject only to Canadian authorities and eliminating this vestige of our colonial past. (In my role in Ottawa after 1968, I managed to change the term from *repatriation* to *patriation*: How could our constitution be *repatriated* I asked, when it had never been *patriated*?)

MY RENDEZVOUS WITH DESTINY

Were I Mackenzie King or John Diefenbaker I might have realized at an early age that my destiny was to help patriate the constitution. A friend from my high school days recently sent me a clipping from our student newspaper to remind me that in December 1949 I had led a debating team in a Regina intercollegiate debate arguing the affirmative of "Resolved that the Canadian government [*sic*] should have the right to amend the constitution." We won.

2

MY INTRODUCTION TO CONSTITUTIONAL REFORM: THE FULTON AND FAVREAU PHASE

My initiation into constitutional reform came with the series of Attorneys-General Conferences on Repatriation of the Constitution in 1960 to 1961.

Upon completing my studies at Oxford in 1957, I accepted a one-year appointment as an Instructor in the College of Law at the University of Saskatchewan in Saskatoon. Fortunately, the Dean assigned to me Constitutional Law as one of my classes, it being my favourite subject. After that we moved to Regina where I articled for admission to the bar at the Department of the Attorney General and where I later worked for most of three years as a Crown Solicitor.

Among the various topics I had to cover in my class in Constitutional Law was the thorny problem of amendment of the Canadian Constitution and the problems of "repatriation." I explained to students that at the time of Confederation no thought was given to providing a process within Canada for amending the most important areas of the *BNA Act, 1867*, and while the United Kingdom Government and Parliament were no doubt willing to be done with making such amendments for us, it had not been possible for Canadians to agree on the terms of a domestic amending procedure. I described to them some of the futile efforts that had gone into trying to transfer the amendment power to Canada—that is, in attempted "repatriation." At that time, the basic authority, nay Bible, on the subject was the book of Paul Gérin-Lajoie, *Constitutional Amendment in Canada*.[1] I felt some affinity for this work as he wrote it as a doctoral thesis

The author and wife Eleanor, Oxford Degree Day, June 1957.

for Oxford, having been a student of my college there, Pembroke. I even later followed his example by successfully submitting my doctoral thesis for Harvard to the same publisher, the University of Toronto Press, where it was published in 1968[2] with a foreword by Frank Scott.

My work in the provincial Department of the Attorney General afforded me considerable exposure to public law issues, and as soon as I was admitted to the bar I had several occasions to represent the Attorney General in court in constitutional and administrative law cases. Within two years of my call to the bar I was in the Supreme Court of Canada as junior counsel in a distribution of powers case. When I read in the summer of 1960 that Prime Minister Diefenbaker had announced the holding of an Attorneys-General Conference, to be chaired by his Minister of Justice, Davie Fulton, on "Repatriation of the Constitution," I called on the Attorney General to tell him of my interest in the subject. I soon found myself the Secretary of the Saskatchewan delegation.

Among the first steps we took was to retain Professor Frank Scott and Dean F.C. Cronkite as advisers to the Saskatchewan delegation (they had served in this role in the 1950 First Ministers' Conferences). In early September, while Attorney General Robert Walker, Minister of Education Allan Blakeney (certainly the most able lawyer in the Cabinet and designated by the Premier to assist in this whole project), and I were attending the annual meeting of the Canadian Bar Association in Quebec City, we arranged to meet with Frank Scott and went to Montreal for a day to see him at McGill. He gave us a brilliant analysis of what was happening in Quebec (in this year that was later seen as the beginning of the Quiet Revolution) and reviewed the possibilities for constitutional reform. Among other things, he urged upon us the need to advocate a constitutional bill of rights. We were also in agreement that the amending formula should be relatively flexible, with due regard to what Frank saw as Quebec's particular concerns.

There followed back in Regina a series of working meetings involving ministers, advisers, and senior officials. Premier T.C. Douglas took a strong personal interest in the subject and attended some of our meetings as well as reading and commenting on the material we generated. I was always impressed with his grasp of the legal issues as well as his commitment to principles such as the entrenchment of rights. He could make the whole thing a good deal more intelligible than many of the lawyers could! We used to say of him, "For a Baptist preacher he's one hell of a good constitutional lawyer!" Among the provincial officials involved in this committee were two of the most senior, both of whom later held high office in the federal public service and played important roles in the constitutional discussions of the late 1960s and the 1970s: A.W. Johnson, who later in Ottawa served as Deputy Minister of National Health and Welfare, Secretary of the Treasury Board, and President of the Canadian Broadcasting Corporation; and T.K. Shoyama (whose family, incidentally, had been interned during the war along with other Canadians of Japanese ancestry), who later in Ottawa was, among other positions held, Deputy Minister of Energy, Mines and Resources, and Deputy Minister of Finance.

My duties as Secretary of our delegation generally included everything from research and drafting of speeches to making hotel reservations and, occasionally, when in Ottawa, going on behalf of the delegation to the stores of the Liquor Control Board of Ontario. For the first conference I

put together an opening statement for the Attorney General, which was vetted and modified in Regina before we left for Ottawa. To be sure, it called for both flexibility in any constitutional arrangements and for the entrenchment of a bill of rights in the constitution.

It is worth considering something of the players at this series of conferences as well as the dynamics of the debate and the interplay of issues, as there was a certain continuum in the next 20 years of the participants and particularly of issues. Among other things, this history demonstrates how the frustration of the process of repatriation and the abortive search for an amending formula ultimately led to the federal focus on a charter.

First, the cast of characters in 1960 to 1961. Among those attending these conferences were Paul Gérin-Lajoie, the author and scholar who was Minister of Youth in the new Lesage government and head of the Quebec delegation. There were two Premiers who were also their own attorneys-general: Louis J. Robichaud of New Brunswick and Ernest Manning of Alberta. (It was said of Mr Manning, who was of course not a lawyer, that he did not have enough faith in any lawyer to entrust him with the role of Attorney General). There were two future Premiers: Sterling Lyon of Manitoba and Allan Blakeney of Saskatchewan. Among the advisers were two future Supreme Court judges, Louis-Philippe Pigeon and Jean Beetz. The chief federal official was Elmer Driedger, then Deputy Minister of Justice and later author of the seminal Canadian text on the interpretation of statutes. R.B. Bryce, one of the greatest of the federal mandarins of his generation and then Secretary to the Cabinet, was also an occasional participant. Among the advisers were other distinguished scholars: Professor Alex Brady of the University of Toronto, Gilbert Kennedy (sometime professor and then Deputy Attorney General of BC), and Frank Scott and Dean Cronkite of the Saskatchewan delegation. The well-known and respected Montreal lawyer, H. Carl Goldenberg, was adviser to the Newfoundland delegation. He and I first became acquainted at that time and were later to be good friends and colleagues. The chairman was of course Davie Fulton, the Minister of Justice, who was a former Rhodes Scholar and one of the strongest intellects in the Diefenbaker cabinet. It seemed, however, that he had been given a rather limited mandate.

The dynamics of the "repatriation" issue that the Conference of Attorneys-General was to address were roughly as follows. There was a general consensus that "repatriation" would be a good thing, and that

the elements of "repatriation" would involve the enactment by the UK Parliament of one final amendment to our constitution, including the putting in place of a purely Canadian procedure for amending our constitution in future, together with some self-denying declaration by Westminster that it would not in future make laws for Canada. But there was of course no consensus on what that domestic amending process should be. Most of the provinces had not changed their basic preferences since the earlier meetings of attorneys-general on this subject in 1936 and 1950. The "have-not" provinces (the Atlantic provinces, Manitoba, and Saskatchewan) generally were more disposed to flexibility in the amendment process, even contemplating easier transfer of provincial powers to the central government because they had learned from experience that the latter was more likely to have the resources and capacity to provide vital services. To this economic motive was added, in the case of Saskatchewan, an ideological disposition toward centralization anchored mainly but not exclusively in socialist doctrine that believed that large economic and social problems had to be tackled by equally large governments.[3] This resulted in Saskatchewan being more resistant to proposals for an inflexible formula as the meetings went on. In contrast were the "have" provinces of Ontario, British Columbia, and Alberta. They were comfortable with the status quo and were in no way interested in making centralization of power any easier. Alberta had obviously forgotten its less salubrious days when it also depended on federal subventions—before oil was discovered in abundance within its boundaries. Not surprisingly, Quebec was a special case. It certainly did not want any possibility of diminutions of provincial powers through any new all-Canadian amending formula. That had been the main concern of Quebec in earlier conferences. But Quebec leaders such as Duplessis had previously had no particular interest in extended powers for the state, even the provincial state. However, even before the Quiet Revolution, Quebec had somewhat belatedly started to experience the implications of both the French Revolution (secular and recognizing the equal rights of individuals) and the Industrial Revolution (with its urbanization and industrialization, its need for a technically educated work force, and its accompanying social problems, which gave rise to increasing need for governmental intervention in social and economic institutions). The Lesage government, and Quebec intellectuals generally, recognized the need for a positive state, and this led to the belief that the government

of Quebec would need more constitutional powers to create Utopia on the St. Lawrence. In other words, Quebec might well want more flexibility in the constitution to allow more powers to be transferred to it. At the same time, however, much as it treasured its own imagined veto over any transfers of powers to or from other provinces, it did not want other provinces having a veto over transfers to it. This objective was combined with a strategic assumption that, as it didn't much care about the symbolism of "repatriation"—it believed this was a precious and pre-eminent goal of "the rest of Canada"—it could exchange its ultimate consent to "repatriation" for not only an amending formula most favourable to Quebec but also insist on something else of substance, such as special powers or special status for that province. This bargaining strategy continued for many years as Quebec rejected one amending formula after another because there were no special benefits for it, until finally its bluff was called in 1981.

And what of the Government of Canada? In previous Dominion-Provincial discussions on the constitution with Prime Minister King or Prime Minister Bennett in the chair, the federal leaders had always taken firm positions in defence of federal powers and the federal role. But in the weeks preceding the first Attorneys-General meeting of October 1960, Mr Fulton sent out a rather astonishing proposal. He suggested that the repatriation process be carried out in two stages. First, that Westminster legislate to provide that thereafter the Canadian constitution could be amended in Canada by the unanimous agreement of Parliament and all of the legislatures; and secondly, that once the constitution had been thus repatriated, the federal and provincial governments could then agree on a better procedure. There was some initial support for this procedure, but Saskatchewan was not alone in rejecting it. We made the obvious point that once the constitution was repatriated with every province having a veto, there would be no chance of getting some of them to agree to anything less than a full veto over every future amendment. To us it seemed incredible that the federal government should be so reckless of its own future that it was prepared to render any prospect of future amendments a hostage to the special interests of any province, no matter how large or small. Yet that seems to have been the attitude of the Diefenbaker government. Throughout the discussions it showed little preference for one formula over another, and thus apparently had no concept of how the constitutional future should unfold. Mr Fulton was quoted as saying

of these discussions, "the Federal government had not taken sides in any of the disagreements over an amending formula, but had acted only as a mediator."[4] In other words, his government was happy to provide the hall but didn't want to appear to have any opinion on a future amending formula for Canada. Mr Diefenbaker seemingly did not know what formula he would like but, as will be seen later, he knew what he didn't like—in particular the Fulton-Favreau Formula of 1964. In a way, this was typical of "the Chief" as a statesman, who was more decisive in Opposition than in Government.

We attended four meetings of the Conference in 1960 to 1961, the last in September 1961, when I combined the trip to Ottawa with transporting my family to Cambridge, Massachusetts, to commence my graduate studies at Harvard. The net result of the 1960 to 1961 conferences was a draft amending procedure that came to be called the Fulton Formula. There was general technical agreement on the draft but no unanimity on the substance. The formula required unanimous consent by all provinces for any amendment "affecting" (a very broad term) any provincial power. While there was an attempt to alleviate this rigidity by a delegation procedure, it would have had limited value. It only permitted delegation of certain provincial powers and it required the participation of four provinces before there could be any delegation. While a number of provinces were prepared to accept this formula, *faute de mieux*, and presumably the malleable federal government would have been willing to accept it, neither Quebec nor Saskatchewan ever affirmed its consent. While Quebec appeared to approve part of the formula, it never did commit itself to delegation. And soon there were voices in that province insisting that the formula must be rejected because it did not delete or limit the federal amendment power in section 91 head 1 of the *BNA Act, 1867*, added in 1949 by Westminster at the sole request of the federal Parliament. By this time the Diefenbaker government had other more pressing problems and it was defeated at the polls in 1963. In the meantime, I had left the public service of Saskatchewan and had taken a position as an Assistant Professor in the College of Law in Saskatoon.

MEDICARE

My last assignment as a public servant of Saskatchewan happened to be one of the most interesting. I had been on a leave of absence from the

Department of the Attorney General while at Harvard, in the academic year 1961–1962. Upon my return to the Department in June, I was given a special research assignment as I was leaving that fall to join the law faculty. This coincided with the coming into force of the provincial *Medical Care Insurance Act*, the fulfilment of a promise by Premier Douglas in the provincial election of 1960. There had been, since that election, an ever sharpening debate about such legislation, which for the first time in North America would establish a publicly funded universal medical insurance program for which every resident would be eligible. Various modalities were debated, but the majority of the medical profession were vehemently against all of them. For them it was pure and simple— "Socialized Medicine"—and they knew they were against *that*. If they had had any doubts, the American Medical Association told them this was a *Bad Thing*. They conjured up the usual bogeymen: state intervention in a patient's assignment to a doctor, state participation in decisions about the treatment to be delivered, and complete loss of privacy resulting from disclosure to a vast array of "bureaucrats" of the intimate details of each person's medical condition. The same nonsense was heard recently in the corridors of Congress in Washington. Saskatchewan doctors, having lost the political battle against a duly elected government, went on strike on July 1, 1962, the day the scheme came into force. Only a dedicated and courageous few continued to work. The College of Physicians and Surgeons did set up a system of emergency care at certain hospitals at which designated doctors voluntarily took turns. Most small hospitals closed entirely. Some pregnant women were warned to leave the province for their deliveries. Within a few days of the beginning of the strike, a small child was rushed by its parents to a local rural hospital for treatment, only to find it closed. They had to drive an hour or so to the nearest open hospital. The child died on the way. Whether the delay had any role in his death was not clear, but the incident heightened tensions and emotions.

About July 3 or 4, I was in an elevator in the Legislative Building in Regina when Allan Blakeney, then Provincial Treasurer, boarded it. He knew I was just back from Harvard and he asked me what I was working on. I said that as I was only there for the summer and I had been asked to work on proposals for a new *Expropriation Act*. He thought for a moment and said, "I think we can find a better use of your time." He must have gone to his office and spoken to the Attorney General because shortly after I had

a call from Allan's secretary saying, "A room has been booked in your name at the Bell City Motel. Please check in by 1:30 as a meeting about medicare will take place there." I duly checked in and there soon arrived Al Blakeney; Al Johnson, his Deputy Minister; Don Tansley, Executive Director of the new Medical Care Insurance Commission (MCIC) that was to administer the insurance plan; T.K. Shoyama, Secretary of the Economic Advisory and Planning Board; and a few other senior officials. They wanted to be free of interruptions at the office and preferred to keep the meeting confidential, hence the motel and myself as registered guest. This was a hastily formed committee to advise Cabinet on the handling and settlement of the medical strike. I was designated legal co-ordinator. As it turned out we met daily, except for Sundays, often well into the evening until the settlement process moved to Saskatoon about July 20.

With the possible exception of the Government of Quebec during the October Crisis of 1970,[5] I have never sensed any peacetime government in Canada to have been faced with such strong forces arrayed against it as was the NDP government of Saskatchewan during this strike. Most doctors have a loyal following of patients, and in the weeks preceding the strike many of them had been eager to dispense to their patients (along with medical care) their side of the story and exaggerated fears of so-called socialized medicine. All major media in the province, including the two largest dailies (the Regina *Leader-Post* and the Saskatoon *StarPhoenix*) were persistent in their opposition and their forecasts of medical disasters if medicare were to become established. The business establishment for the most part sided with the doctors. Local hospital boards, in thrall to their local doctors (whom they desperately wanted to keep) closed hospitals in support of the strike. Such forces formed the Keep Our Doctors Committee (KOD) which, famously aided by an outspoken Roman Catholic priest who saw in medicare a communist plot, campaigned across the province against the government and medicare. The Canadian Medical Association and the American Medical Association each had a large presence in the province, providing public relations and advertising support to the local profession.

The only relief from this constant attack came from the national and international press. For example, the CBC, the *Toronto Star*, Southam Press, the *New York Times*, and the *Times of London* had reporters there and they carried objective coverage untainted by the local hysteria. I used to converse often with a reporter from the Parliamentary Press Gallery

in Ottawa who shared the hilarity with which his colleagues viewed the hyperbole of the KOD.

Our committee soon moved its venue back to the Legislative Building. We continued to look at options, possible compromises, possible mediators. We also became involved in combatting the strike, mainly by urging the recruitment of doctors from outside. We were in regular communication with Graham Spry, Saskatchewan's Agent-General in London, who advertised for British doctors to come to Saskatchewan to provide necessary medical services that our own doctors were withholding. Graham, well aware of the need for high-quality recruits, retained a panel of Harley Street physicians to screen all applicants. Those chosen were flown immediately to Saskatchewan and were assigned to hospitals that were willing to operate but had no doctors. We mainly targeted British doctors because, perhaps as a vestige of colonialism, the provincial *College of Physicians and Surgeons Act* made automatically eligible for its membership any doctor registered with the British Medical Council (BMC). We also had to assist with damage control concerning one or two doctors from elsewhere who turned out to have questionable histories. On July 11 there was supposed to be a massive demonstration in front of the Legislative Building by the KOD and we advised on crowd control. The KOD expected 40,000; only about 4,000 appeared and they were orderly.

At the heart of this government under siege, it was good for morale that various old friends of social democracy came to call to encourage ministers. Frank Scott and David Lewis appeared briefly. George Cadbury worked with our committee for a time. He was a British economist, scion of the Cadbury Chocolate family, who had spent time in Saskatchewan in the 1940s, shortly after the Douglas government came to power, to set up the first Economic Advisory and Planning Board. I well remember what he said the day of the KOD demonstration that we watched and listened to from our offices in the Legislative Building. So apprehensive had we been of a real disturbance, we had the Mayor of Regina waiting near the entrance to proclaim the *Riot Act* if matters got out of control. Amplifiers were poised to play a recording of "God Save the Queen" if necessary: we knew that any unruly Saskatchewan crowd would stop what it was doing and come to attention if that happened! But in fact the KOD speakers calmly addressed their crowd (we had provided the microphones) and then a delegation entered to meet the Cabinet to deliver certain demands.

Thirty minutes later they emerged. We could hear the leader telling the crowd that they had met the Cabinet, which was now considering their proposals. Ministers would reply to them later. Some "boos" rang out. The speaker said, "Now let's be reasonable—they have to have time to think about it." Hearing this, George Cadbury said, "Now that sounds to me like Saskatchewan—just like a Wheat Pool meeting." Shortly after that the crowd drifted off and this was the last major rally for the KOD.

Among the legal issues I had to consider were these: Could federal anti-combines legislation be applied to this strike? Did some of the violent speeches being made against the government constitute the incitement of violence? What controls if any did the government have available in respect of closing of hospitals? I was able to give instructions to counsel in one matter. Although the British doctors as members of the BMC were entitled as of law to be registered as members of the Saskatchewan College of Physicians and Surgeons so that they could practice in the province, the Registrar of the College found the mechanics of registration to be extremely time-consuming. As a result, days of medical care were being lost as qualified British doctors awaited the painfully slow processes of their registration in Saskatoon where the College's headquarters were. Finally I retained Roger Carter, QC, of Saskatoon to take legal steps to effect the registration. I phoned Roger to say we were of the opinion that the Registrar owed an enforceable duty to register the doctors and could be forced to do so by a writ of *mandamus*. I asked him to warn the Registrar of this and see if he could get some quick action. Otherwise we would have to go to court. Invoking the spirit of William Lyon Mackenzie King, I said, "So the word is, Roger: *mandamus* if necessary but not necessarily *mandamus*." Roger, who was an extremely able and imaginative counsel, could see that going to court would result in more delays in getting qualified doctors registered and at work. So instead he hired a bus, put about 20 British doctors on it who were awaiting registration, alerted the press, and had the bus driven up to the very door of the College's head office on Spadina Crescent in downtown Saskatoon. With photographers and TV cameras surrounding his group, he led them into the Registrar's office. Somehow, magically, registration was almost immediate.

About July 20 the strike was settled. The government had brought in a consultant, Lord Taylor of London, a medical doctor and a former Minister

of Health in a British Labour government. As matters developed, the doctors, who were keenly sensing a decline in public support and in their moral position, were ready to talk. They accepted a mediation process with Lord Taylor as mediator. The terms of settlement included the continuation of fee-for-service practice by doctors (this had always been an option under the legislation as passed). One of the key concessions by the government was that while there would be a single payer (the MCIC), doctors would not be obliged to send their claims directly to the MCIC or experience the inhumane degradation of receiving a cheque from the MCIC. Instead, the existing private medical insurers in the province—while they would be put out of the insurance business—could act as post offices to receive claims from doctors, forward them to the MCIC, receive payments from the MCIC, and then cut a cheque on their own accounts for the claimant doctor. So the doctors ended with essentially the scheme as legislated. Patients continued to pick their own doctors. Doctors received payment indirectly from the government agency. To the extent patients' medical records had to be exposed to the Commission for purposes of supporting a claim, they were nonetheless protected by strong privacy protections built into the Act, as had always been planned. One of my last acts before leaving government was to draft regulations establishing and controlling these post office entities to which I gave the modest title "payment services agencies."

It was said that before medicare Saskatchewan doctors managed to collect on average about 60 per cent of their bills. Now they would collect them all. This medicare program, the first in North America, worked so well that within about five years Parliament adopted a measure to pay the provinces 50 per cent of the costs if they would establish such a scheme; within a decade after the Saskatchewan doctors' strike, all provinces had done so. And so the Government of Saskatchewan played a seminal role in the creation of a national icon, our universal medical care insurance system, which no party today would dare abolish.

I do not wish to exaggerate my role in this result. I had no part in the shaping of the plan. I was not around for some of the ugly confrontations experienced by ministers and officials who were advocates of the plan, having been out of the country until a few days before the strike. But I have always felt privileged to have experienced at close hand this crisis of public policy implementation in a free and open society and to see a result

that has had such profound human and social impact on our nation. For once, "the good guys won."

THE FAVREAU ROUND

After the change in government in Ottawa to Lester Pearson's Liberals in 1963, there was a change of government in Saskatchewan, bringing to an end 20 years of moderately socialist government under the Co-operative Commonwealth Federation (CCF) and its successor party, the New Democratic Party (NDP). In its place came the rather right-wing Liberal government of Ross Thatcher. In 1964 the problem of repatriation was taken up once again in intergovernmental conferences. I was by this time working in Saskatoon as a full-time tenured member of the law faculty. Needless to say, because of my identification with the NDP I was out of favour in Regina. I did, at the request of former colleagues, provide some institutional memory of what had happened in this file in recent years but was otherwise not consulted. Out of these further meetings of attorneys-general, chaired by then Justice Minister Guy Favreau, came a slightly revised amending procedure that was dubbed the Fulton-Favreau Formula.[6] It was identical to the Fulton Formula except that it further accommodated Quebec by establishing specific limits on federal power to amend the constitution pertaining to the central institutions of government, as had been given in 1949 in the new section 91, head 1, of the *BNA Act, 1867*. While the new Government of Saskatchewan, along with most other provincial governments, was prepared to accede to this formula, Quebec, as usual, was reluctant, and by 1965 it alone of all the provinces signalled that it would not seek legislative approval for the Fulton-Favreau Formula. At the same time the Official Opposition in the House of Commons, now led by Mr Diefenbaker, mounted a strident campaign to prevent Parliament from endorsing Fulton-Favreau. Again the search for repatriation through a Canadian amending formula had ended in failure.

Before leaving this episode in Canadian constitutional history I must share a personal vignette. While the Fulton-Favreau Formula was still a lively issue, Mr Diefenbaker happened to attend an alumni banquet of his alma mater, the University of Saskatchewan, in Saskatoon, which my wife and I also attended. After the dinner, as we strolled through the reception area in the Bessborough Hotel, we encountered our friend Ray

Hnatyshyn, an active Conservative (later a Member of Parliament, a senior minister in the Clark and Mulroney governments, and Governor General from 1990 to 1995) who was escorting Mr Diefenbaker. He introduced us to the Chief and mentioned that "Professor Strayer has been involved with the constitutional amendment problem." The Chief drew himself up, shook his jowls, and exclaimed, "Oh, that Fulton-Favreau Formula—it would make the constitution as unchangeable as the laws of the Medes and the Persians!" He apparently was not concerned that this formula was virtually the same as that ascribed to his own former Minister of Justice, Davie Fulton, and endorsed by himself in 1961. But then Mr Diefenbaker was never a slave to consistency, the constraint so burdensome to lesser political beings.

3

THE CENTENNIAL
INITIATIVE

Canada's centennial of 1967 proved to be another turning point in my constitutional career. That year there was a widespread expectation in the land that, apart from all the transitory celebrations and Expo '67, there should be some lasting change in our constitution, marking the first hundred years of our existence as a nation. Naturally, the desirability of cutting the umbilical cord to the Mother of Parliaments through patriation of the constitution was frequently suggested. But in the Quebec of the Quiet Revolution, and in many of the other provinces with aspirations for new authority to support new programs or deal with new problems, there was much talk of an overhaul of the distribution of legislative powers in their favour.

I had known Marc Lalonde for some years, having first met him when we were both chosen from our universities (he from the University of Montreal) in 1953 to attend a World University Service of Canada seminar in India. I next encountered Marc in 1955 in Oxford, shortly after my wife and I arrived there. While walking on "the Broad" (as this street was known), I spied Marc on a bicycle. It turned out that, like us, he and his wife had been married that summer and he was there to study for two years, as was I. We kept in touch while there. After our return to Canada, some ten years before the events to be described, he and I had only sporadic contact. In the early 1960s he had worked on the staff of Davie Fulton, Minister of Justice, at the time of the Fulton Formula negotiations in which I had participated. By 1966 Marc was a senior policy adviser to Prime Minister Pearson. Sometime during the winter of 1966–1967, Marc phoned me in Saskatoon where I was teaching law and asked if I would consider coming

to Ottawa to work on reforming the constitution. He was calling me on behalf of Jean Beetz who was serving in Ottawa (on leave from his teaching post in law at the University of Montreal) as an Assistant Secretary to Cabinet for Federal-Provincial Relations in the Privy Council Office. I thought about it and later told Marc I could not absent myself from my teaching responsibilities for the coming academic year of 1967–1968 but could perhaps come to Ottawa for the summer of 1967. In subsequent discussions with Jean Beetz I agreed to meet him in Ottawa in mid-February to explore the question of summer employment.

I arrived on Parliament Hill on the very cold morning of February 14, 1967. I noticed that the Eternal Flame in front of the Centre Block, lit for the first time by the Prime Minister some six weeks before on New Year's Eve at the beginning of Canada's centennial year, had gone out because of ice formation due to the intense cold. I reflected briefly on whether this was a metaphor for Canada and her prospects for ever having a bicentennial! I met Jean in the East Block where he explained to me that, with the spirit of the centennial abroad, growing particularism in Quebec, and the general expectations that something would be done to modernize the constitution, the Government of Canada had launched internal studies on constitutional reform. There was (naturally) an interdepartmental committee discussing various ideas. One unusual feature of the committee was that it included a politician, Pierre Trudeau, the Parliamentary Secretary to the Prime Minister. They were in need of constitutional specialists to develop proposals for the committee. I was of interest to them as I taught and had published in the field of constitutional law and had the experience of the 1960 to 1961 conferences to which Jean had also been a delegate. As we were nearing agreement on terms, I mentioned to Jean that, while I was sure it would make no difference in the question of my employment, I thought he and his superiors and any relevant ministers should be aware that I was a card-carrying member of the NDP. This fact may well have been known to them before: certainly Jean was too much of a gentleman to betray any surprise or dismay. Nothing more was ever said about this but, as I will note later, the fact became well implanted in Pierre Trudeau's memory. Jean and I soon had worked out a plan for me to come on June 1 for three months, subject to me discussing it with my wife.

When I subsequently arrived in Ottawa on May 31 for the summer, I went directly to the East Block to see Jean. After a few pleasantries he

said: "I know you have a contract with the Privy Council Office (PCO) for the summer. You can still work here if you prefer. But some things have changed since we last talked in February. As you know, Pierre Trudeau has been made Minister of Justice and the constitutional file has been assigned to him by the Prime Minister. It might be more useful and interesting if you went to work with the Minister. Why don't you meet him and you two can see if you can work together?" I agreed that this would make sense and Jean arranged the meeting. When I arrived at Pierre's parliamentary office in the West Block I was immediately struck by its opulence. This office, which was virtually unchanged since Confederation and had at one time (it was believed) housed Sir John A. Macdonald, was large and high with a vaulted ceiling, a huge mantel decorated with bas-relief, and splendid carved wood panelling and trim. It was also known to have a secret external staircase where a minister could escape without encountering the press or others in the corridors outside his office: Trudeau used this shortly after he became leader when he made an unannounced trip to Rideau Hall to ask the Governor General for a dissolution of Parliament. Present for our meeting that day in the Minister's office was also Carl Goldenberg, whom I had met at the 1960 to 1961 conferences. Since his appointment as Minister, Pierre had retained Carl as his Special Counsel on the Constitution and it was proposed that for my work that summer I would serve as Assistant Constitutional Counsel. We talked in general terms about the nature of the undertaking and agreed that we could all work together. Carl left before I did. As I was going out I exclaimed to Pierre, "This is a splendid office you have, Minister!" He grinned, shrugged, and said "When a guy joins the Liberal Party he never knows where he'll end up!" (He was obviously speaking from experience—he'd only joined the party less than two years before.)

This not only began a long collaboration with Pierre Trudeau but also with Carl Goldenberg. Carl was a Montreal lawyer who had years of experience in advising governments. He had been chairman of several commissions on municipal government and had been a frequent adviser to governments, federal and provincial. In the sixties and seventies he was doing a lot of labour arbitration work. Apart from his warm personality, he had an uncanny ability for finding common ground among disputing parties. He and Pierre Trudeau had many friends in common in Montreal, including Frank Scott, and they had collaborated in various ways. He was certainly

a mentor to me and I admired his skill in finding compromises. His ability as a diplomat was exemplified in one small incident: one day during a First Ministers' Conference at the Government Conference Centre, it was decided that we should have a discussion with Prime Minister Trudeau over lunch. Carl and I accompanied the Prime Minister in his limousine and went to 24 Sussex Drive, where we joined four or five other advisers. As we were chatting in the sunroom before lunch, Pierre's housekeeper came in. She said, "Excuse me, Prime Minister, but there aren't enough steaks in the freezer. We are one short for lunch." Before Pierre could say anything Carl intervened, saying "Really I would prefer some poached eggs if that is possible." Another problem fixed! Our friendship, which I much valued, continued long after Carl was appointed a Senator and could no longer serve as a constitutional adviser.

It soon became apparent to me that Pierre Trudeau's constitutional priority, which he was in the course of selling to his cabinet colleagues, was the adoption of a charter of rights. In Part II I will dwell on the history of his attraction to a charter. Along with this preference went an antipathy to the discussion of the distribution of powers. Patriation was, I think, of low priority at that time because he had seen the futility of past efforts to get agreement on a domestic amending formula. (He knew the history of attempts since the first conference of 1927, and he had been a junior federal official at the 1950 Dominion-Provincial Conference in Quebec where First Ministers could reach no agreement.)

There were political realities, some of which I was of course already aware, which made it imperative for the federal government to take the initiative in constitutional reform. There had been growing unrest in Quebec for years, feeding the Quiet Revolution that had become manifest in about 1960. There was much talk of special status for Quebec, even among supposedly federalist politicians. By 1967 there was a Union Nationale government in Quebec that wanted to exploit and enhance the Quiet Revolution—albeit that this revolution was against many of the traditional verities embraced by the founder of the UN party, Maurice Duplessis. His posture had been one of running Quebec with its existing powers and the curried support of the Catholic clergy. He rejected the positive state and had no problem with the constitution as it was except for fending off federal encroachments. The leader in 1967, however, was Daniel Johnson. A long-time minister in the Duplessis governments, he

nevertheless adopted a new stance: namely that Quebec represented all French Canadians and that the only way to protect and enhance the rights of this group was greater constitutional powers for Quebec. He had articulated these views in a book, *Égalité ou Indépendance*,[1] published in 1965. To these growing demands of Quebec, of whose tenor of course the federal ministry did not approve, was added the growing belief among Canadians that in Canada's centennial year it was important to update the constitution—particularly for Canada, with its new sense of nationhood and maturity, to be able to amend its own constitution! Outside of Quebec there was also a growing sense of unease concerning the implicit threat to national unity posed by renewed Quebec nationalism.

Among the other provincial Premiers there were some mildly interested in constitutional reform for what they might get out of it. There were others who had a genuine concern for the future of the country in the face of Quebec's blandishments. The most prominent of the latter was Premier Robarts of Ontario. In his view there was a need to come to terms with Quebec for the sake of the whole country, and he considered that Ottawa was showing no leadership in this respect. During that summer he announced a Confederation of Tomorrow Conference to be held in the fall in Toronto. It was to be chaired by Ontario, which would also issue the invitations to all provinces and the federal government.

So the immediate problem facing the federal government that June of 1967 was first, to regain the political initiative for constitutional reform that was clearly and legitimately expected of it, and second, to turn the focus of constitutional discussions away from massive transfers of federal powers to the provinces (which some provinces obviously had in mind). It was this fortuitous set of circumstances into which Pierre Trudeau strode upon his appointment as Minister of Justice. Here was a political opportunity to advance his project of a constitutional bill of rights. Not only would it be a tactical diversion from provincial demands for more powers, but in principle it would also promote Pierre's concept of pan-Canadian biculturalism, where the linguistic and cultural interests of the francophone minority outside Quebec would be guaranteed by the constitution and not be dependent on new powers for Quebec as self-proclaimed defender of the French fact throughout Canada.

Thus, in light of these growing developments, it was necessary to establish a federal policy both for the process and the substance of constitutional

reform. On June 7, 1967, Cabinet considered a brief memorandum on constitutional reform and in particular how to meet the challenge posed by Premier Robarts's proposal of the Confederation of Tomorrow Conference. The Prime Minister was to meet the Premiers on July 5 and it was agreed that on that occasion he should propose to them a federal-provincial conference later in 1967 "to discuss, among other things, the adoption of an overall Canadian Bill of Rights binding upon the federal government and the provinces." This the Prime Minister did on July 5 and a press release was issued announcing that Premier Robarts would invite provincial and federal governments to a Confederation of Tomorrow Conference that fall, it being understood that the federal government would send observers only. The press release also announced that Mr Pearson would invite Premiers to a conference early in 1968 to discuss a constitutional bill of rights.[2] Mr Robarts's Conference was held in Toronto, November 27–30, 1967. The principal observer there for the federal government was Carl Goldenberg. It was the first such intergovernmental conference to be televised, thus setting a precedent for what was to come. While I did not attend this conference, I happened to be in Toronto the day before it was to begin. Carl Goldenberg invited me to his suite at the Royal York that Sunday afternoon and while I was there Premier Robarts arrived for a chat.

Meanwhile, in Ottawa we concentrated on shaping a proposal for a charter of rights, in preparation for the Constitutional Conference of early 1968. I spent most of that summer of 1967 in offices Carl Goldenberg had in the Justice Annex, a "temporary" wooden building beside the Supreme Court of Canada. (This building, among dozens of wood structures hastily constructed during World War II to accommodate burgeoning departments and bureaucrats, today remains standing: now a preserved heritage building as the only remaining temporary building.) The building, of course, had no air conditioning. To get any decent ventilation we had to keep the windows open and use electric fans; this brought into our offices the pungent, sulphurous odours from the pulp and paper mills of Hull. This condition was particularly oppressive with inversions of air on hot humid days. But because of Expo '67, conditions were brightened almost daily by visits of heads of state to nearby Parliament Hill. These arrivals were preceded by the band of the Governor General's Foot Guards forming up outside our office and practising their tunes of pomp and circumstance and the national anthem of the visitor. The Justice Building was yards

away and there I had easy access to the library. In our conference room in the temporary building we held occasional meetings with our advisers and with the Minister. Carl and I also had frequent meetings with Pierre Trudeau in his ministerial office and occasionally lunched with him so there was a regular flow of communication on the project in hand. Apart from Jean Beetz, who had regular input into the work, our outside advisers, with whom we probably met three or four times, were Gerald Le Dain, then lecturing at McGill and practising in Montreal, Gérard La Forest (then at the University of New Brunswick), and Mark MacGuigan (at that time Dean of the Windsor Law School). With their guidance and input I drafted a paper that, with a few additions by others, was published just before the 1968 Conference entitled *A Canadian Charter of Human Rights*[3] over the name of the Minister of Justice, Pierre Elliott Trudeau. (Anyone familiar with Pierre Trudeau's Olympian style of writing would know that he had not composed this rather heavy and pedantic prose).

The Prime Minister duly issued the invitations to a federal-provincial conference to be held in Ottawa, February 5–7, 1968. It was held in the Confederation Room in the West Block of the Parliament Buildings. This is a rather elegant room with much gild and elaborate chandeliers. With Mr Roberts having set the precedent of television in the conference room, Mr Pearson could do no less. One problem was that the Confederation Room was not vented adequately for the hot television lights then required, so participants experienced excessive heat. Also, the bright lights hurt the eyes of Newfoundland Premier Joey Smallwood, who sat throughout with sunglasses on, looking rather like a mafia boss at a congressional hearing. This was a memorable conference, as it gave Mr Trudeau a lot of good and free publicity for his soon-to-be announced candidacy for the leadership of the Liberal Party. Sitting behind him I saw him seize the opportunity to challenge Premier Johnson on the latter's "two nation" and "special status" theories, in the process staking out on national television his own claim to be the defender of a united Canada and the pan-Canadian rights of French Canadians, both within and without Quebec. At one point Johnson referred slightingly to Trudeau as "the member for Mount Royal" (his federal constituency), emphasizing the Englishness of this title. Trudeau referred back to him as the "member for Bagot" (Johnson's provincial constituency), giving it a very anglicized pronunciation. As the debate became more heated, Chairman Pearson, ever the diplomat, suggested a coffee break.

The first televised federal-provincial constitutional conference, February 5–7, 1968, was notable for the debate between Pierre Trudeau and Daniel Johnson of Quebec; the debate boosted Trudeau's campaign for the leadership of the Liberal Party. Seated at the table, left to right, are Trudeau, Minister of Justice; Prime Minister Pearson; Jean Marchand, Minister of Manpower and Immigration; and Premier Johnson. The author is seated behind Mr Marchand.

The publication of *A Canadian Charter of Human Rights* at the time of the Conference, over Trudeau's name, gave his candidacy a further lift. I had the unique gratification of being specifically thanked by name for my efforts as an adviser when Prime Minister Pearson reported to the House of Commons on the Conference.[4] That experience was never repeated!

I will not dwell on the subject matter of that first Constitutional Conference. The Government of Canada focussed the discussion on fundamental rights, including language rights (the first report of the Royal Commission on Bilingualism and Biculturalism had just been published). However, at the end of the Conference First Ministers agreed that there should be an ongoing constitutional review including these and several other topics: distribution of powers, reform of federal institutions such as the Senate and the Supreme Court, regional disparities, an amending procedure (i.e., patriation), and mechanisms of federal-provincial relations. Subsequently, a methodology was adopted in the Continuing Committee of Officials, the ongoing working group that prepared subjects for discussion by the sporadic First Ministers' Meetings, whereby any government could submit "propositions" on all or any part of the constitution. Such

propositions were to state an ideal constitutional arrangement for discussion but were not intended to state final positions of any government.

At about this time, in the early summer of 1968, I came back to Ottawa on a full-time basis, having taken a one-year leave of absence from my teaching position at the University of Saskatchewan. By this time Pierre Trudeau had just become Prime Minister and he had appointed John Turner to replace him as Minister of Justice. While John and his department were to play a major part in the federal-provincial discussions on the constitution, the Prime Minister wanted the principal organizational unit for the federal role in constitutional review to be situated in his department, that is, the Privy Council Office. A Constitutional Review Section was established there of which I was made the Director. Various officers of the PCO were assigned to me and I later recruited several constitutional specialists. I reported directly to the Clerk of the Privy Council and Secretary to Cabinet, Gordon Robertson, a very experienced mandarin in the position often described as head of the public service. He was of course the Deputy Minister of the Prime Minister and was in daily communication with the latter. My work often involved writing memoranda on the constitution to the Prime Minster for Gordon to sign. Another major task was developing and drafting proposed positions in the form of memoranda to cabinet for the Prime Minister's signature. The circulation of these to members of the Cabinet Committee on Federal-Provincial Relations was normally followed by my attendance, along with Gordon and sometimes one of my staff as note taker, at a meeting of the Committee, chaired by the Prime Minister, at which the memorandum was discussed and usually a decision was made. While decisions taken there had to be reported to and approved by full Cabinet, only Gordon and a PCO note taker normally attended those Cabinet meetings. Usually decisions taken by a committee (especially one that had been chaired by the Prime Minister!) were routinely approved. In my unit we did a variety of things: preparation of draft positions, in co-operation with the Department of Justice and other departments; organization of delegations to constitutional meetings of various sorts; preparation of speeches for the Prime Minister on the constitution for constitutional conferences, Parliament, and the public; drafting of talking points and notes on strategy or tactics for the Prime Minister as chairman and head of the federal delegation at constitutional conferences; and of course attendance at countless interdepartmental and

federal-provincial meetings (of officials, ministers, and First Ministers) regarding the constitution. After my first year on leave of absence from the university, I was able to get a further year's extension. By the end of the second year, with no end in sight in the constitutional review, I somewhat reluctantly decided to resign my university post and join the federal public service. I remained in the Privy Council Office until 1974, although after the failure of the Victoria Conference in 1971, the work of constitutional review was essentially over until later that decade. For a time in 1971 to 1974, I occupied a Justice role as Director of the Constitutional Law section there but remained physically located in the PCO, serving in part as constitutional adviser to that office.

Although most of what we did in the Constitutional Review Section during this period did not lead to constitutional reform, I remain proud of some of the studies we launched into a variety of problem areas that demonstrated needs for constitutional change. As it turned out, they involved some of the largest issues in public policy haunting us today. I will mention only two leading reports that were published. One was *Environmental Management* by James W. MacNeill, published in 1971.[5] We had borrowed Jim from his position in the Department of Energy, Mines and Resources and asked him to do an analysis of current and future environmental problems and of the constitutional implications for their future management. Jim was an engineer with economics training in Canada and Sweden. Supported by an outside research group we retained, he wrote a masterful and prophetic analysis of current and predictable environmental problems. Synthesizing the work of others, he described, for example, the phenomenon of global warming and the greenhouse effect, long before these had crept into the consciousness of governments or the public. He demonstrated the many externalities (i.e., harmful effects felt outside the city or province or country of origin) of even local pollution sources, recognizing that these create problems that are not only national but global in their impact. Hence, he argued, there was need for national and international means of management. While he was writing this analysis, Jim and I went to the Federal Republic of Germany and learned how they handled multijurisdictional and multinational environmental problems, such as pollution in the Rhine. Jim's analysis of potential problems for Canada and the world was so novel and alarming that it was only with great

hesitation that the Government of Canada was willing to publish it. We had to include clear messages that the views therein were those of Jim and not the Government! Yet the book has withstood the test of time and is now recognized as prescient—years ahead of informed public debate. As a result of this and other good work, Jim became an international expert on the environment, much in demand by other countries and international organizations. He has served as Chairman of the International Institute of Sustainable Development and Secretary-General of the United Nations' World Commission on Environment and Development.

Another important study to be published was that by A.E. Safarian, then a professor of economics at the University of Toronto. We commissioned him to do a study on Canada's internal common market or lack thereof, and what changes might be desirable in the constitution to strengthen it. His study, published in 1974, was entitled *Canadian Federalism and Economic Integration*.[6] In it he described how lacking we are in free interprovincial movement of services, persons, and capital, free trade being supposedly assured by section 121 of the *Constitution Act, 1867* but only in respect of the movement of goods; and even that assurance is far from perfect (it prohibits only interprovincial tariffs but not other forms of provincial protectionism). He called for a rewriting of section 121 to better protect the free movement of goods and services, as well as the extension of section 121 to cover non-tariff trade barriers for goods. This assessment accurately foresaw the abiding problems Canada has today with engaging in free trade treaties: we are only too conscious that we cannot negotiate a North American Free Trade Agreement that would exclude protectionism by US states and cities because our provinces have insisted on preserving preferences for their own provinces in matters of provincial and city procurements. Some provinces, with the support and assistance of the federal government, also adhere to supply management schemes for agricultural products to protect local farmers. This is a barrier to Canada making free trade agreements for agricultural products with other agricultural exporting countries with respect to Canadian products that otherwise could be profitably exported.

The proposition procedure adopted in the constitutional review in June 1968 soon came to make the discussions more and more discursive. Although some governments, notably the federal, used this approach

in very limited areas, Quebec prepared a complete set of propositions describing a comprehensive logical construct. It struck me during this process that nowhere were the differences between the Anglo-influenced and Gallic-influenced minds so well demonstrated as here. The common law provinces applied inductive reasoning in a pragmatic fashion to conclude (usually on the basis of experience) what would serve as an ideal constitutional provision in a particular area. Quebec began with first principles, such as the right of self-determination and the status of Quebec as a "state" (albeit a special kind of state), representing one of the two nations of Canada, and from which, by deductive reasoning, certain dispositions logically flowed. These two approaches to constitution-making have been elsewhere characterized respectively as Burkean (that is, organic, incremental, ad hoc)[7] and Lockean (that is, proceeding on the first principle that the people are sovereign, a principle from which all else logically follows).[8] In fact, the proposition method only prevailed for a year or so and led quite quickly to discussion of specific provisions of the constitution where chiefly pragmatic arguments prevailed.

Until the Constitutional Conference of September 1970, there had been no discussion of the amending procedure nor of patriation. By this time, after five meetings of the First Ministers, eight ministerial meetings, and 12 meetings of senior officials, all of which focussed on the subject of constitutional reform (plus numerous ad hoc meetings of specialized groups that discussed issues such as death duties and sales taxes!), there had been no final agreement on any subject. The First Ministers were becoming restless (particularly those from some of the common law provinces); they were anxious to demonstrate to their voters that something was being accomplished. They insisted that priorities should be narrowed to a few subjects on which there might be quick agreement. In particular, it was agreed that early consensus should be sought on an amending formula because there might be an early need to make some constitutional changes and a procedure for this should be put in place.[9] It was planned that negotiated agreements on these subjects would be designed for approval by the First Ministers at their next constitutional meeting, planned for Victoria in June 1971 and marking the centennial of British Columbia's entry into Confederation. So in Ottawa there was an immediate need to develop a policy on patriation and an amending formula, matters to

which the government had given little attention thus far in the centennial constitutional review.

The impatience that many First Ministers displayed at the September 1970 meeting was caused in part by what was seen as the cumbersome practice of having multilateral discussions on every subject. It was agreed that preparatory work would be done for the next conference by a series of bilateral discussions between the federal government and each provincial government. This started out with some soundings at the official level and then, after proposals started to take shape, by individual meetings between Minister of Justice John Turner and each Premier. Along with Gordon Robertson, Gérard La Forest, and sometimes Bob Bryce, I accompanied John across the country to meet Premiers, meetings that often included a provincial minister and officials. I remember one occasion when we were descending to land in Regina. John said, "God, Barry, what's Ross going to say when he sees you?" (He obviously had in mind that I had been active in the NDP in Saskatchewan and feared that Premier Ross Thatcher, the right-wing Liberal Premier, would recognize me as one of the "so-shul-ists" he detested. Ross either didn't recognize me or chose to overlook this lapse by the Government of Canada.) We would report to each Premier what we had learned was acceptable and unacceptable to other Premiers. By this process we were able to get tentative agreement on what would be acceptable to all governments, which included the Victoria amending formula. As the date approached for the Victoria Conference, only Quebec seemed uncertain about the total package: Premier Bourassa kept suggesting that he might need "something of substance," particularly enhanced jurisdiction over social policy. We tinkered with proposals that might be acceptable to Ottawa, but on this point there was no tentative agreement before Victoria.

A PHILOSOPHY OF PATRIATION

Patriation was a subject on which I had been reflecting for some years. I had been influenced on the subject of legitimacy of constitutions by some of my reading at Oxford, particularly the writing of Hans Kelsen,[10] whom I had also heard about in the Jurisprudence lectures of Professor A.L. Hart. Kelsen was an Austrian jurisprudential writer who had been widely cited in courts of the Commonwealth. His basic theory was this: a constitution is legitimate if it works, and it can be said to work only if it is

accepted by those governed by it. If it is accepted, it forms the *grundnorm*, or basic norm, of that society: it is the law by which other laws are made. One need not look behind it for its justification as long as it is effective. This analysis contemplates two forms of legitimacy—legal and political. A constitution is legally legitimate if it has been made or amended by the legal procedure authorized by pre-existing law. A constitution is politically legitimate if it is perceived as having been made by processes acceptable to those to be governed by it. In most established states the constitution enjoys both forms of legitimacy: that is, the legally legitimate processes by which it has been made or modified are also politically acceptable as the proper source of a constitution. But in many cases there are legal discontinuities, normally the results of revolutions or coups d'état, whereby an old constitution is rejected and a new one adopted by a process that rejects the old law but is politically endorsed by those to be governed by it. An obvious example is the Constitution of the United States. Prior to 1776, a court in the Thirteen Colonies or England would have treated as lawful only colonial constitutions made by the British Crown. There was nothing in existing English or colonial law to authorize a Continental Congress to issue a Declaration of Independence in that year or the Articles of Confederation in 1781 as a constitution for the United States. Indeed, those Articles even provided the means for their amendment (the unanimous consent of state legislatures), but they were replaced in 1789 by a procedure that did not comply with this requirement. Yet who today would regard the Constitution of the United States as illegitimate? In England the monarch in Parliament is supreme, with the identity of the monarch being established by certain constitutional principles. But in the Glorious Revolution in 1689, the succession to the Throne was unlawfully diverted from the son of James II, the legitimate reigning monarch, and given to William of Orange and his wife Mary (James II's daughter). This should have been done by a proper Act of Parliament that would have required the consent of the reigning monarch. He, however, was not available, having fled to France. Yet for centuries the lineage of the monarchy has been accepted as legitimate, notwithstanding this awkward discontinuity.

Thus, if there is inconsistency between legal and political legitimacy, it is political legitimacy that is the most important. This has been accepted in many Commonwealth courts. Sometimes it is expressed in terms of the doctrine of necessity: even if the previously prescribed constitutive

procedures have been ignored, it is essential to give legal effect to a functioning government.[11] In short, in the language of Kelsen, a politically legitimate constitution that is effective establishes a new *grundnorm*.

In applying these concepts to the constitution of Canada, I remain convinced that Confederation was not the product of the popular will of British North Americans of 1867, nor was it the product of elected colonial legislatures. There was never any referendum in the resulting or future Canada to approve it. While the Quebec Resolutions of 1864 were approved by the Parliament of Canada (then representing parts of the future Quebec and Ontario), those Resolutions underwent modifications during the drafting of the *BNA Act, 1867* in London in 1866 to 1867, and the revised text was not referred back to the Canadian Parliament for approval. The legislatures of New Brunswick and Nova Scotia only authorized their ministers to negotiate some scheme, in London, but never had the opportunity to pass judgement on the draft *BNA Act* before it was enacted. In a post-Confederation election in Nova Scotia, the anti-confederation party won and sent a request to London for the secession of Nova Scotia. Throughout the preparations and political manipulations bringing about Confederation, the Colonial Office used its considerable influence and leverage, including specific directions to colonial governors, to support the project. The British government wanted to unload a financial burden by making the colonies into a viable unit that would no longer be dependent on the mother country.[12] So it is difficult to see Confederation as an expression of popular sovereignty of the inhabitants of the colonies concerned. While those who argue otherwise cite various statements by politicians in colonial legislatures asserting that Confederation would depend on the popular will of the colonial peoples,[13] I cannot see this as other than political rhetoric that was belied by what actually happened in the adoption of the Confederation project. In short, the new Canadian constitution was seen as legally legitimate because it was enacted by the UK Parliament that, for reasons stated earlier, was recognized by the courts as having the power to legislate for the colonies—including the power to make constitutions for them. It was widely accepted as politically legitimate because of a colonial mentality that recognized the propriety of the Imperial government making decisions for us, albeit after considerable consultation with elected colonial representatives. While there was substantial dissatisfaction with some of the details, few questioned the

right of British MPs, unelected by any British North American, to make such laws for us: no tea was dumped in Halifax harbour.

In my early reflections on what would constitute legitimacy in the 1960s, I had to compare conditions then to those at the time of Confederation. If we were to patriate the constitution, what means could be used to result in a constitution that would be recognized by Canadian courts and by Canadian people?

First, I was satisfied that its legal legitimacy would be unquestionable if it were adopted by Westminster in the same way that previous *BNA Acts* had been passed. This was based on the previous jurisprudence, and on the existing provisions of the *Colonial Laws Validity Act, 1865* and the *Statute of Westminster, 1931*.[14] Subsequent decisions of the Supreme Court of Canada confirmed that such legislation was the legally correct way to amend major portions of the Canadian constitution.[15]

But of course such action would have to be initiated by Canada, having regard to our sovereign status. As described earlier in chapter 1, after Confederation British authorities acted to amend our constitution, with rare exceptions of a legislative housekeeping nature, only after a request from Canada, and in the first 40 years those requests were solely on the initiative of the federal government and Parliament. Later it came to be the custom for the provinces to be consulted on most changes affecting them and in point of fact, with perhaps two exceptions, amendments of this nature were sought only where all provinces affected had consented. This is not the place to re-argue the existence and nature of the constitutional conventions for amendment. Suffice it to say that by 1967 political legitimacy for amendments to the Canadian constitution required at least the request and consent of Canadian political authorities.

But when I reflected on the matter, it seemed to me that it might no longer be politically acceptable for the UK Parliament to confer on us a new or revised constitution. Canada was, after all, the oldest autonomous member of the Commonwealth, having enjoyed virtual sovereignty even in international affairs since the 1920s, when most of the now-independent members of the Commonwealth were Crown colonies, protectorates, or League of Nations mandates of the British Empire. The Irish Free State, a dominion, had in 1937 evolved into the Republic of Ireland by the approval of her new republican constitution in a referendum, thus making

it a product of native popular sovereignty. India in 1947 to 1948 adopted its independence constitution by constituent assemblies comprising popularly elected state legislatures (a somewhat attenuated form of popular input). In the 1960s we had seen the care with which the newly independent African Commonwealth nations had avoided having their new constitutions appear to be conferred on them by the British Crown or Parliament. The fashionable word of that era was *autochthony*. An autochthonous constitution was one that was indigenous to a particular country. These countries employed various devices to avoid their constitutions coming into effect by the consent of Her Majesty or of the Governor General.[16] In my first proposals for a constitutional proposition in relation to amendment, as sent to Carl Goldenberg with a letter dated June 11, 1968, I suggested various formats with two elements. First, a new constitution would be adopted by the people of Canada by referendum or on their behalf by Canadian governments and, or, legislatures. Second, as a formality, the United Kingdom would be requested to repeal its legislation extending to Canada. I had in mind here the repeal of relevant parts of the *Colonial Laws Validity Act, 1865* and of the *Statute of Westminster, 1931*. While I suggested as an option that we could leave it to the British to decide whether or not to repeal these sections, I warned that Canadian courts might feel obliged to apply them if they remained in force.

These issues soon had to be studied as a result of the comprehensive constitutional propositions put forward by the Union Nationale government of Quebec in the autumn of 1968. These commenced with the proposal of a constitutional preamble that would assert that Canada is a "sovereign country independent of all others," a "democratic country" whose constitution is "the expression of the popular will," protecting fundamental rights such as "the natural right of nations or peoples to self-determination," that Canada is a "federation of states and an association of two nations" recognizing that Quebec "has a special role to play in bringing about cultural equality." Naturally, the rest of the propositions for a new constitution were deduced from these first principles with fine Cartesian logic. On the subject of repatriation, therefore, Quebec said that because sovereignty rested with the Canadian people, there was no need to repatriate the constitution by approaching "the parliament of another country." All that was needed was to adopt it within Canada by some

democratic process. While this was not yet an urgent matter, in Ottawa we analyzed the Quebec propositions and generally had doubts that we could afford simply to ignore the existing constitution by replacing it with some homegrown product established by a process theretofore unknown to the laws of the UK and Canada. In an internal memorandum circulated among officials it was said,

> If the Canadian Parliament and provincial legislatures were to assert that *legal* power over the constitution now rested in their hands because of the *political fact* of the effective sovereign independence of Canada, the Canadian courts would certainly reject that assertion. They would reject it because they could not face the legal consequences of accepting it....The most important [consequence] is that there would be then no legally constituted authority with power either to settle on a new constitution, or even to amend the old one beyond the limited power of...Parliament in s. 91 ss. 1....It is one thing to get a court to acquiesce in a revolution that has already taken place, and a quite different thing to expect it to make a revolution which would leave us without a constituent authority of any kind.[17]

In general, the memorandum warned against becoming embroiled in a politico-legal dispute about the sovereignty of the Canadian people because this would distract attention from the substance of constitutional reform.

There the matter rested for the next two years, along with the issue of an amending formula because our attentions were devoted to a review of the substance of the constitution. I continued to read and reflect on the issue of the means of patriation. In October of 1969, I was passing through London on the way to the Federal Republic of Germany, where I was to have talks with their officials on the workings of German federalism. Before going to London I contacted Professor S.A. de Smith, a renowned public law professor at the London School of Economics within the University of London. I had read some of his writings[18] on new states of the Commonwealth, particularly in Africa, and how they had established

autochthonous constitutions. He was good enough to agree to meet with me and I discussed with him the dilemma we faced in Canada in finding a means to patriate our constitution consistently with our status as a sovereign country.

With the acceleration of discussions of an amending formula and patriation in the autumn and early winter of 1970, I drafted a memorandum for the Prime Minister to submit to Cabinet, exploring the options. On the matter of patriation I followed the analysis of legal legitimacy and political legitimacy. Using the approach that I have earlier described, I pointed out that perfect legal legitimacy would require enactment of any new amending formula by the United Kingdom Parliament as its last exercise of legislative authority over Canada. It was observed, however, that this would not appear to be consistent with Canada's avowed sovereignty and it could offend Canadian nationalists. It would most certainly be objected to by the Government of Quebec, which, as mentioned before, had already asserted that any reference to the "parliament of another country" for its approval would be contrary to the rights of peoples to self-determination, such choices being properly made as an expression of the popular will of Canadians. I therefore suggested that if a new amending formula and other changes to the constitution agreed to at this time were clearly the product of a political consensus in Canada, there might be ways to minimize the British role in their adoption. In other words, by analogy to the Kelsen principle, if—because of their acceptability—constitutional changes were seen as politically legitimate and thus effective, history would suggest that we could afford something less than the perfect legal legitimacy that enactment by Westminster would provide. In the context of the ongoing constitutional discussions, it was assumed that the end product would be agreed to by every executive government, federal and provincial. If this were the outcome, then such changes would readily be recommended to, and approved by, resolutions in both Houses of Parliament and every provincial legislature. This would surely give these changes as much political legitimacy as possible. In such circumstances, any British action should not appear to confer such constitutional changes but only to recognize them while making consequential changes in British laws.

This was the approach that Cabinet adhered to and it was successfully presented to the provinces. At a closed First Ministers' Meeting on February 8 and 9, 1971, the following conclusion was stated:

The Constitutional Conference agreed on a procedure to be undertaken in Canada at a very early date in order to bring home the Constitution and to transfer to the people of Canada, through their elected representatives, the exclusive power to amend and to enact constitutional provisions affecting Canada. This procedure would involve:

(a) Agreement among the governments as to changes and procedure.
(b) Approval of a resolution in the usual way, by legislatures plus the two Houses of Parliament, authorizing the issuance of a proclamation by the Governor General to contain the amendment formula and whatever changes are agreed upon.
(c) Recommendation that the British Parliament legislate to:
   i) recognize the validity of the Canadian proclamation and its provisions;
   ii) provide that no future British law should have application to Canada; and
   iii) make any consequential repeal or amendment of British statutes affecting the Canadian Constitution.
(d) Issuance of the proclamation by the Governor General on a date to coincide with the effective date of the British law.[19]

This formed the framework for preparations for patriation. In Ottawa we began to contemplate the kind of legislation we should be recommending to British authorities. We presented some options to Cabinet; it did not in the end settle on one, but recognized the need for flexibility in approaches to the British since we wished this to be their legislation and not made to order at our request.

I was soon in regular contact with the Deputy High Commissioner for the UK in Ottawa. He was John Morrison, 2nd Viscount Dunrossil. He was a gracious and amiable interlocutor and Eleanor and I came to know the Dunrossils, sharing a few social occasions. He was very sensitive to Canadian politics and particularly to Quebec nationalism. He had been closely involved with the plight of the family of James Cross, the British

Trade Commissioner kidnapped the previous autumn in Montreal by the FLQ, and with efforts to secure his release. On the subject of patriation he made contact with the relevant British authorities, both political and official, and paved the way for us to have discussions in London in May. He proposed that I should go over in advance to meet with officials in preparation for the ministerial meetings to be held by Minister of Justice John Turner with his counterparts there. In preparation for my meetings, on May 17 I provided to the High Commission for transmission to London a memorandum setting out the background and Canadian objectives.

NEGOTIATING CANADA'S LIBERATION

My wife, Eleanor, preceded me to London. We were both delighted to be there as we had had little opportunity to visit England since the mid-1950s when we had lived there as newlyweds. When I arrived, she happily moved from her modest bed and breakfast in Ebury Street to my spacious room at the Dorchester (that splendid hotel on Park Lane, chosen because that was where the Minister would be staying). It happened to be remarkably sunny May weather. Happily, my meetings were spread out, taking place on a Friday, Monday, and Wednesday, so we were able to spend the weekend in Oxford visiting old friends, the Fowlers, there. Perhaps for the first time I grasped the mystique of being an Oxonian, or "member of the University," as they are called. Our friends—he was a fellow of Brasenose College—were taking us to dine on Saturday night in the Senior Common Room at his College. As we proceeded through the inner quadrangle of the College, Jenny and Eleanor ahead of us following the sidewalk that surrounds the grass, Alistair touched me on the shoulder and said, "Come on, you're a member of the University!" and he led me straight across the lawn to the door we sought, arriving well ahead of our wives. This, indeed, is one of the perquisites of being a member of the university!

Before going to Oxford for the weekend, I had spent part of a day in meetings at the Foreign and Commonwealth Office (FCO) in Whitehall, with the Deputy Head of the North American Division and the Deputy Legal Adviser to the FCO. They were particularly alerted to the political overtones and wanted to be able to brief the Attorney General, Sir Peter Rawlinson, before his meeting the following week with John Turner. I explained the need for the UK legislation to precede the coming into force of the intended Proclamation by the Governor General, which would contain

the new constitutional provisions and the amending formula. The UK legislation would thus give legal recognition to the Proclamation when issued, but not appear to authorize that Proclamation and its contents. They said for their part they would prefer that the UK legislation should come into force when passed and not appear to be dependent on the Proclamation date, although it would have no practical effect until that time. We worked out a rough draft of a short statute that they despatched to Sir John Fiennes, Chief Parliamentary Counsel, with whom we were to meet the following week.

On Monday afternoon, May 24, I met in Whitehall with Sir John Fiennes and the two senior officers from the FCO. The two main drafting issues were what form the UK legislation would take so as to recognize the Proclamation and its contents, and to what degree it should repeal UK statutes that up to then applied to Canada. On the first point Sir John felt the British Act should provide some authorization for future changes in Canada of the constitution, but I said that should not be necessary and was politically undesirable. He did not press the point. On the matter of identifying the Canadian Proclamation that was to be recognized by the British Act as having legal effect, we discussed the possibility that the draft Proclamation and all its contents, including the actual constitutional amendments decided upon by Canada, could be tabled with the bill at Westminster and somehow referred to in that fashion. This would underline the fact that these constitutional changes were the choice of the people of Canada as represented through their elected representatives. The other legal issue was about whether or not the UK should repeal its own legislation extending to Canada. Our proposed scheme was as follows: the changes to be made in the Canadian constitution would be specifically spelled out in our document (which came to be referred to as the Victoria Charter). Our draft had a schedule that provided for the repeal or amendment (and renaming) of the *BNA Acts*, and the repeal of certain other British legislation still applicable to Canada, such as section 4 and subsection 7(1) of the *Statute of Westminster, 1931*, the provisions that recognized the authority of Westminster to pass laws for Canada. We in Ottawa felt that the new regime would appear more autochthonous if these changes were brought about by the homegrown Victoria Charter. Sir John, however, was concerned that the repeal brought about only by the Canadian instrument would not allow him to consider these statutes

repealed from the British statute books, a matter of importance at least in the preparation of Revised Statutes of the United Kingdom. I was fairly persuaded by this but we left the matter for further discussion among draftsmen.

We discussed two other matters with more political content. First was the question of what to name this UK legislation. Sir John, a courtly and benign gentleman, thought it would be logical to call it the *British North America Act, 1971*, as the last in a long series of Westminster's similarly named enactments of Canada's constitution (the most recent having been 1964). I firmly rejected this idea: it could not be squared with the concept of an autochthonous constitution springing from the soil of Canada! We considered other names: the *Canadian Constitution Act*, rejected because it still had the air of Westminster conferring the constitution; and simply the *Constitution Act*, rejected because the UK already had on its statute books similarly named laws. Finally, I suggested the *Canada Act, 1971*. This seemed bland and ambiguous enough. We agreed on this as a tentative working title, subject to other direction from ministers. (This remained the proposed title until the whole project came to naught after the Victoria Conference. However, when patriation really was effected in 1982, it was by means of a UK statute entitled the *Canada Act, 1982*,[20] the name chosen on that sunny May afternoon in Whitehall in 1971). The other matter was more contentious. Following instructions from our Cabinet, I said that we were not excluding the possibility of requesting this patriation legislation without unanimous provincial agreement. Sir John cautioned that if we found ourselves in that situation it could raise a "significant" issue for his government; he saw it somehow having internal implications for the UK in its decision to enter the Common Market, a matter then under active consideration. Finally we agreed that Sir John would incorporate the legal points agreed upon into a draft for our ministers to consider two days later.

Minister of Justice John Turner, Cabinet Secretary Gordon Robertson, and Assistant Deputy Minister of Justice Gérard La Forest arrived by government jet the next evening. They, of course, were still oriented to Canadian time—7 p.m. in Ottawa but midnight in London—so I was summoned to John's suite at the Dorchester at midnight to brief them on my meetings. I had for them Sir John Fiennes's preliminary draft of the *Canada Act* and I reported on our discussions. We met again the next morning for further discussion of the draft and noted a few small changes

we thought should be made. There was general satisfaction with the tone of the document.

From there we proceeded to Lancaster House for the ministerial meeting. Lancaster House is a luxurious mansion near St. James's Palace, the former residence of the Queen Mother and now of the Prince of Wales. Lancaster House, a one-time home of the aristocracy, had been presented to the UK government and was used for receptions and conferences. Perhaps it was destined for a role in the liberation of the colonies: apart from our meeting on patriation in 1971, it was in 1979 the site of the meetings that produced an agreement on the independence of the Colony of Rhodesia, turning it into Zimbabwe. There, John Turner first met privately with Sir Peter Rawlinson, Attorney General of England, and then we and the British officials joined them. Apart from some discussions of the draft, John made the point that we were not waiving our right to request such legislation even in the absence of unanimity among the provinces. This discussion was followed by lunch that, in addition to the above, also included Sir Geoffrey Howe, then Solicitor General; Charles Ritchie, Canadian High Commissioner; Sir Burke Trend, Secretary of the British Cabinet; and Sir Vincent Evans, Legal Adviser to the FCO. I sat beside Sir Geoffrey and discussed recent Canadian history.

Incidentally, many years later Sir Geoffrey Howe was, unwittingly and indirectly, to have an effect on my career. In June 1989 he was Foreign Secretary in Margaret Thatcher's government when the People's Republic of China fiercely suppressed pro-democracy demonstrators in Beijing's Tiananmen Square. Because, by that time, there was an agreement between Britain and the People's Republic that Hong Kong would pass to Chinese sovereignty in 1997, there was much angst in Britain, as well as in Hong Kong, about the possible future of Hong Kong under Chinese rule. Questions were asked in the House of Commons in London regarding what Her Majesty's Government intended to do to restore confidence within Hong Kong. Sir Geoffrey replied, announcing various initiatives and ending with a promise that there would be a bill of rights adopted by Hong Kong. This was apparently the first time the colonial government of Hong Kong had heard of it. Its law officers quickly looked for outside advice. Knowing that Canada had within the same decade adopted the *Charter*, they looked for expertise here by approaching the Government of Canada. The Department of Justice asked my Chief Justice if I could

be spared, and soon my wife and I were off to Hong Kong, where I spent three months at the end of 1989 developing the concept and assisting in the drafting (in both English and Cantonese) of a bill of rights that was adopted the following year.

Our mission to London in 1971 was completed by getting a further draft of a bill by Sir John Fiennes that we carried back to Canada as evidence of a tentative agreement as to how we could proceed to patriation once we had a political agreement in Canada. The return flight was for me a bit unusual because I accompanied John Turner and the other officials on a government executive Jet Star. While I had travelled in these craft many times, I had not realized before that they did not have sufficient range to cross the Atlantic without refuelling. We had to depart from Heathrow Airport before 9 a.m., as small planes could not use it after that time. Charles Ritchie personally organized our departure from the Dorchester with two High Commission limousines and we arrived in adequate time to board our plane and depart. We were driven directly onto the field. However, at the VIP departure office we were asked for our passports. We all quickly produced them except for Gérard La Forest, who had packed his in his suitcase. There was much impatience, particularly on the part of the Minister, as this future Supreme Court Justice rifled through his baggage in search of his passport. It finally appeared and we successfully departed before the 9 a.m. deadline. Because of our need for refuelling, we flew up over Scotland and then over the North Atlantic to Iceland, where we refuelled at Reykjavik and visited the duty free shop. Landing and refuelling once again, at Goose Bay, Labrador, we flew on to Ottawa to end a rather long day of travel.

THE VICTORIA CONFERENCE: END OF THE CENTENNIAL INITIATIVE

As long since planned, the next Constitutional Conference of First Ministers opened in Victoria on June 14, 1971, and lasted three days. The federal delegation, apart from the Prime Minister and his immediate entourage, travelled westward in a Canadian Armed Forces Boeing 707. Some of us were accompanied by our spouses, and the plane also carried some provincial delegations and many journalists, both Canadian and foreign. Among the latter was Edith Iglauer of the *New Yorker* who had published a long article on Pierre Trudeau and the Canadian North[21] after his election

as Prime Minister and was still following his constitutional struggles. In that era, the Victoria airport could not accommodate a 707 landing, so we landed in Vancouver and crossed the Georgia Strait by ferry. On the ferry crossing I was assigned to brief Edith Iglauer on the lengthy background to this constitutional conference. We had a long, pleasant conversation on the sunny deck of the BC ferry. On arrival we were all located in the Empress Hotel, across the street from the provincial legislative building where the Conference was to take place.

The public sessions, televised, were held in the legislative chamber, a rather sombre space that was adorned for the occasion with huge bouquets. Some irreverent journalists referred to it as "Mr Bennett's funeral parlour." Premier Bennett was ever the thoughtful host, although the sessions were of course chaired by the Prime Minister. One evening the Premier took us on a dinner cruise on a government ferry. The one disappointment for many was that, true to his abstemious nature, the Premier had ordered it to be a dry cruise—officially with no liquor or wine on board. Many delegates and ministerial aides came aboard with laden briefcases, even though no business was to be done that evening. Private staterooms were much in demand.

In the months leading up to Victoria, through our repeated consultations with the Premiers in their capitals, and through the working session of the Constitutional Conference in February, most issues had been settled and required only limited discussion at this June, mostly public, conference. It is remarkable how much agreement there was—on an amending formula that we had proposed in February (the Victoria Formula), the method of patriation (to be discussed later), a modest charter of rights, provisions on regional disparities, structure and appointments of the Supreme Court of Canada, federal-provincial consultation, and the repeal of powers of reservation and disallowance of provincial laws. Some of these required last-minute bargaining to reach agreement, but there remained little doubt about their acceptability. The one contentious area was that of social policy. Essentially, Quebec asserted its logical imperative that social policy is a matter of culture, and provinces (or at least Quebec) have a monopoly on culture. Therefore, Quebec initially wanted a withdrawal of federal jurisdiction in this area, including the power to legislate for unemployment insurance, family allowances, old-age pensions and their dependants' benefit features. Ottawa was not prepared to yield all these programs: some

it regarded as economic in nature, others it saw as the means to provide some national standards for all Canadians. Politically, federal ministers resisted the idea that cheques should not be sent into Canadian homes bearing the name and logo of the Government of Canada. Privately, this debate had gone on with Quebec for months. Premier Bourassa, although he found acceptable most of the package, which included important gains for Quebec with its veto under the Victoria Formula and its new proposed constitutional role in the appointment of Quebec judges to the Supreme Court, kept saying he "needed something of substance" that he could use to justify to his nationalist skeptics that this was a good deal for Quebec. This something was a new, exclusive provincial jurisdiction over social policy. Ottawa and provinces other than Quebec were prepared to affirm concurrent federal power over pensions, and over family, youth, and occupational training allowances, even with the proviso that such laws could not affect the operation of provincial laws in respect of these matters: in other words, provincial paramountcy would be established in these areas. There would also be a requirement that before introducing such federal legislation, Ottawa would consult the provinces. This was a compromise worked out in closed sessions by the First Ministers, with a doubtful Premier Bourassa obviously having to resist pressure from some ideologues in his delegation. Consequently, he was not prepared to approve the so-called Victoria Charter without consulting his government. In the end it was agreed that all First Ministers would report back to their colleagues and advise the Secretary of the Conference within 12 days as to whether they were prepared to recommend the Victoria Charter to their legislatures or not.

The subject of most interest to us here was the agreement on patriation. The Secretary's Report[22] states that the Conference accepted the federal proposal that had been circulated to all governments on May 11, 1971. That paper reiterated the agreement[23] reached at the February working conference but added to it the following specifics concerning the anticipated United Kingdom legislation.

THE UNITED KINGDOM ENACTMENT

After resolutions of approval have been adopted by legislative bodies in Canada, the British Parliament would be requested to pass appropriate legislation. The British enactment would refer

to the approval expressed by legislative bodies in Canada for such constitutional changes, and would specifically recognize the validity of the Proclamation (containing the Canadian Constitutional Charter) to be issued subsequently by the Governor General. This recognition of validity is essential to remove any possibility of challenge in some court of law at some time concerning the legal and constitutional basis for the new provisions. The UK legislation would also terminate all remaining formal legislative authority which the British Parliament now has with respect to Canada.

Discussions will be held with the British government before the Victoria Conference to be sure that there are no legal or procedural problems that could cause difficulty and to ensure that preparations for this aspect of patriation may be effected as smoothly as possible.

Achievement of patriation will also involve the repeal of parts of the Statute of Westminster, 1931 as it applies to Canada. The provisions requiring repeal are section 4 as it applies to Canada, section 7 (1), and the references to Newfoundland as a separate Dominion in sections 1 and 10 (3).

These changes in the Statute of Westminster, 1931 have been provided for in the text relating to Modernization of the Constitution (already distributed) which will form part of ·the Canadian Constitutional Charter to be given effect by the Governor General's Proclamation.[24]

The important point to note here is that all governments agreed that we should not have Westminster enact these constitutional amendments as it had done for a century in exercise of its recognized parliamentary sovereignty over Canada's constitution. *We were consciously departing from strict legal legitimacy.* We believed, however, that if the UK Parliament "recognized" what we had done, no court in Canada at least would impugn the validity of the Victoria Charter. This was all possible because if the Charter were agreed to by all governments and all Canadian legislative

bodies, it would be seen to have perfect political legitimacy and thus be, in Kelsen's analysis, "effective."

At the Victoria Conference we did not share with the provinces the details of our conversations to date with the British government nor the preliminary draft done by Sir John Fiennes.

The last day at the Victoria Conference remains memorable to me because of its length and stress. That day began for me, along with a few other federal officials, with a meeting with the Prime Minister in the salon of his suite at the Empress Hotel, overlooking Victoria's inner harbour. Some remnants of his breakfast with Margaret (they had been married only a few months then) were on a side table. After discussions with the PM, we accompanied him across the street and up the broad steps of the British Columbia legislative building. The Conference went into closed session in another room during the morning and continued through part of the afternoon. There emerged from the closed sessions agreement on matters not yet covered by drafts, the main ones being the provincial role in appointment of Supreme Court judges, and the abolition of the federal power of reservation and disallowance of provincial legislation. These agreements required new or modified drafts and I worked with our draftsmen (Jean Beetz for the French version and Gérard La Forest for the English). After the Conference reconvened in public session, I carried new drafts in to the Prime Minister and explained them before he discussed them with the Premiers. Although it had been expected that the Conference would be completed by late afternoon, and a closing reception had been planned accordingly, we did not complete formal discussion and tentative agreement on the substance until about 9 p.m. We then all retreated to the Empress Hotel for the reception. But the day's work was not over. The Conference Secretariat was still pulling together the text of the entire Victoria Charter and it was agreed that when this was done representatives of each government would return to the legislative building to give final approval to the text as representing the tentative agreement. At about 1 a.m. Gordon Robertson and I, and I believe Gérard La Forest, accompanied the Minister of Justice, John Turner, to that meeting. The discussion went on until after 4 a.m. I recall that I earned the gratitude of John Turner for catching one error: the Charter would have required the retirement of Supreme Court of Canada judges at age 70, but it had also been agreed by First Ministers that current judges of the Court would be

grandfathered, that is, they could continue to serve until age 75. I noticed that the Secretariat's draft had not provided for the latter exception and when I raised it the draft was corrected. John was glad he didn't have to return to Ottawa to face the wrath of senior judges of the Court! After the text[25] was approved, Gordon and I went to John's suite at the Empress where we were joined by Jean Beetz and Julien Chouinard, then Secretary of the Quebec cabinet and later also, with Jean, a judge of the Supreme Court of Canada. In a weary discussion over drinks, it seemed apparent to me that Quebec would not agree to this package. I got to our room after 5 a.m. Yet we were up by about 8 a.m. to pack and get ready for the ferry trip to Vancouver to take our plane. In Vancouver we discovered that our plane was having mechanical problems and could not take off. We spent nearly six hours waiting at the Vancouver airport. Fortunately, we were friends of Marg Munro, then wife of Minister of National Health and Welfare John Munro, who had been part of the federal delegation. He had already returned to Ottawa by other means. But Marg had access to the VIP lounge at the airport. She recognized my state of fatigue and ensured that we had a few hours of rest in comfortable surroundings. My final memory of that day was our arrival at Uplands Airport in Ottawa at about 4 a.m. There were of course no taxis immediately available. As I wearily reclined on the grass verge beside the taxi stand, fellow passenger Larry Zolf, renowned CBC journalist and an acquaintance of ours, recognized my plight and graciously yielded to us his cab.

It was an anti-climax when little more than a week later Premier Bourassa advised the Conference Secretary that his government was not prepared to recommend the Victoria Charter to his legislature. All other governments except Saskatchewan had already given their assent. Saskatchewan had not yet taken action because it was in the middle of an election, and once Quebec renounced the deal Saskatchewan thought it no longer necessary to state a position. And so Quebec walked away from an agreement that would have given it the best amending formula for which it could ever have hoped: giving it the veto it believed was its due while denying that veto to every other province except Ontario, the one province with a larger population than Quebec's.

And so the great centennial hopes for a patriated and improved constitution came to naught.

4

A NON-CONSTITUTIONAL
INTERLUDE

There was great disappointment across the country when Premier Bourassa announced that his government would not recommend the Victoria Charter to his legislature. Thousands of person-hours of preparation, weeks of meetings, continents of travel, had all been for nothing. Although many of us in Ottawa were aware of what a close thing it might be given the state of mind within the Quebec government, we nevertheless had dared to hope that the deal could be saved. For a few days there was some discussion of a possible new compromise, but that did not last long. I don't think that Pierre Trudeau had the appetite for more bargaining with Robert Bourassa. In spite of the fact that in discussions with British officials we had reserved the possibility of proceeding without the unanimous agreement of the provinces, I am satisfied the inarticulate premise was that we might proceed to patriation if only one or two of the smaller provinces rejected the Victoria Charter. Few in Ottawa would have contemplated proceeding over the objections of Quebec or Ontario.

Once it became clear that the constitutional review that had been ongoing since 1968 was not likely to recommence soon, I started considering what steps should be taken in my Constitutional Review Section of the Privy Council Office. I asked each of the officers to prepare comprehensive summaries of the work done, research carried out, and, where applicable, the negotiations carried out, in respect of each of the constitutional subjects we had worked on. I felt that someday many of these subjects would be reopened in constitutional discussions of some kind and the work done

should not be lost. This historical work took several weeks to complete.

Gradually, various members of the staff began to drift away to other jobs or were reassigned by the PCO. I stayed in my office, which was finely located in a corner of a Sparks Street building where I overlooked Confederation Square. From my windows I could observe demonstrations, fireworks displays on Parliament Hill, and Remembrance Day ceremonies at the National War Memorial.

I still participated in PCO staff meetings but the focus of my work gradually shifted from constitutional reform to constitutional law. After the constitutional review wound down, I started performing more work for Justice at the request of the Deputy Minister, while at the same time giving constitutional advice to the PCO on a variety of matters.

NEWFOUNDLAND CAPERS

Of the special assignments given to me by the Deputy Minister of Justice, two involved Newfoundland (the name by which the province was then known in the Constitution, not Newfoundland and Labrador, renamed as such by a constitutional amendment in 2001). The first was in the fall of 1971. It was well known that Premier Smallwood of that province had to call an election soon and that his position was tenuous since he had been in power some 22 years. He was busy shoring up his political support. One group he wanted on his side was the Pentecostal Assemblies, an evangelical church that was rapidly proselytizing and gaining adherents in Newfoundland. Now, among the constitutional curiosities in the Terms of Union of Newfoundland with Canada of 1949[1] was a provision guaranteeing tax-supported schools for the denominations that had enjoyed such status by law before Confederation. These were the Roman Catholics, the Church of England, the United Church, and the Salvation Army. The Terms of Union constituted in this case a constitutional obligation on the provincial legislature to make the necessary provisions for financial support for their schools. These churches all ran schools in places where they had adherents. There was no state-run system of schools at that time. After Union in 1949, the Pentecostal Assemblies started to grow and to set up their own schools. In fact, they did receive tax support like the other denominations, but they came to feel themselves discriminated against because their financial support was not constitutionally guaranteed like that of other churches. They pressed Joey for a constitutional amendment.

Such an amendment, by the constitutional law and practices at that time, would have to be enacted by the United Kingdom Parliament, but only with the approval of the Parliament of Canada and the Government of Newfoundland. Joey had asked Pierre Trudeau several times to initiate the necessary action but Trudeau had left the matter in abeyance. As the provincial election approached, Joey became more pressing. Pierre had a certain fondness for Joey, who had been the first Liberal Premier to endorse Pierre as a candidate for the leadership of the federal Liberal Party. So the word came down from the Prime Minister's Office that something had to be done about a constitutional amendment of the Terms of Union with Newfoundland. Don Thorson, Associate Deputy Minister of Justice and chief of legislative drafting, and I were despatched to St. John's to meet with the Premier. I recall that in preparation for the meeting I had placed a call to the Premier's executive assistant. To my surprise, the phone was answered with a bark: "Smallwood here!" I had often heard that he ran a one-man government but I had never believed it! I certainly hadn't expected to be making administrative arrangements with the self-styled Last Living Father of Confederation.

The day Don Thorson and I arrived by plane from Ottawa we were met by a provincial government driver. He whisked us to the Legislative Assembly building in St. John's where the Premier was to preside at a lunch. He was accompanied by two or three provincial ministers of the Crown, and the guests were several ministers of the cloth representing the Pentecostal Assemblies. As the meal proceeded, Joey was in full oratorical flight. He first assured his guests that he and the Prime Minister took their request for a constitutional amendment very seriously. The Prime Minister was so concerned that he had sent "two of the most senior lawyers in Ottawa" to prepare such an amendment. Joey then proceeded with a monologue, as was his custom, about the book he was then reading. (It is true that Joey was very widely read. It was also true that he liked to impress his audience: he had a habit of name-dropping. I can recall in other gatherings with him where he would mention what "Dick Nixon" or "President Ceausescu" of Romania had said to him.) On this day, the book he was reading was a biography in six volumes of the author of "Onward Christian Soldiers," which was bound to impress the reverend gentlemen with his piety. Still musing about religion, he said that he was of course a Baptist. One day during a cabinet coffee break,

he had said to one of his Roman Catholic ministers, "You know, if I had it to do over again I think I would become an Anglican." That minister said, "Why not come all the way over to us?" Joey replied, "No, one step enough for me." I was the only one at lunch who laughed. He turned to me and said, "Do you know where that's from?" I said, "Yes, it's from 'Lead, Kindly Light.'" He asked, "Do you know who wrote it?" I said, "Cardinal John Newman" (he who had gone "all the way"). After that I could do no wrong in Joey's eyes.

After the lunch we met with the Premier and his Attorney General in Smallwood's office. We discussed the constitutional issues and possible solutions. Don and I then retired to our rooms at the Holiday Inn where Don took out his pen and lined foolscap, the tools of his trade, and we worked out two possible drafts for the necessary changes to the Terms of Union. We had these typed up and then we returned the next morning to meet with the Premier. This time he had no advisers present. We showed him the two drafts and explained the pros and cons of each. Without summoning any help, he paced up and down his office for a few minutes looking at each draft. Suddenly he said, "I'll take that one"—and that was the end of our meeting. We flew back to Ottawa (after being fogged in for a further 24 hours in Newfoundland) and turned the chosen draft into a Joint Resolution for submission to the Senate and House of Commons. The day we left Newfoundland the Premier announced a provincial election. No doubt to bolster the provincial Liberals, the federal Liberal Minister of Transport (who was from Newfoundland) introduced the constitutional amendment resolution in the House of Commons with some fanfare. Of course it was not expected to get through Parliament in Ottawa before the Newfoundland election, and it didn't. After some very close races and recounts it was finally determined that Premier Smallwood had lost the election. That was the last ever heard of that so-cleverly-crafted constitutional amendment. It is thus always for constitutional reformers.[2]

A year or two after that, I was once again sent to Newfoundland to discuss another possible constitutional issue. The Deputy Minister of Justice of Canada had been contacted by the staff of a provincial Royal Commission that was considering the future status of Labrador, which of course was administered as an integral part of the province. There had been much disaffection among residents of Labrador complaining of a lack of adequate provincial services and a perceived indifference in St. John's,

and this aroused some separatist sentiment in Labrador. The provincial government established a Royal Commission on Newfoundland, chaired by Donald Snowden, to look at possible alternatives for its administration. There was some interest in the federal-territorial relationship and I was asked to discuss this with the Royal Commission staff. It was a pleasant interlude but, again, to the best of my knowledge, nothing concrete ever arose out of it. The Commission did recognize that many of the complaints of Labradorians were justified and it recommended, among other things, a Labrador Regional Advisory Council. But the federal-territorial model that I was asked to discuss with Commission staff and members was not adopted.

ABORIGINAL LAND CLAIMS

Aboriginal peoples lived in North America millennia before Europeans "discovered" it. They used some portions of the land, usually for hunting, fishing, and trapping, but also in some cases for agriculture. Some of them were nomadic, but often within areas frequented by them and no others.

The French regime in Canada generally did not recognize any prior rights of the Indigenous peoples to the use of the land. However, after the British conquest of Canada in 1759, a Royal Proclamation was issued in 1763 broadly defining the treatment of Aboriginals in respect of their customary territories. It ordered that Indians "should not be molested or disturbed in the Possession of such parts of our Dominions and Territories as, *not having been ceded to or purchased by Us*, are reserved to them, or any of them, as their Hunting Grounds" (emphasis added).[3] The Proclamation went on to reserve "for the use of the said Indians" all lands beyond the boundaries of the three governments (all in eastern and southern North America) established by it. It generally prohibited anyone from purchasing Indian lands, reserving that right to the Crown or with the consent of the Crown.

I should say at the outset that I use the term *Indian* advisedly, conscious that it is largely out of favour with Indigenous peoples because it is a reminder of the white man's (that is, Columbus's) misconception that North America, when first "discovered" by Europeans, was in fact India. Nevertheless, it is a term that is deeply entrenched in our laws and in our constitution. It has a legal meaning and it is that to which I address my comments.

As the European occupation of Canada followed, the Crown[4] entered into treaties with many tribes or bands, particularly in Ontario and the Prairie provinces whereby the Indians ceded their Aboriginal rights to their customary territories in return for the grant of certain reserves for their exclusive use, and miscellaneous other benefits including very small annuities to members of the group ceding territory. But this policy was not systematically followed as European settlement expanded. For example, very little of British Columbia was covered by treaties; white settlers and their governments proceeded with settlement there without regard to the possible prior rights of the Indians. At Confederation it was the Parliament of Canada, and thus also the Government of Canada, that became responsible for "Indians, and Lands reserved for the Indians."[5] That government was not diligent about negotiating treaties in areas not ceded by the Indians but nevertheless occupied by Europeans. It also failed in many cases to live up to the terms of the treaties, particularly in the matter of designating the amount of land promised by treaties to members of the ceding band.

There were many protests by the Indian peoples over the years, but little attention was paid by a succession of white governments, either federal or provincial (the latter having made lucrative grants of unceded Aboriginal lands to settlers and entrepreneurs). By the 1960s, Indigenous peoples were becoming more organized and more articulate about their interests. In the mid-1960s there were some court cases involving Indian hunting rights where it was recognized in *obiter dicta* that, prior to the adoption of a treaty for an area of unoccupied Crown lands, the Indians had a right to hunt and fish there.[6] From 1966 to 1967 the federal government funded an outside study entitled *A Survey of the Contemporary Indians of Canada: Economic, Political, Educational Needs and Policies*.[7] Generally known as the Hawthorn Report, it advocated a "Citizen Plus" status for Indians: that is, they should have all the rights of citizens plus special rights flowing from their prior occupation of Canadian territory. But after Trudeau formed a government in 1968, it rejected the Hawthorn recommendations. Instead, it published a White Paper entitled *Statement of the Government of Canada on Indian Policy, 1969*.[8] The thrust of the Paper was frankly assimilationist. The major premise was that Indians were disadvantaged in Canadian society because they were treated separately—in the constitution, in our laws, and in social services. The Paper's

principal approach was that Indians would only achieve equality with the non-indigenous population if they were declared legally equal. This would involve abolishing their constitutional assignment to the responsibility of the federal government and the abolition of Indian status. It would involve the repeal of the *Indian Act* and a transfer to the provinces (along with the necessary revenues) of responsibility for the social services of Indians. It envisaged the eventual abolition of "Indian lands"—that is, communally held land making up the existing reserves created under treaties—with simple ownership ultimately being transferred to individual Indians. Of Aboriginal land claims it said this: "These are so general and undefined it is not realistic to think of them as specific claims capable of remedy except through a policy and program that will end injustice to Indians as members of the Canadian community. This is the policy that the Government is proposing for discussion." In other words, the government did not recognize any legal obligations in respect of Indian claims for compensation for, or a share in, their unceded traditional lands not already covered by treaty.

While I had no part in the formulation of this 1969 policy, it was, I think, based on goodwill and a sincere desire to change the unhappy status quo of Indian peoples. There was a good deal of logic to it. While put out over the name of the then Minister of Indian and Northern Affairs, Jean Chrétien, it represented government policy and most certainly the current views of Prime Minister Pierre Trudeau, whose stated belief was "reason before passion." It appealed to his preference for individual, not communal, rights, and to his desire to guarantee equality of all citizens. He also said on many occasions that the goal of leaders should be to "do justice in our time" without regard to the sins of the past.[9] He also said, "No society can be built on historical might-have-beens." For Trudeau, this was a forward-looking policy that was unencumbered by our collective history, one that would enable all Canadians of whatever race to march together into the rest of the 20th century on an equal legal footing. He was aware of the world's history of endless conflicts ostensibly designed to correct the wrongs of the past, a phenomenon that is still all too prevalent today.

Unfortunately, the White Paper policy was hopelessly naive, probably because there had been inadequate consultation with Indian leaders and this had led its authors to underestimate the importance that First Nations peoples attached to their historical rights. Predictably, First

Nations peoples rejected the proposed policy as assimilation, a denial of their particular history, and a rejection of any historic claims they had to lands they regarded as traditionally their own and that had been despoiled by the white newcomers since contact (the term that came to be used to describe the arrival of the Europeans). The White Paper was answered by a "Red Paper" entitled *Citizens Plus* (the concept endorsed by the Hawthorn Report) and published by the Alberta branch of the National Indian Brotherhood (the gender-insensitive title of the national organization of status Indians). It argued that Indians should have the same rights as other Canadians and should, in addition, retain their historic treaty and other rights to special treatment for their further benefit. *Citizens Plus* became the catalyst for general opposition by Indians to the policy proposals in the White Paper. It forced the federal government to discuss the concerns of the Indians with Native representatives. On the subject of Indian land claims in respect of unceded lands, the subject with which I became involved, Ottawa came to realize such claims could not be airily dismissed as they were in the White Paper passage quoted above, that is, as being "so general and undefined" that it was unrealistic "to think of them as specific claims capable of remedy."

In January 1973 the *Calder*[10] decision was released by the Supreme Court of Canada. This involved a major lawsuit brought in British Columbia in 1967 by the Nisga'a First Nation against the Government of British Columbia. The claim covered thousands of square kilometres in northwestern British Columbia in the Nass Valley. This area had never been the subject of a proper treaty, yet for more than a century there had been non-Indian intrusions on and exploitation of parts of the land. The action, brought in 1967 in the name of Frank Calder, then President of the Nisga'a Tribal Council, on behalf of the Council, sought a declaration that the Nisga'a had Aboriginal title to this land, a title that had not been ceded or extinguished by government action. This claim was rejected entirely in the BC courts. On appeal, the Supreme Court of Canada was divided on the question. Of the seven judges, six found that Aboriginal land claims have a legal validity and that the Nisga'a had had such rights at one time. Three of the judges (Martland, Judson Ritchie JJ) found, however, that their rights had been extinguished by the assertion of the sovereign powers of the colony of British Columbia prior to Confederation. Three of the six judges (Hall, Spence, and Laskin JJ) held that such rights had not been

extinguished by governmental action in respect of this territory because such action was not specifically directed to extinguishment of Indian title. The seventh judge (Pigeon J) simply held that the action could not be brought against the Government of British Columbia without the grant by that government of a Petition of Right. Thus the legal nature of Aboriginal land claims was upheld by six judges, even though the Nisga'a could not succeed in this action. The six judges who recognized such rights said that they were based on the historic use, since time immemorial, of a defined area by a defined group still using such lands. The uses contemplated at that time were hunting, fishing, and trapping.

In Ottawa it was realized that a new policy was required because of the Indian reaction to the White Paper and the nature of the *Calder* decision. The Department of Justice was to play a major role in shaping this new policy. Gérard La Forest, then Assistant Deputy Minister in the Department (and my immediate superior and predecessor as Assistant Deputy Minister), personally undertook the preparation of a masterful paper on the legal aspects of land claims.[11] As it happened, he had done personal research on this subject before joining the Department and was readily able, single-handedly, to produce a comprehensive paper in short order. I did not make a contribution to this paper other than participating in several meetings with the Deputy Minister (by then Don Thorson), Gérard, and others to discuss successive drafts. It was viewed as a major departmental task to advise the government on its legal obligations in respect of unceded Indian lands, given that successive governments in the past had manifested such attitudes as those expressed in the quoted passage from the White Paper. There had been an assumption for many decades that sovereignty trumped all—that as Canada successfully asserted sovereignty over all of the former British North America, its Indian subjects had no legal claim to lands other than those recognized by treaty. Federal lawyers tended to see all sorts of practical reasons why all other claims could not succeed in court: for example, evidence to establish traditional uses of particular land by the ancestors of a current claimant group would not be available. In addition, the normal rules of prescription for title to land and limitations of actions laws that prevent court claims after a long passage of time from first awareness of the injury seemed to preclude practical recourse through the courts. I was skeptical at first about the current legal reality of Aboriginal land claims; however, once I understood that

they did not challenge Canadian sovereignty but only the right to use of land, I accepted Gérard's conclusions and later had to explain and defend them often to other departments of government.

The paper developed by Gérard La Forest in the Department of Justice examined the history of Aboriginal lands throughout the British Empire and the legal treatment accorded them by Imperial and Commonwealth courts including, in particular, the Judicial Committee of the Privy Council on appeals from Canada. The doctrine that emerged was essentially this: where a defined Aboriginal claimant group could establish traditional uses (hunting, fishing, and trapping) since time immemorial over a defined area, they were entitled to continue such use unless they ceded that right to the Crown, or until the relevant governmental authority by express terms extinguished such rights. In most cases it was the Crown in right of Canada that was responsible, but in some areas it was the province that had been given the responsibility of settling Indian land claims. This Aboriginal right, *as we understood it at that time*, was in the nature of what in Roman Law would be called a usufructuary right, the right to enjoy the fruits of the land as traditionally used; however, it did not equal *dominium*, or conventional ownership.[12] If governments or anyone else wanted to use the land for other purposes it was incumbent on the relevant Crown to negotiate with the entitled Aboriginal group and to obtain from that group a release consenting to that use in return for appropriate compensation. This was the principle that had underlain the making of treaties over large parts of the country where Indians had ceded their use of most of their territory in return for payments and for land reserves subject to their *exclusive* use, held in the name of the Crown for their benefit. The Justice paper provided an overview of what parts of the country were still not "cleared" of Aboriginal title through treaties; these included much of Quebec, most of the Maritime provinces, some parts of northern Ontario, and most of British Columbia and the northern territories.

This Justice paper provided the intellectual framework for the development of a new federal government policy on the reception and settlement of land claims, which came to be referred to as the *comprehensive claims*. This policy was announced by Jean Chrétien, Minister of Indian and Northern Affairs, on August 8, 1973. It spawned a large federal bureaucracy to manage this process, as well as a large cottage industry of lawyers, negotiators, historians, sociologists, and others to support Aboriginal

claimants, much of it funded by the federal government. As a result, I found myself immersed in two comprehensive claims negotiations in the mid-1970s.

The first concerned the claim of the Council for Yukon Indians, representing at that time both status and non-status Indians. Only a small area in the southeast corner of the Yukon had been covered by any treaty, in this case Treaty 8. But starting with the gold rush in 1898, and followed by numerous mining ventures for other minerals, the construction of the Alaska Highway during World War II, and the influx of various entrepreneurs along with federal public works and officials, the traditional hunting and fishing grounds of the Indigenous groups had been severely disturbed. These negotiations had started in the late 1960s before the federal government had clarified its position on Aboriginal rights. Gérard La Forest was the original Justice member of the federal negotiating team until I took over this responsibility in the fall of 1973. The talks took on new vigour after the announcement of the government's new policy. We met in Ottawa, Vancouver, and in Whitehorse before I left the team. It was my first experience in negotiating with First Nations representatives. One of their practices that I found unusual but effective was their frequent silences. We would make a suggestion and their team would sit across the table in silence. This I found unnerving. It instinctively made one think one had said something outrageous and that it should be withdrawn. It was their cautious way of proceeding: often they would not respond but then, after a long silence, would announce that they wanted to withdraw for a caucus.

Another recollection that stands out concerned a question I raised one day. Because Aboriginal land claims (as we understood them) had to be based on traditional uses of the land "from time immemorial," I said at one point, "You are claiming the whole of the Yukon except the small treaty area; did your people really use the whole territory for hunting, fishing, and trapping?" The President of the Council for Yukon Indians (CYI) who headed their negotiating team was Elijah Smith, a very wise and canny man. He had considerable experience in the outside world and was a veteran of World War II. He said, quite pleasantly, "Why don't you folks stay on here a week or two and I'll take you around the whole territory. I can show you the traplines, the fishing cabins, the hunting grounds that our people have always used." This was said in Whitehorse

in late January, to a group of city-dwellers from Ottawa and Victoria. That idea was quickly dropped.

Incidentally, the territory-wide agreement that ultimately emerged from these negotiations was rejected by the constituent First Nations of the Yukon. In 1990 the new Umbrella Final Agreement was reached and accepted. It laid down some parameters for further separate negotiations with each of the 14 First Nations, and several of these have now been successfully completed.

My next involvement with land claims concerned those of the Cree and Inuit in the James Bay area of Quebec. In 1971 the Bourassa government of Quebec had announced a very large hydroelectric project for James Bay. This caused protests from the Cree and Inuit of northern Quebec, whose traditional uses of these territories would be seriously impinged by the development. They managed to get an injunction against the project in 1973, and though this was set aside by the Quebec Court of Appeal there was a clear recognition in the courts of their Aboriginal rights. Negotiations followed between Quebec and the Cree and Inuit claimants. An agreement in principle was reached in November 1974. At about this time the federal government was also brought into the negotiations because of the history of Quebec's territorial accretions. It must be remembered that Quebec came into Confederation only with the territory of New France—essentially the valley of the St. Lawrence. The rest of Quebec was made up of lands ruled by the British since before the Conquest of Quebec in 1759 and that were conferred on the new Dominion of Canada after Confederation and eventually bestowed on Quebec by the Parliament of Canada. The first transfer to Quebec in 1890 was of an east-west tranche to the north of the original French province running up as far as the Eastmain River on the James Bay coast, with the northern boundary running generally eastward from that point until it reached the Labrador border with Quebec.[13] The second grant, in 1912, was of the remainder of Ungava, extending as far north as the Hudson Strait.[14] The 1898 transfer was simply a new boundary definition and was silent on the question of Indian rights, thus leaving the responsibility with the Government of Canada in respect of surrender and compensation; the 1912 Act, however, required that the province be responsible for these matters in the immense area transferred by that Act with such surrenders to be subject to the approval of the Governor in Council. Thus the federal government had continuing responsibilities in

protecting Indian rights to land in both the transferred areas, such areas being involved in the James Bay project. The agreement contemplated with the Cree and Inuit would also involve devolution to them of extensive powers with respect to wildlife administration, and the federal government had constitutional responsibilities with respect to, for example, migratory birds and sea coast fisheries. A final consideration was that the Government of Canada was expected to contribute many millions of dollars to the settlement.

I joined the federal team in the fall of 1975 as it was trying to finalize the agreement with respect to the matters of federal concern. The meetings were held in the Department of Justice in Ottawa and involved representatives of the Cree, the Inuit, and the federal and Quebec governments. At times the discussions were heated. They also became very technical. I remember the last late evening of discussion—required to meet the deadline for the conclusion of the talks. We became involved in a debate about whether or not there are freshwater seals: if so, they would be under provincial or Cree/Inuit jurisdiction, but if the seals were saltwater mammals, they would be under federal jurisdiction. Oh, the marvels of federalism! Near midnight, federal scientists explained to us that there are indeed some freshwater seals inland from Hudson's Bay and somehow this enabled us to complete the agreement.

While I can seek no credit for the change of government policy in respect of Aboriginal land claims, I am proud to have been part of this historic development. It formed another part of a legal revolution that Canada experienced in the last half of the 20th century. I did have a part later in safeguarding this development by the constitutional guarantee of Aboriginal land rights in section 35 of the *Constitution Act, 1982*,[15] to be discussed in connection with the patriation of the constitution in that year.

OWNERSHIP OF PROVINCIAL LAND BY FOREIGNERS AND NON-RESIDENT CANADIANS

This became a public issue in the early 1970s. For some time, Prince Edward Island had been concerned about acquisitions of land within the province by non-residents of that province, whether aliens or Canadians resident in other provinces. In 1972 it adopted legislation[16] requiring that any non-resident person or corporation wanting to acquire more than ten acres of land in the province or more than five chains of its shore frontage would

require the consent of the provincial cabinet, which was left with complete discretion in the matter. This reflected the growing concern in that province—with a small land base and no Crown lands—that outsiders would continue to acquire more and more land, mainly for recreational purposes and at inflated values, to the ultimate exclusion of most islanders. A Royal Commission had estimated that by the year 2000, one-half of the province would be owned by non-residents if no controls were imposed. Shortly thereafter, Saskatchewan was publicly contemplating legislation to limit the acquisition of farm lands by non-residents, reflecting a growing trend at that time of Americans and Europeans, particularly corporations, purchasing farms in the province. In due course it adopted the *Saskatchewan Farm Ownership Act, 1974*,[17] which limited the acquisition by non-residents of land to an assessed value of $15,000 or more. Corporations owned by persons, a majority of whom were not residents of Saskatchewan, would be limited to holding 160 acres.

This type of restriction had attracted discussion in a First Ministers' Conference of May 1973. The Prime Minister had expressed concern about this seeming restriction on the ability of Canadian citizens to move about, to carry on business, and to own property anywhere they wished within Canada. He also raised the possibility of this kind of restriction being found to breach some of our obligations in treaties or other international laws. Some other Premiers expressed at least mild concerns about possible restrictions on the rights of their residents to own a holiday cottage in other provinces, or to expand their farming operations across provincial borders. As a result, the First Ministers established a federal-provincial committee of officials with terms of reference to identify "legal, constitutional and land use problems" related to ownership of land in Canada by aliens, and of land in a province by a Canadian resident in another province. It was to examine ways in which governments might co-operate to deal with these problems "and to make recommendations for any legislative or administrative changes which could overcome or avoid possible legal and constitutional difficulties." The Prime Minister designated me as Chairman of this committee.

I launched some research work on the constitutional issues and on the practices in some 18 other countries, including federal states such as the United States, Australia, the Federal Republic of Germany, Mexico, and Switzerland. In the work of the Committee I was aided greatly by André

Millar of the Canadian Intergovernmental Conference Secretariat, who served as Secretary of the Committee. I visited several of the designated provincial members for preliminary discussions and then we had three meetings of the whole committee in Ottawa. I submitted our report to First Ministers in September 1975.[18] We reported on the state of restrictions on land acquisitions in the various provinces. Apart from the two that had passed the legislation described above, most provinces did not seem too concerned about the problem. Although lacking such legislation to restrict private sales of land, most provinces did impose some restrictions on the granting or leasing of Crown lands: there were often limitations on, or special fees attached to, acquisitions by non-Canadians. Apart from these, many provinces saw this as a land use problem, not an ownership problem. In examining the legal and constitutional issues, we identified some potential conflicts. For example, Parliament has jurisdiction over "Aliens" under head 25 of section 91 of the *Constitution Act, 1867*,[19] whereas the provinces have jurisdiction over "Property and Civil Rights in the Province" under head 13 of section 92 of the same Act. In the report we speculated about possible difficulties that might arise. Parliament, in its exercise of its "Aliens" power, had enacted section 24 of the *Citizenship Act*,[20] which provides that aliens have the same rights as Canadian citizens to acquire and dispose of real and personal property in Canada. Could this be reconciled with a provincial property law such as PEI's that limited the rights of aliens and other non-residents to acquire land there?[21] In reality, there was no consensus in the Committee for any particular solution. It was recognized that some provinces had a problem. It was hoped that many of these could be solved by taxation and land-use measures not directly tied to the owner's place of residence. I strongly advocated on behalf of the federal government the principle that the right to own land should not be denied by a province to a Canadian resident in another province. While there was some sympathy for this point of view, there was also a strong feeling from some provinces that this was really none of our business. I achieved inclusion in the report a statement that First Ministers might wish to consider a constitutional amendment that would guarantee the rights of aliens to own land and the rights of Canadians to own it anywhere in Canada. But because the recommendation of constitutional amendments was not in our terms of reference, we refrained from actually recommending that such an amendment be made. The report also

included a lot of useful reference material on how such problems are dealt with in other countries.

No concrete results came from this report. I think it did help to clarify some issues. It also provided useful material for the federal government during the negotiation of the Charter some years later to propose an additional mobility right for inclusion in what is now section 6, the right of every citizen and permanent resident to move to, take up residence, *and own property* in any province. As a result of many provincial objections, however, the right to own property in any province was not included in the final text.

NON-CONSTITUTIONAL PROTECTION OF HUMAN RIGHTS

By the time of the failure of the Victoria Charter in mid-1971, by which we had lost any early prospect of achieving a constitutional bill of rights, we had been working in Ottawa for four years toward such a goal. After a few weeks of reflection following the Victoria Conference, I began to urge in the Privy Council Office that we should turn our minds to what we could achieve for human rights without constitutional change. There was ample scope for federal improvements through legislation and policies. I of course was not alone in suggesting such initiatives. These came from members of Parliament and from other departments, such as Justice and External Affairs. There emerged two large initiatives in the last half of the 1970s: the development of the *Canadian Human Rights Act*,[22] and Canada's accession to the *International Covenant on Civil and Political Rights*, in both of which I played a substantial role.

CANADIAN HUMAN RIGHTS ACT

On the legislative front, the federal government compared unfavourably to many provinces in respect of the protection of equality rights. There was no general legislation prohibiting discrimination in federally regulated employment and services. Although there were specific provisions in labour legislation concerning gender and racial discrimination in federally regulated employment, and in respect of equal pay, enforcement was carried out by labour inspectors, and individual complaints or complainants played a small role in the process. Moreover, there was no independent commission for enforcement. Equal pay for women was cast in terms of

a requirement of "equal pay for equal work." "Equal work," though, was narrowly interpreted to require as a comparator virtually the same job in the same occupation classification. Within the federal public service the laws also prohibited a certain number of forms of discrimination, and these were enforced internally by ultimate recourse to the Public Service Commission.

As early as 1947, Saskatchewan had passed a *Bill of Rights*,²³ a comprehensive prohibition on racial, religious, and gender discrimination in employment, housing, and services normally available to the public. (That *Bill* also proclaimed freedom of speech and religion). After the Saskatchewan initiative, most provinces had adopted similar anti-discrimination laws. By the 1960s and early 1970s, most had also created independent commissions to administer such laws, to receive and investigate complaints from individuals, and to promote human rights through educational programs and research. The federal government had no such apparatus. Some of its critics questioned Ottawa's insistence on a constitutional Charter when its own legislative protections for rights were so deficient.

Cabinet had in early 1974 approved in principle the development of comprehensive federal human rights legislation, before I undertook full-time duties in the Department of Justice. I went there from the Privy Council Office in April of that year as Assistant Deputy Minister, replacing Gerárd La Forest. One of the first files handed to me was the development of the *Canadian Human Rights Act* (CHRA).

I should say at the outset that this was a project in which I had long believed. While a junior lawyer in the Department of the Attorney General of Saskatchewan, I had observed some of the inadequacies of the provincial *Bill of Rights* in matters of enforcement. The only sanctions it provided for breaches of its anti-discrimination provisions were either prosecution for an offence or an injunction issued by the Court of Queen's Bench. The latter obviously would have required resources to hire counsel. The former would normally have required police action. The complaints we used to hear of in the Department usually involved refusal to serve Indians in restaurants or hotels. When asked to follow up on one of these complaints, I found the police to be remarkably uninterested. There was no one who regarded it as his or her responsibility to see that the *Bill of Rights* was obeyed. While I was later a professor of law in Saskatoon during the mid-1960s, I had served for a time as chairman of the provincial Legal Policy Committee

of the Saskatchewan New Democratic Party. One of our members was Roy Romanow, then a young lawyer in Saskatoon and later, in the 1970s, to be Attorney General and, subsequently, party leader and Premier in the 1990s. During my tenure we recommended the establishment of a Human Rights Commission for the province and the strengthening of human rights legislation. The NDP was then in opposition and this policy was not to be adopted until the time of the Blakeney NDP government, elected in 1971, when Roy Romanow as Attorney General introduced the legislation, after I had left Saskatchewan. As a result of my experiences and of our Committee's study, I firmly believed in the importance of a Commission dedicated to the protection and promotion of human rights. If in the narrative to follow I seem unduly pragmatic in compromises that would allow the legislative project to move forward, it was because I was convinced that even if we ended up with an Act with some imperfections, it was of overwhelming importance to get the Commission established and operating. I felt the Commission, if properly established, would become a dedicated engine for change in the ongoing enlargement of human rights. I was only too familiar with the aphorism that "the best is the enemy of the good," and feared that interest groups, by insisting on achieving the perfect Act, might well prevent any Act from being passed. I knew the currents of resistance we had regularly to deal with in getting such legislation through Parliament. I therefore often counselled compromise in order to achieve the main goal.

I spent many weeks intermittently developing instructions for the legislative drafters. We largely based it on successful provincial models. As the project unfolded, we were obliged to consult many other departments and to participate in federal-provincial discussions of the modalities. There were many stages at which we had to seek further Cabinet guidance. And the bill, once introduced and given first and second reading, was examined minutely by the Justice and Legal Affairs Committee of the House of Commons, where I spent many days with the Minister of Justice whose bill it was. I will describe some of the more important problems that we encountered. But before doing so I should acknowledge the valuable assistance we had from Professor Walter Tarnopolsky, who was our main outside consultant on the project. Walter was then a professor of law at Osgoode Hall Law School of York University and was former Dean of Law at the University of Windsor. He was one of the leading authorities on

human rights law in Canada, having authored a seminal book[24] on the *Canadian Bill of Rights, 1960* and written numerous articles on the subject. Walter and I had been contemporaries as Arts students at the University of Saskatchewan in the 1950s, and colleagues on the law faculty of that university in the mid-1960s.

One of our first problems was to persuade other departments of government that they could and should accept the imperatives of a human rights Act. Some were receptive and supportive but others, when consulted, would express support for the principles of the Act but explain why it should not apply to them. Among these departments was National Defence. I was fortunate to have among my senior staff on contract a retired Brigadier General who had served as Judge Advocate General in the past. I don't know what his personal views were on some of the proposed requirements of the Act, but he was perfectly loyal to the project and helped us assess the merits of the military objections. As an example of the attitude of some military minds in those days, I recall an incident after the Act had come into force. A complaint had been made to the Canadian Human Rights Commission against the Armed Forces because, in recruiting and training summer students for the Governor General's Foot Guards to perform the ceremonial Changing of the Guard on Parliament Hill, they refused to employ women. Eventually the current Judge Advocate General came to seek my advice. I asked him why they did not recruit women for this purpose. The military command's position was, he related, that they would only recruit personnel for this activity who would be eligible for combat. In those days women were not used in combat—hence they could not march around Parliament Hill in the heat and humidity of an Ottawa summer wearing big black fur hats and scarlet wool uniforms! I advised that this was not a valid explanation, a "bona fide occupational requirement" that could by the terms of the Act justify such gender discrimination. The rule was soon changed.

Another formidable opponent was the Department of Labour. It had for years administered the anti-discrimination and equal pay requirements of the *Labour Code* through a system of inspections. According to many victims of discrimination and informed observers, this system was not effective. In its place, we proposed to give a right of complaint by any employee or prospective employee to an independent body, the Canadian Human Rights Commission. Labour insisted that it had the

With first members of the Canadian Human Rights Commission. At left, Walter Tarnopolsky; centre rear, Chairman Gordon Fairweather; to his left, Hon. Ron Basford, Minister of Justice; Commission member Father MacDonnell; and the author.

expertise and the ongoing relationship with employers that enabled it to resolve problems in a non-confrontational way. We were convinced that a change was needed and a complaints procedure administered by an independent Commission, the model adopted by most provinces and many jurisdictions abroad, would be the more effective approach. This issue was fought over in Cabinet, and Labour succeeded in having the bill modified to retain most of its inspection jurisdiction, though not without a lot of stress and effort on the part of all concerned. But Justice had its little triumph. When this matter was before the parliamentary committee, many questions were raised both by Government and Opposition members as to the wisdom of this exception to the Commission's jurisdiction. Walter Tarnopolsky, who was in attendance, and I had lunch one day with Mark MacGuigan, then a leading Liberal member of the committee, and Gordon Fairweather, then the Conservative Justice critic in the committee (and later the first Chairman of the Canadian Human Rights Commission). Both were opposed to this exception for Labour. From our conversation they realized that Justice shared their views and that it was because of the adamant position of Labour that the bill was as it was. After lunch Gordon moved, and Mark seconded, an amendment that would remove the exception for Labour. The Minister of Justice, Ron Basford, was in a difficult position: he had instructions from Cabinet to

advance the bill as then drafted, but he had the normal problem of any minister trying to get consensus in a parliamentary committee who had to consider whether he could vary Cabinet's instructions for this purpose. We advised him to accept the amendment in the interests of a committee consensus and he did. This later required considerable explanation to the Minister of Labour, John Munro.

One of the most difficult issues was that of equal pay, essentially a gender issue. The traditional requirement had been "equal pay for equal work," a test that had first been adopted internationally in 1919[25] and was employed in Canadian labour legislation. With the encouragement of certain feminist organizations, I thought we should adopt the broader concept of "equal pay for work of equal value." This would overcome the familiar acceptance that typical "women's jobs" were per se entitled to less remuneration: they did not count as "equal work" with jobs that were typically male. This broader concept of "work of equal value" had been adopted by the International Labour Organization in 1951,[26] and Canada had ratified the 1951 Convention in 1972. Admittedly, the concept of "work of equal value" was hard to define and apply. When we proposed its inclusion in the Act, our strongest opposition came from the Treasury Board staff and, to a lesser extent, from the Privy Council Office. They saw it as at best a nebulous concept incapable of application to the public service, and at worst a ruinous drain on the Consolidated Revenue Fund. This subject hovered for months in interdepartmental and cabinet committees. At one time I warned the Minister of Justice that unless we could rally support from the Minister Responsible for the Status of Women and from some outside feminist groups, I thought the matter would have to be dropped. In the end he was able to get enough support in Cabinet and the "work of equal value" phraseology was adopted. I had heard enough, however, to recognize that the new Commission would have a difficult challenge in applying this test to any given complaint. As soon as the Act was passed in early 1977, and before the Commission was appointed, I started organizing some interim staff for it, and the first project we undertook was to establish a task force to work on the definition and application of "work of equal value." To be fair, the opponents of the adoption of this principle have been proven in many ways to be right: its application has been the subject of a multitude of litigation, many of the cases ending in the Supreme Court, and many issues remain to be solved some 30 years

after its adoption. But these contests have also revealed many situations of an irrational undervaluing of women's employment.

Another matter that lurked—often beneath the surface—was our failure to include in the definition of proscribed discrimination the ground of "sexual orientation." This had been considered and rejected in Cabinet's study of the bill, it being concluded that there was in the 1970s no sufficient consensus on this subject to support in Parliament a bill containing such a provision. Needless to say, however, its absence was quickly noted in the press and in the Commons committee. An amendment was moved in Committee by the Opposition to include sexual preference as a prohibited ground of discrimination in employment, housing, or services. So persistent was the pressure for a change that the Minister decided to take the matter back to Cabinet. A memorandum was prepared, reporting to Cabinet on the situation in the Commons committee and seeking further direction. Unfortunately, when the matter was scheduled for consideration in an evening Cabinet Committee, the Minister of Justice told me he was not available. As a result, I had to represent him at the meeting where our chief antagonists were representatives of the Canadian Armed Forces, the Royal Canadian Mounted Police, and the Department of External Affairs. It will not be difficult for the reader to guess the nature of their objections to being obliged to recruit otherwise qualified gay personnel. The military and the RCMP officers assured us *they* had no personal objections to such persons but the "men in the barracks" would object. At one point I observed that they sounded like restaurant owners in the Old South who said they had nothing against black customers but that other customers would object to their admission. External Affairs had their traditional lament that gay officers would be subject to blackmail and would therefore constitute a security risk. In short, we did not get approval for the addition of "sexual orientation" or "sexual preference" to the list of prohibited grounds of discrimination.

During the period when we were developing the Act, the Attorney General of Ontario, Roy McMurtry, came under pressure from various groups to do something about telephonic hate messages. There were a few of these "services" available in Toronto that one could phone and then listen to a recorded message of a scurrilous nature, usually directed against blacks, Jews, or visible minorities. Representatives of these targets pressed the Attorney General of Ontario to take action. He had concluded that

the messages probably did not contravene the *Criminal Code* provisions for the incitement of hatred. It was also true that in Ontario the principal phone carrier at that time was Bell Canada, a federally regulated enterprise. Roy pressed my Minister, Ron Basford, to take action. We looked into the matter and found no existing federal instruments of control. Bell Canada insisted that there was nothing it could do: as a common carrier it had no right to interfere with its customers' messages. The Canadian Radio-television and Telecommunications Commission said it had no regulatory power to control the content of telephone messages. Roy continued to press Ron, and Ron continued to press me to find a solution within the context of the pending human rights bill. I was particularly concerned that we might, in a human rights measure, be seen to be stifling freedom of speech. I expected that we would encounter objections in Parliament against setting up a "new bureaucracy" to censor telephone conversations. I was conscious of judicial strictures, particularly by the US Supreme Court, that the law should not impose "prior restraints" on speech but confine itself to punishing harmful speech, if necessary, only after the event. I was also aware that we were being asked to control speech that the law did not otherwise prohibit or punish: not the law of defamation (because groups cannot be actionably defamed); nor the criminal law, which, as Roy McMurtry had rightly concluded, did not go so far as to punish this type of message. With the collaboration of Fred Gibson, then Director of Legislation in Justice, and our English-language draftsman, we came up with what became section 13 of the *Canadian Human Rights Act*[27] to make telephonic hate messages a discriminatory practice. We circumscribed the offence: the messages had to be communicated repeatedly over a federally regulated telecommunications undertaking (other than a broadcaster) and contain such matter that "is likely to expose a person or persons to hatred or contempt by reason of the fact that person or those persons are identifiable on the basis of a prohibited ground of discrimination." The owner of the telephone system could not merely as owner be liable unless it also participated in the message. The sole remedy provided was a complaint to the Commission against the originator of the messages, which could refer it to adjudication before a Tribunal panel; that panel could then issue a cease and desist only *after* adjudication. In other words, the provision was carefully constructed to avoid prior restraints and censorship prior to publication. However, this section and similar sections in some provincial

laws have been frequently attacked by libertarians as undue restraints on freedom of speech. A private member's bill to repeal section 13 was approved by the House of Commons on June 6, 2012, and was awaiting consideration by the Senate as this book went to press.

I did have further contact with this section in my later judicial life. Perhaps I suffered from (or had the advantage of) too much knowledge as to its background, with the result that my judgement was reversed by the Supreme Court of Canada which apparently did not. The origins of this case arose in December 1991 with several complaints under section 13 against Canadian Liberty Net, a Vancouver organization. Persons dialling its number could hear messages denigrating Jewish and non-white persons. The complaints to the Commission were found by it to be substantiated and it referred them to a Human Rights Tribunal panel for adjudication. That panel was very slow to move, so in the meantime the Commission applied to the Federal Court Trial Division for an interlocutory injunction. The injunction was granted that stilled the hate messages for some 18 months before the Tribunal disposed of the matter, issuing a cease and desist order in September 1993. The respondents appealed the Trial Division's injunction decision to the Federal Court of Appeal where I wrote the majority judgement.[28] I allowed the appeal on the grounds that the Trial Division had no jurisdiction to issue the injunction. The only federal law that was arguably being violated by the respondents was section 13 of the CHRA. It was part of the fundamental scheme of that Act that it had its own discrete enforcement mechanism, essentially the Commission and the Tribunal. A deliberate decision had been taken by Parliament at the outset not to rely on the courts for the Act's enforcement as had been done in some other jurisdictions. No judicial remedies were intended. Also, in particular reference to section 13, care had been taken to ensure that no speech was prohibited prior to an adjudication in the Tribunal. A normal interlocutory injunction hearing falls far short of an adjudication on the merits. On appeal to the Supreme Court, however, this history and context were ignored: the Court found that the provisions of section 13 "nourished" as a "law of Canada" the general power granted the Federal Court by statute to issue injunctions against violations of federal law.[29] This obscured what I had identified as the basic problem, which was the slowness of the Tribunal system: if it were functioning efficiently, it could have heard the evidence and made a considered adjudication sooner, and

it would thus have evaded the criticism of "prior restraint" that Parliament had intended to avoid.

Another abiding difficulty in the development of the CHRA was the treatment of Indians as constitutionally defined. It was an easy white, liberal assumption that it was time to treat Indians equally and that the CHRA should apply to them without exception. As noted earlier, this view did not accord with the constitution, which contemplated a separate regime for Indians under Parliament's power and responsibility (stated in section 91, head 24 of the *Constitution Act, 1867*[30]) to legislate specially for "Indians and Lands reserved for the Indians." Representatives of status Indians expressed their concerns about the seeming negation of their distinct status that the general application of the CHRA to them would imply. In particular they were concerned about the preservation of paragraph 12(1)(b) of the *Indian Act*,[31] which provided that an Indian woman who married a non-Indian man would lose her Indian status. (The Act also provided that when an Indian man married a non-Indian woman, the wife *acquired* Indian status). With such loss of status went an Indian woman's right to live on the reserve of her former band. Indian representatives, mostly male, objected to the application of the CHRA to give such a woman the right to accommodation on the reserve without discrimination because she had married a person of another race. There was also uncertainty about how the courts would treat seemingly contradictory provisions in the *Indian Act* and the CHRA. To avoid prolonged opposition from the Indian organizations, we put section 67 in the Act, providing that nothing in it would affect the *Indian Act*. Of course this provision was not without its detractors. When I appeared before the Senate Committee studying the bill, I was questioned by a woman Senator. I gave the official explanation: that Indian leaders were concerned about Indian women who married non-Indians bringing their spouses home to live on the reserve. There was concern that such persons would assert undue influence in the management of the reserve. Also, there generally wasn't enough room for non-Indians on existing reserves. The Senator said abruptly, "Do you believe that?" I looked at her piously and said, "Senator, it is not for me to believe or disbelieve. I am only telling you why ministers have decided to recommend this provision." This provision has since been repealed.[32]

An abiding concern as the Act developed was the hostility or lack of support shown by some provinces to the introduction of comprehensive

federal human rights legislation and the establishment of a federal commission. We had at least two meetings with provincial administrators
and tried to keep them informed—as much as parliamentary government
can permit—of our plans prior to their submission to Parliament. Some
provincial representatives thought it was quite unnecessary to have a federal agency; they saw no reason why they could not administer federal
laws on behalf of Ottawa. We, on the other hand, were certain that to
ensure speedy and uniform administration a central agency was needed.
There were also concerns about the disruption of federal departments
and agencies by provincial investigators. In particular, it was recognized
that at times investigations would lead to confidential matters touching
on national security or sensitive policies. While this would be a problem
even under a federal Commission, we believed we could establish rules
and procedures that would have the confidence of federal administrators
while permitting the effective administration of the CHRA. We built in
provisions encouraging co-operation with provincial human rights agencies, and I believe once the national Commission was in place there was a
high order of federal-provincial co-operation at the official level.

A major challenge peculiar to developing the federal Act was that we
were instructed to create and incorporate within it a regime protecting
the privacy of Canadians in respect of their personal information held by
the Government of Canada. Ours was the first Canadian jurisdiction to
so legislate. There was a US law that we studied as a model, but much of
the scheme had to be original to our system: from the definition of government institutions that would be subject to the law; to the definition
of what constitutes personal information; to the procedures provided
whereby individuals could find out and request corrections in respect of
their personal information on government files, including rights of appeal to a Commissioner and the courts where access was refused; to the
definition of grounds upon which the government institution could refuse
disclosure; and to the permitted use of personal information by government institutions. I was very fortunate to have working with me Stephen
Skelly, a very able colleague in the Department of Justice who, like myself,
had spent time as a law professor in the west (in his case, Manitoba). He
had become an expert in the infant science of jurimetrics—essentially
the use of computers in the legal system—and advised the Department
on such matters. Indeed, he was one of the few people I knew in the

1970s who was computer-literate. He was also well informed about current privacy issues and their regulation and had a very innovative mind. He is entitled to much of the credit for the development of our first privacy legislation. (He later also played a major role in the drafting of the *Access to Information Act*.) One difficult part of our mandate was to provide for the office and role of the Privacy Commissioner. It had been decided that rather than establishing a separate agency for the administration of privacy legislation, it should be the special duty of one of the members of the Canadian Human Rights Commission who would be so designated. I suppose the rationale, other than a bureaucratic one of saving costs, was that privacy should be seen as a new human right. We so designed the office of Privacy Commissioner, and the first person appointed to it was Inger Hansen. A native of Denmark, she had trained and worked as a lawyer in Canada and became the first prison ombudsman of the federal corrections system, visiting prisons and listening to the complaints of prisoners that she would then take up with the authorities. She was an effective first Privacy Commissioner, but in time the inclusion of this Office as part of the Canadian Human Rights Commission became less and less satisfactory for the Privacy Commissioner and the rest of the Commission. In time, a separate office of Privacy Commissioner was established by law.

One other aspect of the Act as originally drafted deserves consideration, if for no other reason than that it was emphatically struck down by the courts in later years. It was typical of human rights legislation in the 1970s that a commission received a complaint and made an initial determination as to whether it had prima facie validity. If so, the commission would then refer the complaint to an adjudicative person or body. We were largely following the Ontario legislation in this respect but felt its provision for adjudication was unacceptable: it provided for the Minister responsible for the Human Rights Commission to choose a hearing officer to make the adjudication of a complaint referred by the Commission. In that era this was seen by many human rights commentators as unfair because it allowed a political selection of an adjudicator for a particular complaint; this was particularly objectionable where the government was a respondent, or defendant, in the complaint proceeding. With this in mind, I suggested a structure whereby the Governor in Council (a body otherwise entrusted by the Constitution to appoint judges) would name a number of members of a Human Rights panel and, when the Commission

referred a complaint for hearing, the Commission Chairman would choose up to three members from that panel to hear the case. In the context of the more relaxed standards of impartiality in the 1970s, this seemed like a major improvement on the Ontario model: the Governor in Council would only name a list from which tribunal members could be drawn but could not designate the trier(s) of any particular case; furthermore the Commission, as an independent body, would not have free rein to pick just anyone, but would have to choose among those persons the Governor General in Council thought to have the necessary ability and integrity to decide such cases. This system went unchallenged for nearly ten years but was finally struck down by the Federal Court of Appeal in *MacBain v Canada*.[33] The Court laid stress on the Act's provision that the Commission must first find a complaint to be "substantiated" before referring it to a Tribunal; however, the Tribunal was also charged with determining whether a complaint was "substantiated" before it could impose sanctions. The Court concluded that there was a reasonable apprehension of institutional bias in such circumstances: the Commission having first determined "substantiation," its Chairman could then choose such Tribunal members as he thought might agree in finding "substantiation." I cannot fault that decision, although in our defence I would say that the original scheme was thought to be a major improvement in independence when compared with certain provincial models of that time, and that in the 1980s, and since, there has been a progressively heightened judicial sensitivity to issues of bias and the appearance of bias. In any event, Parliament, after the *MacBain* case, amended the CHRA to provide for an independent Canadian Human Rights Tribunal, still appointed by the Governor in Council but with its own President who would in future determine which members would sit on a particular case. Still, further attacks were mounted against the Tribunal in the 1990s because there was no security of tenure and because the Commission fixed the salaries of members. These matters were corrected by later legislation.

Once the Act was passed, and before the Chairman or members had been appointed, I had the responsibility of determining interim steps to ensure a smooth launch for the Commission. I borrowed some temporary staff from other departments and we conducted some preliminary planning, including the study on equal pay, as mentioned earlier. An important first step was to get authorization for and find suitable office space for the

Commission. Perhaps one of my last errors connected with that Act was to approve quarters to which, it later emerged after the Commission had moved in, were not wheelchair accessible—for a Commission intended to protect (among others) the physically disabled!

INTERNATIONAL HUMAN RIGHTS COVENANTS

My other major human rights activity in this decade arose out of Canada's wish to accede to two United Nations instruments, the *International Covenant on Civil and Political Rights* along with its *Optional Protocol*, and the *International Covenant on Economic, Social and Cultural Rights*. The drafting of these instruments had been completed by the United Nations in 1966 and each provided that it was to come into effect when at least 35 member nations had ratified it. In 1976 the Department of External Affairs was pressing for Canada's ratification. Justice had been asked to consider the domestic legal implications of ratification.

The *International Covenant on Economic, Social and Cultural Rights* (*ICESCR*) holds the generous promise of rights to work and to favourable work conditions, trade union rights, the right to social security, and an adequate standard of living, to the "highest attainable standard of physical and mental health," to education, and many others. These may be seen as positive rights, obliging action and expenditure by states rather than negative rights only requiring the state to refrain from many harmful or oppressive activities. The Covenant was to apply without exception to the component units of federal states. Canadian politicians had for a long time been wary of any sort of legal obligations on governments and legislatures to spend money without regard to their own view of public priorities and fiscal ability. It was hard to contemplate the concept of a legal right to work. Rights similar to these had been enunciated in the 1948 *Universal Declaration of Human Rights*. At that time, Parliament had recommended adherence to the *Declaration* only on the assumption that it was intended to state social goals rather than legal imperatives.[34] In the development of the Charter both before and after 1976, a similar approach had been taken: we did not attempt to implement the positive rights enunciated in the *ICESCR*.[35] Fortunately, that Convention, Article 2, section 1, clarified that states parties to the Covenant were simply undertaking their best efforts to achieve the goals it announced as rights. On this basis we were able to advise Cabinet that the *ICESCR*, if ratified, would not impose legal

obligations on the federal or provincial governments but only express certain worthy ideals for us all.

But the *International Covenant on Civil and Political Rights* (*ICCPR*) was another matter. By its Article 2, section 1, it obliged states parties to it to ensure all their inhabitants the rights recognized in the Covenant. These included the whole gamut of right to life, equality rights, legal rights, political rights and liberties, rights of the family, freedom from slavery, et cetera. One of the potentially controversial rights was stated up front in Article 1, section 1: the right of "all peoples" to self-determination. (Of this I will speak later in connection with Canada's first report to the UN under this Covenant). Adding importance to the status of such rights in a signatory country was Canada's determination to sign the *Optional Protocol* to this Covenant. A signatory to that *Protocol* would be subject to complaints by individuals against it in respect of failure to respect the rights stated by the Covenant. Such complaints would go to the Human Rights Committee provided for in the Covenant. This was the first such instrument to allow individuals (and not just other states parties) to complain to the UN of a failure by a signatory to comply with a treaty or covenant. In assessing the potential conflicts that there might be between existing federal and provincial laws and institutions and the Covenant, we had to keep in mind that any perceived conflict might bring us before the UN Human Rights Committee in response to individual complaints of aggrieved Canadians. After a careful but not exhaustive examination of this Covenant, we recognized that there were at least grey areas of our laws, federal and provincial, that might attract unfavourable comment from the UN Human Rights Committee. But External Affairs made a strong argument for Canadian ratification and our advice to Cabinet was in effect that while there was some uncertainty, the risks were sustainable. In the result, Canada acceded to both Covenants in 1976. Ours was one of the last accessions numerically required to bring the Covenants into effect, as they soon were.

We then had to consider nominating a Canadian to sit on the UN Human Rights Committee. Because it was limited to 18 members, not all signatories would be represented there. The nomination of our candidate would go to New York where it would be vetted by the signatory states that would have a vote. External Affairs raised with me the possibility of nominating Walter Tarnopolsky. I was much in favour of this and I was delegated to consult Walter. This I did, and though he was quite willing to be

nominated, he was sure he would not be chosen: he cited to me objections that other states might have to him, and in particular the Soviet Union. I minimized these problems and urged Walter to let his name go forward, which he did. It turned out that some of his pessimism was warranted. We later heard that the Soviets had some reservations about Walter's candidacy because, according to their records, he had been Canadian Chairman of the Free Moroz Committee. And this was true. Valentyn Moroz was a dissident Ukrainian intellectual who had been imprisoned by the Soviet Union. A protest was organized in various countries including Canada, where Walter, a leading intellectual of Ukrainian descent and a human rights advocate, had led the protest, including a march on the Soviet Embassy in Ottawa. This fact had obviously not escaped Soviet intelligence. Nevertheless, the Soviets did not object to his candidacy and Walter served on the Committee with distinction from 1977 to 1983.

The ICCPR came into effect for Canada on August 19, 1976. Before long there was a litany of complaints against her by residents of Canada to the Human Rights Committee. These ranged over a variety of alleged infringements of equality and legal rights, for the most part. It was said that in the first year the number of complaints against Canada were second only to those against Paraguay! I took it as the mark of a truly free and open society that would tolerate such attacks on it before an international body. But it did keep my branch occupied from time to time, as we were in effect counsel for the defence. We had much collaboration with the Department of the Secretary of State that had a proficient human rights unit au courant with developments in Canada. Our largest and most difficult defence during the period of my responsibility in the late 1970s and early 1980s concerned the complaint of Sandra Lovelace, filed with the Committee in Geneva on December 27, 1977. She had been a Maliseet Indian living on her band's reserve in New Brunswick. She had married a non-Indian and hence had lost her Indian status and had to leave the reserve because of the provisions of paragraph 12(1)(b) of the *Indian Act* as discussed earlier. She complained of two kinds of violations of the Covenant: discrimination based on sex, invoking Articles 3, 23, and 26; and denial to her as the member of a cultural and linguistic minority in community with others to enjoy her own culture and language, invoking Article 27. When the Committee asked Canada for a response to this complaint, it fell to my officers in consultation with Indian Affairs to draft a defence. I think our

heart was not in it, as we had been discussing with Indian Affairs for some time the need to get rid of paragraph 12(1)(b). Our main submissions were that Canada had obligations under treaties to preserve reserves as exclusive to Indians, which this paragraph was designed to do, and that remedial legislation was being developed. The UN Committee set aside the complaints of sexual discrimination on the basis that the marriage of May 23, 1970, had predated the coming into force of the Covenant. But it accepted the complaint based on denial of the right to share her culture and language in community with others, and Canada was declared to be in violation of Article 27.

The aftermath of *Lovelace* makes a good case study of the utility of international commitments to universal principles in driving domestic reforms. The Committee's condemnation of our legislation added greatly to the sentiment in Canada in favour of a legislative change. When the *Canadian Charter of Rights and Freedoms*[36] was adopted in 1982, the guarantees of equality in section 15 were unqualified. While the coming into force of that section was postponed for three years, it gave the impetus to the amendment of the *Indian Act* in 1985[37] in order to repeal paragraph 12 (1)(b) effective April 17, 1985, the day that section 15 of the *Charter* would come into force. This amendment also contained elaborate provisions for restoring status to women who had lost it through marriage and to their offspring.

In passing, I find it remarkable that I had such a long and varied experience with the issue of loss of status by Indian women marrying non-Indians. First I was involved in evading the issue at the time of the adoption of the CHRA. Then I participated in the defence of Canada before the UN Human Rights Committee in the *Lovelace* case because of that paragraph. Then I helped draft a Charter that we knew would almost certainly void paragraph 12(1)(b). And after I went to the bench, the paragraph was repealed, but I was involved in two hearings of different aspects of the same case involving a challenge to the validity of that repeal.[38] I also heard a case involving the right of newly restored women band members, for whom there was no room to live on the reserve, to vote for the band council.[39]

My final major commitment to Canada's accession to the ICCPR came with the initial report we were obliged to make to the Human Rights Committee on the state of human rights in Canada in relation to our compliance with the Covenant. By Article 40 we were required to make

a first report within a year of the coming into force of the Covenant, and thereafter as requested by the Committee. We asked for and requested several extensions of time because of the complexity of making such a report for a federal state. My branch in Justice and the human rights section in the Department of the Secretary of State, under Gerald Rayner, Assistant Deputy Secretary of State, led this exercise. We did the analysis of federal laws and policies and sought to demonstrate where possible that they met the requirements of the Covenant. We also gained the co-operation of provincial governments to prepare reports on their laws and policies, to be part of Canada's report to the UN Human Rights Committee. The territorial governments were unable to perform this task so we drafted their reports for their approval. In time, the report was completed and sent off to Geneva in 1979, three years after the Covenant came into force. A hearing by the Committee in respect of our report was fixed for March 1980 in Geneva.

In preparation for this hearing, we recognized that members of the committee might ask us anything about the state of human rights in Canada whether dealt with in our report or not. We therefore had extensive briefing notes prepared to cover any possible question we could imagine. We knew that a vulnerable area would be that of the condition of our Aboriginal people and we assembled lots of statistics, many of them not reflecting well on our society: for example, rates of infant mortality, tuberculosis, illiteracy, unemployment, incarceration, and alcoholism. But we also had positive statistics showing an improvement in many of these areas, growth in higher education for Indigenous people, new land claims policies, and the growth of vibrant organizations successfully representing them (largely funded by government).

We assembled in the Peace Palace in Geneva in the last week of March 1980. The delegation was headed by Canada's permanent ambassador to the UN in Geneva, with Gerald Rayner and me as his chief advisers. Alice Desjardins, a senior colleague in my Department, was the other Justice representative. We had invited some provincial representatives, including those of Quebec and Saskatchewan, to act as advisers, as the report had to cover provincial compliance as well. The format of this proceeding was typical of many international bodies including the International Court of Justice. Our written submission had already been studied (no doubt with varying degrees of acuity) before the meeting. We then sat at a table

and were asked questions by members of the committee. But this was not the free exchange of question and answers with which we are familiar in public affairs in Canada: we were only expected to note the questions but not answer at that time. After a day of questions we were given about two days to prepare our answers, which we would then come back and deliver. The two most difficult subjects we were asked about were the right of self-determination of "peoples" proclaimed in Article 1 of the Covenant, and the denial of equality to Canada's Indigenous population.

The sensitivity of the self-determination issue will be appreciated if one considers the date of this appearance before the Committee: it was a week at the end of March 1980, and back home the Quebec Referendum campaign was in full stream leading up to the vote fixed for May 20. That referendum sought authorization for the separatist Parti Québécois (PQ) government to negotiate "sovereignty-association" with the rest of Canada. Most Canadians, including a majority of Quebecers, understood this to be a step on the road to separation. The referendum was well known to many foreign observers, particularly the well-briefed members of the UN Human Rights Committee. Early on the first day, a committee member from one of the Soviet-bloc Eastern European states asked the question: Does "Quebec have the right of self-determination?" (I am satisfied that this was simply a mischievous question designed to embarrass a NATO member.) We were conscious that the PQ was well aware of what was going on in the Committee hearings in Geneva: a provincial minister was in Paris keeping in touch with the Quebec representative on the Canadian delegation. It was the hope of the Quebec government, apparently, that federal representatives would answer the question with a simple yes or no. In the former case the separatists could broadcast it as confirmation of Quebec's right to do what the PQ proposed; in the latter case it would be used to arouse hostility among the Quebec population against Ottawa and perhaps invite a rebuke of Canada from the UN Committee. Fortunately, we had two days to draft a reply. The Prime Minister's Office, the Department of External Affairs, and the Minister of Justice (Jean Chrétien, who was leading the federal government's role in the referendum campaign) were on high alert. I was asked by our Ambassador to do an initial draft text. The text was faxed to Ottawa and numerous were the suggestions for revision, particularly by External Affairs. The Deputy Minister of Justice, Roger Tassé, phoned me several times so he could brief the Minister and to

pass on to me ministerial instructions. The approved answer as it emerged in part argued that the guarantee of "self-determination for peoples" had long been understood to apply to colonial or politically oppressed groups. We affirmed that Quebec was a multi-ethnic society that was neither a colony nor politically oppressed. We described the federal and democratic system of our government. The people of Quebec were fully in control of their provincial government and they also elected representatives to the national Parliament. Quebec representatives played a leading part in the affairs of the national government. We also stressed that we had methods of amending our constitution in a democratic way and that if a consensus were reached by Canadians that a change should be made it could be made. When we delivered this nuanced answer it attracted little reaction from the Committee or coverage by the press.

With respect to Indigenous persons, there were several questions concerning the state of their social condition. In our answers we frankly recognized some serious problems but tried to demonstrate the extensive efforts and expenditures devoted to ameliorating those conditions. One question, however, was obviously designed to humiliate us. "How," it was asked, "does your system of Indian reserves differ in any way from South Africa's apartheid policies?" The answer I drafted to this was simple. Indian reserves are created for the exclusive use of Indians. No one else has the right to reside there. But Indians are not obliged to live there and are free to move anywhere they wish. With apartheid, the areas designated for blacks and coloureds are where they must live and they may not live elsewhere. Of course, this answer avoided all the many deficiencies of reserve life and the difficulties of status Indians becoming established and employed off-reserve, but I felt that a simplistic question deserved only a simplistic reply.

With this hearing in Geneva my major involvement in Canada's international human rights obligations came to an end as I became almost fully absorbed with the constitutional negotiations, legislation, and litigation that followed the outcome of the Quebec Referendum, where the "No" side—the federalist side—won on May 20, 1980, by a vote of 60 per cent compared with 40 per cent for the "Yes" side.

This experience with the two Covenants happened to help me in later years and in respect of other countries. As I have mentioned before, I was loaned to Hong Kong in 1989 to advise its Government on the drafting

of a bill of rights. The United Kingdom had acceded to the *International Covenant on Civil and Political Rights* (but not to its Protocol, with the result that, unlike Canadians, UK residents could not make complaints against their country to the UN Committee on Human Rights) and to the *International Covenant on Economic, Social and Cultural Rights*. The UK had also applied these covenants to certain of its Overseas Territories, including Hong Kong. When the *Sino-British Joint Declaration on the Question of Hong Kong* was signed by the two countries in December 1984, providing for the return of sovereignty to China on July 1, 1997, it contained the following among China's commitments on its basic policies regarding Hong Kong: "156. The provisions of the International Covenant on Civil and Political Rights and the International Covenant on Economic, Social and Cultural Rights as applied to Hong Kong shall remain in force." The colonial government, heavily influenced by the very cautious hand of the British Foreign Office, was fearful of doing anything in the adoption of a bill of rights that would upset the gerontocracy then ruling in Beijing. It was the accepted wisdom that Hong Kong, because of the above passage in the Chinese Government Declaration of Policy quoted above, had to confine its Bill to the ambit, and even the language, of the Covenants. The most surprising view urged by some was that, to be on the safe side, they should just pass a short statute attaching the two Covenants as schedules and declaring them to be law.

At the outset I tried to persuade them that the economic, social, and cultural instrument was not suitable for adoption as domestic law: it merely constituted an agreed set of goals for the signatory countries. Enacted as a statute, such goals would have no judicially enforceable value. I was finally able to persuade them that although the civil and political rights document did oblige the protection of the rights and freedoms set out in it, much of the language was unsuitable as a basis for judicially enforceable rights and freedoms. We agreed to use it as a guide to drafting a statute legally proclaiming and protecting those rights by means of judicial enforcement. While I was at a loss to know why they believed the Sino-British declaration placed a ceiling on civil and political rights that Hong Kong was permitted to enact for itself some seven years before the transfer of sovereignty, I urged that the drafting of a bill of rights in our own language with reference to the specific legal system of Hong Kong would be a legitimate implementation of that declaration that the civil and political

rights covenant should remain in force. Throughout the piece there was a lack of understanding by the representatives of the Foreign Office of the difference between an international covenant stating principles and an operating domestic law with legal force. (At that time Britain had no experience with a domestic bill of rights. Their only related experience was the operation of the *European Convention on Human Rights* to which they are a party: violations of it first had to be the subject of special proceedings in British Courts, with ultimate resort to the European Commission on Human Rights and then to the European Court on Human Rights—obviously not remedies readily available to the average citizen). We proceeded to draft a made-for-Hong Kong measure, in both English and Cantonese. In some ways this was reminiscent of my years in Ottawa participating in bilingual drafting, except that in Hong Kong I was not tempted to challenge the Cantonese text as I was, back in Ottawa (sometimes to the distress of my francophone colleagues), to question words in the French text. My experience with Canada's problems dealing with complaints under the *International Covenant on Civil and Political Rights* and our appearance before the UN Committee served me well in this work of implementing the Covenant in the domestic laws of another jurisdiction.

My last experience with the concepts of the Covenants came in Nepal in 2007. I had agreed to serve on a voluntary Advisory Committee of the Canadian Bar Association (CBA) to advise on a joint project the CBA had with the Nepal Bar Association (NBA), to assist the latter with participation in the drafting of a new constitution for Nepal. At that time Nepal was operating under an Interim Constitution and was awaiting the election of a Constituent Assembly to draft the new constitution. The Interim Constitution was a rather hastily drafted instrument that had helped end a revolution. But it was obviously going to be an important point of reference in the drafting of its replacement. It was the avowed purpose of the CBA not to attempt to tell its Nepal counterpart what a new constitution should contain. Much of the CBA effort was directed to helping the NBA consult its members and many previously neglected groups (most particularly women) in this diverse society regarding what the constitution should contain. But Canadian experts did from time to time identify problems that should be considered in preparing a new constitution. To this end, while I was in Nepal for a few weeks in the fall of 2007, I addressed a group of members of the NBA in Kathmandu, urging them to consider

how much social policy should be defined in the Constitution (and thus left to future judicial choices in application), and how much should be left to future legislatures and governments to decide in the circumstances of the time. I pointed to a number of provisions in the Interim Constitution that contained guarantees along the lines of the *International Covenant on Economic, Social and Cultural Rights*—what I would describe as "positive rights," which in Canada we had declined to try to guarantee in the constitution. These included rights set out in Part 3 of the Interim Constitution to live in a clean environment, to get basic health services, to get basic education, and the right to employment. While the three latter rights were all qualified by the phrase "as provided for in the law" (thus presumably leaving it to legislators to define the scope of the right), there was some discussion of removing those qualifiers. The right to a clean environment was not so qualified. I asked them to consider whether they wanted the standards of implementation for such social objectives to be fixed by future judges or future legislators. This was a choice they should make. My impression was that they were more willing to take their chances with the judges. Perhaps this was the result of their history, which involved repeated disappointments with autocratic governments.

CONCLUSION

In retrospect I am grateful for this non-constitutional phase in my public law career. It was in its own way as creative, innovative, and historic as patriation and the *Charter*. The change in policy for the recognition and negotiation of Aboriginal land rights has put in train a long process for the righting of historic wrongs. The advent of the *Canadian Human Rights Act* with its human rights watchdog, the Commission, has done much to correct injustices within federal jurisdiction and to contribute to the growth of a human rights culture in Canada. And our accession to the UN Covenants on human rights has committed us internationally to standards and goals that will continue to inform our domestic policies.

5

CONSTITUTIONAL DIALOGUE
BEFORE THE QUEBEC
REFERENDUM

After the failure of the Victoria Charter in mid-1971, there was very little federal-provincial discussion of constitutional reform for several years. The provinces were generally bored with the subject and the federal government had many other priorities in what were difficult economic times.

THE JOINT PARLIAMENTARY COMMITTEE, 1970 TO 1972

The principal sustained effort of constitutional review was made in these years by the Molgat-MacGuigan committee, otherwise known as the Special Joint Committee of the Senate and the House of Commons on the Constitution.[1] It had been appointed by the two Houses by resolutions of January 27, 1970, (House of Commons) and February 17, 1970, (Senate), while the comprehensive federal-provincial constitutional review was still underway. Its mandate included the study of federal proposals made during that review as published, as well as the development of its own proposals for change. The Committee heard hundreds of witnesses and received written submissions from many more. I appeared as an invited witness before the committee to talk about a possible charter of rights. Mark MacGuigan, co-chairman from the House of Commons and a personal friend from our days in academe, was a former professor of constitutional law and former Dean of Law at the University of Windsor and took the committee's work very seriously. It produced a very insightful

report published in 1972. Unfortunately, in that post-Victoria era there was not much interest in further constitutional negotiations. The report still deserves consideration, however. Indeed, it was cited in 1978 as providing a rationale for the attempt of the Government of Canada to write a new constitution. The Joint Committee reported that, from its hearings, it was satisfied that the Canadian public desired a new constitution, in part because the existing constitution was silent on some very important principles of government and therefore provided neither guidance nor inspiration to Canadians. The public also demanded reforms in the constitution (albeit there was no consensus on what those reforms should be).[2] While the drive for a new constitution in 1978 and 1979, to be discussed below, failed, some of the Committee's other ideas were later adopted in the *Canadian Charter of Rights and Freedoms*, Part I of the *Constitution Act, 1982*.[3] For example, the Committee was critical of the numerous and expansive limitations permitted on specified rights as they appeared in some of our early drafts. The Committee suggested instead that there should be only one general limitation clause, and such a clause did later find its place in section 1 of the *Charter*. The Committee recommended that such a clause should only permit such limitations on the rights in the *Charter* "as are reasonably justifiable in a democratic society,"[4] very close to the formulation of "as can be demonstrably justified in a free and democratic society" ultimately adopted in section 1. Also, in respect of the guarantees of life, liberty, and security of the person, the Committee rejected the early drafts that allowed derogation of such rights in accordance with "due process." The committee objected to "due process" because of the American interpretation of that term, which "gave judges leeway to substitute their socio-economic views for those of legislatures." Instead, the Committee suggested derogations should be permissible only when in accordance with "the principles of fundamental justice,"[5] the controversial provision that was later (in 1980) adopted by the drafters of the *Charter* in section 7. We did not then foresee that the Supreme Court of Canada would, within five years of that drafting, equally consider "principles of fundamental justice" to be an invitation for judges to "substitute their socio-economic views for those of legislatures."[6] In spite of its later influence, the Molgat-MacGuigan Report did not at the time of its publication attract much public interest.

Pierre Trudeau nevertheless continued to be interested in achieving patriation of the constitution with an amending formula. In a meeting of April 1975, he obtained the agreement of the Premiers to attempt to find such a formula upon which patriation could be based without getting into the difficult issue of the distribution of powers.[7] After some ongoing private intergovernmental discussions, the Prime Minister wrote to the Premiers on March 1, 1976, enclosing a draft resolution that might be the basis for seeking a constitutional amendment from the UK Parliament. He understood the resolution to reflect the suggestions that the federal government and the provinces had made in the intervening discussions: patriation; an amending formula (based on the Victoria Charter); some provisions concerning the Supreme Court; the entrenchment of language rights at the federal level; a special guarantee for the French language and culture; and the relief of regional disparities. He followed this up with private discussions with the Premiers in May 1976 to see if there could be such agreement as to permit going forward with a small package of amendments as proposed. The Premiers promised to give him a reply later. They met in August and October and their reply was given by Premier Lougheed as Chairman of the Annual Conference of Premiers in a letter of October 14, 1976. In it he said that while the Premiers agreed on patriation (although they hadn't agreed on an amending formula), they considered that a number of other matters should be included in any package of amendments. Most of these changes involved the enlargement of provincial powers. The federal cabinet gave some further study to the provincial proposals but authorized the Prime Minster to distribute in early 1977 a proposed resolution for constitutional amendments confined to patriation, an amending formula, regional disparities, a change in Senate representation to give the western provinces more senators, a provincial role in appointments to the Supreme Court, and a few other matters.[8] Instead of transferring more powers to the provinces, it provided a requirement that the federal government consult the provinces affected before exercising its powers in many of the areas of jurisdiction sought by the provinces. But these proposals did not produce much further discussion. In the Quebec provincial election of November 15, 1976, the Parti Québécois (PQ)—dedicated to the ultimate separation of Quebec from Canada—had emerged victorious.

In the face of this development, traditional discussions of constitutional change seemed for the time irrelevant.

TASK FORCE ON NATIONAL UNITY

It was a time for sober reflection in Ottawa. It seemed impossible simply to rest on the status quo. The Prime Minister and his advisers retained the hope of a patriated constitution and a charter of rights, but combined this with aspirations for a genuine constitutional renewal that could capture the support of Canadians across the country, including Quebec. Canadians, other than perhaps the hard core of separatists who could be found among PQ militants, looked to the federal government for a response to this threat to national unity. For a time, the government waited and watched as the unity debate developed in the country among concerned individuals and elements of civil society that became engaged with national unity issues.

Among the early governmental responses was the appointment on July 5, 1977, of a federal study group: the *Task Force on Canadian Unity*. It was co-chaired by Jean-Luc Pépin, a former federal Liberal minister, and John Robarts, a former Progressive Conservative Premier of Ontario. In retrospect, this initiative seems to me to have been designed more to provide an outlet for public concerns than as a source of inspiration for constitutional reform. From my observations of Pierre Trudeau and Jean-Luc Pépin in cabinet committees, I had the impression that Trudeau liked Pépin but had serious reservations about some of the former political science professor's ideas of the nature of Canada. Robarts was of course no close ally, but he was seen by the public as an eminently respectable federalist Canadian who, as a Premier of Ontario, had shown a sensitive concern for Quebec's linguistic and cultural interest. It was he, after all, who beat the federal government to the draw by being the first to call a conference on the Future of Confederation in Canada's centennial year. There were six other members of the Task Force and a considerable staff aided by consultants. Its mandate was to hear from Canadians on the question of national unity and to make recommendations about how it could be strengthened. The Task Force held hearings across the country and received many written submissions. It reported in January 1979 and I will refer to its recommendations later.[9] Suffice it to say that it analyzed Canada's unity problems as arising mainly from a duality of language and culture and from regionalism engendered by the sheer geography of

Canada. I had no contact with this initiative other than to read the Task Force recommendations, often in summary form, in 1979 when we were completely immersed in ongoing federal-provincial negotiations on the constitution. It is fair to say that the recommendations had little influence on the outcomes of those negotiations.

BILL C-60

While the Task Force was only part way into its work, Pierre Trudeau, on June 12, 1978, published a White Paper entitled *A Time for Action*. Its opening paragraph announced, "With this document the government launches a new and intensive effort towards the renewal of the Canadian Federation."[10] The fundamental but unarticulated premise for this bold initiative was that something had to be done because a separatist government had been elected in Quebec. But nowhere was this awkward fact mentioned. It did at one point refer to "the crisis threatening the stability, unity and prosperity of the country."[11]

Some parts of the Paper were almost lyrical, betraying an authorship that was more literary than bureaucratic. Some greats were quoted— Jean Talon, Bruce Hutchison, Anne Hébert, Edward (not William!) Blake, Archibald Lampman, Pierre Chauveau, Hugh MacLennan, and Henri (not Robert!) Bourassa. It was said that "too many myths and old hang-ups persist *in various parts of the country*" (emphasis added). It went on to declaim, "Let us forget once and for all about the Plains of Abraham: the vanquished and the vanquishers are dead. Let us 'decolonize' Quebec in our own minds: Quebec is in full *renaissance*." It went on to deny the validity of the stereotypes of the other regions: the Atlantic provinces were, instead, full of vitality; Ontario could no longer be seen as a "bastion of selfishness"; and the Western provinces enjoyed a success that had removed their earlier dependence on the East. The Paper continued: "This watershed in Canadian history gives us a unique opportunity to reshape our national destiny and to reshape it as we see fit. To this destiny, our whole country, all our regions and all our people must be committed. To accomplish it we require a political framework; this will be considered in the following chapters. We require much more—a new openness of spirit, a new dedication stirring and moving in the hearts of Canadians."[12] Stirring words, but as we shall see they fell mostly on deaf ears. There were too many vested interests among the political classes, and not enough

imagination among the electorate and the media, to seize the opportunity thus described.

The White Paper went on to pronounce on the principles to guide such a renewal of the Federation: the "pre-eminence of citizens over institutions"; a full recognition of the "legitimate rights of the native peoples"; full development of the "two linguistic majorities"; respect for cultural diversity; avoiding excessive centralization; promotion of national solidarity among people and regions; clarification of the respective roles of the central and provincial governments, but also recognizing their interdependence; and the production of a Canada that has the strong support of all Canadians.

The remainder of the Paper then accepted and built on the recommendation of the Molgat-MacGuigan Joint Parliamentary Committee Report of 1972, discussed above, that Canada needed a new constitution that should be expressed in contemporary terms and be both a guide and an inspiration to its citizens. The Paper noted that the government had indicated in October 1977 that it would be bringing forth constitutional proposals and it confirmed that such proposals would soon be tabled in Parliament for debate. It then went on to list the main elements of such legislation, which I will describe more fully in an analysis of that legislation, Bill C-60.[13] The Paper ended by proposing a timetable for constitutional change. Phase I, the portion that Parliament could enact, should be adopted by July 1, 1979; Phase II, which would require negotiation and agreement with the provinces, including an amending formula so as to permit patriation, should be completed by July 1, 1981.

The preparation of Bill C-60 had started the previous year when Don Thorson retired as Deputy Minister of Justice and was appointed to a special counsel role in the Privy Council Office. He worked in association with Gordon Robertson, who had moved from being Clerk of the Privy Council and general Secretary to Cabinet to being Secretary to Cabinet for Federal-Provincial Relations. He was carrying much of the responsibility for developing the policy that would emerge as *A Time for Action,* as well as the legislation that would create a new constitution. Don, a veteran legislative draftsman before he became Deputy Minister of Justice, was to be responsible for the constitutional drafting. I and my staff participated by doing legal research on some of the issues raised, and I participated in many meetings where successive drafts were discussed. At one point Don asked me what the elements of a charter of rights should be. I sat

down at the kitchen table in our cottage in the Gatineau Hills and made a summary of the contents I would like to see in such a document. I drew on previous drafts we had developed since 1967 and on the work of the Molgat-MacGuigan Committee. I proposed, I think for the first time, that there should be an enforcement clause ensuring that there would always be a means for an individual to seek a judicial remedy to assert Charter rights. Don built this into section 24 of the ill-fated C-60, but in later years it was revived as section 24 of the *Canadian Charter of Rights and Freedoms*.[14]

On June 20, 1978, Bill C-60 was tabled in the House of Commons, for purposes of debate. It was never intended to proceed to second reading in that form but instead to be the basis of parliamentary and public debate. It was an ambitious and a complex measure: ambitious because it undertook nothing less than to restate the existing constitution and to add to it many new elements, including the crystallization in legislative form of much of the unwritten constitution found in constitutional conventions or practices; and complex because, while in form it was a complete restatement, it was recognized that only part of it could be enacted by Parliament alone, the rest having to await the approval of the provinces for the constitutional amendments proposed by the Bill.

Major contents of the Bill included a statement of "aims of the Canadian federation," a kind of preamble setting out the characteristics and goals of Canada and Canadians. There were definite Trudeauesque assertions of the importance of fundamental individual rights, popular sovereignty, reduction of regional disparities, respect for multiculturalism, and the implicit denial of the two nation theory. It spoke instead of the "new nationality created by [our] forebears." It spoke of the equal respect required for the English and French languages "throughout Canada." As for the separatist view of Quebec as the sole representative of the French fact, this preamble asserted instead the aim that "inasmuch as the North American majority is, and seems certain to remain overwhelmingly English-speaking, to recognize a permanent national commitment to the endurance and self-fulfilment of the Canadian French-speaking society centred in but not limited to Quebec."

The Bill then went on in its first substantive provisions to propose a constitutional bill of rights. This was a Part that, it was recognized, Parliament could not give permanent constitutional effect to in relation to federal jurisdiction but could only give it legislative effect in that domain:

further action would be required by the provinces to give it constitutional permanency and application to provincial jurisdictions as well.

In Part IV the Bill purported to define the "Elements and Composition of the Canadian Federation." As part of the effort to make the constitution an inclusive description of our system of government, it described our head of state (the Queen), our flag, and our motto (*a mari usque ad mare*). Most of this was uncontroversial. When it turned to describing the office and functions of the Governor General, however, it ruffled more feathers. The Governor General was specifically to have precedence as "First Canadian," an idea that attracted some derision. One controversial provision specified that the Governor General was Commander in Chief. (In spite of the fact that this had been so provided in the Letters Patent issued by the monarch to define the role of Governors General of Canada since at least 1931, the proposal was met with paranoid concerns that a Canadian Prime Minister, having arranged the appointment of his willing stooge as Governor General, would somehow illicitly gain an authority over Canada's Armed Forces that, I must confess, I have always hoped that the head of our elected government already had.)

There were many other provisions concerning the Executive Government of Canada that sought to describe the current reality of our institutions that were either not mentioned in the original *British North America Act, 1867* or whose functions were not explained there. In some cases more meaningful titles were applied to old institutions. The Privy Council would have become the Council of State of Canada. The Cabinet would for the first time be mentioned in the constitution as a committee of the Council of State with its composition explained. For the first time an attempt was made to spell out constitutional conventions on the roles of the Prime Minister and the Governor General in case a government lost the confidence of Parliament. (I will return to this later as it seems we misdescribed one of the conventions.)

As for Parliament, little new was added concerning the House of Commons. But in respect of the Senate, that *soi-disant* Chamber of Sober Second Thought would have been abolished and replaced by the House of the Federation. In devising this change, we tried to implement a concept for an Upper House that we thought most consistent with our history: the need for better representation of regional (but not necessarily provincial government) views at the national level, without setting up

a chamber with the same political legitimacy as, and powers equal to, the House of Commons. First we gave more seats to the Atlantic and the Western provinces than they have in the Senate, increasing the former by 2 to 32 and the latter by 12 to 36 (reflecting the great growth in population and wealth of those four provinces since their respective entries into Confederation). Most importantly we wanted members of this House to reflect current popular opinion across the country unrestrained by the kind of party discipline that must prevail in the House of Commons to enable a government to have the confidence of that House as it must to stay in office. Therefore, instead of having ordinary direct elections for members of the House of the Federation, elections that would normally fall under the control of the usual party systems, members of this House were to be chosen for each province by these means: one-half by provincial legislatures on the basis of the distribution of votes by party in the last provincial election, and one-half by the House of Commons on the basis of the distribution of votes by party in that province in the last federal election. It was our view that this method of selection would introduce an element of proportional representation into our existing system (which typically allows parties with less than 40 per cent of the popular vote to run monolithic regimes), and because the distribution of seats would vary from one election to another, it would reflect contemporary political preferences (not, as in the existing Senate, whose members are the choice of a present, or many past, Prime Minister(s) reflecting varying political views over perhaps two or three past decades). But because the members of the House would be thus chosen by indirect election, they would not be able to assert a political legitimacy equal to the members of the House of Commons directly elected by the public. Consistent with this approach, we gave the House of the Federation only a suspensive veto over measures approved by the Commons, with one exception: any measure concerning the use of either of the two official languages would have to be approved in the House of the Federation by a majority of English-speaking members and a majority of French-speaking members in that House.

In discussions in Cabinet on June 7, 1978, just a few days before the tabling of Bill C-60, the Prime Minister responded to criticisms from some ministers who feared such a House of the Federation would make government difficult or impossible. Trudeau responded in part as follows: "*The Prime Minister* noted that the government was attempting

to change the power relationship in the country by bringing the regions to Parliament Hill. He fully agreed that it represented a gamble but the alternative was the decentralization and fragmentation of the country. With the regions represented at the centre, he believed that the debate on division of powers would be more rational."[15] In effect he was arguing that if regional points of view were seen to be promoted in the Upper House by persons who represented current public opinion in the regions, Premiers would not be perceived as the only legitimate spokesmen for those interests in national affairs. Thus their role, and the importance of federal-provincial conferences as a means of consultation by the federal government on matters of regional concern, would be diminished. The perceived legitimacy of decisions taken by such a bicameral Parliament would be greatly enhanced.

I was always proud of this nuanced proposal for Senate reform. It seemed to me it re-emphasized the purpose of regional representation that had informed the original concept in the *British North America Act, 1867*, a concept that has been largely displaced by the requirements of party government in the House of Commons. Our proposal would have made possible regional representation in Parliament to include many smaller parties reflecting contemporary political thought: imagine the diversity this could bring to debates and committee work in the Upper House! Yet, save in the matter of official languages, the indirectly elected Upper House would not have a veto over the representation-by-population members of the House of Commons. This approach in my view was and remains far superior to most proposals for Senate reform, which include simplistic notions such as direct election of senators, equal representation for all provinces, and powers equal to those of the House of Commons, including a complete veto over Commons measures (said to be the means to make the Senate "effective"). These proposals are apparently based on a rather mindless embrace of the United States Senate model, which is part of a seriously flawed system that frequently results in deadlock. Unfortunately, as I will later explain, this proposal in Bill C-60 never received the attention it deserved because of attacks on the federal assumption that Parliament could alter the Senate without provincial approval as part of its power under section 91, head 1 of the *British North America Act, 1867* to amend the "Constitution of Canada." This provision up until then had been thought to authorize amendments by Parliament of the institutions of the central

government and had been so employed successfully on several occasions, including many changing the distribution of members in the House of Commons and the means for their election.

In the proposed new constitution were included, for the sake of completeness, provisions concerning the executive governments and legislatures of provinces. The Bill clearly indicated with an asterisk that such provisions could only be adopted by or with the consent of provincial legislatures. Yet there were some provisions concerning the office of Lieutenant-Governor that the provinces could not at that time amend. We had added one such provision giving the Governor General in Council a new power, to exercise at the request of a province, to appoint an administrator for the province to perform the functions of the Lieutenant-Governor during the absence or incapacity of the latter, or when the office of Lieutenant-Governor was vacant. While provision is made federally for such an administrator to act in place of the Governor General, or during a vacancy in that office, there was not, nor is there today, any comparable provision in the case of a vacancy in the office of Lieutenant-Governor. Not long after we unsuccessfully debated with the provinces the adoption of such a provision, I had a good illustration of the need for this change. One morning I had a call from Esmond Butler, Secretary to the Governor General. He asked me to call the Secretary of the Lieutenant-Governor of Saskatchewan, whose employer had died suddenly the previous day. There had been some important regulations recently adopted by the provincial cabinet and sent to the Lieutenant-Governor for signature. He died without signing them. The government was very anxious to put the regulations into effect as they involved millions of dollars in tax revenues on oil production. The Chief Justice of the province, who also held the title of Deputy Lieutenant-Governor, was prepared to sign, but the Secretary sought advice as to whether this was legally possible. I phoned her and discussed the matter. Fortunately, I knew what the advice of the Department of Justice had been since Confederation: indeed, I had seen a copy of an opinion on the matter signed by Sir John A. Macdonald when he held the post of Minister of Justice along with that of Prime Minister shortly after Confederation. That advice was that in the absence of a living Lieutenant-Governor, his deputy ceased to have any authority to act in his place. I think my advice caused much chagrin in the office of the Chief Justice and the Attorney General of the province. Soon I had a call from

Roy Meldrum, Constitutional Adviser to the Saskatchewan Government and a former Deputy Attorney General for whom I had once worked. He was at first incredulous that such could be the case, but I explained the reasoning of the Department going back to the time of Sir John A. I ended by saying "Don't call me, Roy, phone the Prime Minister's Office and ask for a quick replacement for the Lieutenant-Governor!" Within a few days there was a new Lieutenant-Governor.

Bill C-60 reproduced the same distribution of powers provisions as were found in the *British North America Act, 1867*, except for a new limitation on the rights of both federal and provincial legislatures to amend their own internal constitutions so as to prevent them from infringing on the new political rights proposed to be included in the *Bill of Rights*. Care was taken not to prejudge further negotiations on the distribution of powers, this part of the constitution being carefully flagged as subject to agreement with the provinces; nevertheless, we did not avoid acrimony. We had dropped section 109 of the 1867 Act, a section confirming continuing provincial ownership of provincial lands at the time of Confederation. We believed the effects of this transitional section to have been exhausted by the passage of time and in the interests of modernization had not repeated it in the new formulation. Some provinces—Alberta being one of the most aggressive on this point—saw this as a Machiavellian federal plot to seize provincial lands and protested vehemently.

Bill C-60 went on to introduce some completely new constitutional provisions: a commitment for easing regional disparities; mechanisms for conduct of federal-provincial relations; and, for the first time, rules for the existence, appointment of the judges, and jurisdiction, of the Supreme Court of Canada. These included elaborate provisions for participation by provincial governments in the appointment of judges.

Finally, the Bill had complicated provisions for its implementation. The essential approach here was that if approved by Parliament, the Bill would be deemed to have changed the constitution with respect to those matters within Parliament's power to amend; approval of the Bill in respect of other matters would be deemed to be a resolution by Parliament in favour of such constitutional amendments that would be subject to similar approval by legislatures in accordance with some future amending procedure. The whole initiative was of course based on the premise that before Parliament approved Bill C-60 there would have been intensive

discussions on the contents, reaching a consensus with the provinces on those texts requiring provincial consent.

It was the Prime Minister's intent with this Bill to revive fundamental constitutional discussions for the purpose of, to use the White Paper's language, "the renewal of the Canadian Federation." It was hoped that the federal government would regain the initiative on constitutional reform in the face of the implicit threat from the election of a separatist party in Quebec. Discussion it certainly did provoke, but we were not prepared for the degree of hostility coming from most provinces, and from federalist senators, members of Parliament, and academics. There was a widespread and persistent view that the Bill concealed a variety of hidden agendas threatening the Crown and provincial powers and property. This hostility played out mainly in two parliamentary committees established to examine the bill. It soon also became manifest in federal-provincial discussions at the official and ministerial level.

Bill C-60 was tabled on June 20, 1978, and before the end of that month two parliamentary committees were established to study it: the Special Joint Committee of the Senate and House of Commons on the Constitution of Canada (the Joint Committee) and the Special Committee of the Senate on the Constitution of Canada (the Senate Committee). I appeared with federal ministers throughout most of the public sessions of the Joint Committee, and as the lead representative of the government, without ministers, before the Senate Committee. At that time it was not customary for ministers to appear before Senate committees. This left me, with the able assistance of various lawyers from my branch, to explain to the senators why the Senate should be abolished and replaced with the House of the Federation.

Without prolonging the details of these hearings, which occupied much of the hottest weather during the summer of 1978 and several all-day and evening sessions, I will briefly describe a few of the main issues. There was of course no paucity of criticism of the drafting. In fairness, one could say that the drafting was overly technical in places and not particularly inspirational in tone: not surprising, perhaps, because the principal drafter was recognized as one of the best and most experienced authors of income tax legislation. We knew that technically it was an outstanding draft, but the language did not exactly sing. That aside, one of the big issues was the perceived undermining of the monarchy. We were accused of *lese-majesté*

for having tried to "Canadianize" the monarchy by spelling out the reality that it is the Governor General who performs all important functions of the head of state in Canada. Thus we defined Parliament as consisting of the Governor General (not the Queen as in the *BNA Act, 1867*), the Senate, and the House of Commons; we vested the Executive Government in the "Governor General of Canada, on behalf of and in the name of the Queen" instead of simply vesting it in the Queen, as did the *BNA Act, 1867*; and we made the Governor General the Commander in Chief of the Canadian Forces (while the *BNA Act, 1867* had made the Queen the Commander in Chief). From the issues with which we were confronted, both in the parliamentary committees and in federal-provincial meetings, I was surprised by the number of adult Canadians who seemed to think that the Queen regularly devotes part of her normal day to managing the affairs of her Dominion of Canada. In fact, by now about the only decision the Queen makes with respect to our governance is who the Governor General will be, and she does this on the advice of her Canadian Prime Minister.

I experienced a clash (one of many) with Senator Forsey in the Senate Committee on the subject of the Crown. I had known Eugene Forsey since 1953, when he was one of the faculty and I was a student at a World University Service of Canada (WUSC) seminar in India. At that time he was Research Director for the Canadian Labour Congress on loan to WUSC, and was a long-time member of the Co-operative Commonwealth Federation (CCF), the democratic socialist formation that was the predecessor of the New Democratic Party (NDP). I was also a member then of the CCF and I thought this established a certain affinity between us. At an amateur night in Mysore, India, where we were entertaining our hosts, I joined a group led by Forsey singing boisterous socialist songs. He was particularly well known at that time for his ability to mimic Mackenzie King and other politicians.

Here in Ottawa, 25 years later, Forsey was sitting as a Liberal Senator, appointed by a Liberal Prime Minister with whom he had an intellectual affinity, particularly in matters of national unity. And there was I, whose only party allegiance had ever been CCF or NDP but having been attracted to Ottawa by a Liberal Minister of Justice, Pierre Trudeau, with whom I also found I had an affinity on national unity questions. None of this tempered Forsey's scathing attacks on this legislative initiative of that same Prime Minister nor on me, the messenger, who was there to explain and defend

Trudeau's project. His attacks were not confined to the committee room; he took every opportunity to broadcast his trenchant views to journalists in the corridors who knew he was always good for a quotable quote. This was an arena in which a public servant had no place. Forsey was a brilliant, wise, and usually charitable person, and could be an amusing companion, but he had a strong belief in his own constitutional expertise. Although he always prefaced his constitutional pronouncements with the self-deprecating "of course I'm not a constitutional lawyer, but," he never hesitated to give a constitutional opinion, and an emphatic one at that. As a political scientist who had written his thesis on the power of the Governor General to refuse dissolution of Parliament,[16] he did have a profound knowledge of constitutional history and conventions. I had the feeling that summer that he was really affronted because some bureaucrats had the temerity to try to define the conventions in a legal text without consulting him. I was well briefed for most of his assaults but he bested me once. I had been explaining to the Senate Committee that it was the long-standing opinion of the Department of Justice that when the Queen is in Canada she cannot perform the function of giving royal assent to Acts of our Parliament. This conclusion was based on the language of the *British North America Act, 1867*, section 55 which says that when a bill passed by both Houses is presented to the Governor General, he must either assent in the Queen's name or state that he withholds her assent. It was our view that the Imperial Act had specifically designated the Governor General to perform this function, not the Queen. I also pointed out that this was the same interpretation as the Government of Australia gave to a similar term in its constitution; in fact, in that country they had adopted a special law providing that when the monarch is in Australia, he or she may perform the same functions as their Governor General. After my little explanation, Forsey snapped, "George VI gave assent to six bills in Ottawa in May, 1939!" I could only undertake to look into it. That night my lawyers discovered that, indeed, His Majesty had given such assent during the Royal Tour in May 1939. After further research in which I became satisfied that the six resulting Acts were of a minor nature whose force had been spent well before 1978, I reported back to the Committee as follows: it was true that such assent had been given but that we could find no advice given by the Department that such was legally correct, and that our opinion remained as before. My own guess was that Justice was not consulted at the time and

King George simply acted on the advice of Prime Minister William Lyon Mackenzie King. Some years before, I had had occasion to go through many of the Privy Council Office files on the Royal Tour of 1939, and it was apparent that Mackenzie King's ardent wish was to be seen during this, the first tour of Canada of a reigning monarch, as enjoying the same role of first adviser to the King as his British Prime Minister would perform were the King back in London. To this end I'm sure it appeared entirely appropriate that the King should give royal assent to bills of the Canadian Parliament while in Ottawa. I would also guess that Mackenzie King chose not to consult his Minister of Justice on such a matter.

The only other loss I suffered at Forsey's hands, in my view, related to the way we had tried to express in Bill C-60 the advice that a resigning Prime Minister can give to the Governor General. We expressed what we thought was the convention in this form: if the Government is defeated in the House of Commons, the Prime Minster should so inform the Governor General and advise him or her whether the House should be dissolved and a new election held. This was uncontroversial but we went on to say that, as an alternative, the Prime Minister could, "if the dissolution of Parliament on that account is not advised by the Prime Minister or is refused by the Governor General, [advise] whether the Prime Minister should be invited to form another administration, or whether the resignation of the Prime Minister and of the other members of the Cabinet should be accepted to permit some person other than himself or herself to be called upon by the Governor General to form the administration for the time being of Canada."[17] Forsey latched onto this and insisted it misstated the conventions, and in this I think he was right. A further review indicated, according to most opinions on the subject, that a Prime Minister defeated in the House must advise dissolution, and if that advice is rejected by the Governor General, then the Prime Minister must resign and he has no right or duty to express an opinion on whether he or someone else should be invited to form a new government. Whether or not it had been thought when our proposal was drafted that the formulation in Bill C-60 would improve on the functioning of government, it could not be defended as simply the status quo.

There was a certain amount of duplication in the debate in the Joint Committee with that in the Senate Committee. But one of the major issues before the Joint Committee was the jurisdiction of Parliament to alter the

institutions of the central government without approval of the provinces, the most controversial changes being those in respect of the Senate. Otto Lang, back serving as Minister of Justice in addition to his Transport portfolio, delivered to the Joint Committee an opinion that I had prepared and he had approved. We based our case for the jurisdiction of Parliament on section 91, head 1, which grants it the power to legislate in respect of the following: "The amendment from time to time of the Constitution of Canada, except as regards matters coming within the classes of subjects by this Act assigned exclusively to the Legislatures of the provinces, or as regards rights or privileges by this or any other Constitutional Act granted or secured to the Legislature or the Government of a province.... [Other exceptions were not relevant to the Senate.]" It was our thesis that changes to the composition, powers, and method of selection of senators had nothing to do with the legislative subjects assigned exclusively to the provinces, nor to any "rights or privileges" of any provincial *government* or *legislature*. The Senate was not the creature of the provinces, nor does it represent provincial governments or legislatures; it represents regions of the country not necessarily geographically coterminous with particular provinces, and it is chosen by means that are federal, not provincial. I think that the logic and the text of the constitution were on our side, but in that summer of discontent sentiment was against us. The committee called other witnesses and preferred their advice. One of the most influential was Dean W.R. Lederman, of Queen's University, a distinguished constitutional lawyer (and, along with Otto and myself, a graduate of the universities of Saskatchewan and Oxford). Bill Lederman had for years been able to find hidden, implied principles in the constitution that more literal positivists such as myself could not find. His presentation to the Committee, essentially, was that provincial legislatures and governments do have some sort of mystical interests in the Senate, a federal legislative body. He was sufficiently persuasive that the Joint Committee recommended that there be referred to the Supreme Court, among other issues, the question of whether or not Parliament could unilaterally alter the Senate in this way (assuming, of course, that senators could be persuaded to vote for such a measure). My greatest disillusionment with politics as I watched this vote came from seeing Stanley Knowles, venerable NDP Member of Parliament, champion of the pensioners and the little guy, vote along with the others for this reference to the Supreme Court. I had

long been an admirer of Mr Knowles and had indeed benefited from his support when I was national president of the Co-operative Commonwealth University Federation in 1953 and 1954. But here was this saint in politics, this paragon of rectitude, voting for such a reference even though almost every year from his first arrival in Parliament in 1942 he had introduced a bill to abolish the Senate! During all those years he apparently had had no qualms about Parliament's power to do just that—to go further than our proposals in Bill C-60.

A few days after this resolution passed, I attended a meeting about it in the Prime Minister's Office in the Langevin Building across Wellington Street from the Parliament Buildings. He was there because the House was not in session. He sat at a desk originally belonging to Sir John A. Macdonald, our first Prime Minister. It was a beautiful sunny morning in August and, as we finished, the Governor General's Foot Guards were approaching to perform the Changing of the Guard in front of the Centre Block of the Parliament Buildings. Also present were Gordon Robertson, Secretary of Cabinet for Federal-Provincial Relations, and Otto Lang, Minister of Justice. My consistent advice was not to take a reference to the Supreme Court. I said that the text of the Constitution was adequately clear as to Parliament's jurisdiction to revise the Senate. I argued that the kind of analysis given by Bill Lederman, which seemingly had impressed the Committee, was based on extra-constitutional considerations—a web of alleged conventions or practices that supposedly gave provincial governments or legislatures some veto over Senate changes. As such, I said, such considerations were essentially political, and to refer the question to the Supreme Court would politicize the Court. (That was in the days when I assumed the Court did not *want* to be politicized.) I also felt that if the amendments to the Senate were passed, with the support of the Senate, the Court would be much less likely to question them—but if asked to give its prior approval, the Court would be more likely to find the path beset by lions. In the end, however, the Prime Minister felt it was not politically feasible to proceed without such a reference. The reference was held and we lost.[18] I believe this was the beginning of an activist trend in the Supreme Court in constitutional matters that continues to this day.

I had a hand in the drafting of the reference questions for the Court. It should first be noted that the Court was asked whether or not such amendments *would be within the legislative authority* of Parliament, not

whether it would be nice or wise or contrary to political practices (conventions) to make such changes without the consent of the provinces. Yet in deciding what was within Parliament's legislative authority, the Court declined to apply the precise words of section 91, head 1, which gave Parliament jurisdiction to amend "the Constitution of Canada" except (for present purposes) in respect of those matters coming within "the classes of subjects...assigned exclusively to the Legislatures of the provinces" or as regarding "rights or privileges...granted or secured to the Legislature or the Government of a province." These were the only matters excepted by the written constitution from Parliament's power to amend it unilaterally. The Court instead indulged in the pursuit of non-textual or implied limits on Parliament's power, notwithstanding the fact that the UK Parliament in adopting section 91, head 1, had not imposed such limits. In the first place, it found in effect that "the Constitution of Canada" did not include the whole of the *British North America Act, 1867*. Admittedly, the term *Canada* can have different meanings, depending on the context. But the Court insisted that "Constitution of Canada" meant only the "constitution of the central executive government" and some parts (but not all) of the national legislature of Canada. If this is so, the UK Parliament was extraordinarily careless to use the loose language it did, as these are very significant limitations on the term *Constitution of Canada*. One must also wonder why, if the UK Parliament understood its words to be so limited, it added all the exceptions such as the powers, rights, and privileges of the provinces, as quoted above. If these had to be specifically excepted, and there was no qualification such as "for greater certainty," one is tempted to think that such matters were otherwise believed to be covered by the term *Constitution of Canada*: the normal rule of interpretation is that "the exception proves the rule" or, as we used to say at Oxford "*exceptio probat regulam de rebus non exceptis.*"

The Court then looked to constitutional practice to conclude that, in addition to the narrow view it took of section 91, head 1, Parliament could not unilaterally make such changes in the Senate. It satisfied itself by finding that Senate reform "affected federal-provincial relationships," and any such change could be made by Parliament only with consultation and prior agreement with the provinces. For this Damascean insight the Court relied on the federal paper[19] published in 1965 to justify the then-pending Fulton-Favreau Formula, a proposed amending formula that was never in

fact adopted. In a summary of previous amendment practices it concluded with a statement of some general principles based on past practice, one of which was that "Parliament will not request an amendment directly affecting federal-provincial relationships without prior consultation and agreement with the provinces." This statement was hedged about with various qualifications. And of course it did not purport to state a legal rule but rather to describe a political practice. Its whole purpose was political—to sell this product. But the Court used this 1965 pronouncement to interpret the meaning of section 91, head 1, enacted some 16 years earlier![20]

While purporting to give a legal interpretation of Parliament's legislative authority, the Court relied on all manner of extra-legal considerations. And at the base of its reasoning was the assumption that only provincial governments and legislatures can be relied on to determine and defend regional interests. The people—as represented through their Members of Parliament—cannot be trusted with something so important, even though nowhere in the constitution are provincial legislatures and governments assigned rights or interests in these matters. The Court was implicitly adopting the thesis of Quebec nationalists that the interests of Quebecers can only be represented by the government and legislature of Quebec.

Thus ended the initiative to reform the Senate. No doubt the scheme for the House of the Federation had its imperfections. The sad thing is that instead of parliamentarians and representatives of the provinces earnestly addressing the problems we were trying to resolve, and refining the federal proposal to produce an agreement on fundamental reform, the whole debate was derailed by the question of federal jurisdiction to reform the Senate. As a result, we have endured a further 30 years of an appointed Senate with tenure of senators until age 75, a body with legislative powers essentially equal to those of the elected House of Commons.

RENEWED FEDERAL-PROVINCIAL DISCUSSIONS

One of the main purposes of the White Paper *A Time for Action* and Bill C-60 was to bring about some fundamental constitutional discussions that would be a sign of the renewal of federalism in the nervous period between the election of the PQ in Quebec and the holding of their anticipated referendum on separation. In this effort the federal initiatives were successful, even if the discussions were not exactly what we had anticipated.

Shortly after the publication of these documents, we went in late June

to a meeting of senior federal and provincial officials in Halifax for a pre-liminary discussion on how talks might proceed. The initial provincial First Ministers' response came after the annual meeting of the Premiers at Regina in August. Premier Allan Blakeney of Saskatchewan, as Conference Chairman, wrote to Prime Minister Trudeau on August 22, 1978, forward-ing to him the Conference Communiqué and his comments thereon.[21] With respect to constitutional matters, the Premiers had affirmed their belief in the importance of constitutional reform and looked forward to a First Ministers' Meeting on the constitution scheduled for the following October. But Premier Blakeney reported that the Premiers had serious doubts about the authority of Parliament to move unilaterally, as contem-plated in Bill C-60. They opposed what they regarded as changes in the office of the Crown and Governor General and the changes proposed in respect of the Senate. They rejected the federal government's proposed timetable for constitutional revision. Additionally, he reminded Trudeau that the Premiers had in 1976, in response to Trudeau's proposal for early action on patriation and an amending formula, proposed that in addition many other constitutional matters be addressed as follows: immigration, language rights, resource taxation, the federal declaratory power, the an-nual Conference of First Ministers, creation of new provinces, culture, communications, Supreme Court of Canada, the federal spending power, and regional disparities and equalization. (When faced with this list of mostly distribution of powers issues, Trudeau had at that time abandoned hope for an early agreement on patriation alone). Blakeney reported that the Premiers felt there had been no adequate response by the federal government in 1976 to this provincial consensus on what needed to be discussed. In his reply[22] of September 13, 1978, Trudeau—while denying that his proposed timetable was too rigid—emphasized that his govern-ment "does, however[,] feel that some effective start should be made on constitutional change at the earliest possible moment, and in any event, *before* the electors of Quebec are called upon by their provincial govern-ment to choose between political independence on the one hand, and on the other, the preservation of a status quo which federal and provincial governments have proved incapable of changing despite 51 years of effort." He went on to say that his government wanted a full exchange of views on constitutional reform and recognized that agreement is desirable: "The question is whether, if the complete agreement of all provinces cannot

Constitutional Conference, October–November 1978. Left to right—front row: Roy McMurtry, Attorney General of Ontario; Premier of Ontario William Davis; Otto Lang, federal Minister of Transport; Rt. Hon. Pierre Trudeau, Prime Minister. Second row: the author; Roger Tassé, Deputy Minister of Justice; Gordon Robertson, Cabinet Secretary. Third row, directly behind author: Fred Jordan, Department of Justice. Fifth row, left end: Stuart MacKinnon, Department of Justice.

be achieved, nothing whatever can be done—as nothing has been done in eight previous attempts to achieve major and far-reaching agreements on constitutional change, undertaken by six Prime Ministers of Canada, starting in 1927." He explained that for this reason his government had set a target of one year in which to implement those constitutional changes that were within Parliament's exclusive authority.

He went on to defend the proposed provisions concerning the Crown as merely descriptive of current reality and in no way constituting a change. While the government had already announced that a reference would be taken to the Supreme Court on the powers of Parliament to reform the Senate, he had no doubts about Parliament's jurisdiction but was acceding to the parliamentary committee's recommendation as "it seems undesirable to allow allegations of uncertainty in this regard to continue to impede concentration on the substance of the question of a second chamber in a revised Constitution." As for the subjects listed in the 1976 communiqué that the Premiers still wanted to discuss, Trudeau said that several were already covered in the Bill C-60 proposals, and that his government was prepared to discuss the rest. He indicated clearly that he was prepared to

discuss the distribution of powers generally, something that he had for years been reluctant to do.

The planned meeting of First Ministers on the Constitution was held from October 30 through November 1, 1978. To give it a special gravitas, many others were invited: leaders of the federal Opposition, some senators, MPs and members of provincial legislatures, members of the Pépin-Roberts Task Force on Canadian Unity, Aboriginal representatives, and representatives of the Federation of Municipalities of Canada. The purpose was to highlight the importance attached to constitutional reform and the seriousness of the effort being undertaken to achieve it, all to impress Quebec voters who, within a year or two, would be called upon to vote in a referendum on that province's future within or without Canada. The First Ministers in their communiqué at the end of the meeting agreed on the urgency of constitutional change and on the need for all governments to devote the necessary resources and to take a flexible approach. A Continuing Committee of Ministers was established to carry on negotiations and report back to the First Ministers before their next Constitutional Conference.

There then followed three months of intensive work for ministers and their officials. We met in Mont Ste. Marie, Quebec (a resort about an hour's drive north of Ottawa), in Toronto, Ottawa, and Vancouver. These meetings were to prepare the ground for the next First Ministers' Constitutional Conference to be held on February 5 and 6, 1979. The details of the discussions are now not important, other than providing the background for the critical discussions after the "No" side won the Quebec Referendum, to be discussed in the next chapter.

In retrospect I believe these sessions, held between November 1978 and February 1979, were, for me, the most depressing. Our bargaining position was weakening for two reasons: first, the concern felt strongly by the federal delegation about the need for real progress before the pending referendum was not always shared by many of the provinces, and second, the Trudeau government was in a politically tenuous position, being in the fifth year of its mandate, facing an inevitable election soon, and being down in the polls. In the circumstances we were obliged to discuss seriously large areas of the distribution of powers, with all proposals being for the enlargement of provincial powers. The only federal proposal was for a charter that would limit both federal and provincial powers;

for this we got no provincial support at that time. As for an amending procedure, the Victoria Formula favoured by the federal government, and approved in 1971 by all provinces, was under attack. Even the weather was depressing for most of these meetings. At Mont Ste. Marie in late November, shortly after we arrived in cars, there was a severe ice storm, with freezing rain making the highway impassable; even walking outside the hotel was dangerous. Federal ministers who came late or left early had to travel to and from Ottawa by helicopter. In Toronto in December it was exceptionally cold for that city. In Vancouver in January it was dark and rainy most of the time. Needless to say, we were far from agreement when the time came to report to First Ministers in early February. On top of all this, the Task Force on Canadian Unity issued its report while we were in Vancouver. That report provided no comfort for the federal delegation. Based on its analysis of Canada as being shaped principally by regionalism and duality (linguistic and cultural), it recommended a recasting of the distribution of powers with major shifts to the benefit of the provinces. The report recommended that residual powers be given to the provinces (in theory, at least, the existing Constitution gives them to Parliament), and that the Senate should be replaced by a body appointed by the provinces. Worse still, in Mr Trudeau's eyes, was the recommendation that we should countenance an asymmetrical union where provinces, notably Quebec, would enjoy special status. The federal government gave this but cursory consideration and constitutional discussions went on as before, although some provinces liked to quote from the Task Force Report ideas that suited their case.

The report of the Continuing Committee of Ministers on the Constitution to the First Ministers for their meeting of February 5 and 6, 1979, included the following items. On an amending formula, the federal government had moved as far as to present a tentative draft somewhat in keeping with the pattern of the Fulton-Favreau Formula. Alberta reportedly preferred an opt-out provision whereby an amendment that required unanimous consent could still take effect without unanimity but would not apply to a province or provinces that refused assent. This provision ultimately found a place in subsection 38(3) of the *Constitution Act, 1982*.[23] There were several "best-efforts" drafts representing some kind of consensus in the Continuing Committee of Ministers on the Constitution that were submitted for consideration by First Ministers.

One best-efforts draft concerned Resource Ownership and Inter-provincial Trade. This was an extremely important topic for Alberta and Saskatchewan. Their attitude throughout (and apparently it remains so today) is that things extracted from provincial ground are provincial prop-erty or permanently subject solely to provincial control or taxation; more-over, they should not be subject to federal control or taxation. The federal view was that once minerals are extracted, sold, and enter the stream of commerce, they are commodities subject to federal taxation and federal jurisdiction over interprovincial and international trade. Saskatchewan in particular resented this position and protested two Supreme Court of Canada decisions striking down a provincial oil income tax and controls on the export of potash.[24] On the other hand, the Government of Canada, which had intervened in both these cases to argue against the provincial position, was demonstrating a renewed concern about the preservation of a common market within Canada and a defence of the much-ignored federal power over interprovincial and international commerce. I had become aware of such concerns after coming to Ottawa and joined in support of the federal trade and commerce power. I and my branch had assisted in the constitutional interventions in these two cases. I regret to say that my home province and Alberta characterized such initiatives as a "smash and grab" raid on their natural resources,[25] and they wanted ad-ditional powers to prevent a repetition. Thus we spent many days trying to enlarge provincial control over exports: the draft would have given the provinces jurisdiction over the export of non-renewable natural resources and forestry products, with provincial laws being paramount over federal laws relating to interprovincial (but not international) trade and commerce unless such a federal law could be shown to serve a "compelling national interest." This would have been a major concession by the federal govern-ment and we also remained concerned that such provincial export controls could involve discrimination against certain other provinces.

Another best-efforts draft would have given provinces power over in-direct taxation, provided that its implementation could not be used in effect to create import or export duties or be primarily designed to pass on tax burdens to non-residents of the province.

A best-efforts draft would have put the structure and jurisdiction of the Supreme Court in the constitution and required consultation with provincial attorneys-general before an appointment of a judge was made.

A particularly salient concession of Parliament's powers was pro- posed under the rubric "Family Law": it would have turned over to the provinces complete jurisdiction over marriage and divorce, except that Parliament would be able to legislate on the recognition of provincial divorces throughout the country.

There was proposed a constitutional commitment to equalization and regional development. While on its face this engaged both federal and provincial responsibility, there was little doubt that if such a section had any force at all, the principal burden would be on Ottawa. There was also a proposed limitation on Parliament's power to declare intraprovincial works (such as grain elevators or uranium mines) to be for the general advantage of Canada.

Apart from these best-efforts drafts that showed major tentative conces- sions by the federal government, seemingly with some degree of provincial acceptance, there were a few other proposals by the federal government that were considered by the First Ministers. Communications was at that time the subject of much controversy: Quebec in particular saw telecom- munications as an essential part of its cultural mission. The courts had, however, found that Parliament had exclusive jurisdiction over radio and television and cable television transmission and, over the largest telephone systems in the country as well. The proposal proffered by the federal gov- ernment in early 1979 would have given the provinces concurrent power over cable television distribution (then the cutting-edge technology), with provincial paramountcy over federal laws except where the latter concerned Canadian content and technical standards.

In those days, when offshore oil exploration near Newfoundland was very promising, there was still a hotly contested debate about who had the right of exploitation of that offshore resource: Newfoundland or Canada. Newfoundland wanted to regulate as well as profit from that exploitation. There was a strong belief in Ottawa that it was the federal government that had the necessary jurisdiction and ownership. By international law, in our view, the relatively new continental shelf doctrine—about to be enhanced by the United Nations Convention on the Law of the Sea then under negotiation—gave the right of exploitation to adjacent sovereign states. But Newfoundland had elaborate historical claims: it had once been a self-governing Dominion before it went into receivership in 1934 and reverted to a kind of colonial status under British tutelage. There was

a widespread, somewhat mystical, belief that Newfoundland had resumed Dominion status one minute before midnight when it joined Canada on March 31, 1949. Thus, it was said, Newfoundland had the same rights as sovereign nations have under the law of the sea to exploit its offshore. They could not be disabused of this notion until the Supreme Court of Canada decided in 1984 that it was Canada, not Newfoundland, that held those sovereign rights.[26] (Given current political rhetoric, one would never detect that Newfoundland is not the owner of, or lacks sovereign authority over, those resources that lie *beside* its territory, to the same extent that Saskatchewan or Alberta own or control the resources that lie *under* their territory.) So, in an effort to meet pressures from Newfoundland, a federal proposal would have conferred concurrent jurisdiction to coastal provinces concerning the *management* of offshore resources "without prejudice to the ownership of the resources in question." Certain areas for paramountcy of federal laws were prescribed.

Finally, the federal delegation had submitted a draft Charter, revised from the version that had appeared in Bill C-60. There was of course no best-efforts draft of a Charter because no province was prepared to commit itself in principle to such an instrument. As this was the only "gain" that the federal government sought in this round of negotiation, it naturally wanted to ensure that a Charter proposal was still on the agenda of First Ministers.

The First Ministers' Conference that met February 5–6, 1979, was, needless to say, inconclusive. No one was prepared to make a final commitment on any of the drafts. Trudeau was being pressed by Premiers who knew he had to call an election within weeks. He did sound conciliatory on many matters, and many provincial delegations left with the feeling that we were on the verge of some major federal concessions. Matters were referred back to the Continuing Committee of Ministers for further work.

One idea that gained some respectability at this time was the possibility of a Charter with an override or notwithstanding clause, permitting a declaration in a law that infringed the Charter would apply notwithstanding the Charter. It was Premier Lougheed of Alberta who suggested it: it appeared he had borrowed the idea from section 2 of the *Canadian Bill of Rights, 1960*,[27] which contemplated that any Act of Parliament could override the *Bill* if it specifically stated that it was to apply "notwithstanding the *Canadian Bill of Rights.*" This possibility had also been noted for

consideration in Pierre Trudeau's publication of 1968, *A Canadian Charter of Rights*,[28] which I had drafted in the summer of 1967. As is now well-known, this device became the deal-maker in November 1981 when nine provinces agreed to have a Charter if it contained the "notwithstanding clause" now found in section 33 of that document.

There was some unease in the federal cabinet after this Conference. Some ministers were said to believe that the Prime Minister had made too many concessions, tentative though they might have been. It was even suggested that Trudeau had "given away the farm." In the weeks that followed, there was little ministerial attention for constitutional affairs as the government prepared for an election.

I escaped the worst of the remaining winter by going to the Republic of Seychelles, an Indian Ocean archipelago on the equator several hundred miles off the coast of Kenya. It is a member of the Commonwealth and there had been a coup d'état there in 1977. The new President had promised to have elections under a new constitution within two years. A large commission had been holding hearings around the islands and had a list of recommendations for the constitution. But time was running out and they needed help to draft it. The Commonwealth Secretariat in London asked Canada that I be loaned for the purpose. I worked there for three weeks with a professional draftsman. We then forwarded the draft to the President. The next day my driver took us to the President's Palace where we met with His Excellency. After a discussion of an hour or so, and a few minor changes in the draft, we left. Three weeks later he proclaimed it as the new constitution and elections were held. My last efforts had been to leave a lengthy memorandum addressing the steps required to put the new constitution into operation. I realized afterward that cleaning up after coups is a thriving industry in Africa. One wag told me that in the former French African colonies they have a saying: "Chacun à son coup."

Back in Canada, the election occurred on May 22, 1979, and the Progressive Conservatives under Joe Clark were called upon to form a minority government, with 136 seats compared to the Liberals' 114. Constitutional reform was not at that time a high priority for the Clark government, which naturally wanted to familiarize itself with more pressing issues and to put its own mark on national policies. Those of us in the bureaucracy concerned with constitutional reform did come to understand that this government wished to be more conciliatory toward

the provinces in most matters. The only federal-provincial constitutional meetings held during the Clark administration were two meetings of the Continuing Committee of Ministers on the Constitution, held in Halifax in October 1979 and in Toronto in November 1979. At Halifax it was noted that the February Conference of First Ministers had identified 14 subjects for discussion and the Committee sought to canvass these areas to see if there were changes in the positions of various governments. It was also agreed that subjects should be prioritized depending on the degree of progress, and likelihood of progress, being made on each. The Committee agreed to a short list of constitutional items for immediate attention: Resource Ownership and Interprovincial Trade; Offshore Resources; Communications; Senate Reform; Family Law; Equalization and Regional Development; and a Charter of Rights. In looking at the record of these discussions, it is apparent that there was no agreement on anything. There were dissenters on every topic. Some provinces even objected to *acquiring* jurisdiction. To try to appease the provinces on the matter of a charter, a new watered-down federal draft was presented by the Clark government. It contained no equality rights. But there was still no consensus to adopt a charter. The Halifax meeting did agree to consider "powers affecting the economy," a federal concern that contemplated better guarantees of the free movement of goods, services, capital, and persons; this topic was often referred to as the "common market issue" and had the potential to involve new federal powers to act in times of economic emergency.

In Toronto, in November, the federal government, as planned at Halifax, introduced a preliminary discussion paper on powers affecting the economy. The ensuing discussion led to no conclusion. The federal delegation again submitted a revised draft Charter, again without an equality rights clause. There was no final agreement on any text on any subject, although there did seem to be an emerging consensus on the "Family Law" topic, going in the direction of concurrent provincial powers over divorce—this to accommodate those provinces that did not want to exercise legislative power on this subject.

Further sustained work on constitutional reform was put aside within weeks in the face of surprising political developments. On December 13 the Clark government was defeated in the House of Commons on its budget—a matter of confidence. Parliament was dissolved and a new election was set for February 18, 1980. Pierre Trudeau, who had announced his resignation

as leader following the Liberals' defeat the previous May, was persuaded to stay on as leader. He campaigned vigorously, including promises for constitutional reform. His party was returned with a majority of 147 seats in a House of 282 members and he was once again Prime Minister.

While Pierre was experiencing a quiet summer in 1979 out of office, and after he had announced his resignation as Leader of the Opposition, he was kind enough to autograph for me a photo of himself and me with his other advisers taken at a First Ministers' Conference on the Constitution. The inscription was "For Barry Strayer, with the best of memories of our 12 years working together on the Constitution." As it turned out, it was too soon for valedictories.

6

POST-REFERENDUM
NEGOTIATIONS

THE REFERENDUM CAMPAIGN

The return of Pierre Trudeau's Liberals with a majority suddenly changed the dynamics of the Quebec referendum campaign. The new Cabinet was sworn in on March 3, 1980. The referendum had been set for May 20, 1980. The Clark government had generally taken a hands-off attitude to the referendum and was not in a strong position to campaign in Quebec because few of its members were from that province. The attitude of the Liberals was quite the opposite. The head of the "No" committee was Claude Ryan, the leader of the Quebec Liberal Party and former editor of *Le Devoir*; he had been a staunch critic of the Trudeau government in the past and was an uneasy federalist at best. He did not have a natural talent as a stump campaigner; nevertheless, he and Trudeau agreed to co-operate. Trudeau named Jean Chrétien, Minister of Justice in the new government, to lead the federal Liberals' efforts in the campaign. Chrétien—more than Trudeau and much more than Ryan—was a scrappy street campaigner, and he livened the "No" campaign immeasurably. He protested the con- voluted referendum question (the English version had 106 words) that softened the idea of separation from Canada with the hope of a continuing economic association. As May 20 grew closer, Chrétien was on the road in Quebec almost every day, speaking wherever they would have him. His day would usually start with a meeting in Ottawa with his officials from Justice and from the Federal-Provincial Relations Office. We lawyers were there to advise on legal and constitutional issues, of which there were many

concerning the federal role in a campaign mainly governed by provincial law. Occasionally broader constitutional issues arose out of claims and promises being made by the "Yes" side. We at Justice did not, of course, concern ourselves with the purely political issues, although those were inevitably discussed with others. Chrétien was quick-minded and had limited patience for briefings. As soon as he had grasped the essence of the advice he fell to talking about his adventures on the campaign trail. He had to follow the leadership of the aloof and austere Montreal intellectual Claude Ryan, whom he referred to sometimes as "the pope." But on the campaign trail he had the common touch and he liked to recount to us some of his bons mots. For example, at one country gathering he exclaimed, in deriding the ambitions of the separatist elite, "Que voulez-vous? Un ambassadeur du Québec au Gabon, dans une Cadillac avec un *flag* sur le *hood*?" Trudeau was used more sparingly in the campaign but he made three impassioned speeches, one in Quebec City and two in Montreal, which many thought were of enormous effect. In the first two he mainly criticized the referendum question for its ambiguity, assuring his audiences that the "rest of Canada," including the federal government, would not be prepared to negotiate "association" with a Pequiste government even if the "Yes" side won. But in his final speech on May 14 at Paul Sauvé Arena in Montreal, he gave a solemn pledge on behalf of himself and his Quebec MPs that if there were a "No" vote in the referendum, they would immediately put in motion a mechanism for renewal of the Constitution ("mettre en marche immédiatement le mécanisme de renouvellement de la Constitution"). He also warned the rest of Canada that a "No" vote would not mean that nothing would change or that things could remain as before. He said that he and the other Liberal MPs from Quebec were putting their seats at risk to achieve this (that is, presumably, to achieve a mechanism for renewal of the constitution, apparently meaning that if they did not achieve it they would resign). Read carefully,[1] this statement could be taken as a promise to patriate the constitution with a Canadian amending formula (a mechanism for renewing the constitution). But for years after he was accused by Quebec nationalists, and a number of well-meaning federalists inside and outside Quebec, of thereby having promised to accept large transfers of jurisdiction to Quebec or to the provinces generally. Few who knew Pierre Trudeau's constitutional views would have jumped to the same conclusion.

When the referendum votes were counted, the "No" side had won a solid victory. With an 85 per cent turnout of voters, 59.56 per cent had voted against separation and 40.44 per cent in favour.

CONSTITUTIONAL DISCUSSIONS
ARE RENEWED AND FAIL

The next day Jean Chrétien was despatched to cross the country, meeting the Premiers to discuss their views on constitutional reform. He was able to meet with them all except Premier Lévesque of Quebec, who declined to see him. What he learned was that Premiers were willing to have constitutional negotiations as long as their own favourite topics were included, these being mostly distribution of powers matters. As a result, in preparation for a meeting of the Premiers with the Prime Minister at 24 Sussex Drive in Ottawa set for June 9, Trudeau tabled in the House of Commons his list of priorities for these discussions, incorporating items the Premiers had identified in their discussions with Jean Chrétien. These items were mainly but not entirely gleaned from the discussions of 1978 and 1979 that were sparked by Bill C-60; they included the following:

1 A statement of principles
2 A Charter of Rights, including language rights
3 A commitment to sharing and/or to equalization: the reduction of regional disparities
4 The Patriation of the Constitution
5 Resource Ownership and interprovincial trade
6 Offshore resources
7 Fisheries
8 Powers affecting the economy
9 Communications, including broadcasting
10 Family law
11 A new upper house, involving the provinces
12 The Supreme Court

The meeting of the First Ministers on June 9 at the Prime Minister's residence endorsed this agenda and agreed on accelerated discussions throughout the summer, to be conducted by the Continuing Committee of Ministers on the Constitution, reporting back to a full First Ministers'

Conference in September. The other Premiers agreed to this urgent process in recognition of the need to show a response to the "No" victory in Quebec. A subdued Lévesque felt obliged to agree that there should be new and urgent discussion for constitutional reform. He was a democrat who, at that time at least, was conscious of the fact that a majority of Quebecers had voted to remain in Canada and he could not appear to be rejecting discussions about its constitutional future. On the other hand, the role his government played in the subsequent discussions revealed a lack of commitment to their success.

It is important to realize that the determination with which Pierre Trudeau helped launch this new round of discussions in June 1980 was very different from his rather defensive stance in February 1979 in the dying days of his previous administration. Things had changed. He had just won a new majority in Parliament with 74 out of 75 seats from Quebec (constituting over half of his caucus of 147), and he had successfully helped the victory of the "No" side in the Quebec referendum. He probably—even then—was determined not to seek another mandate in 1984, the year the next federal election would normally be expected. He and most of his ministers were determined to achieve a constitutional settlement that included at least their own priorities.

Another indication of a new aggressive attitude on the part of Trudeau was evidenced by his appointment of Michael Kirby as Secretary of Cabinet for Federal-Provincial Relations. Michael had strong experience in politically oriented posts. Coming from an academic background, with a PHD in applied mathematics, he had served as Principal Assistant to a Liberal Nova Scotia Premier and as Assistant Principal Secretary to Prime Minister Trudeau. After Trudeau's return as Prime Minister in 1980, he appointed Kirby to the Cabinet Secretary role for Federal-Provincial Relations with his prime focus to be the constitutional discussions. This post had for some years been filled by Gordon Robertson, who had retired during the Clark administration. Gordon had a wealth of governmental experience going back to the days when he had been a rising star in the office of Prime Minister Mackenzie King, and including many years as Cabinet Secretary. He had in particular been involved with the constitutional patriation and reform files intermittently since 1950. His patient and courteous conduct of federal-provincial relations and his deep understanding of the constitution had been widely respected.

In the summer of 1980, however, patience and courtesy were not the Prime Minister's first priorities. Kirby's political skills were more valued by the Prime Minister at that point. Like Trudeau, Kirby was prepared to be combative in furtherance of the Prime Minister's objectives. Some of us who had been engaged in the constitutional discussions for years had some difficulty adjusting to this strategy. I well remember a meeting of some of the key players from the Federal-Provincial Relations Office (FPRO) and Justice, chaired by Kirby, where someone had spoken of the difficulties we faced. Michael observed that "When the going gets tough, the tough get going!" One of those present was a very wise man, Reeves Haggan, then of the FPRO, born in Northern Ireland, former member of British Intelligence, former Canadian Broadcast Corporation associate producer of the controversial 1960s program *This Hour Has Seven Days*, and senior to most of us in years. In his slight Irish lilt Reeves quietly observed, "Well now, Michael. In my life I have found that when the tough get going the going gets tough." Nevertheless, we all "got going" to sustain a huge effort to advance the federal goals throughout that summer.

In Justice we were soon assigned our priority. In the first meeting of the constitutional team after the referendum with our new Minister, Jean Chrétien, he opened by saying, "The boss wants this Charter." He had also brought with his staff his long-time aide Eddie Goldenberg (son of Carl Goldenberg), whose title during the next two years was Special Constitutional Adviser to the Minister of Justice. Eddie contributed much to the planning of strategy, to sensitive contacts with other parties and interest groups, and to focussing the Minister and his office on the constitutional file.

This new aggressivity is well demonstrated in the minutes of a Cabinet meeting on June 3, 1980, called especially by the Prime Minister to consider constitutional discussions.[2] Jean Chrétien reported to his colleagues on his meetings with the Premiers (except Quebec's). The federal approach had been revealed at the outset with his presentation of two lists of subjects for discussion. The first list contained the federal priorities (a preamble, a Charter with language rights, and a patriation/amending formula). This soon came to be referred to by federal representatives (somewhat tendentiously) as the People's Package. The second list contained the priorities of the provinces, including institutions and the distribution of powers. Even at this stage some provinces were warning that they would not accept

the People's Package without some trade-off—some concessions by the federal government on the second list. Chrétien said he had made no commitment to the Premiers that Ottawa would not take unilateral action if there were no agreement by September. The Prime Minister spoke of the urgency of accomplishing some change. He indicated, even then, that if discussions were not successful ministers should consider the possibility of Ottawa "going alone" with its preferred amendments, namely the People's Package. The sentiment in favour of this in Cabinet seemed fairly general. Trudeau's Quebec ministers assured him that his "personal authority" in Quebec had never been greater. Several ministers suggested there should be means to encourage public participation in the constitutional renewal process. (Although no precise mechanism was suggested at that time, such public participation came to be achieved in an important way with the Special Joint Committee of the Senate and of the House of Commons on the Constitution of Canada, established that autumn to consider the "unilateral" federal proposal for constitutional change.) Both Ontario and Quebec ministers stressed the need for quick action while the post-referendum public mood would still sustain bold measures.

This Cabinet Discussion was followed by another on July 2 in the Priorities and Planning Committee where there was agreement on the federal approach to the upcoming discussions. The salient points of agreement were these:

1 The People's Package (at this point also including equalization) is distinct for bargaining purposes from the items related to institutions and the distribution of powers. The federal government is not prepared to bargain one list against the other.
2 Negotiation on the People's Package must be concluded by the time of the First Ministers meeting in September, 1980.
3 While the government is prepared to bargain on distribution of powers items this is in the context of arriving at a fair distribution of powers: and notice should be given that Ottawa would seek some strengthening of federal powers over the economy.

These conclusions were confirmed by full Cabinet on July 3.[3]

Meetings of the Continuing Committee of Ministers on the Constitution (CCM), with two or more ministers from each government and dozens

of officials, meeting together and separately to conduct detailed ne-gotiations, were held with great intensity during the summer of 1980: Montreal, from July 8–11; Toronto, July 14–18; Vancouver, July 22–24; and Ottawa, from August 26–29. The ministerial sessions were co-chaired by Jean Chrétien, federal Minister of Justice, and Roy Romanow, Attorney General of Saskatchewan. One was my minister, the other a friend and one-time fellow political activist in Saskatchewan. Both were destined in later years to head their respective governments. The chairmanship was fair and for the most part good-humoured, in spite of growing fatigue and the prolonged, forced associations in hotel conference rooms in mid-summer.

Most provincial representatives were taken aback by the new aggres-sivity of the federal delegation, reflecting its determination to achieve results this time as well as to defend federal interests. This new stance was demonstrated in the discussions in many ways—for example, our division of the topics into two lists with a goal to see at least the People's Package adopted by September. In his opening statement (described in a press release), Mr Chrétien signalled there would be no trade-offs between the People's Package and the distribution of powers (as Pierre Trudeau put it, "we are not going to trade rights for fish"). He emphasized that in any reform of the distribution of powers there would have to be both give and take. In the following weeks we brought in new demands for clarified or extended federal powers in respect of the economy, the first time Ottawa in 12 years of constitutional discussions had the temerity to suggest that the governance of our country might be enhanced with some new *federal* powers. In particular, we insisted on linking discussions on resources and interprovincial trade (areas where the resource-exporting provinces wanted extended powers over those subjects) with those on powers over the economy more generally where we sought new federal jurisdiction and guarantees of the internal common market. Finally, although there was not much said publicly on the subject, some of us were encouraged to take the opportunity to explain quietly to our provincial counterparts that Ottawa was prepared to proceed unilaterally with the United Kingdom Parliament to achieve adoption of the People's Package if there were no agreement with some or all of the provinces by September. I engaged in several such conversations.

About the only fun I can recall having at the CCM was during an evening spent in Montreal at the Olympic Stadium (the "Big O") at a major-league

baseball game. Eddie Goldenberg, Jean Chrétien's principal aide, arranged for a group of us, including Jean Chrétien and Roy Romanow, to use the private box of the Bronfman family at the stadium to see the game.

Without going into details of these summer negotiations, a brief summary will indicate the large area of disagreement left by the time the First Ministers' Meeting of September 8–13 was to commence.

First, the People's Package—the items the federal government was determined to move on if there were no agreement by September. There remained a debate over a possible preamble to the Constitution. The federal government's priority was to ensure that the preamble recognized that the will of the Canadian people is the ultimate basis for the federation, and that the continuance of that federation was not exclusively dependent on the will of provincial governments. British Columbia and Quebec instead wanted it clear that the existence and continuation of the federation depended on the will of provincial governments. To their credit, the Ontario delegates presented a draft they correctly referred to as poetic, a draft which declared that "We, as Canadians...choose federalism as the system for sharing government best suited to the achievement of unity in diversity," thus making it clear that our Union was the will of the people, not the provinces. Unfortunately, this draft seems to have attracted no other provincial support. There was also a dispute regarding how the French fact in Canada should be affirmed in the preamble. The federal government wanted a recognition that French-speaking society is "centred in though not confined to Quebec," whereas that province wanted recognition of "the distinctive character of Quebec with its French-speaking majority."[4] These differences remained unresolved, and were referred to the First Ministers for decision in September.

As for patriation and an amending formula, it was reported to the federal cabinet that we had indicated the intention of the government to move unilaterally if necessary to have the People's Package adopted by the UK Parliament. We had informed the Continuing Committee of Ministers that in our view this would be legally possible. Saskatchewan agreed with this but Ontario said it had an opinion to the contrary. (This will be discussed more fully later). On the matter of an amendment formula, most provinces were supportive of the "Alberta draft" that indeed later formed the basis of the formula ultimately written into the *Constitution Act, 1982*.[5] The general formula required the approval of Parliament plus legislatures of seven

provinces having at least 50 per cent of the national population. If such an amendment affected the legislative or other rights of a dissenting province it would not have effect in that province. A short list of items would require for their amendment the unanimous consent of the provinces. While the federal delegation found this formula unattractive, particularly the opting-out provision that it feared could lead to a checkerboard effect of federal and provincial powers across the country, it was reluctantly willing to contemplate such a formula if there were a real provincial agreement on it: we realized that, in the event an amendment were to be approved by the seven provinces/50 per cent of population rule, and if it became apparent that there would be substantial opting out so as to create a checkerboard effect of laws made under the proposed amendment, Parliament could always withhold its approval of that amendment.

In respect of the Charter there was only limited provincial support for the idea of an entrenched Charter (Ontario, New Brunswick, and, with qualifications, Newfoundland) and even less agreement on its contents. Provinces were generally opposed to equality or language rights or mobility rights. There was some support for a notwithstanding clause, although the federal delegation wanted a special majority in any legislative vote to be able to override the Charter with a particular law. For the first time in 12 years of discussion, the provinces finally produced on August 26, 1980, a draft Charter,[6] but it was put forward only on the basis of "In the Event there is Going to be Entrenchment," a matter not yet agreed. And it was a disappointing document: it contained no equality, language, or mobility rights.

There was apparent agreement on the text that addressed the subject of equalization, which Ottawa had come to regard as part of the People's Package. So, in the run-up to the September First Ministers' Meeting we had some optimism for substantial agreement on Package provisions concerning the preamble, an amending formula, and an equalization text. It was almost certain we could not get agreement on an entrenched Charter and, absent agreement, there would be a fight over unilateral patriation.

But on the remaining topics of distribution of powers and institutions there was clearly not much agreement. On the subject of powers over the economy there was very limited consensus even after a summer of discussion. The Government of Canada had published in June 1980, a booklet entitled *Securing the Canadian Economic Union in the Constitution*.[7] It

described the very limited protection in section 121 of the 1867 Constitution for the Canadian common market, guaranteeing as it does only tariff-free movement of goods between provinces. It compared this to superior guarantees for the free movement of goods, services, and people found in the constitutions of other states and in international agreements for free trade among independent countries. It also described some of the uncertainties in federal jurisdiction over matters such as competition and product standards that require control on a national level. Relying on this background material, we put forward several proposals: the inclusion of personal mobility rights in the Charter; the strengthening of section 121 to guarantee free movement of persons, goods, services, and capital; and the strengthening of Parliament's power in section 91, head 2 of the 1867 Act ("the regulation of trade and commerce"), specifically to cover commerce in services and capital as well as to regulate competition and products standards. It was also our position that the new section 121 should be enforceable by the courts. The provinces generally resisted our proposals, although they were somewhat sympathetic to a broadened section 121 if its enforcement was to be in the hands of a political body (some sort of intergovernmental commission). That was the state of disagreement when September arrived.[8]

Discussions in the committee on Resources and Interprovincial Trade, which I attended, were tough from the beginning. When this matter had last been discussed in February 1979, the federal delegation had tentatively accepted a draft that would have given provinces concurrent jurisdiction over the export of resource products from the province. Federal laws in respect of interprovincial trade would have paramountcy over provincial laws only if it were "necessary to serve a compelling national interest." In July 1980 we took this offer off the table, much to the shock of some provincial representatives. We also said that any federal concessions on trade in natural resources would be dependent on acceptance of our proposals for protection of the national economy. While we made some concessions later, this subject was not much advanced during the summer's discussions.

With respect to discussions on the reform of the Senate, they never advanced beyond a partial agreement by the provinces on the creation of an interim Council of the Provinces, which would operate at least until there was adequate discussion of and agreement on the Senate. This Council, on which the federal government would not be represented, would consist of

provincially appointed members, three from each province. Its functions would be limited to reviewing and ratifying federal measures thought to affect the provinces, such as use of the spending power in areas of provincial jurisdiction, exercise of the declaratory power, and appointments to certain federal agencies. So absorbed by this was British Columbia that at one point it said it would not agree to any of the other 11 subjects under discussion if there were no agreement on this Council. There was no solution in sight before the September meeting.

Discussions on Fisheries were diffuse and inconclusive. At issue was the continuing exclusive federal jurisdiction over "Sea Coast and Inland Fisheries" as provided in section 91, head 12 of the 1867 constitution. Newfoundland led several provinces that wanted concurrent provincial jurisdiction. The federal approach was instead to divide up exclusive jurisdiction, with provinces being given a new power over inland fisheries. As the talks proceeded, a variety of thorny problems arose, such as what to do with anadromous species (e.g., salmon) that move from inland to sea and back, aquaculture (fish farming), marine plants vital to fisheries, and the protection of native fishing rights. These were issues hardly soluble by constitutional lawyers, or indeed administrators.

The Communications discussions involved mainly a federal wish to retain exclusive jurisdiction over the broadcast spectrum, interprovincial and international aspects of telecommunications, technical aspects of carriers, and broadcasting. Ottawa was willing to concede concurrent provincial jurisdiction over cable television. The provinces instead sought concurrent jurisdiction over other matters and exclusive jurisdiction over cable. Just before the September First Ministers' Conference, federal ministers were advised of a probable impasse, and it turned out that there was disagreement within Cabinet on the federal proposals already made.[9]

On the subject of Family Law, the federal government had been willing in earlier discussions, in 1979, to give up its exclusive jurisdiction over "Marriage and Divorce" and see it given to the provinces, subject to Parliament retaining jurisdiction to provide for recognition in other provinces of divorces granted in any province. This was to ensure that there would be "full faith and credit" accorded across the country to provincial decrees, a legislative equivalent to the guarantee in Article IV of the United States Constitution. As discussions unfolded in the summer of 1980, some refinements were considered, such as the enforcement of maintenance and

custody orders across the country and the recognition of nullity as well as divorce decrees. There probably could have been a consensus reached in September on these matters had circumstances been otherwise more auspicious. Manitoba remained reluctant to see divorce transferred to provincial jurisdiction. It must also be said that there were many women's groups who objected to divorce being made provincial.

Discussion of the Supreme Court largely revolved around a Quebec proposal for some incorporation of dualism in its functioning. The initial suggestion was that all constitutional matters should be decided by a panel of five judges consisting of two common law judges, two civil law judges, and the Chief Justice. It was also proposed that the position of Chief Justice should be filled alternately by common law and civil law judges. In response, some other provinces suggested instead an enlarged court of 11 judges but with a common law majority. There was never agreement among the provinces on this structure. While provinces were generally agreed that they should have a role in the appointment of Supreme Court judges, there was again no agreement on the details. Ottawa went into the September meeting willing to accede to any plan the provinces could agree on, but that was not to be.

This was a hectic summer for the ministers and officials of all governments involved. I found that one of my problems was, in trying to deal on an urgent basis with the numerous legal issues raised by the negotiations, to keep abreast of the changing goals and negotiating postures of our political masters. I was on occasion confronted with issues in committees for which I had no guidance with respect to the government's current position. Our occasional meetings with the Minister were valuable but not always sufficient.

If I had any abiding influence on our negotiating positions, it was mainly in respect of pressing the concept of concurrent powers as a means of resolving conflicting federal and provincial claims to control certain matters. What is normally meant by *concurrent powers* is an express constitutional authority given to both levels of government to regulate the same matter, with provision for "paramountcy" of one level where its legislation conflicts with that of the other. In the 1867 constitution there was only limited express provision for concurrent powers: by section 95, where Agriculture and Immigration are concurrent, with paramountcy of federal laws in case of conflict; and by section 94A, added in 1964, which gives

Parliament concurrent powers over old-age pensions and supplementary benefits (in effect, the authorization for the Canada Pension Plan) but with recognition of the paramountcy of provincial laws in this field. I had for a long time advocated concurrent powers in many fields because I felt they would overcome unnecessary rigidities in the distribution of powers. If, for example, some government wants to regulate a matter that is of concern to it, even if it has potential implications for other governments who do not wish to legislate, why should that government not be able to regulate at least until such time as the government(s) with the paramount power wishes to enter the field? An obvious example of provincial paramountcy is the Canada Pension Plan, which Parliament legislated for nine provinces that did not wish to enter that field, while Quebec insisted on legislating its own scheme and used its paramount power to exclude the operation of the Canada Pension Plan in that province. Indeed, I have argued that there are already many implicitly concurrent powers in the constitution, where both levels of government may regulate the same phenomenon even though it may be described by various terms in the constitution.[10] An example is that of highway traffic: provinces generally regulate the use of highways but Parliament punishes seriously harmful driving amounting to criminal conduct under the *Criminal Code*. So it was natural that, in our constitutional discussions over jurisdiction concerning matters in which both provinces and Canada have a strong interest, I suggested both interests be recognized, with the stronger interest being protected by paramountcy. This approach was tried in discussions over interprovincial and international trade in provincial resource products, communications, and fisheries. Only in respect of resource products did such a proposal finally find adoption in the constitution, which occurred as a result of further negotiations after the failure of the September 1980 First Ministers' Meeting to reach agreement on anything.[11]

My willingness to contemplate more concurrent powers reflected a certain disagreement I had with Prime Minister Trudeau's approach to federalism. He insisted on symmetrical federalism, where each province had exactly the same powers as every other one and federal powers were always distinct from provincial powers. Federal lawmakers should be able to vote on laws applicable to the whole country: special status for Quebec would mean MPs from that province should not be able to vote on federal laws for the rest of the country in subject areas under the control of

Quebec because of its special status. In this I think he was being more Trudeau than Elliott: he preferred Gallic logic and deductive reasoning to British pragmatism and inductive reasoning, or, muddling along with any system that works. As an example of the latter, how else can one explain the many anomalies of the Union of England and Scotland in 1707? For example, until recently there were many laws passed at Westminster that were only applicable to Scotland. Yet MPs from England, Wales, and Northern Ireland could vote on them. Conversely, since the *Scotland Act, 1998* created a separate Parliament for Scotland that has exclusive jurisdiction over a wide range of legislation applicable only to Scotland, Scottish MPs at Westminster can vote on legislation over similar matters that applies only in England, Wales, and Northern Ireland. This anomaly is known as the West Lothian Question.

While a concurrent power would not legally make one province more powerful by its exercise than another, the practical effects of a province exercising its concurrent power over a subject, while other provinces are content to see federal regulation of that subject, would be asymmetrical. I was surprised that Trudeau was willing to entertain as many proposals for concurrent powers as he did.

In my earlier days as a young constitutional lawyer I would have gone even further with asymmetry: I once advocated an amending formula that would allow Quebec (but no other province) to opt out of amendments affecting her language and culture.[12] After all, Prime Minister Pearson had himself referred to Canada as a "nation based on dualism"[13] and I was inspired by that thought. Later, after reflecting on the greater implications of dualism, I thought better of it.

A steady preoccupation for me that summer was the marshalling of a case for the federal government to proceed to achieve adoption of the People's Package without the consent of any or all of the provinces. As has been noted, the Cabinet, as early as June, had noted a willingness to do this if necessary and a firm decision was taken to that end on July 3. While there was a general belief in Ottawa that this could be done I was asked early in the summer to prepare a comprehensive opinion on the subject. I was of course travelling and meeting in various cities outside of Ottawa with the CCM during much of this time. But I had the good fortune to have some excellent lawyers in my branch, including Fred Jordan, Barbara Reed, Louis Reynolds, and Louis Davis, who researched a variety of sources with some

general direction from me. I can recall many summer evenings spent in my hotel room after a day of CCM proceedings, going over memoranda and drafting passages on this subject. The government of course also wanted reassurance from eminent private practitioners that we had a strong case in law. Two of the Quebec practitioners forming part of our legal team were Michel Robert (later Chief Justice of Quebec) and Raynold Langlois, both leading counsel. Pierre Genest, an outstanding Toronto lawyer, was a member of our team, and we also consulted a leading academic, Professor Peter Hogg of Osgoode Hall Law School. The private practitioners reviewed the drafts we were generating in the Department of Justice and we had to find the time during the federal-provincial negotiations for meetings to discuss and strengthen these drafts. We had formed a strong opinion that the Canadian Parliament had the legal right to request, and the United Kingdom had the legal right to enact, a package of amendments including a preamble, patriation, an amending formula, a Charter, and an equalization commitment. I set out our views to the Deputy Minister in a memorandum of August 13 and these views were duly reported to the Prime Minister. The main lines of these opinions were later included in the so-called Kirby Memorandum of August 30, 1980,[14] which constituted the final report by the federal delegation presented to Cabinet regarding the summer's work in preparation for the First Ministers' Conference scheduled for September 8–12, of which I will write later. During the meeting of the Continuing Committee of Ministers in Ottawa from August 26–29, the co-chairmen, Jean Chrétien and Roy Romanow, invited me to brief provincial ministers on the federal government's conclusions regarding its entitlement to take unilateral action if necessary. Needless to say this presentation was not met with much enthusiasm or acceptance. Meanwhile, the government had also retained the services of one of Canada's most accomplished counsel, Mr John J. Robinette of Toronto. I had sent to him a memorandum describing the intentions of the government along with our opinion on its right to seek patriation without provincial approval. On September 3 I flew to Toronto for a few hours to obtain his views. This was the first time I had met this iconic figure, and I was struck by his modesty and straightforward expression of complicated issues. I could appreciate why he had such success before appellate courts. He was satisfied that patriation legislation by the UK Parliament, passed at the request of the Parliament of Canada, would be legally valid in Canada. He too doubted

that there was any constitutional convention to the contrary or that, if there were, that it would affect the legality of such a measure. He subsequently confirmed his views in writing.

With the last meeting of the Continuing Committee of Ministers ending in August with no complete agreement on anything, a series of best-efforts drafts were to be reported to the meeting of the First Ministers scheduled for September 8 through 12 (it actually continued into September 13 in hopes of reaching agreement). In preparation for this assembly, the federal delegation prepared a lengthy memorandum for Cabinet of some 64 pages, setting out the areas of agreement and disagreement and recommending positions for the Prime Minister to take at the First Ministers' Conference. It also advised on the legal and political issues of proceeding, if necessary, to request legislation from the UK Parliament without provincial agreement. While this document was the product of perhaps 10 to 15 authors, including myself, it was signed by Michael Kirby and thus came to be known as the Kirby Memorandum. Its final paragraph was certainly Kirbyesque: "The probability of an agreement is not high. Unilateral action is therefore a distinct possibility. In the event unilateral action becomes necessary, Ministers should understand that the fight in Parliament and the country will be very, very rough. For as Machiavelli said: 'It should be borne in mind that there is nothing more difficult to arrange, more doubtful of success, and more dangerous to carry through than initiating changes in a state's constitution.'"[15] A salient fact about this memorandum, which was intended as strategic and legal advice of the utmost confidence, is that it was leaked to the Government of Quebec a few days before the First Ministers' Conference.[16] That Government distributed it to the other provinces the night before the opening session. Many Premiers took umbrage at what they regarded as evidence that the federal government had no intention of negotiating in good faith. But some saw it as evidence that we had fairly assessed the possibilities of agreement, had suggested positions that might help achieve consensus, and had carefully advised the government as to its options if there were no agreement. In fact, the memorandum was widely distributed later in some schools of public administration as an example of good public service policy advice.

As the memorandum was made public there could be no lingering claims to its confidential nature. First, it is important to note that as early as this stage, the paper suggested the use of a parliamentary committee to

review our "unilateral package" if such were to be advanced by the government.[17] This is important because the Official Opposition later asserted that it had forced the government to have such a committee. The paper also reported our opinion that unilateral action would be legal. But we warned that some would argue that there were conventions (i.e., political customs) of the constitution that require provincial consent (in some undefined form) for such amendments to be sought from Westminster. A unilateral process breaching such constitutional conventions could be described as "unconstitutional"—even if legal. We argued that at best the conventions were debatable, that there was no precise precedent for amendments of the kind we would be seeking from Westminster, and that at most the alleged breach of conventions could not affect the legality of the measure once adopted there. We therefore advised against the federal government taking a reference to the Supreme Court of Canada on this subject: "Any reference to the Supreme Court would put that Court in a very difficult position, and the Government of Canada would be seen to be responsible. The major issue involved would be more of a political than of a legal nature, since the debatable area was essentially that of the conventions. Conventions are rules of political conduct which are usually imprecise, unwritten, and changeable by time and circumstance. The request for their definition by the court would come in the midst of a widespread political controversy which the Court would be obliged to solve."[18] In retrospect, I realize that the concerns expressed here were partly drawn from my own writings and my understanding that courts are properly confined to "justiciable" questions, issues that cannot be dealt with better by other institutions of the state and for whose determination there are discernible objective criteria available for a court to apply.[19] As history has demonstrated, I was far too solicitous of the Supreme Court, the majority of which seemed not at all embarrassed to decide purely political questions as to the "nice" way to do constitutional reform. The Kirby paper went on to say this: "that if the question somehow came before a Canadian court, it would uphold the legal validity of the UK legislation effecting patriation. The court might very well, however, make a pronouncement, not necessary for the decision, that the patriation process was in violation of established conventions and therefore in one sense was 'unconstitutional' even though legally valid."[20] Consequently, we advised that the federal government—the only authority entitled to do so—not take a reference directly to the Supreme

Court. We observed, however, that "it would...be open to a province to refer the question of the validity of federal and UK action to its Court of Appeal whose decision could then be appealed to the Supreme Court of Canada. This is very likely if the federal government is not willing to refer the matter directly to the Supreme Court."[21] It will be seen that this confidential legal advice intended for the federal cabinet became a guidebook for subsequent provincial challenges to the patriation package, suggesting to them their best arguments and a means of getting them before the Supreme Court.

It was a premise of our advice that the chances of getting a favourable decision from the Supreme Court would be greatly enhanced if the UK Parliament had already acted on a request from the Parliament of Canada and legislated the patriation package.[22] Our reasoning ran that such a response from Westminster would be consistent with its practice of acting on the advice of the federal Parliament and Government, something for which it needed no authorization from the Supreme Court of Canada, and that once it had acted this would emphasize the legitimacy of such a procedure. My advice in effect was, borrowing from Shakespeare, "If it were done when 'tis done, then 'twere well / It were done quickly."[23] Mr Robinette agreed with this approach. As events unfolded, however, it became politically impossible.

The First Ministers assembled in Ottawa the afternoon of Sunday, September 7, the day before the Conference was to open. That evening First Ministers were dinner guests of the Governor General. The dinner proved to be a very tense affair, with many Premiers irate at the Prime Minister. Later that night they received a copy of the Kirby Memorandum. This intensified the ill will, which carried over into the week of proceedings that followed. It is difficult to discern in any detail what happened that week. The most vital discussions were held by Premiers meeting separately, or by closed meetings of all First Ministers with perhaps a minister and one or two officials each. There were a few days of disharmony in public sessions over specific outstanding issues, and the differences that we had identified at the end of the summer's meetings of the Continuing Committee of Ministers on the Constitution largely remained unresolved. But it appears the real impasse developed on Friday, February 12, in two closed meetings. That day began with the Premiers meeting over breakfast at the Chateau Laurier, across Wellington Street from the Conference

Centre. Quebec had distributed to provincial delegations the day before a document entitled "Proposal for a common stand of the Provinces"[24]: it contained drafts on all 12 agenda items, many of which had already been rejected by the federal government and on some of which there was no unanimity among the provinces. Over breakfast the Premiers were seemingly able to agree on six of the topics as forming their "common stand" for any settlement at the Conference. The degree of real consensus is not clear. It appears that some provinces soon tried to distance themselves from aspects of it. They transmitted such a proposal that day to the Prime Minister. This document, soon dubbed the "Chateau Consensus,"[25] said that in return for agreeing to patriation and an amending formula along the lines of the "Alberta formula" (but no Charter) they would want new provincial powers in the following areas:

- interprovincial and international trade in resources,
- ownership and control of offshore resources,
- regulation of offshore fisheries,
- telecommunications,
- appointment of members of the federal Upper House (in the manner of the German Bundesrat), and
- appointments to the Supreme Court of Canada.

As I said a year later at a meeting of the American Political Science Association in New York, "this was an offer which the federal government had no difficulty refusing." It is apparent from the public proceedings of Saturday, September 13, that in closed discussions the previous evening the Prime Minister rejected these terms. The public meeting the next day allowed all First Ministers to vent their frustrations. Peter Russell, a very perceptive long-time observer of such conferences, described it as "one of the most acrimonious on record."[26] The account of the Canadian Intergovernmental Conference Secretariat simply states, "[t]he Conference concluded, without agreement being reached, with closing statements made by First Ministers on the morning of September 13."[27] It is nevertheless instructive to see the nature of the exchanges, as these laid the groundwork for the battle that was to follow.

First, there was considerable hostility shown by several Premiers toward the Prime Minister. Many of them saw the breakdown as essentially a

struggle between two Quebec politicians, Trudeau and Lévesque. Premier Blakeney perhaps put it most charitably when he said "there were two agendas before us, one constitutional renewal for Canada and the other the continuing contest for the hearts and minds of the people of Québec. In that latter contest, it seemed to some of us that nothing offered was enough and everything being demanded was too much."[28] Premier Bennett was less tactful. In lamenting the fact that an agreement had not been reached notwithstanding the measure of accord among the Premiers at their breakfast meeting the day before, he made a point of expressing confidence in Mr Lévesque (and by implication his lack thereof in Mr Trudeau): "I believe the Premier of Québec when he said he came here in a spirit of goodwill to achieve an agreement. Others may doubt him, but I don't have a long-term battle. My personal feelings aren't mixed up in my ability to achieve an agreement. God help the country if personal vendettas can prevent the achievement of an agreement." I could see that this much annoyed Trudeau and he did not let the remark pass unanswered. In his response to the Premiers explaining why the Government of Canada could not accede to their "common stand," he said

> Canada is more than just the sum of its parts, more than
> the sum of 10 provinces, more than the sum of 10 regional
> economies and that is my view. It is one view that I hold very
> dearly and I was a little bit chagrined this morning when
> Premier Bennett described that as a personal vendetta. I
> don't think there is anything personal between Mr Lévesque
> and myself.

> I see laughs again from British Columbia and that shows
> how little they know Quebecers, but I ask Mr Lévesque and
> he can inform you if in our personal relationships there has
> ever been anything mean and I know he will say no because
> we talked about that very point as recently as Sunday night.
> So it is not a personal matter. It is two views of Canada.

Several Premiers, particularly Lévesque, Sterling Lyon of Manitoba, William Bennett of British Columbia, and Brian Peckford of Newfoundland, characterized the Conference as a failure and laid the blame on the federal

government because it had rejected the Chateau Consensus. Others, such as Ontario, Nova Scotia, New Brunswick, and Saskatchewan, were more conciliatory, expressing hope for some future accord that would be possible without the federal government's "artificial deadline" for agreement on its "People's Package." Premier Davis of Ontario and Premier Hatfield of New Brunswick gave signals of their support for early patriation and some form of Charter, positions that they later confirmed in supporting the federal package tabled in Parliament in October.

Prime Minster Trudeau, in responding to these attacks that suggested the failure of the Conference was due to his intransigence in the face of the Chateau Consensus, pointed out that his government had been willing to make many concessions, including provincial powers over indirect taxation, family law, some regulation of interprovincial trade in resource products, inland fisheries, a sharing of jurisdiction over communications and of revenue from offshore resources, and constitutionalization of the Supreme Court and of equalization. This was not deemed to be enough. He also pointed out that his government had tried to convince the provinces that Canadian citizens should have the constitutional right to move anywhere in Canada, to work and own property there, with better guarantees of a common market throughout the country. He reminded them of his efforts to have a Charter of Canadians' rights, including linguistic rights. He reminded them again of the two views he said emerged from the private meeting the night before. One view [theirs], he said, was that where the provinces all agreed on some demand for increased powers, the federal government must give in. The other view [his] was that there is a national interest that transcends provincial interests and where there is a conflict the national interest must prevail.[29]

Premier Blakeney responded to this briefly by saying that the issue was not that simple:

> I do not believe that the national interest is represented
> by a consensus of all provincial governments. The federal
> government has a role to play. It is not a creature of the
> provinces. This is not a confederation. Nor, however, do I
> believe that the national interest is to ascertain [sic] by the
> majority will of Canadians. This is something more than a
> collection of citizens and, accordingly, the national interest

cannot be stated by the majority view in the House of Commons. That is the view of a unitary state....The essence of Canada is that it is a federation. The essence of Canada is therefore that on major matters we need a double majority. We need the majority of citizens as expressed by the popular will in the House of Commons and we need the majority, however defined, of the regional will. That is the essence of a federal state.[30]

This was a position he held consistently during the months to follow as the battle in the courts unfolded.

Trudeau responded to Lévesque's complaint that he was abandoning his promise to Quebecers, made in his Montreal speech during the referendum campaign, that if they voted "No" he would press for the "renouvellement" of the Constitution. He argued that for renewal we needed a viable Canadian amending formula, one that did not require British legislation and unanimity for every constitutional change to be effective across the country. The so-called Alberta formula, with its opting-out provision as proposed, did not provide that. He also stressed the importance of constitutional language rights for francophones outside Quebec—something the Quebec government adamantly opposed. In this way Trudeau justified his position as fulfilling the promise in a way meaningful to the Quebecers, to whom he had made a commitment to put in motion a mechanism for the renewal of the constitution.

It should be noted here that the authors of the Kirby Memorandum did not escape a few bruises during this tumultuous week. Premier Lyon attacked this document: "that document spoke not of reasoning or good faith negotiation, but of elaborate efforts to put those around this table who might disagree with your government on the defensive. It outlined a plan for unilateral action by the federal government together with elaborate plans to blame the provinces for the failure of this conference, a *failure that only those who wrote the document for you seemed to find desirable*" (emphasis added).[31] Premier Blakeney had this to add: "nobody can deny that that document and the increasing evidence of the federal cabinet's acceptance of it struck deeply at the attitude of accommodation which was so crucial if we were to succeed."[32] Prime Minister Trudeau responded to these comments by stating the following: "If an honest examination of

that document is made, it will be clear that our first hope, our first choice, our first preference, our preferred course was to reach an agreement and that is why in the course of the summer not only the federal ministers who flank me now, but other ministers and other departments met many times to see what concessions we could make in giving up powers to the provinces and they were many."[33]

That Trudeau, by June of 1980, was firm in his belief in popular sovereignty, which he felt by the end of the summer had been rejected by most of the Premiers, is shown in a speech he made in 1991 at the University of Toronto. He recalled the history of negotiations on the amending formula, going back to 1927. He attributed the failure of that conference to the advocacy of the "compact theory" of Confederation articulated by Ontario and Quebec and that implicitly located the sovereignty of Canada in the provinces collectively. He said that the failure of further attempts up to 1971 occurred because the First Ministers could not decide whether sovereignty rested with the provinces or in some combination of the federal state and the provinces in numbers yet to be defined. Trudeau said it was obvious that no federal government would capitulate to the compact theorists. He went on to comment,

> During the 1980–82 constitutional exercise, the federal
> government proposed to cut the Gordian knot by arguing
> that the sovereignty of Canada ultimately resided neither
> in the provinces nor in the federal government, but in the
> Canadian people. The provincial governments collectively
> rejected that view, even objecting to the use of the words
> "the people of Canada" in a preamble to the constitution
> and proposing instead a description of Canada as a country
> made up of "provinces...freely united," thus returning to the
> selfsame concept that had prevented patriation in 1927.

> The Premiers also made it abundantly clear, by the so-called
> Chateau Consensus, on September 12, 1980, that they would
> never permit the patriation of the Canadian constitution
> until jurisdictional powers had been drastically reallocated
> in favour of the provinces.

The federal government took the position that a reallocation of powers between the two orders of government was a legitimate subject of negotiation, but that the right of Canadians to have a constitution of their own should not be subordinated to the open-ended process of satisfying any premier's insatiable desire for increased provincial powers.[34]

While Trudeau may have oversimplified the issue in this description of the debate, there is little doubt that from the beginning of the summer he had expressed—by threatening to "go it alone" if necessary to achieve patriation and a Charter—a determination to proceed on the basis of a public consensus for the People's Package that he intended to achieve with or without provincial government consent. This pointed the way for what was to follow the failed Conference of September 8 to 13.

7

PREPARING THE
PATRIATION PACKAGE

At the conclusion of the First Ministers' Conference on Saturday, September 13, 1980, members of the federal team had little doubt as to our next task. We rapidly assembled a draft of our proposed measure for the United Kingdom Parliament to enact to effect patriation, which we proposed to call the "Canada Act" (the same name given to the abortive draft of 1971 prior to the Victoria Conference). It would be designed to give legal effect to the substantive changes in the Canadian constitution to be set out in a document called the "Constitution Act, 1980." Initially at least we expected the latter to include a Charter and an amending formula. We quickly prepared and despatched to London a draft of the *Canada Act* and its Schedule, the *Constitution Act, 1980*. The latter was based on our many draft proposals in the federal-provincial discussions and our best estimate of what Cabinet would approve for the joint resolution to be tabled soon in Parliament. It was understood by the British that the draft *Constitution Act* was still undergoing modifications back in Ottawa, but we wanted to work out with them the mechanics of patriation. We indicated that it was the Prime Minister's objective to have the patriated constitution come into force on July 1, 1981.

The Prime Minster had had lunch with Prime Minister Thatcher at 10 Downing Street on June 22, 1980, and discussed the possibility of an early request by the Canadian Parliament in the fall or winter for a patriation measure. He later told reporters that she had undertaken to put it through Parliament using party discipline (the "three-line whip") if necessary. He later admitted that she had also said her government would prefer a request supported substantially or unanimously by the provinces.[1]

Thus it was that by September 24—some 11 days after the close of the last constitutional conference—I found myself on the way to London for the second time in my career to help arrange for Canada's legislative independence. But this time the delegation was larger. It was led by Roger Tassé, Deputy Minister of Justice, and included Edythe MacDonald of our department, at that time the English-language drafter, and Léonard Legault, Legal Adviser to the Department of External Affairs (as it then was). When Léonard's inclusion was suggested to me by a senior official of External Affairs I objected on the ground that this was not a matter of "external" affairs since in this respect the Parliament of the United Kingdom was acting as our domestic legislator. The law applicable was not international law but domestic law, on which the Department of Justice was the authorized source of advice. This was the position that had been accepted in 1971 when I had previously been involved in similar discussions. However, my view did not prevail, presumably because in the circumstances of a "unilateral" request to the UK for legislation there would be many elements of diplomacy required. I hasten to say that I had no personal objection to Léonard Legault joining our team. He was well known to me because he had been a student of mine at the College of Law, University of Saskatchewan from 1957 to 1958. He was undoubtedly one of the brightest students I ever taught, apart from being an erudite, charming, witty friend whom we had seen socially in Ottawa since our arrival. Léonard held many important diplomatic posts during his career, including Ambassador to the Vatican and Deputy Ambassador in Washington, as well as later serving as the Chairman, Canadian Section, of the International Joint Commission that oversees US–Canada boundary waters.

In London we were met by an official at the Horseguards entrance to the Foreign and Commonwealth Office (FCO) in Whitehall. When I was introduced he said, "Oh, we know about you. You were here the last time to talk about this business." (They obviously had good files spanning the intervening nine years.) We proceeded to our meeting in the FCO, held in the splendid Indian Office Chamber. This was part of what had originally been the India Office, built in the 19th century (at the expense of Indian taxpayers) to house the imperial administrators based in London. The Chamber itself is a very large, splendidly ornate room featuring much gilding, marble, tapestry, and statuary. It had been used often for formal meetings and ceremonies with Indian maharajahs and princes. After the

independence of India in 1947, the India Office space was incorporated into the Foreign Office. This Chamber was apparently deemed a suitable ambience for discussing the independence of Britain's oldest self-governing territory.

We were accompanied at this meeting by Christian Hardy, Deputy High Commissioner in London. We met with Sir Ian Sinclair, Legal Adviser to the FCO, and with other legal and diplomatic officers. The FCO personnel were very co-operative, accepting this as a responsibility to help out an old friend and fellow member of the Commonwealth to put an end to the anachronism of Westminster amending the Canadian constitution. They pointed out, however, that the proposed package of changes (particularly the Charter) was more extensive than they had anticipated and that there could be problems in clearing enough time at Westminster for its passage by the target date. This was a theme to be repeated many times by British officials and politicians as events unfolded. After this amiable morning we were entertained at lunch by D.M. Day, Deputy Under Secretary of the FCO, at the Oxford and Cambridge Club in Pall Mall, which was a pleasure for me as an alumnus of one of those universities.

The afternoon session was markedly less amiable when we met in Whitehall with Sir Henry Rowe, First Parliamentary Counsel. What we were proposing for the UK Parliament to legislate was a short statute entitled the *Canada Act, 1980* that would give the force of law to the *Constitution Act, 1980* as a Schedule. The latter measure would contain the substantive changes in our constitution, including the Charter and an amending formula. The *Canada Act, 1980* itself would effect the repeal, as part of the law of Canada, of various British statutes, including subsection 7(1) of the *Statute of Westminster, 1931*[2] that specifically had preserved the right of the UK Parliament to amend the Canadian constitution. The proposed *Canada Act, 1980* would also have declared that no future legislation of the UK Parliament would apply to Canada. Basically, Sir Henry thought it was absurd that the UK Parliament should still be legislating for Canada by the proposed *Canada Act*. He had prepared a written commentary to this effect. In his view the *British North America Act, 1867* and its amendments were not part of the law of the UK. Whatever its history, it was now the law of Canada and not of the UK; Canada was now a sovereign state and the UK was not in the habit of legislating for other sovereign states. He expressed a view, with which most of us could at least sympathize,

that it was "inconceivable that the power of a sovereign state to change its constitution should depend on the willingness of the government and Parliament of another sovereign state to play a part in the change." When we pointed out that section 7 of the *Statute of Westminster, 1931* expressly reserved to the UK Parliament the power to amend the *BNA Acts* he said that Statute had no relevance to the problem, that it was largely "a historical document rather than living law." I said "Sir Henry, I might be inclined to agree with you, but there are hundreds of lawyers in Canada who still believe that the matter is governed by the *Statute of Westminster* and unfortunately several of them sit on the Supreme Court of Canada.[3] We do need the repeal of that section for patriation." He snapped back, "Well, we didn't do that for Rhodesia!" (Rhodesia was, I guess, fresh in his mind as the most recent colony to be liberated, having gained its independence as Zimbabwe in April of that same year. I didn't point out to him that the *Statute of Westminster* never did apply to Rhodesia.)

Sir Henry also had problems with our proposal to have the *Canada Act, 1980* enacted in both the official languages of Canada. We had presented to the British officials bilingual side-by-side draft texts of that Act and its Schedule that was to be the *Constitution Act, 1980.* "My dear fellow," Sir Henry said to me, "you could never get the clerks [he of course pronounced it *clarks*] of the two Houses to accept a bill in a foreign language!" This partly flowed from his emphasis that the *Canada Act* would be a British statute (not one to which the Governor General of Canada could give assent, this being one of the scenarios we had considered) and that the Parliament at Westminster only legislates in English. I resisted the temptation to remind him of the medieval use of Law French and instead suggested an alternative: noting that the British Parliament often gives legal force to treaties that have foreign as well as English texts, and that they do this by adding the treaty text in all its languages as a Schedule to the British Act, I suggested that the French version of the *Canada Act* could be treated as a Schedule to that Act. In the British statute books it could appear at the back of that statute as Schedules normally do, but in any Canadian printing of the Act the French version could appear beside the English version in the bicolumnar form with which we are familiar in Canada. (I was aware, but did not mention, that a similar approach had been accepted by British drafters in 1965 when arrangements were being discussed for legislation at Westminster to adopt the ill-fated Fulton-Favreau Formula.)

This procedure was agreed to and ultimately implemented. As we had always planned the *Constitution Act, 1980* to be made a Schedule to the *Canada Act* with English and French versions side-by-side, and as French in a Schedule caused Sir Henry no concern, we had no further problems concerning language.

We also agreed, consistently with Sir Henry's view, that actual changes in the law of Canada, such as British statutes still applying to Canada that we wanted repealed for Canadian purposes, should be dealt with in the *Constitution Act, 1980* and not in the body of the *Canada Act, 1980*.

In subsequent weeks the FCO apparently persuaded Sir Henry that our need for legislation was real and with few changes our drafts as they evolved were accepted. I did have a few transatlantic telephone discussions with him but only on matters of detail.

After conversations with Mrs Jean Wadds, our High Commissioner in London, we returned to Ottawa fairly confident that we had worked out the mechanics of patriation, recognizing some of the political hazards yet to be overcome. We so reported to our ministers.

In the meantime in Ottawa, there were last-minute ministerial discussions regarding the precise content of the package. There had been further debate about the terms of the mobility clause and about minority language rights in education. More importantly, there was still some question as to whether the Charter would be made applicable to the provinces. The Prime Minister was still uncertain about the amending formula and felt a growing determination to provide a referendum mechanism as a "tiebreaker" in the event that enough provincial legislatures opposed an amendment to prevent its adoption and the federal government wanted the final decision to be made by the public in a referendum.[4] I remember being involved with a small group of officials in a discussion about this with the Prime Minister in his sunroom at 24 Sussex Drive overlooking the Ottawa River, on a bright morning in late September. I think it was there, for the first time, that I appreciated that his wish to involve the people directly in the process was more a matter of philosophy than of political strategy. It was this attitude that Peter Russell later aptly described as "Gaullist": an appeal directly to the people over the heads of elected representatives.[5]

On October 1 the Prime Minister met separately with Joe Clark, Leader of the Official Opposition, and Ed Broadbent, Leader of the New Democratic Party. He apparently advised them that the government planned to proceed

with a joint resolution in Parliament that would provide for patriation, an amending formula, and a Charter. He did not share the text with them as it was still in the last stages of drafting. According to his report to Cabinet the next day, they both said they could support a resolution "that was not divisive" but that their ideas about what would be divisive "varied greatly." He had the impression that for Mr Clark any unilateral action would be divisive, whereas Mr Broadbent had some particular concerns but was generally supportive.[6] (He had told Trudeau he would want some changes to protect better the jurisdiction of the provinces over their natural resources, a particular concern of the NDP government of Saskatchewan.) At this meeting Cabinet finally agreed on a package that would impose the Charter on the provinces as well, on the amending formula, and on certain questions of detail. That night Prime Minister Trudeau went on national television to announce this initiative, explaining the history of what had brought the government to the conclusion that it had to proceed with patriation and certain other changes even without the approval of some or any provinces, and he outlined the nature of the package. Concurrently, texts of the joint resolution containing the proposed amendments were made available to the Opposition leaders and then to the press.

That same evening Messrs Clark and Broadbent had national television time to reply. Mr Clark immediately opposed the initiative because of the unilateral process involved. He also specifically attacked the idea of the referendum option built into the proposed amending formula. Mr Broadbent was generally supportive, although wishing to make some amendments to the proposal. The next day Premier Davis of Ontario announced that his government would support the measure and expressed the hope that federal MPs and senators of *all* parties would support it as well.[7] On October 17 Premier Hatfield of New Brunswick also announced his support.

The package that was tabled in Parliament on October 6 was in form a proposed joint resolution of the Senate and House of Commons addressed to the Queen and requesting that she lay before the Parliament of the United Kingdom the specific changes to our constitution as spelled out in the legal drafts attached.[8] This was the manner and form in which previous amendments had been obtained by Canada to our constitution. Apart from a technical change (moving the specific repeal of British laws as they applied to Canada to a Schedule of the *Constitution Act, 1980*)

and the manipulation of the language issue to meet the concerns of the British, the proposed *Canada Act, 1980* was essentially what we had put forward to officials in London: the *Constitution Act, 1980* as a Schedule of the *Canada Act, 1980*—the former to be given legal effect by the latter—that embodied a Charter, an amending formula, and a statement of constitutional principle in favour of equalization and the reduction of regional disparities. It also had a section and a Schedule dealing with the modernization of the constitution. This involved renaming all the *British North America Acts* as *Constitution Acts*, and the repeal of various pieces of UK legislation as they applied to Canada, including section 4 and subsection 7(1) of the *Statute of Westminster, 1931*. Some other spent laws were to be repealed as well. Most of the content of the package had at least been discussed with the provinces, some as early as the Victoria Conference of 1971; the precise amending formula, on which the federal cabinet had but recently agreed, had not.

This amending formula was quite complex. It first provided for an interim formula that would require unanimity of Parliament and provincial legislatures for any general amendment not otherwise authorized by the constitution (for example by head 1 of section 91 and head 1 of section 92 of the 1867 Act) and affecting more than one province. This procedure for amendments would obtain for two years, at which time it would be replaced by the procedure (the federal preference) set out in Part V, which was essentially the Victoria Formula that at one moment in 1971 had enjoyed the support of all provinces. If, however, there were within those two years provincial objections to the Victoria Formula and if at least eight provinces with at least 80 per cent of the national population agreed on a different formula, then the federal government could hold a referendum under federal rules to give the public a direct opportunity to choose between the Victoria formula and the new proposed provincial formula. The net effect would be as follows: immediate patriation, with an interim period of two years wherein unanimity would be the rule while provinces could attempt to reach agreement on a different plan; if they did, the federal government could challenge that plan through a referendum so that the Canadian people could decide which one they liked—the federal or the provincial formula.

As soon as the proposals had been made public on October 2, the federal government launched a public relations program to sell it. On October

3 all federal caucuses were briefed in Ottawa. (I had once or twice in the past declined to brief the government caucus on other legal matters when I found it was the only caucus being briefed by officials. I accepted this assignment because all caucuses were to get similar treatment.) Presumably because of my past connections with the NDP while in Saskatchewan, I was assigned that afternoon to brief that party's caucus, including such members as Stanley Knowles, Bob Rae, and Svend Robinson. After the briefing I proceeded directly to the airport to board an executive jet with Senator Hazen Argue, Minister of State (Canadian Wheat Board) from Saskatchewan, to accompany him at press conferences in Saskatoon and Regina where we explained the federal initiative.

After the Regina press conference I took the opportunity to call on John Whyte, a leading constitutional scholar and, at that time, Constitutional Adviser to the Government of Saskatchewan. Saskatchewan had not yet taken a position on the federal proposals and we discussed the possibility of the province supporting them, perhaps with some changes in the package. I reported back to my superiors in Ottawa and urged contact at the political level.

In the meantime, before the actual tabling of the resolution on October 6, the Prime Minister had had another meeting with Mr Broadbent. The latter had pressed his demands for changes to clarify provincial ownership of resources, to give the provinces the power of indirect taxation of resource products, and to give them a concurrent power over interprovincial sales of resource products. Trudeau agreed to these changes and agreed to make them public by an exchange of letters.[9]

So, with this side agreement, the patriation package was launched by being tabled in Parliament on October 6, 1980.

Abundant have been the criticisms of this proposed package of amendments. Many of these have come from human rights advocates who found the Charter particularly faulty. Some of the fault has been attributed to unimaginative or regressive drafting and the defective policy analyses that lay behind the drafting. While I will return to some specific issues later, I would not like it to be thought that the text, particularly of the Charter, represented the federal team's idea of perfection or the outer limits of our intellects. At all times we were working under great pressure. We were engaged in a highly politicized process, and politics, as we know, is the art of the possible. On the basis of our years of discussion with the provinces,

we sometimes chose less than our preferred draft and used language we thought might make the Charter acceptable to at least some provinces. Compromises were abundant and, happily, many of them became unnecessary or irrelevant in the months that followed. And undoubtedly important improvements were made as the result of public representations and suggestions mainly received through the parliamentary committee process, some involving matters of which we had not known nor thought.

I might also add that I had not expected to be engaged that year in this high-velocity political and legal tornado. During the winter of 1979–1980, I had been making arrangements to take a senior executive sabbatical from the Department of Justice during the 1980–1981 university term. I had arranged with my alma mater, Harvard, to be based at its Center for International Affairs in Cambridge, Massachusetts as a Research Associate. There I would be free to research and write with some modest duties to perform in connection with the University Consortium on North American Research based at the Center, where I would be a Visiting Scholar. (This Consortium, an arrangement between Harvard and Brandeis universities, was essentially a Canadian Studies program). As events unfolded in the spring of 1980 with Mr Trudeau back in office and the Quebec Referendum pending, I agreed to stay in Ottawa for the following year to participate in a renewed effort to reform the constitution. When I finally did take up the Harvard offer in the fall of 1981, I was still inextricably linked to the constitutional process as will become apparent.

8

A YEAR OF CONFLICT

From October 2, 1980, when the Prime Minister announced the federal government's patriation initiative and made public the proposed joint resolution, to September 28, 1981, when the Supreme Court of Canada released its opinions on the constitutionality of that resolution, a great public debate rocked the country. It was a very demanding year for members of the federal team. While I will relate here the major events and my role in them, I will not attempt to describe much of the political disputes and the efforts at negotiation. These have been well described by others.[1] My role was principally that of a legal adviser: as Assistant Deputy Minister for Public Law in the Department of Justice, I was the head of the branch responsible for providing constitutional advice to the Government of Canada and subject only to the final approval of the Deputy Minister. During this critical period I was mainly focussed on the legal issues and, unlike earlier periods of federal-provincial discussions, I was not involved, except occasionally and incidentally, in negotiations. I was throughout helped immeasurably by my personal staff which included my Secretarial Assistant, Francine Roy, and my Executive Assistant, Louis Davis.

There were essentially three fields of activity, often concurrent: the improvement and political "selling" of the patriation package in Canada, whether to Parliament, the public, or the provinces; the defence of the government's legal right to do what it was doing, in the courts; and the persuasion of the British government and Parliament to enact our patriation package.

In this process we had two main objectives. The first, and most difficult, was to get the package adopted in Britain, and as soon as possible. Timing was important for two reasons. The Canadian reason was that the Prime

Minister had adopted the goal of passage by July 1, 1981. Apart from the magic of a July 1 date, he and his colleagues had from the outset seen the year following the Liberal return to office and the defeat of separatism in the Quebec Referendum as a window of opportunity to effect important changes while they sensed a widespread public consensus in support.[2] The British reason for urgency was that Mrs Thatcher and British officials had urged the early delivery of the package to them to fit it into their legislative program if they were to enact it by July 1, 1981. Another reason for speed was given by the government's legal advisers: specifically, that it would be best to have the measure through Westminster before Canadian courts had the opportunity to rule on any questions raised about the constitutional conventions. Nothing would persuade a court more that we were pursuing an acceptable route than Westminster's acknowledgement of its ability and obligation to accede to Canada's request. There was no rule, we pointed out, that a government cannot act in accord with the legal advice it receives even if there are other opinions being advanced on the matter elsewhere. Of course, of even greater importance, timing aside, was achieving the adoption of the measure once it reached Westminster. It became apparent that, notwithstanding Prime Minister Thatcher's undertakings to Prime Minister Trudeau to pass whatever we sent, her MPs might not be so obliging. It was obvious that the more controversial the measure was in Canada, the more difficulty we might face in London. The more consensus we could establish in Canada, whether in Parliament, the provinces, or the public, the easier it would be to gain early passage at Westminster. Passage there could also become difficult if Canadian courts made findings regarding non-compliance by the Government of Canada with the law or the conventions of the constitution in the submission of the joint resolution.

The second objective was to take the opportunity during Parliamentary consideration to fine-tune the elements of the patriation package that had, of necessity, been hurriedly assembled, responding in the process to public, parliamentary, and provincial suggestions and criticisms.

Achieving these objectives involved a massive effort on the part of the Department of Justice, as well as of the many outside counsel we retained for various phases of the work.

I will recount our activities on three fronts: the domestic political, the judicial, and the British.

The centrepiece of the public and parliamentary debate was the Special Joint Committee of the Senate and House of Commons on the Constitution of Canada, set up by orders of both houses in late October and early November 1980. It consisted of 15 MPs and 10 senators, jointly chaired by Senator Hayes and Serge Joyal, MP. Other senators and MPs could and sometimes did attend as well. The committee was charged with considering the Proposed Resolution for a Joint Address to Her Majesty as had been announced by the government.

Considering the importance this committee was to have, its development was somewhat haphazard. The Kirby Memorandum had signalled the fact that a committee would be required. But the government proposed at first to limit the proceedings of the committee to two weeks, a period consistent with the felt need to get the finished resolution through the Canadian Parliament and off to England within a few weeks to meet the British government's request for an early receipt of the measure if it was to be passed in London by the following July 1. Debate on the joint resolution started in the House of Commons in early October. There was apparently division within the Progressive Conservative caucus about whether it should even participate in the Committee. For their part, the Liberals were insisting on a very short Committee mandate, and they were opposed initially to televising it, fearing further delays would flow from that. An opposition filibuster in the debate on the joint resolution developed in the House with the result that the government terminated debate by referring the resolution to the Committee sooner than had been planned—over the strong objections of the Progressive Conservatives. Hearings opened in the Committee on November 6. Pursuant to a decision taken in the House, but seemingly against the government's recommendations, the proceedings of the Committee were televised live on national television.[3] It was finally agreed that the Committee would hear witnesses and receive written submissions and, before long, it was submerged with requests and representations. In spite of its controversial beginning, the Committee proved to be an invaluable forum, both for informing the public and for generating a national consensus on the desirability of the *Charter*. It held 106 meetings over 56 hearing days, heard 104 representations, and received over one thousand written submissions.[4] I had to ensure that lawyers from my branch were present at all the hearings to keep our Minister informed

Author with Justice Minister Jean Chrétien appearing before the Special Joint Committee of the Senate and House of Commons on the Constitution, January 1981.

and to prepare responses to new issues raised by witnesses. We were at the same time engaged in an internal, ongoing review of the draft resolution to consider ways it might be improved.

My personal role with the Committee mainly consisted of accompanying the Minister of Justice, Jean Chrétien, at his appearances there. He spent many days there, first with an opening statement at the beginning on November 7, on which he was questioned by members, and then, starting on January 12, he or a colleague had to be there for clause-by-clause consideration. At the beginning of clause-by-clause consideration, the Minister tabled changes in the package that the government was already prepared to propose. The Minister's appearances usually involved questions from committee members regarding the intended meaning of each section, in addition to consideration of the changes they often proposed. Normally I sat on his left side and Roger Tassé, the Deputy Minister of Justice, on his right. As I understood it, this arrangement reflected the Minister's hearing abilities. He had an affliction in his right ear originating in a childhood malady. When he turned to Roger for advice on how to answer a question, the response would normally be in French, Jean's mother tongue, which he could absorb even with defective hearing on that side; when he turned

to me, I would respond in English and he wanted the aid of his best ear to understand. These sessions were held as committee members were available and could be in the morning, afternoon, or evening; on one occasion we sat most of a Saturday. During the weeks of these sittings the Minister at one point took ill and was absent for a few days. He was replaced by the acting Minister of Justice, Solicitor General Robert Kaplan.

Much of the time when the ministers were there, they were answering questions about the meaning of the various sections of the proposed *Constitution Act*, most frequently about the *Charter of Rights and Freedoms*. On these issues the Minister would frequently turn to Roger or me for advice. Sometimes, on the more technical issues, he would ask one of us to reply to the question. It was such responses as Roger and I made about the meaning of section 7 of the *Charter* that were later cited to the Supreme Court of Canada in 1985 in the *Reference re Section 94(2) of the Motor Vehicle Act*.[5] The question concerned the meaning of "fundamental justice" used in section 7 of the *Charter* in reference to the protection of "life, liberty and security of the person and the right not to be deprived thereof except in accordance with the principles of fundamental justice." I testified,[6] as did Roger Tassé, that we used this language rather than that of "due process," as used in the comparable section of the US Constitution, because in that country "due process" had been interpreted to include a requirement of both a fair procedure and a fair law in order to limit or deny such rights. A "fair" law had come to mean a law that the American courts agreed with as to its policy or provisions, a concept usually described as "substantive due process." I explained to the committee that the federal government and the provincial governments that had discussed this in our negotiations objected to the importation of substantive due process and did not intend to embrace it in the language of "fundamental justice."

We used the "principles of fundamental justice" as the standard by which such rights were to be protected, and we intended this to mean "fair procedure" or "procedural due process." As will be explained more fully in chapter 12, the Supreme Court rejected this evidence of the understanding and intention of the political decision makers in finding that indeed this was a guarantee of substantive due process.

While the appearances before the Committee were long and sometimes trying, there were, nonetheless, some pleasant moments. I was laughingly told by a member early in the process that my appearance, while sitting by

the Minister in quiet contemplation, reminded him of the "young Henry Fonda." I had a beard at that time, which perhaps added a false gravitas to my appearance. On one occasion Ray Hnatyshyn, an old friend from university days (he was a year behind me in law school in Saskatchewan), who was attending the committee as a Conservative M P, prefaced a question to me by telling the committee that in law school he had passed constitutional law only because he had borrowed my notes. (Many years later, in 1992, when he was Governor General of Canada, he and his wife Gerda were guests of honour at a dinner at the Rideau Club to mark the 125th anniversary of Confederation. He was the guest speaker and I had been designated to thank him. I referred to this public acknowledgement of his use of my constitutional law notes and told the dinner guests that when I had first heard of Ray's appointment as Governor General I had rushed to my notes to see if I had dealt adequately with the conventional limitations on the powers of the Governor General!)

But as the days and weeks went by, relations between the Committee and the Minister and his officials became more frayed. One of the causes of annoyance for members, I suppose, was that often when they suggested certain changes in the drafting, officials were called upon to reply, and officials often had to say that there were good reasons why the change was not desirable—often because of the possible implications for interpretations of other sections. For example, a member would typically want some meaning or some exception specifically spelled out in one section; we would point out that this would bear an implication for the interpretation of other sections where the same term was not spelled out or excepted. Or we would be aware of jurisprudence that might cause problems not immediately apparent. We tried to be as flexible as possible, and certainly at times changes were adopted about which we had lingering concern. But I imagine we were often seen as obstructionist. I must admit that probably I annoyed some members as I am not always good at concealing my boredom or irritation. There is a tendency among a few senators and members of parliament to treat officials as either stupid or malevolent, and they feel at liberty to display such attitudes but do not tolerate a response in kind. After having worked on this project intermittently for some 13 years, I could become impatient with criticisms about drafts we had composed after sometimes years of study and of discussion with provincial governments. I probably, at times, also displayed flashes of amusement at the

constitutional mythology to which some committee members subscribed. The attitude of some toward me was revealed in the comment made by one opposition member to another purposefully as I walked past them in the cloakroom: "There but for the grace of God goes God."

While we were busy attending the Committee we were also engaged, when our presence was not required there, in developing certain improvements to the package, often in response to pressures from one quarter or another. I will speak of these changes here briefly, except for those concerning the *Charter*, which I will discuss in Part II.

One small change was made in the *Canada Act*, revising its long title. Our original draft used this description: "An Act to amend the Constitution of Canada and to transfer to Canada all authority of the Parliament of the United Kingdom in respect of Canada." As political difficulties surfaced in London and British officials became concerned that members of the House of Commons or of the House of Lords might be tempted to move amendments to the bill as presented by Canada, we advised the Minister in December 1980 to change the long title to the following: "An Act to give effect to a request by the Senate and House of Commons of Canada." As we understood it, this would preclude amendments at Westminster: legislators would be limited to voting for or against the measure as requested by Canada. This change was adopted in the set of amendments proposed by the Minister to the Committee on January 12, 1981, and these words appeared in the *Canada Act, 1982* as it finally was enacted at Westminster on March 25, 1981. As will be seen, however, it did not later prevent the Speaker of the British House of Commons from allowing amendments to be moved and debated.

A more weighty issue was that of Aboriginal rights. The immediate political significance of this was that Trudeau, in seeking to build a national consensus without the wide support of provincial governments, particularly needed political legitimacy in the west. As a result of the 1980 election, the Liberals had only two members of Parliament from west of Ontario, both from Winnipeg. On the other hand, the NDP had 27 members from the west. For this reason the Prime Minister sought the support of Ed Broadbent, the NDP leader and, as already noted, he received a positive response in discussions starting as early as October 1, subject to some possible changes in the package. The first change discussed was that of adding new protections for provinces in respect of

their natural resources. This will be discussed later. The next important demand was the recognition of Aboriginal rights. This became an imperative for Broadbent if he were to maintain unity in his own caucus. By late 1980 Broadbent was pressing the government to accept an amendment guaranteeing such rights. I attended meetings with the Deputy Minister in Broadbent's office, meeting with him and Vancouver MP Ian Waddell. We were, at that time, warning the government about the problems of such a guarantee. Our position was that if the constitution simply guaranteed "Aboriginal rights" in so many words, we could not give much meaningful advice about what that might mean. The jurisprudence up to that time had given some precision to Aboriginal land rights, but there were many potential aspects of such rights that were the stuff of rhetoric but not of legal definition: for example, the right of Aboriginal self-government, the right to define who is an Aboriginal, hunting and fishing rights unrelated to traditional lands, et cetera. Further, as the proposed guarantee was to apply to Indians, Inuit, and Métis, we had to point out that there was no generally accepted determinant of who is a "Métis." While we were criticized as essentially opposing the protection of Aboriginal rights, we were simply doing our duties as lawyers in trying to advise ministers on the meaning and effect of the language they were being asked to endorse.[7] For a time the Prime Minister and the government took our advice: the official position was that while a guarantee of Aboriginal rights should not be put in this package, there should be a constitutional commitment to negotiate with Aboriginal people the definition of such rights before they were constitutionalized by a future amendment. However, the NDP was still threatening to withdraw support for the whole package. And then on January 6, 1981, Aboriginal groups started making submissions to the Committee. Even when they were not making formal presentations they remained in the Committee room and made their presence felt through conversations with the Minister and committee members. Pressure was growing for a change and finally the Prime Minister decided to accept the risk: the Minister of Justice proposed an amendment that was then to be section 33 of the *Constitution Act, 1981*, as follows:

33. (1) The aboriginal and treaty rights of the aboriginal
peoples of Canada are hereby recognised and affirmed.

(2) In this Act, "aboriginal peoples of Canada" includes
the Indian, Inuit and Métis peoples of Canada.

Such a provision was included in the amended draft reported by the Committee to Parliament on February 13, 1981.

As part of the effort to broaden consensus for the package, especially in the west, Trudeau for some months continued to hope to gain the support of at least two other provinces, Saskatchewan and Nova Scotia. These two had not been as vehement in their opposition to the *Charter* during the difficult summer debates in 1980. Saskatchewan had an NDP government and that party, and its predecessor, the Co-operative Commonwealth Federation (CCF), had a history of support of human rights and even their constitutional protection: this had been an important factor in the support of the federal NDP caucus for the package. Neither Saskatchewan nor Nova Scotia had joined the six provinces that banded together in October 1980 to challenge the "unilateral" package in the courts. I had a strong personal interest in seeing my native province support the *Charter*, which I firmly believed in and that I had helped endorse as a member of the then Saskatchewan delegation in constitutional discussions in the early 1960s. I did everything on a personal level to encourage that result, starting with my previously mentioned meeting in Regina with John Whyte of the provincial Department of the Attorney General on October 4. During the fall and winter I had the opportunity to see Roy Romanow in Ottawa a few times and informally explored with him areas for compromise. On one occasion I was able to arrange a breakfast meeting for him with Jean Chrétien at the Chateau Laurier where we considered some possibilities in the current state of the discussions.

The negotiations with Saskatchewan first focussed on natural resources. The province felt particularly offended by two decisions of the Supreme Court of Canada of the 1970s.[8] The first of these, *Canadian Industrial Gas & Oil Ltd. v Government of Saskatchewan*,[9] had struck down a provincial oil income tax and royalty surcharge as invalid. This was legislation designed to enable the province to collect by taxation and royalties the windfall profits from oil produced in the province and exported nationally and internationally (the windfall having been created by the actions of the Organization of Petroleum Exporting Countries, which arbitrarily raised crude oil prices in response to political conditions in the Middle East).

The Court held that the scheme amounted to indirect taxation, being in effect an export tax, and a regulation of interprovincial and international trade through the provincial government fixing the export price. The second of these cases was *Central Canada Potash Co. v Saskatchewan*.[10] This involved the validity of regulations limiting the amount of potash that could be produced annually in Saskatchewan. Nearly all potash produced there was being exported, and the purpose of the "pro-rationing" scheme was to prevent a collapse in export prices through overproduction. The Court held that this amounted to the regulation of interprovincial and international commerce, a matter for Parliament.

The province, and in particular Premier Blakeney, saw these cases (in which the federal government had participated as a party or as an intervener) as an assault on a province's power to control its own resources. The federal government, of course, saw it as the vindication of federal jurisdiction over trade and commerce regarding resource products once removed from the ground and marketed as articles of commerce. We had been made amply aware, however, of the fundamental nature of Saskatchewan's feelings on the subject, feelings that were shared to varying degrees by other resource-laden provinces whose support we had little hope of attracting. Ed Broadbent made enhanced provincial powers over resource management and exports his first condition for supporting the constitutional resolution in his meeting with the Prime Minister on October 1, 1980. He was anxious to show solidarity with the only provincial NDP government by making this a condition of his support, hoping that Trudeau's acceptance of this condition would enable the province of Saskatchewan to join Ontario and New Brunswick in endorsing the package. On October 21 Trudeau confirmed by letter that he was prepared to include a section on natural resources as requested by Broadbent. There then ensued private discussions with Mr Broadbent's office and Saskatchewan officials to articulate the precise wording of such an amendment. Saskatchewan wanted confirmation of provincial rights of management of natural resources (they thought the *Potash* case had diminished such rights) as well as a power of indirect taxation over natural resource products being exported, as well as a concurrent jurisdiction over interprovincial and international trade. Basically, the federal position was to limit the provincial concurrent power to interprovincial trade, to leave an unqualified paramountcy for federal laws over interprovincial trade, and to prevent provincial laws over

export of resources to other parts of Canada from discriminating between provinces of destination. (This would presumably frustrate the fulfilment of the Alberta bumper sticker wish of the 1970s: "Let the Eastern Bastards Freeze in the Dark"). On December 19 Premier Blakeney presented to the Committee the changes Saskatchewan wanted in the package, including the broader provincial powers over resource exports. In the end we persisted with the somewhat narrower federal version—one that the NDP caucus was prepared to support—and this was included in the amendments, the Committee agreed to, as moved by the Minister of Justice in the House of Commons on February 17, 1981. It later was enacted as section 92A of the *Constitution Act, 1867*. Nevertheless, on February 19 the government of Saskatchewan announced that it would oppose the joint resolution and within a few days became part of the "Gang of Eight." This heightened tensions between the NDP provincial government and the federal NDP caucus, causing some division in the latter in respect of support for the package.

I do not think that Saskatchewan's failure to get all it wanted on resources caused its ultimate decision in February to withhold support of the package and to become part of the Gang of Eight in opposing the federal initiative in political measures, in the courts and in Britain. In the end the position of the province turned on its distrust of the federal government and in particular on Trudeau's position that the Senate must retain its existing powers of veto over constitutional amendments requiring the approval of Parliament. I think the former problem could have been avoided by more adroit management of the relationship; but the latter had its roots in the political need of the Prime Minister to keep the support of the Senate for his constitutional package. This would not have been an imperative, I think, if he had had support from Saskatchewan and perhaps a few more provinces. In a political battle where the Prime Minister would have a clear national mandate, the Senate would I believe have bowed to the inevitable, facing up to its democratic deficit. But in the circumstances of 1981 Trudeau could not take that risk. Allan Blakeney was persistent in his position that the Senate could have no veto and that was the direct cause of breakdown in discussions.[11] Knowing both men reasonably well, I could see that although both were brilliant there was a gulf between their intellectual processes. On one occasion I was in the Prime Minister's office to be present when he was to speak to Premier Blakeney on the phone. Although I could not hear what the Premier was

saying, I could discern from Trudeau's responses where the difficulties lay. Allan Blakeney had a clear and precise legal mind with a complete attention to detail. He wanted an assurance that there would not be any further changes after he agreed to the text. Trudeau by this time was immersed in a giant and fluid political struggle in which he had to appease a large array of potentially hostile forces. In the end there was no reconciling the positions of the two First Ministers.

Throughout the duration of the Committee process we were often engaged in behind the scenes discussions with those concerned about the contents of the Charter. The Prime Minister had representations from the hierarchy of the Roman Catholic Church of Canada on their wish to see abortion precluded by the *Charter*. We had to provide analysis and commentary for the Prime Minister in this dialogue. Eddie Goldenberg, of the Minister's office, and I met with the Archbishop of Newfoundland on another matter—his concern that the guarantees of equality in the *Charter* might abolish the privileged position the Church's tax-supported schools in Newfoundland enjoyed under the constitution as compared with some other denominations. We had several meetings with representatives of the Advisory Council on the Status of Women as well as other feminist groups on equality rights and other elements of the *Charter*. We had representations from the Jewish Students Association concerning the prohibition in what is now paragraph 11(g) of the *Charter* against conviction for acts that were not contrary to law at the time they were committed. The original formulation could be interpreted as applying only to acts prohibited by domestic law. As a result of these and other representations, we broadened the meaning of law to include international law or "criminal according to the general principles of law recognized by the community of nations." This alteration was designed to preserve the right to try war criminals on the same basis on which the Nuremberg Trials proceeded. Changes the Minister agreed to were subsequently made to the package in the form of these amendments.

One change for which I can find no record of a formal submission (I believe suggestions had been made in private to the Prime Minister by the Roman Catholic hierarchy) was the addition of a preamble to the *Charter* that was duly enacted as follows: "Whereas Canada is founded upon principles that recognise the supremacy of God and the rule of law." The first trace I can find in the record for this bold statement is in

the minutes of Cabinet for April 16, 1981, as the debate in Parliament was about to draw to a close. The minutes state: "*The Prime Minister sought counsel on the inclusion of God in the government's amendments. Ministers generally agreed that God should be referred to in these amendments.*"[12] The matter was left for the Prime Minister, the Minister of Justice (Jean Chrétien), and the President of the Privy Council (Yvon Pinard, the House Leader, later to be my valued colleague on the Federal Court) to work out the details. While it is a trite saying that "the devil is in the details," here it was God in the details! I was never consulted on this: if I had been I would have observed that structurally it is an odd preamble because of the reference to God. There is no clear causal link between the recognition of God in the preamble and what follows. Also, it seems to me it is full of ambiguity. One must ask "Which God?" or "Whose God?" It clearly refers to the God of a monotheistic religion, yet we know that many Canadians adhere to polytheism while others are atheists. And there is a basic inconsistency in this declaration of the existence of one God when no more than six lines below, in paragraph 2(a) of the following document, there is the recognition and guarantee of "freedom of conscience and religion," a document designed to permit Canadians to have their own beliefs or non-beliefs about God. This amendment must have sprung from the devout beliefs of the Prime Minster and his ministers, but there were some who saw it as political bait to attract the religious faithful who might have lingering doubts about this otherwise secular document. One newspaper at the time carried a cartoon depicting the amendment being made in Parliament. There is a stentorian voice coming from on high saying, "THAT'S ALL VERY WELL, BUT YOU STILL NEED [Alberta Premier] LOUGHEED ON SIDE!"

I must mention another amendment made at the Committee stage that was of my own initiative and that found its way into the opening words of section 52 of the *Constitution Act, 1982*—namely the declaration that "The Constitution of Canada is the supreme law of Canada," added as one of the amendments to the joint resolution proposed by the Minister of Justice to the Committee on January 12, 1981. It has always been my conviction, and no court to my knowledge has ever denied it, that as part of the former British Empire the superiority of British laws over Canadian laws, where both applied to Canada, was confirmed and clarified by section 2 of the *Colonial Laws Validity Act, 1865*,[13] which provided that where Imperial

laws expressly or by necessary intendment applied to a colony, and if there were a conflict between such law and a colonial law, the colonial law would be invalid to the extent of the conflict. The *BNA Acts* were such Imperial laws. And that is why federal or provincial laws that were inconsistent with the distribution of powers in the 1867 Act were struck down by Canadian courts and the Judicial Committee of the Privy Council. This constitutional rule in respect of Canada was preserved by the *Statute of Westminster, 1931*, subsection 7(1),[14] which retained the rule that one set of Imperial laws, namely the *BNA Acts*, would remain supreme over any Canadian legislation, federal or provincial. In other words, this was the textual underpinning of the supremacy of the Canadian constitution. It suddenly struck me one morning in early September of 1980, as I was shaving, that the structure we had in mind for patriation might eliminate that rule. While in the provision that became section 52 we had described the statutes that were specifically to be considered part of the Constitution of Canada, that description nowhere mentioned section 2 of the *Colonial Laws Validity Act, 1865*. Furthermore, it was our plan to seek the repeal of subsection 7(1) of the *Statute of Westminster, 1931*, which had so far preserved for our constitution the supremacy rule in section 2 of the *Colonial Laws Validity Act, 1865*. It therefore seemed important to reaffirm the constitutional supremacy principle in the revised constitution we were adopting. I asked for some work to be done on this in the Department, which confirmed my concerns. As a result, a declaration of the supremacy of the Constitution was added to section 52, paraphrasing Article VI, section 2 of the Constitution of the United States. At times this declaration has been treated matter-of-factly by the Supreme Court as a simple continuity of the principle of supremacy of the constitution.[15] At other times, however, the Court has waxed eloquently on the profound change in our constitutional system effected by section 52, from one of "Parliamentary supremacy to one of constitutional supremacy,"[16] and from this perceived fundamental change it has inferred a large license for the Court to redefine the contents of the constitution.[17] The notion that in 1982 we suddenly became a nation of "constitutional supremacy" has become the stuff of after-dinner speeches wherever lawyers are gathered, but it has no basis in reality. All that section 52 does is to maintain the continuity of our system, which has known judicial review to enforce constitutional limitations on our legislatures and executives since before Confederation.

As mentioned earlier, the government had originally hoped the Committee hearings would be brief, in order to get a resolution passed through Parliament and sent to England within the short time frame the British had said they needed in order for adoption at Westminster by July 1, 1981. Once the Conservative Opposition stopped objecting to the early reference to committee (in lieu of further debate in the House), they were determined to make the Committee process as thorough (and lengthy) as possible, their strategy being to delay the submission to Westminster until opposition to it in Canada could be maximized, including possible negative pronouncements by one or more Canadian courts on the propriety of the Liberal government's process. The government had finally set its goal to get the package out of Committee before Christmas. But this was protested by the Opposition and ultimately there was a compromise agreement for the Committee to finish its work by February 9, 1981. On January 12 Chrétien proposed some amendments and on January 20 the Official Opposition proposed its changes. These latter included a proposal for a Charter, but one to be adopted only after provincial consent. By this time the Progressive Conservatives had actually noticed that there was a growing tide of support for the Charter in the country, so they decided they would only oppose it on procedural grounds. The Committee voted on numerous proposed amendments and then reported a revised joint resolution to the Commons on February 17, 1981. There then ensued a boisterous debate in the Commons that the Liberals tried in vain to terminate by April. By this time the Opposition was filibustering to prevent the resolution from passing before the appeals in the three provincial cases challenging the process had been heard in the Supreme Court. For reasons already stated, the government had been determined to send the matter to Westminster and get a determination there before the Supreme Court had made its decision and, as late as April 16, the Cabinet was still planning on a completion of the debate in the Commons by April 21 and in the Senate by April 24.[18] In the end this became politically impossible: as the date for the Supreme Court hearing had been set for April 28, 1981 (it had originally been expected much later), the three parties in the House agreed to complete voting on the amendments before the House prior to that date and then to adjourn debate on April 23 until after the Supreme Court had ruled on the questions before it.

With the Committee having finished its work, and the debate in Parliament having been adjourned, my colleagues and I could put aside our long-standing efforts to improve the package or adapt it in response to political pressures, and concentrate instead on the battles on the judicial and British fronts. This is not to say that during the Committee process we had had the luxury of ignoring these other aspects. While before the committee we also had to contend with other challenges: on January 29 there was issued in London the Report of the Foreign Affairs Committee of the British House of Commons on *British North America Acts: the Role of Parliament*.[19] This came to be known as the Kershaw Report after its chairman, Sir Anthony Kershaw, whom I had the dubious pleasure of meeting a few months later at an Oxford seminar. This committee had heard a variety of British academics and Canadian provincial witnesses and concluded that Westminster should not enact the measure to be requested by Canada unless there was sufficient provincial support for that request. It even went so far as to define what would be "sufficient support." Needless to say, this caused quite a stir in the Committee room in Ottawa. But then on February 3 the Manitoba Court of Appeal released a judgement in the reference to that court on the patriation measure: it found in favour of the federal position by a majority of 3 to 2. This decision generated another cause for comment at the Committee and more briefing notes for our ministers. Once the Committee had terminated its work, these other matters became the prime focus of my attention, as will be seen.

One other activity that followed the adjournment of the debate in Parliament was forward planning for the application of the *Charter*. We were very conscious of the limited impact that the *Canadian Bill of Rights* of 1960 had had after its adoption. The bar had invoked it sparingly and the courts had construed it narrowly. We did not want the same thing to happen with the *Charter*. Thus, although the adoption of the *Charter* was as yet by no means sure, in my branch we planned for its launching. In June 1981 we made a contract with the Human Rights Institute of the University of Ottawa to plan a series of studies on the various sections of the *Charter*, in order to analyze their probable interpretations and to identify issues, some drawn from foreign jurisprudence, that might arise. These studies were then to be edited and published in book form, and did in fact appear in 1982 in both languages, the English version being Tarnopolsky and Beaudoin, *The Canadian Charter of Rights and Freedoms*.[20] The Institute

was to choose the authors and do the editing. We only retained the right to delete any confidential information we might have provided. Similarly, as the months went by and the enactment of the *Charter* became more imminent, we made grants available to the Canadian Institute for the Administration of Justice and other independent bodies to organize seminars open to judges and lawyers, with specialist speakers to familiarize participants with its contents, issues likely to arise, and sources of legal writing and jurisprudence that might be helpful. Again this was an arm's length operation, with the Department having no control over the program other than to suggest possible areas of likely concern. Finally, in anticipation of the coming into force of the *Charter*, we undertook surveys of existing federal laws to try to identify possible conflicts with the *Charter* and to advise relevant departments of the possible need for change. As it turned out, we need not have feared that the bench or the bar would neglect the *Charter* once it came into force. Instead, there was a race among lawyers and judges to find and decide *Charter* cases!

THE JUDICIAL FRONT

It will be recalled that in the Kirby Memorandum, which had been intended as confidential political and legal advice to Cabinet, we had expressed the view that unilateral patriation was in accordance with constitutional law. We also noted that some would argue, and some court might hold, that unilateral patriation would be contrary to the conventions of the constitution. We emphasized that in our view (and in the view of most authors on law and politics) the existence and definition of a constitutional convention was essentially a political question determined by political actors, not a matter for determination by the courts; however, we warned that such an obvious principle would not necessarily be recognized by every court. And we warned, too, that even if the Government of Canada (the only government empowered to do so) declined to refer such an issue to the Supreme Court of Canada, it would be open to one or more provinces to refer similar questions to their provincial Court of Appeal and decisions of those courts could then be appealed to the Supreme Court. The Memorandum was leaked and became a litigation manual for the provinces.

On October 14, a few days after the debate on the resolution had commenced in Ottawa, the ten Premiers met in Toronto to consider what

they should do.[21] It emerged that at that time only six were prepared to mount an opposition: these were British Columbia, Alberta, Manitoba, Quebec, Prince Edward Island, and Newfoundland. Within three weeks of the tabling of the joint resolution, these six met in Winnipeg and developed a legal strategy of opposition.[22] There it was agreed that Manitoba, Quebec, and Newfoundland would each take references to their respective ·Court of Appeal. Apparently these three were chosen as representatives: Quebec as an original province in Confederation, Manitoba as a creature of the Parliament of Canada, and Newfoundland as a province of Canada through its consent. The questions they posed differed slightly but in each case they raised the issues of whether this "unilateral action" would be legally effective, and whether it would be in accordance with constitutional conventions. The underlying issue was whether such action required the consent of the "provinces," but none of the questions specified how such consent would be expressed.

Two observations must be made about these references at the outset. First, the statutes under which such references are taken really allow executive governments to refer any question, whether legal, factual, or otherwise. However, it is open to a Court to refuse to answer non-justiciable questions, as the Supreme Court itself confirmed in the appeal from these provincial reference decisions in the case that has come to be known as the *Patriation Reference*.[23] Having said that, a majority nevertheless went on to decide that there was a convention requiring a "sufficient measure of provincial consent" for such amendment requests to be made to Westminster. Yet it seems clear that in conventional litigation (that is, in a dispute between two parties not involving a reference to the court by an executive government) a court would not undertake to define constitutional conventions[24] nor should this Court have done so when it had the right to refuse.[25]

The second observation is that the government of Quebec very deliberately launched a process in its Court of Appeal that it knew would end up before the Supreme Court of Canada. This is abundantly clear from its actions. While most if not all other provinces had long provided by statute for a right of appeal to the Supreme Court of Canada from a decision of its provincial Court of Appeal on a reference, Quebec had never done so. But suddenly it adopted such legislation[26] for the specific purpose of this case in early December 1980, and its reference questions were then announced. So determined was the Lévesque government to obstruct the

federal initiative, it committed itself in this way to having the question of its alleged right to veto constitutional amendments to be determined by an Ottawa tribunal. Nonetheless, it refused to abide by that decision.

Faced with the prospects of fighting three court cases in three courts of appeal, federal lawyers were obliged to make hasty preparations. In my Public Law Branch of the Department of Justice we had for many months, of course, been researching and writing opinions and consulting outside counsel on the option of the federal government seeking patriation and amendments from the UK Parliament without the consent of some or all provinces. We now had to focus on the preparation of factums (written briefs of argument) for use in the courts of appeal of Manitoba, Quebec, and Newfoundland. As representations on behalf of the Government of Canada, it was essential that these factums be in both official languages in the two provinces where, according to the constitution, both English and French are official, namely Quebec and Manitoba. The Justice lawyers doing much of the drafting of the factums included Fred Jordan, Barbara Reed, and Louis Reynolds, with valuable input from experienced litigation lawyers such as Associate Deputy Minister Don Christie and Senior Counsel John Scollin. I reviewed successive drafts and made suggestions.

The speed at which the whole process moved was almost breathtaking by any normal standards of litigation. When we had speculated during the summer of 1980 on a possible reference being taken by a province, we thought it would take many months for the first hearing to be held and perhaps two years before the Supreme Court could dispose of the matter. Yet within about seven weeks of the three provinces deciding to take references, the argument opened in the Manitoba Court of Appeal in the first week of December. Our counsel in that Court included J.J. Robinette, John Scollin of the Department of Justice, and Professor Dale Gibson of the University of Manitoba Law School. There were 16 counsel from the various provinces and argument took four days. I went to Winnipeg to hear the argument and to discuss issues with our counsel as they developed. Our most vocal critic among the judges was Mr Justice O'Sullivan, who brusquely intervened frequently during argument, particularly to challenge Mr Robinette. Again, with surprising speed in a case so complex, the Court issued its judgement on February 3, 1981.[27] It split three to two in favour of upholding the federal initiative as being in conformity with constitutional law. As for the conventions, these three judges either declined

Author as one of federal counsel at the Supreme Court of Canada in the Patriation Reference, April 1981. In the centre is James Thistle, one of counsel for Newfoundland, and to the right is Fred Jordan of the federal Department of Justice.

to answer that question or found no conflict between the conventions and what was proposed by Ottawa.

The Quebec reference was heard in its Court of Appeal by a five-judge panel in early March 1981. I went to Montreal to attend one day of the hearing and had lunch with counsel to discuss the case. We were represented in that Court by Michel Robert, Raynold Langlois, and Louis Reynolds. There were 14 counsel representing the various provinces. Judgement was rendered on April 15, 1981,[28] the Court splitting four to one with the majority finding that the federal proposal was neither contrary to constitutional law nor the constitutional conventions.

I had a much more active role in the hearing of the Newfoundland Reference, which took place in St. John's February 10–12, 1981, before three judges. I acted as one of the counsel in that case, as did another lawyer in my branch, Barbara Reed. We were there to assist our chief counsel, prominent Newfoundland lawyer Clyde Wells, QC, and Clyde had arranged with the Newfoundland bar for Barbara and me to have temporary admission for the purpose of this case. Clyde had been a minister in Joey Smallwood's cabinet until he left over a disagreement with the Premier.

He had since been a very successful practitioner in Corner Brook and had argued many important commercial and constitutional cases. (He was later to become Premier of Newfoundland and then Chief Justice of the province.) With us we also had a St. John's lawyer, Douglas Hunt, QC, whose firm fortunately had an office across the street from the Court House where we could meet and gown for court. In court we were of course faced with an array of 13 counsel representing the Newfoundland and other provincial governments. The court, while judicious, did not betray much sympathy for our arguments. I did not entirely grasp the hostility of our surroundings until the morning of the last day when a *Globe and Mail* reporter asked me if we were attending the dinner that evening. I asked "What dinner?" It emerged that the Attorney General of the province had invited to a private dinner all the lawyers appearing in the case except those representing the Government of Canada! It was no great surprise when the Court announced its decision on March 31, 1981,[29] unanimously finding against us that the federal initiative was contrary to constitutional law and conventions. Thus it was the only court to find the process to be illegal, and in doing so it relied on the *Statute of Westminster, 1931*, the statute that Britain's Chief Parliamentary Counsel had told us the previous September was no longer living law!

I remember that week in St. John's as being particularly hectic because of other responsibilities. In my spare time I was on the telephone to Ottawa and London in respect of preparations for a trip I had to make to Britain the following week to further the patriation project. Along with Barbara Reed I also spent a long evening in a meeting with officials of the provincial cabinet office, of their Department of Justice, and of the provincially owned electrical utility on a complex constitutional matter. Newfoundland has extensive hydroelectric production facilities in Labrador and a great potential for more, most of it being surplus to the province's needs. It believed there was a major market in the United States for much of its surplus, but geography intervened: land lines carrying electricity to the United States must pass through the province of Quebec. While Hydro Quebec was always willing to buy Labrador electricity (at bargain prices because of improvident contracts made by Newfoundland back in the 1960s) and to sell it at a profit in the United States, Newfoundland wanted to market its own product to the Americans at current market rates. It was the view of the province that the federal government could, through its

jurisdiction over interprovincial and international undertakings, either force Hydro Quebec to "wheel" (that is, transmit as a carrier but not as a middleman) Labrador electricity through Quebec to the US border, or to authorize the construction through Quebec territory of a dedicated power line for such transmission. We had a long and inconclusive discussion of the constitutional issues, a discussion that was continued in Ottawa the following month. There was a strong suspicion on the part of Newfoundland that Ottawa had little stomach for forcing this issue with Quebec, even if there was federal jurisdiction to do so. In my view they had correctly assessed the situation.

The following week I was in London. Returning to Canada the next Monday, I landed at Mirabel where I had left my car and drove into Montreal to join that afternoon a meeting of several of our counsel then underway.

Incidentally, when the decision of the Newfoundland Court of Appeal was announced on March 31, we had a tense morning in Ottawa. As St. John's time is one and one-half hours ahead of Ottawa, the radio and television news of the result was available at the opening time of offices in the national capital. But we did not have the text in hand. Today such a decision would be issued electronically and be available instantly throughout the world. But in those days it was strictly hard copy—at best, the text would have to be transmitted by fax. One of the few fax machines on the island of Newfoundland was owned by a corporate client of Clyde Wells that Clyde used to transmit the text of the decision and that was not particularly fast. The judgement was lengthy and we waited impatiently as it emerged page by page from our fax machine in the Department. Tempers were even more frayed by the arrival of Svend Robinson, M P, who had been an NDP member of the Special Joint Committee and one of our severe critics. Having been told by phone that copies of the judgement were not yet available, he came to the Department insisting that he receive a copy. I had to tell him he would have it as soon as the rest of us and he finally left. The full set of reasons was not available until noon.

From these provincial arenas the action shifted to the perfection of appeals in the Supreme Court. The Attorney General of Canada was of course supporting the decisions of the Manitoba and Quebec appeal courts and appealing against the judgement of the Newfoundland Court of Appeal. Few could have imagined (certainly I didn't) that these appeals could all

be argued by the end of April. The Manitoba judgement had only been entered on February 3. As the end of March approached, we were still awaiting the Newfoundland and Quebec decisions. Yet Kerr Twaddle, QC, counsel for Manitoba as appellant from the decision of their Court of Appeal, was pressing the Supreme Court to fix an early date for a hearing, for fear that the joint resolution would be passed by Parliament and sent to London before the Supreme Court could pronounce on the matter. That in fact was precisely what we hoped would happen. Kerr arranged a scheduling meeting with Chief Justice Laskin to which we were invited to send representatives. The meeting was held in the Chief Justice's office—as it happened one floor directly above an office I came to occupy some 14 years later as a judge of the Federal Court of Appeal and Chief Justice of the Court Martial Appeal Court of Canada. John Scollin, Senior Counsel from the Department, and I attended for the Government of Canada. Kerr made a forceful presentation of the need for an early hearing date in order to have the matter determined before Parliament approved the resolution. At a certain point the Chief Justice said, "Surely the government does not plan to proceed with adoption of the resolution before our hearing," and he looked pointedly at John and me. John (although he was a senior counsel of record in the Manitoba appeal) said, "Perhaps Mr Strayer can speak to that." So I was obliged to say to the Chief, "My lord, our instructions are that the debate will proceed to a conclusion in Parliament whether or not the Court has heard this matter." This was a true account of the state of Cabinet's determination at that time. But it seemed to shock the Chief and I was the unfortunate messenger. I think if I had not known Bora for years through academic circles I might have received a judicial blast. As it was, he grimaced and said that he would fix an early date for the hearing to commence, a little over a month later, on April 28. We expressed concern that this would be too soon to hear the appeals from the other provinces as their decisions were not yet announced and we pointed out the importance of having the appeals all heard together. (As already noted, Newfoundland's was subsequently announced on March 31 and Quebec's on April 15.) While we expected the Newfoundland decision momentarily, I expressed concern that we didn't know when Quebec's would be issued, and this early date made it unlikely an appeal could be heard from that Court at the same time. But the Chief Justice persevered in his determination of April 28 as the starting date for whatever appeals were ready to be heard.

In the event, we were able to perfect all three appeals and have them heard together. But the timetable was without precedent; three provincial appeal court decisions on complex matters made respectively approximately seven weeks, five weeks, and two weeks before the opening of their appeals in the Supreme Court! Needless to say, this took an extraordinary amount of work under pressure to prepare our appeal materials, with factums in both official languages. Throughout this whole process we had to consult and seek the input and agreement of our four outside counsel who were to participate in the argument before the Supreme Court. Word processors had not come into general use in the Department of Justice at that time; they were confined to the Legislation Section, where they were invaluable for drafting and revising legislation. We were able to get the use of these machines during the height of our preparations and, incidentally, demonstrate to the Department the wisdom of making such devices generally available.

On one occasion Mr Robinette, who was to lead off in the appeal from Manitoba, was in Ottawa at the Justice Building to discuss the factum. I received a message that the Prime Minister wanted to meet him that afternoon in the Centre Block. After lunch I told Mr Robinette that he and I had to go to a meeting in the Centre Block and I arranged for a car. As we were in the car he said, "What is this meeting about?" I said, "We're going to meet your client." And so we arrived to meet with the Prime Minster in a small conference room near his office. Trudeau was obviously curious to meet Robinette (I'm not sure they had ever met other than casually) and to explore some of the intellectual niceties of the case. It was a lively discussion on both sides.

Our final preparatory meeting was held in the Justice boardroom the day before the hearing was to open. It was chaired by the Minister of Justice, Jean Chrétien, and included federal counsel as well as some other federal advisers, and the counsel team for Ontario, led by Attorney General Roy McMurtry, as well as New Brunswick. A journalistic account has it that there were more than 50 people present, such as to cause the Minister some distress.[30] As for myself, I felt great relief that we had our team assembled and all the arguments ready for the next day—no small achievement in the time that had been available for the task!

When the argument of the *Patriation Reference* opened in the Supreme Court of Canada chamber on April 28, 1981, the room was packed. There

were 38 lawyers at counsel tables, straining the available space. On either side of the chamber were chairs facing to the centre, occupied by guests of the justices, including some judges' wives and law clerks. The central spectator area was completely full: most seats were simply available on a first-come, first-served basis, meaning that there was a long lineup each morning in the foyer of the Court starting an hour or more before the sitting opened. There were a very few reserved seats. One of these was used on occasion by Jean Chrétien, as Attorney General of Canada. The federal team consisted of J.J. Robinette, John Scollin, Clyde Wells, Michel Robert, Raynold Langlois, Barbara Reed, Louis Reynolds, and myself. The federal arguments were presented in both official languages in respect of the Quebec and Manitoba appeals. We were placed near to our allies, Ontario and New Brunswick, which had, respectively, four and two counsel present. Notables among provincial counsel included Lucien Bouchard (later founder of the Bloc Québécois and separatist Premier of Quebec) appearing for the Lévesque government, and Roy McMurtry, the Attorney General of Ontario performing what had been at one time a customary function of a chief law officer to represent his government in a constitutional case. Roy of course later became Canada's High Commissioner to the United Kingdom and then Chief Justice of Ontario. In between these posts he had practised law in Toronto and I once had the pleasure of him appearing before me in a Competition Tribunal hearing that I chaired as a judicial member of that Tribunal. Later still we were colleagues, as were Michel Robert and Clyde Wells, in the Canadian Judicial Council, the assembly of Chief Justices.

The federal position before the Supreme Court remained as it had throughout the summer of 1980 and in the provincial courts of appeal, as follows: the UK Parliament still had the legal authority, confirmed by the *Statute of Westminster, 1931*, to amend our constitution, the *BNA Acts*. There were no *legal* preconditions to the exercise of that power, even though by convention Westminster would not act without a request from the Canadian Parliament. We argued that the provinces could not attack the passing of a joint resolution by the Parliament of Canada because that was an instrument of no legal effect. It was just a request to the Queen to pass on a request to the UK Parliament. J.J. Robinette, who had a remarkable talent for making complicated issues simple, told the Court a joint resolution had no more legal effect than a resolution by the Canadian

Parliament wishing the Queen a happy birthday. Some of the judges rather choked on that. As for the questions raised as to the conventions, we argued that the Court should not answer such questions. They were not justiciable, as there were no legal standards to apply to answer them. We cited numerous authors to the effect that conventions are based on political practice, that they are defined by political actors not the courts, and may change from time to time with changing circumstances. Even assuming the Court would address the convention questions, we argued that the history of past amendments was unclear and there were many examples where amendments had been made affecting provincial rights without unanimous provincial consent. Further, and I think this should have been the most telling argument, whatever past practices might indicate, it is the nature of conventions to evolve. On the assumption that unanimity was required, Canada had been trying since 1927 to reach agreement among all the provinces on an amending formula without success. This alone justified a new departure in which a national government, the government responsible for national sovereignty, was justified in severing this last element of legal dependence on the Parliament of another country on the basis of what it apprehended to be a public consensus. Further, the amendment formula proposed by the national government could by its own terms ultimately be put to the people of Canada in a referendum.

Of the Gang of Eight, seven provinces argued that both legally and by convention all provinces must agree on any amendments affecting them. Some relied on the compact theory of Confederation, a historical myth. Others argued that this logically flowed from the inherent sovereignty of provincial legislatures: their powers should never be limited without their consent. Many of the justices also seemed sensitive to this sovereignty argument. (Did any of them ever notice that when ten executive governments later signed the accord of November 5, 1981—the result of which was to reduce the powers of both Parliament and the legislatures—only three legislative bodies ever voted on these changes: namely the Parliament of Canada and the legislature of Alberta that approved, and the National Assembly of Quebec that disapproved?) And of course they rehearsed ad infinitum the past practices to demonstrate in their view that nothing was ever done without the consent of all provinces, thus confirming the convention on which they relied. Only Saskatchewan took a different approach. Its counsel, Ken Lysyk, did not argue that unanimity of the

provinces was required, only "a sufficient measure of provincial consent." He hastened to assure the justices that they did not need to define "sufficient measure." All they had to do was state the obvious: that the support of Ontario and New Brunswick for these changes did not amount to a "sufficient measure." This was enough to provide a comfort zone for six judges (the "Conventions Majority").

At the end of five days the Court reserved its judgement and we were relieved from further legal battles for the summer. My own efforts switched to the British front as I will discuss later. I also spent some time finalizing my arrangements to take a sabbatical at Harvard starting in September; in fact, before the Court's judgement was rendered I had taken up residence there along with my posts as a Visiting Scholar at the University Consortium for Research on North America and a Research Associate at the Center for International Affairs. My main project was to be the production of a second edition of my book first published in 1968[31] and by then needing much updating. To this end I had obtained a Social Sciences and Humanities Research Council grant in Canada and had a student researcher working part-time in Ottawa. But when word arrived that the Supreme Court judgement was to be released on September 28, I was called back to help with the aftermath. This was to be the first of many trips to Ottawa that autumn and winter to participate in follow-up work. When I was sworn in as a Judge of the Federal Court, Trial Division in August 1983, the Minister of Justice Mark MacGuigan spoke at the ceremony. He described my role during these events and said that I was a "familiar figure" on the Boston-Ottawa flights that fall. He was correct.

On the morning of September 28 we were all gowned and in our place in Court. For the first time, television cameras were allowed in the room. The Chief Justice slowly read a synopsis of the judgement. Unfortunately, the sound cables had become disconnected so that there was no sound on television, and it was with difficulty that we listened intensely to decide whether we had won or lost. Even with the best of hearing it was not easy to tell.

It emerged that seven judges (the Legal Majority) agreed with us that what we were doing in seeking the amendments from the UK Parliament would produce legally valid amendments to the Canadian constitution. This majority included Laskin, CJ, and Dickson, Beetz, Estey, McIntyre, Chouinard, and Lamer, JJ. However four of these judges—Dickson, Beetz,

Chouinard, and Lamer—joined with the two dissenters from the Legal Majority (Martland and Ritchie, JJ) to form the Convention Majority, holding that this manner of proceeding was contrary to the "federal principle," which, they said, required a "sufficient measure of provincial consent," as was argued by Ken Lysyk for Saskatchewan. These four seemed unembarrassed by the statement they had all subscribed to as members of the Legal Majority, that "There is not and cannot be any standardized federal system from which particular conclusions must necessarily be drawn."[32] And indeed this is so: there are federal states (for example the United States, Australia, and Switzerland) where neither the legislatures nor the executive governments of the component units have a necessary role in constitutional amendments. Yet somehow the majority believed that the "federal principle" at least dictated a role for provincial executive governments in Canadian constitutional amendments. (The Court never prescribed a specific role for provincial legislatures and as we have seen there is apparently no such role guaranteed by the "federal principle": the legislatures of eight provinces ultimately supporting the 1981 Accord never had the opportunity to vote on it).

This is not the place for a detailed critique of the decision of the Convention Majority. I have pointed out elsewhere both its illogicalities and its harmful consequences. Briefly, I am still convinced the Court should have refused to answer what was a political question concerning the existence of a convention and its definition as to the need for provincial consent. I was surprised and disappointed that this seemed to cause such little concern to academics and wondered what they would say if one day the Court was asked, for example, whether a government had lost the confidence of the House of Commons because it refused to hold a sitting where it was almost certain to be defeated. This is every bit as much a matter of constitutional convention as the provincial role in constitutional amendments. Can anyone imagine the Supreme Court of the United States having told Franklin Roosevelt he could not seek a third term in 1940 because the clear constitutional convention since the first years of the Republic was that no president should serve more than two terms? Instead, it required the Twenty-second Constitutional Amendment in 1951 before that became a judicially enforceable norm. In the *Patriation Reference* the Court was using its position to dictate a rule of constitutional amendment with which politicians had struggled unsuccessfully

to establish for over 50 years. And the Convention Majority reasons were sadly lacking in intellectual rigour, both with respect to the historical record and with respect to their assumptions about the requirements of the "federal principle." For the latter they had scant regard for what actually happens in other federal states. Finally, as I have said elsewhere, this form of judicial activism was an early example of what later became a growing trend, based on the Court's premise that if there is an important problem of public policy that politicians have not resolved, and if somebody with a private interest or a public interest group will be good enough to bring the issue before the Court, it will solve that problem.[33]

In the hours immediately following the release of the judgement we were heavily engaged in analyzing it and preparing briefing materials for ministers. The Prime Minister was in Seoul, Korea, having meetings there on his way to Melbourne, Australia, for a Commonwealth Heads of Government meeting and briefing materials were also prepared for him. In the early days after the judgement, both sides were asserting that they had won.[34] Soon federal representatives were hinting that because the Court had said unilateral patriation would be legal, we could proceed without more consultation if necessary. Provincial spokesmen spoke of their moral victory. We in Justice did our part to reinforce the federal view. We had a meeting of our working group in the Justice boardroom and allowed in a crew from the National Film Board (of which my son Colin was a member) that was filming for a movie later released as *The Road to Patriation*. As the cameras rolled, we turned the pages of the Supreme Court judgement with exclamations such as "We really won that point" or "On a gagné!"

The ensuing political fallout and the patriation finale will be described in chapter 9.

THE BRITISH FRONT

Here transpired what other authors have aptly described as the "Battle of Britain."[35] As Hitler had found in 1940, it was much tougher than expected.

Why did we underestimate the difficulties of having this last amendment made by the British Parliament? In retrospect it seems to me there were several factors. We relied too much on precedent: since the beginning of the 20th century. Westminster had always acted in accordance with a request from the Parliament of Canada. We had never committed ourselves to making such requests only with unanimous provincial agreement: in the

last discussions on patriation in 1971 we had made it clear that we reserved the right to ask for an amendment without unanimity and British ministers did not reject that possibility. One problem in 1980–1981 was that we were relying on the reassuring promises that Prime Minister Thatcher had made to enact whatever we requested, without an appreciation of the looser party discipline that prevails in Parliament at Westminster. In retrospect I think Pierre Trudeau assumed that Mrs Thatcher exercised the same degree of control over her Conservative caucus as he did over the Liberal caucus in Ottawa. This did not take into account the fact that the leader of the British Conservative party is chosen by the caucus, which can always replace her or him. The leader of the Canadian Liberal party can claim a wider mandate from the party at large, expressed at the last leadership convention, which members of caucus must respect. Further, in 1980 and 1981, Mrs Thatcher's policies, such as privatization and free market reforms, along with growing unemployment, had become unpopular in large sectors of the population, which led many of her MPs to question her leadership. It was not until she successfully proclaimed and executed the war against Argentina in the Falkland Islands that her position was solidly established: that war did not start until April 1982, the month after the *Canada Act* was passed at Westminster.[36] But we continued to treat this as an arrangement between two national governments, as amendment processes had always been in the past. In doing so, we underestimated the potential for obstruction by parliamentarians that could be promoted in London by opposing provincial governments and First Nations groups. We had also not appreciated the lingering imperial nostalgia that stirred some Britons to resist the grant of legal independence to Canada for our own good—mostly in the supposed interests of protecting our minorities. One can find close precedents in the public debates in London during the 1930s and 1940s over the granting of independence to India.

Finally, and quite importantly, our insistence on having a Charter enacted for us along with patriation created many difficulties that probably would not have arisen if patriation alone had been sought.

Initially, reassurances from senior British sources had seemed clear. To put the pressure on the provinces in the negotiations of the summer of 1980, Prime Minister Trudeau and Mark MacGuigan, Minister of External Affairs, went to London in late June. Trudeau had lunch with

Prime Minister Thatcher to discuss the patriation matter. No written record was kept of these discussions, but Trudeau told the press afterward that Mrs Thatcher did undertake to recommend to her Parliament whatever measure the federal government might present. He did acknowledge later that she had also said that her government would *prefer* a federal request that had substantial or unanimous provincial support. Mark MacGuigan had similar discussions with Lord Carrington, the Foreign Secretary.[37] I attended a meeting in mid-June in 1980 that Jean Chrétien had in Ottawa with Nicholas Ridley, British Minister of State for Foreign Affairs and Ridley certainly indicated that they would enact whatever we sent over.

We officials were warned, however, when we met with Foreign and Commonwealth Office officials on September 26, 1980, before the patriation package was disclosed in Ottawa, that the package we had outlined was more extensive than they had anticipated (meaning the inclusion of the *Charter*) and this could cause difficulties in Parliament. They said that if it were confined to patriation and an amending formula this would be less controversial.

Nevertheless, as soon as the package was released in Ottawa on October 2, Mark MacGuigan and John Roberts, federal Minister of the Environment, went to London and briefed the Queen, Prime Minister Thatcher, and Michael Foot, leader of the Labour Party and Opposition Leader, as to the precise contents of the joint resolution intended to be submitted in due course. There was no rejection in principle of such a measure.[38] And on December 9 Mrs Thatcher told the House of Commons that her government would deal with the Canadian request "expeditiously and in accordance with precedents."[39]

Yet there were disturbing signals from other ministers. Norman St. John-Stevas, then House Leader in the British House of Commons, warned Mark MacGuigan that the British government might not proceed as long as there were challenges pending before Canadian courts.[40] Shortly before Christmas, Mrs Thatcher asked Trudeau to meet Francis Pym, then her Minister of Defence but soon to become House Leader, during his impending visit to Ottawa. I prepared briefing notes for the Prime Minister on the subject of the provincial references. By the time of this visit all the reference questions had been announced and the Manitoba case had already been argued. But this was not the central focus of Pym's interest. He told Prime

Minister Trudeau that the British Parliament would not pass a measure containing the *Charter*.[41] It is said that some very firm statements were made on both sides and the meeting was far from pleasant.

As far as I could understand at the time, the British government was apprehensive of the *Charter* because it saw this as the salient cause of controversy in Canada. If there were controversy, it would become very difficult to use party discipline to bring its backbenchers into line and get a speedy resolution of the matter, particularly when there was really no political gain or loss to be experienced by any MP whether the measure passed at Westminster or not. Further, I always suspected that many British parliamentarians had intellectual problems with the idea of a constitutional Charter that is the antithesis of parliamentary sovereignty—the hallmark of the British constitution. If Canada and its provinces were to limit the sovereignty of their legislative bodies in this way in favour of individual rights, some misguided people might see this as the model for a new British constitution!

Before long there were dissident British MPs, mostly Conservatives, who were threatening to oppose the Canadian measure. In this they were encouraged by the Canadian provinces opposed to the federal scheme. As early as November 1980 the Agent-General for Quebec in London was trolling for disgruntled MPs and was soon encouraging the other opposing provinces to do the same.[42] Much lobbying was done over lunches and dinners hosted by various provinces, and before long the federal government joined in this venture, hoping to reinforce support for our package. Reeves Haggan, attached to the Federal-Provincial Relations Office for this patriation exercise, was sent to London as a special member of the High Commission staff. Reeves knew London well, particularly the best restaurants. He and his wife Hilary were installed in an apartment not far from Grosvenor Square where the main office of the High Commission was. I enjoyed their hospitality while in London on support work for the project. One irritating aspect of the public debate in Britain was that the most vocal opponents among British politicians seemed to be those who were looking for easy publicity. After all, it cost an MP at Westminster nothing in political terms to oppose legislation for Canada when encouraged to do so by provincial lobbying and hospitality. There could be nothing in this to offend any of their constituents and it seemed to be a sure attention-getter in the press.

On one of my visits to London that winter I suggested to Canadian officials that they lease one of those garish electronic billboards in Picadilly Circus, and put a large red maple leaf on it with the message (paraphrased from what God told Moses to say to the Pharoah) "Let Our People Go!" But no one took my advice.

An early result of the Quebec lobbying in London was a decision taken by Sir Anthony Kershaw, Conservative MP and chairman of the Select Committee on Foreign Affairs, to hold hearings on the role of the UK Parliament in responding to a request from the Parliament of Canada for constitutional amendments. In Ottawa we viewed with growing concern the work of this committee. It was receiving submissions from various of the provinces opposed to the federal initiative. It also heard from three English academic witnesses, none of whom claimed to be experts on the Canadian constitution and two of whom indicated they had been consulted by provincial governments. The Government of Canada had not made representations to the committee: it took the position that it was not appropriate for the national executive government of a sovereign state to give advice to a parliamentary committee of another sovereign state. Indeed, throughout the whole period of our pursuit of patriation, the federal government conducted its formal discussions as from one executive government to another; and the British government was equally careful not to have formal discussions with provincial governments.

We soon concluded that we might have to be prepared to reply to an unfavourable report of the Kershaw Committee. Accordingly on January 9, 1981, I retained Professor Dale Gibson of the Faculty of Law, University of Manitoba to make preparations for this. I chose Dale because I considered his to be one of the "fastest pens in the west." He had published several works on law and history and he was fully conversant with the current issues in the patriation wars because he had served as one of federal counsel in the December reference hearing in the Manitoba Court of Appeal.

The Kershaw Report[43] was issued on January 30. While it recognized that the UK Parliament had a duty to fulfill any "proper request"[44] made by the Canadian Government and Parliament, it would be contrary to the "established constitutional position" for the Canadian Parliament to make such a request without a "sufficient level and distribution of Provincial concurrence."[45] It even went so far as to spell out what a proper number and distribution of provincial consents would be: Ontario and Quebec

and provinces containing 50 per cent of the voters in the Atlantic and the western provinces (essentially the Victoria Formula on which Canadian statesmen had never been able finally to agree unanimously). These conclusions, presumptuous and ill-founded as they may have been, of course gave enormous moral support to all those good Canadians who opposed the federal initiative. Those provincial politicians who applauded Kershaw (including the Parti Québécois government) were apparently crypto-colonialists who seemed to have no problem seeking the aid of the Mother Country, for whose government they had no means to vote, to protect them from the Government of Canada, for whom many of their citizens had voted. Pierre Trudeau, however, speaking in Toronto the next night, summed up the Report mockingly in one phrase: "The Empire Strikes Back!" (the name of a then current science fiction movie in the popular *Star Wars* series).

Dale Gibson proceeded rapidly to draft a paper for publication by the federal government to respond to the Kershaw Report. Although ostensibly written for Canadian MPs and senators, as well as for the Canadian public, we hoped it would have a certain readership in Britain among those who had a genuine interest in the proper role for Westminster. It provided the background history of the problem; the need for patriation; the years of unsuccessful attempts to arrive at an agreed amendment procedure; the desirability of the substantive changes sought, such as the *Charter,* and the grant of additional powers to provinces over natural resources; and the entrenchment of the equalization principle. It pointed out that these new changes transferred no provincial jurisdiction to the Government or Parliament of Canada: the only change proposed for distribution of powers was the grant of more power to provinces over trade in natural resource products. It explained that there was no clear convention that important constitutional changes required provincial consent. And it underlined what the precedents *did* establish: that the UK Parliament would adopt such amendments to the *BNA Acts* as were requested by the Parliament of Canada. It concluded by saying this:

> Canadians have reason to be very grateful to the
> Government and Parliament of the United Kingdom for
> the patience, understanding and co-operation they have
> consistently displayed throughout Canada's prolonged

constitutional amendment stalemate. Deeply steeped in democratic traditions, British authorities have always known that political judgements concerning the amendment of the Constitution of Canada can only be exercised by those who hold a political mandate from the people of Canada. They have, therefore, always respected the wishes of the Government and Parliament of Canada when amendment requests have been made. Canadians are confident that when this final request for British constitutional assistance arrives at Westminster, it will be treated in the same understanding and co-operative manner that has always marked the relations of these two cordial associates in the Commonwealth of Nations.[46]

So deftly had Dale worked that within two weeks of the issue of the Kershaw Report we had a draft of our reply paper, which had been reviewed in Ottawa by many players and had been sent to the Foreign and Commonwealth Office (FCO) in London for their reactions. By February 18 (a week after my appearance in the Newfoundland Court of Appeal), Dale and I were in London meeting with officials of the FCO. They apprised us of one or two areas of sensitivity but generally had few problems with our draft. We returned home, made some revisions, got ministerial approvals, and sent it for translation. It was published in early summer. It was distributed as intended to Canadian parliamentarians and to the Canadian public. We sought wide distribution in Britain but I am not sure the paper ever received much attention there except from those who were already favourably disposed to our project and wanted some documented arguments in our support.

On this and other visits to London I became involved in some of the representational work in pressing our cause. While in London in February 1981, I had some business to do at the Legal Division of the Commonwealth Secretariat at Marlborough House in the Mall. While there I was told that the Secretary-General of the Commonwealth, Sir Shridath (Sonny) Ramphal had asked me to call on him. I had known Sonny for a number of years through attending meetings of Commonwealth Law Ministers. I visited him in his splendid office, no doubt at one time one of the public rooms where the Prince and Princess of Wales (later Edward VII and Queen

Alexandra) had entertained during their long residence there awaiting the demise of his mother, Queen Victoria. Sonny was much interested in the Canadian proposals and was very supportive of our request to Britain, seeing this as a matter of maintaining good Commonwealth relations. I was able to brief him on recent developments and he suggested some avenues within the British government that we should explore. He warned of misgivings certain British ministers had about proceeding with legislation in London while there were still the references before the Canadian courts. I duly reported this back to the Deputy Minister and the Minister. The next time I was to see Sonny was over a year later, on April 17, 1982, when we were seated near each other on Parliament Hill in Ottawa to see the Queen sign the proclamation of the *Constitution Act, 1982.*

On another visit to London the following May I was among the guests at a reception and lunch at the then residence of the Canadian High Commissioner in Upper Brook Street in Mayfair. This was to be an opportunity for informing some members of the Conservative caucus in the House of Lords of the case for patriation. One of the first British guests I met was a peer whose expertise about things Canadian was apparently based on the fact that his grandfather had been Prime Minister of Newfoundland (in the early part of the 20th century, long before it was part of Canada). I asked him when he was last in Newfoundland. "Oh," he said, "I was there in the war with the RAF." (Of course he pronounced it *raff.*)

At lunch I was seated beside Lord Avon, son of Anthony Eden, first Lord Avon. Anthony Eden had of course been Chamberlain's Foreign Secretary, resigning in protest over Chamberlain's policy of appeasement of Hitler. He then became Churchill's Foreign Secretary during the war, and later Prime Minister in the mid-fifties. The second Lord Avon was a junior minister of the Environment in Mrs Thatcher's government. He told me that morning his departmental officials had taken him on a tour of the wartime Cabinet bunker under Downing Street, which they had recently unsealed with a view to making it a kind of museum. (I have since visited this museum.) This led to a discussion of wartime conditions. I said that I had read that Prime Minister Churchill could function with only a few hours of sleep a day, taken at random times. "Yes," said Lord Avon, "but the problem was that he thought his ministers could too! I can remember my father often being summoned in the middle of the night to meet the

The author (second from right) at a Commonwealth Law Ministers
Conference in Lagos, Nigeria, February 1975.

Prime Minister." After that we had only desultory conversation about the
Canadian constitution.

At about this time I was also despatched by the High Commission to call
on Lord Elwyn-Jones at the House of Lords. He had been Lord Chancellor
in the Labour governments of Harold Wilson and James Callaghan. I had
met him at meetings of the Commonwealth Law Ministers in Lagos in
1975 and in Winnipeg in 1977. He had apparently requested some information about the Canadian court cases, so I went along with an envelope
containing all the judgements of the provincial courts, prepared to explain
them. We had a very pleasant cup of tea in one of the Lords' lounges while
I quickly briefed him. I had the feeling that I had exceeded his attention
span.

The most intense and challenging encounter I had in Britain in defence
of the federal position was at a seminar on the Canadian constitution held
at All Souls College, Oxford, on May 8 and 9, 1981. This was the inspiration of Patrick Neill, QC, Warden of All Souls (later Vice-Chancellor of
Oxford University and then Baron Neill of Bladen), who presided over
the seminar. All Souls is an august, ancient institution at Oxford that
has no students as such but houses some of the most eminent scholars,
many of whom lecture in the University. While a student at Oxford I

had only once gained admission there, to attend a sherry party given by the Regius Professor of Civil Law, David Daube, for his Roman Law students, of which I was one, on the eve of our final exams. For this seminar on Canadian constitutional developments the Warden had assembled a distinguished array of British scholars (lawyers and political scientists), some British politicians, and representatives of both the federal and provincial governments of Canada. British politicians included Sir Anthony Kershaw, Chairman of the Select Committee already discussed, as well as Mr Kevin McNamara, a Labour MP who had been a member of the Kershaw Committee and was very critical of our position. Sir Ian Sinclair, Legal Adviser to the FCO, generally supported our position that the UK Parliament should act on a request from the Canadian Government and Parliament. Sir John Foster, QC, a prominent senior barrister and former Conservative minister proved to be helpful to us. There were three provincial governments represented: Quebec, British Columbia, and Saskatchewan. Their chief spokesman was Mr Yves Pratte acting as an adviser for the Lévesque government. There were two lawyers identified with Canadian First Nations: Professor Ian Brownlie of Oxford (and Fellow of All Souls), and Professor Michael Jackson of the University of British Columbia. The federal team consisted of Hon. John Roberts, Minister of the Environment (whom I had known as a fellow student at Oxford); Serge Joyal, MP and Joint Chairman of the Special Parliamentary Committee on the Constitution; Professor Dale Gibson; and myself. Our political colleagues stated the political situation in Canada to support the federal project. I described the Canadian court proceedings. Dale spoke of the matters covered by our pending publication, *The Role of the United Kingdom in the Amendment of the Canadian Constitution.* (Incidentally, at least one of the English professors said he had read this paper and found it persuasive). The provincial representatives made their expected presentations, although Mr Pratte, who was the most familiar with the legal issues, missed a substantial part of the seminar because of travel arrangements. While Sir Anthony Kershaw was relatively restrained in his comments, his committee colleague McNamara was quite vehement in his attacks on the substance of our proposals and assured us they would not get through Westminster. I was delighted therefore when Sir John Foster, the venerable ex-minister, said that the Kershaw Committee had completely invented the doctrine that the British Parliament could make

a determination of its own as to whether the Canadian people supported a request. He also dismissed McNamara's interventions as highly political and quite inappropriate.

While I felt that we had adequately put our case before this seminar, I harboured a growing resentment as the proceedings went on that such a group should even be discussing decisions taken by Canadians about their own constitution. I sensed a lingering imperialism in the air and I thought patriation could not come too soon!

I was delighted to find attending parts of the seminar an old acquaintance from Saskatchewan, James McConica. Jim had been a Rhodes Scholar from there in the early 1950s. After taking a degree in history and later a doctorate at Oxford, he went on to become an internationally renowned scholar in Tudor and Renaissance history. He was also ordained as a Basilian priest. He happened to be residing at All Souls in the spring of 1981 in order to write one volume of a commissioned history of Oxford. As I was also staying at All Souls, we dined together in hall and then retired to the Senior Common Room for cigars and port. Cigars and port in the Senior Common Room at All Souls was something I could never have aspired to as an Oxford undergraduate some 25 years before!

One further opportunity arose from the All Souls seminar. Before leaving for England, I had been instructed by the Deputy Minister to retain a certain London barrister for the Canadian government to assist us in London if necessary in the period after the Supreme Court of Canada had rendered its judgement. This was Sir John Foster, the same gentleman who, as it happened, appeared at the seminar at All Souls. He was not only a former Conservative minister with many good contacts in the Thatcher government, but he was also known to have good relations with the Labour Party, particularly with the Rt. Hon. James Callaghan, former Labour Prime Minster. So after I had observed him at the seminar saying things favourable to our position, on the second day during intermission I went over to speak to him. I had long since been well informed of the ritualistic division of the English legal profession between barristers and solicitors: one could only retain a barrister through the intermediary of a solicitor. However, I made bold to say to him, "Sir John, my government would like to retain you." He replied as graciously as he could: "Yes, yes, well have your solicitor's clerk [*clark*] ring my clerk [*clark*]." "Yes, of course," I replied.

I went back to London on a Sunday evening and the next day asked officials at the High Commission to instruct their solicitors to retain Sir John Foster. They in turn set up an appointment for me with the head of the High Commission's firm of solicitors, Sir Charles Russell & Co. in Lincoln's Fields, asking Sir Charles at the same time to arrange an appointment with Sir John Foster. This firm had been Canada's solicitors in London for at least 80 years: the first example I can find of them acting for the Canadian government in a case before the Judicial Committee of the Privy Council (when it was our final court of appeal) was in 1899.[47] I spent a few hours in my hotel room drafting a memorandum of instructions for Sir John and had it typed at the High Commission. At the appointed time the next morning I went to Sir Charles's office. He served me tea and we talked briefly of the instructions I had drafted. He thereupon summoned a cab to take us to the City of Westminster where Sir John was working at home that morning. On the way I said, "Sir Charles, my government is not accustomed to retaining lawyers without knowing the rates they charge. Can you tell me what Sir John's rates are?" He replied, "I'll have my clerk talk to his clerk." With that unsatisfactory reply we preceded to Sir John's where we found him comfortably ensconced in his sitting room. A manservant hovered, in due course serving us coffee and biscuits. Sir John was an engaging man and he recounted to me his first visit to Ottawa during World War II. It seems that at that time he had a position in the Treasury. Canada had made a large loan to Britain for war *materiel* (in the order of one billion dollars, I believe). Payment was soon due and Mr Foster, as he then was, had been sent to Ottawa to negotiate more favourable terms of repayment. He told me he had expected a prolonged negotiation and, not sorry to leave the hardships of wartime London, he had packed a steamer trunk good for a month or so and had established himself at the Chateau Laurier in Ottawa. His first appointment was with C.D. Howe, Minister of Munitions and Supply, who was closely involved with wartime credits for the British. When the young John Foster started to explain his mission to get better terms for repayment of the defence loan, C.D. cut him off by saying, "No, no, we're going to forgive that loan." The young Foster said something to the effect of, "Well, that's excellent, Minister, but I expected to be here for some weeks to settle this matter." C.D., immediately understanding, said "Quite so, Foster. Look, these matters take time. Come back in a week and we'll speak about it again."

Eventually I was able to explain to Sir John that we wanted him to hold a watching brief on the situation, particularly after the results of the Supreme Court decision were known. I handed to him my memorandum outlining our needs. Sir Charles Russell then took me in a cab for lunch at his club, the Garrick near Leicester Square, a club with historical links to the theatre. During an excellent lunch he told me that his firm still had its files on the Oscar Wilde trials. His firm had acted for the Marquess of Queensbury in Wilde's abortive prosecution of Queensbury for criminal libel in 1895, a prosecution that grievously backfired on Wilde, eventually putting him in jail.

So I had a very agreeable day but learned in the process the intricacies of hiring an English barrister.

After that, until the Supreme Court decision of September 28, 1981, I had little further contact with the British front. In spite of all the private warnings from British sources of difficulties ahead, within the federal government our official position was that, whatever happened, the British government would act in accordance with the precedents and the comity owing between two sovereign states of the Commonwealth, and do what they were asked to do by the Parliament and Government of Canada. This was not merely an empty mantra. I believe it reflected the conviction of Prime Minister Trudeau that he was dealing with the Prime Minister of the United Kingdom and that if she made a commitment to the Government of Canada, she would fulfill it. I think he still believed that she had the same degree of control over her caucus as he had over his. In this I think he was not well informed or chose not to believe the reality.

But, anglophile as I might be, the whole British scene made me angry as a Canadian—seeing British politicians and academics occupying themselves with matters on which they had little information and nothing at stake.

9

THE DENOUEMENT

"Free at Last! Thank God Almighty
we are free at last!"[1]

In early September 1981 I had settled in a small apartment in Cambridge, Massachusetts, and moved into an office at the Harvard Center for International Affairs where I was to be a Research Associate for the next nine months while on sabbatical from the Department of Justice. There I became acquainted with the principals in the University Consortium on North American Research and with several Canadian colleagues at the Center who, like me, were Visiting Scholars of the Consortium. We were expected to take part in its work, in particular to attend and participate in seminars the Consortium held with outside speakers on subjects mainly concerned with American-Canadian issues. I started to organize my main project, which was to revise my book first published in 1968. Also during this period I appeared in New York in a roundtable discussion sponsored by the University Consortium at the annual American Political Science Association conference on the subject of recent constitutional developments in Canada.[2] Also at the roundtable were some American academics, and two Canadians whom I could not expect to be in sympathy with the federal position. One was Daniel Latouche, a McGill Professor and sometime Parti Québécois strategist. The other was Dr Peter Meekison, the able and amiable Deputy Minister of Intergovernmental Affairs in the Alberta government. I of course supported the federal initiative for patriation and the *Charter*. Latouche confidently predicted that the Supreme Court (expected to deliver judgement later that month in the *Patriation Reference*) would decide in favour of the federal government, that the

patriation measure would go through the British Parliament, and that the country would be ruined. Meekison criticized the haste of the federal government and its refusal to accept the "convention" of the requirement for unanimous provincial agreement for such constitutional changes. He got at least one thing right: he said the *Charter*, if adopted, "will generate more business for lawyers than anything since Magna Carta." The only other panellist sympathetic to our cause was Professor Samuel Beer of Harvard who entitled his paper "The Empire Strikes Back" (the same film reference Trudeau had used the previous January in mocking the Kershaw Report). Beer said that the objections of some British parliamentarians to enacting what the Parliament of Canada requested it to do had "an imperial resonance." He said some British parliamentarians believed that it was "all right for Canadians to be at the mercy of the UK Parliament but not the Canadian Parliament." This was the kind of academic analysis which, I regret to say, was rarely heard in Canada during this hectic period.

AFTERMATH OF THE
SUPREME COURT DECISION

The Supreme Court decision was scheduled for release on September 28, 1981, and I returned to Ottawa for the occasion, to join the other federal counsel in Court to hear the verdict, all as recounted in chapter 8. I stayed for two days to help with the analysis and briefing of ministers and then flew back to Boston. When I left, there was in Ottawa and in provincial capitals a great air of uncertainty about what would happen next. There was a widely held view that Pierre Trudeau, it having been confirmed that our course of action was legal, would immediately proceed with his unilateral initiative. The Gang of Eight provinces, however, did their best to portray the Supreme Court decision as a victory for them because the Court had ventured its political opinion that there must be a substantial measure of provincial consent before the resolution could be sent to London. This would mean no action by Ottawa until there was a further effort to achieve that consent.

Trudeau was at this time on his way to Melbourne, Australia, to attend a Commonwealth Heads of Government Meeting. Once there, he arranged a meeting with Prime Minister Margaret Thatcher. As a result, they issued a formal joint statement that confirmed Prime Minister Thatcher would introduce and support whatever measure the Canadian Parliament

requested.[3] This certainly strengthened Trudeau's hand for his return to Canada and his confrontation with the Premiers. On October 13 the Cabinet met in the morning in Ottawa in preparation for the meeting scheduled later that day between Prime Minister Trudeau and Premier Bennett of British Columbia who was that year Chairman of the Premiers' Conference. Bennett had consulted widely among his colleagues in preparation for this meeting with Trudeau. Cabinet confirmed that one last attempt should be made for agreement with the provinces on a package and, if that failed, the government should proceed with the resolution in Parliament and a request to Westminster. There was a feeling that the Canadian public would want to see one more attempt at agreement, and Mark MacGuigan, Minister of External Affairs, believed this would be important with respect to how the British Parliament would receive the request for an amendment. If the Canadian government did not appear to be conciliatory toward the provinces, "there would not be enough co-operation from Conservative backbenchers to ensure passage." Cabinet, even at this stage, noted the possibility of a final compromise in which it would accept the provincial amending formula in return for provincial acceptance of the *Charter*[4] (essentially the deal reached over three weeks later). Trudeau accordingly met with Bennett later that day and after some difficult discussion they agreed, and announced, that there would be a further First Ministers' Conference on the constitution commencing on November 2, 1981.[5]

I was in Cambridge during most of the pre-Conference preparations, speaking on the telephone frequently with my colleagues in Justice, including the Deputy Minister. Among other views I conveyed was that, if necessary for an agreement, we could live with a notwithstanding clause. I returned to Ottawa on November 1 feeling somewhat out of touch with the current political situation and with federal strategy. One thing I soon learned was that recent polls had shown widespread public expectations that an agreement would be reached in addition to broad public support for a Charter.[6] Presumably, the Premiers had read the polls too and felt strong pressure to reach a compromise.

THE "LAST CHANCE" CONFERENCE

There are many accounts[7] of this Conference and I will limit my account mainly to the aspects where I was involved. Much of the discussion

went on in closed session involving only First Ministers, one minister and one or two officials each. The federal officials usually involved were the Deputy Minister of Justice (Roger Tassé) and the Secretary to the Cabinet for Federal-Provincial Relations (Michael Kirby). The first morning was spent in public session and the whole federal delegation was seated behind the Prime Minister. The opening speeches were mostly conciliatory in tone, with the notable exceptions of Lévesque and Lougheed. Trudeau made it clear that he would insist on the adoption of the Charter but was prepared to compromise on timing and on drafting. It was apparent that there would have to be a compromise on the amending formula: while Ottawa had proposed the Victoria Formula, the former members of the Gang of Eight wanted the formula they had agreed to the previous April.

The Conference went into private session in the afternoon of the first day, Monday, November 2, and continued in that manner until an agreement was reached on the afternoon of Thursday, November 5, whereupon they went into public session to sign and announce their Accord. For the first two and one-half days of private sessions there was much discussion of possible compromises, none of it conclusive. On the evening of November 3, the federal cabinet met and the Prime Minister reported on discussions to date. He said he wanted to know what the government's "bottom line" should be. He reported that he had proposed that the question of an amending formula be decided by a referendum, to which most Premiers had vehemently objected. He suggested to his ministers the possibility of a referendum on the adoption of the *Charter* but this did not seem to attract much support in Cabinet. Two salient ideas do emerge from the minutes: that the *Charter* was essential, but that it might be acceptable to include within it a notwithstanding clause.[8]

Wednesday's session opened with Lévesque saying he would be leaving by noon because the National Assembly was scheduled to open the next day. But later that morning, the Prime Minster proposed that the whole package be submitted to a referendum within two years if no agreement were reached in the meantime. (He later clarified this by saying that the package would first be enacted by the British Parliament but would not come into effect unless later approved by a referendum). Trudeau cleverly appealed to Lévesque's partiality to referenda, subtly suggesting that they were fellow believers in popular sovereignty (which they were). Without much hesitation, Lévesque appeared to agree with such an approach.

It interested him sufficiently that he decided to stay at the Conference. Trudeau seized on this and, when I saw his brief press conference at lunch time, he was pleased to say (I thought rather mischievously) that at least Canada and Quebec were in agreement. This had the immediate effect of alienating the other members of the Gang of Eight who had agreed in an Accord of April 1981 on a united front against the federal government. That Accord in effect presented to Ottawa a take-it-or-leave-it proposal for patriation and an amending formula that permitted opting out by any province for amendments affecting provincial rights. It did not include a Charter in any form. The understanding had been that no member of the Gang would make or endorse a proposal different from their April 1981 Accord without informing other members first. Yet here was Lévesque apparently agreeing, without consultation, to something that most of them found unacceptable. Thereafter, the rest of the Gang of Eight used this as a justification for their compromise with Ottawa, which they reached during the following night without consulting Lévesque.

The immediate effect of this noontime "agreement" was that federal officials were given instructions to draft a statement of the proposal making the package subject to a referendum. I was responsible for this work, in conjunction with the professional drafters in both official languages. By about 4:30 that afternoon I was able to take a draft to the federal ministers. I was looking for Jean Chrétien and found him upstairs in a small kitchen with Roy McMurtry and Roy Romanow where, it later appeared, serious discussions had begun on the final compromise.[9] Hugh Segal from Premier Davis's office was nearby. Our drafts were distributed to all delegations. Premier Lévesque, who by this time had realized he should not have indicated a tentative agreement to the referendum proposal, was quoted as scornfully dismissing our draft as "chinoiserie." In any event, we were given further instructions by federal ministers to convert the proposal into legislative drafts. That evening, while secret negotiations were going on among the politicians sans Quebec's—the so-called "night of the long knives"—I worked with our drafters on the principles to be incorporated until perhaps 10 p.m. and then they continued with their meticulous drafting work until the small hours of the morning to implement the earlier Trudeau-Lévesque "accord."

When my colleagues and I arrived at the Conference Centre at about 8 a.m. the following morning, November 5, we had not yet had time to

Government Conference Centre, November 5, 1981. Federal officials are assembling and drafting remaining parts of what became the *Constitution Act, 1982*, while the First Ministers continue discussions downstairs on the tentative compromise on inclusion of the *Charter* with a "notwithstanding" clause and the amendment formula proferred by the "Gang of Eight" provincial governments. This compromise had been agreed to by some ministers and officials overnight November 4–5 and federal officials here were incorporating that compromise on the assumption it would be confirmed. From left to right: Mary Dawson, Fred Jordan, the author, Gérard Bertrand, Bea Guilbault.

review the drafts carrying out the instructions from the previous afternoon when a message came that there had been a new deal tentatively agreed to overnight. It was simply described as "the provincial amending formula, and a Charter with a notwithstanding clause." While this compromise would not be approved by First Ministers until later in the day, we were to have a complete draft of the whole package (essentially the whole of what became the *Constitution Act, 1982*) in both official languages ready for review by provincial officials for their approval by 5 o'clock that afternoon. As I perceived it, the reason for this haste was that those endorsing the compromise wanted to have it committed to print within hours before the fragile consensus could crumble.

This was a major undertaking, carried out by myself, Fred Jordan of my branch, Mary Dawson (the English-language drafter), and Gérard Bertrand (the French-language drafter), with much secretarial support. We worked steadily all day in an upstairs office at the Conference Centre, receiving bulletins from time to time concerning the First Ministers' decisions. One

task was the editorial revision of the provincial amending formula that had been drafted by provincial officials. Our drafters wanted to apply to it the stylistic practices of the Justice Department in order to make this part of the future *Constitution Act* consistent in style with the rest of that document. While we otherwise had drafts of most of the elements of the proposed package, we had never had a draft of a notwithstanding clause—what became section 33 of the *Charter*. This provision was to authorize Parliament or provincial legislatures, when enacting legislation, to declare that such legislation would operate notwithstanding section 2 or sections 7–15 of the *Charter*. (Instructions changed from time to time during the day about the *Charter* sections intended to be subject to such an override, as the First Ministers continued their fine-tuning of the proposal). At the Prime Minister's insistence they had agreed that such a declaration could only have this protective effect for 5 years, although it could be renewed for another five years by another debate and vote in the relevant legislative body.

Word also came that some provinces would not accept the section recognizing and guaranteeing Aboriginal rights—what later became section 35 of the *Constitution Act, 1982*,[10] so we removed that from the drafts. But in its place First Ministers would accept a provision requiring a constitutional conference to be held within one year to identify and define such Aboriginal rights as should be included in the constitution. The Prime Minister would be required to invite representatives of Aboriginal people to participate in such a conference. We developed a text to cover this change. There was also agreement among First Ministers on some minor changes in the amending formula that we incorporated.

About 4 p.m. we heard that the First Ministers were returning from their private session to the public conference room to announce the agreement of the federal and nine provincial governments, not including Quebec, and to sign an Accord. This brief Accord had been drafted as a political agreement in the private session and simply summarized the essential features of the settlement. Although our legislative drafting work was not quite complete, I went downstairs to see the final act of the drama: after 21 years of intermittent work on patriation and the *Charter*, I felt compelled to be there. I saw the final stages of the signing by the Prime Minister, eight Premiers, and the representative of Manitoba's Premier Lyon, who had left earlier because of the election campaign underway

in his province. Premier Lévesque, of course, had refused to sign. In the milling about afterward, I was able to shake the Prime Minister's hand to congratulate him and have a small glass of the champagne, which by that time was flowing for the politicians and such advisers as were not to be engaged in the immediate task of approving the text of the package.

It was to this task that I hastily returned, finding my colleagues at the end of their drafting. The Conference Secretariat immediately made copies of our texts and distributed them to all delegations for the meeting of officials scheduled for 5 o'clock. Naively assuming that this would be a meeting of two hours at most, I phoned my wife to say I would be home for dinner a bit late.

Roger Tassé, federal Deputy Minister of Justice, chaired this meeting. Many provincial officials were in a truculent mood when we assembled. They had the natural suspicions of any lawyers presented suddenly with a document they haven't seen before. But this could not account for the degree of hostility we first met. Quebec, the dissenting province, did not send any representatives, of course, but it became apparent to me that several officials from other provinces were disgruntled that any agreement had been reached. They were obviously out of sympathy with the concessions their First Ministers had made. The spirit of the Gang of Eight was still informing their thought. They were suspicious because we had made editorial changes in their amending formula and were only slowly persuaded that these were innocuous. They had never seen a draft of a "notwithstanding" clause and required some time to absorb it. We made one or two changes in detail after discussion.

But the strongest and most prolonged argument was regarding what the First Ministers had agreed to in respect of the application of the override section to what is now section 28. That section now reads: "Notwithstanding anything in this Charter, the rights and freedoms referred to in it are guaranteed equally to male and female persons." This section had been put in the previous winter during the hearings of the Special Joint Committee of Parliament, at the urging of feminist organizations. They feared that certain other sections such as 25, which purported to preserve the rights and freedoms of Aboriginal peoples notwithstanding the *Charter*, and section 27, which required the *Charter* to be interpreted "in a manner consistent with the preservation and enhancement of the multicultural heritage of Canadians," might attenuate the guarantee of

gender equality in section 15. These sections had been added to reassure Aboriginals and ethnic communities that the guarantees of equality in the *Charter* would not undermine their cultural particularities. But the feminists feared that these provisions might have the effect of preserving customs based on assumptions of male superiority. Therefore, to trump those provisions, section 28 was put in to say, in essence, "whatever sections 25 and 27 may mean, they can't result in protecting male chauvinism." This process of adding trumps and super-trumps I described privately at the time as "ascending paranoia." The federal government was definitely committed to section 28 as approved in the parliamentary Committee. But we were told by some provincial officials who had been in the First Ministers' closed meetings that it had been agreed there to make section 28 subject to the "notwithstanding" clause. However, the Accord that the First Ministers had just signed only called for "a 'notwithstanding' clause covering sections dealing with Fundamental Freedoms, Legal Rights and Equality Rights."[11] Those categories of rights obviously referred to headings in the draft Charter. Section 28 was under none of those headings. Federal officials present had no instructions that the override clause should apply to section 28. In fact, I think there was uncertainty regarding what First Ministers intended. Romanow, Whyte, and Leeson (at least two of whom would have been present) say in their book that "all participants" in the closed session agreed to the override of section 28 by section 33.[12] However, when this matter was later discussed in the federal cabinet on November 12, 1981, Jean Chrétien, who was also present at the closed session, "noted that the problem seemed initially to have arisen as a consequence of *misdirected negotiations at the officials' level*" (emphasis added).[13] As the discussion continued among the officials that evening, I was still not satisfied that First Ministers could have intended to attenuate section 28 in this way. I said to the most insistent provincial official, "I don't know how it is in your province, but in the federal jurisdiction women have the vote and they are going to object to this very strongly." However, he was supported by many of the other provincial officials and as we had no hard information to the contrary, Roger accepted for the time being an amendment of section 28 so that it would read as follows: "Notwithstanding anything in this Charter except section 33, the rights and freedoms referred to in it are guaranteed equally to male and female persons." As section 33 was the notwithstanding clause, the net effect would be that Parliament or provincial legislatures

could declare that a law discriminating against women would apply in spite of sections 15 (the general equality guarantee) and 28. Roger indicated at the time that this change might have to be reviewed.

With a few other problems eventually overcome, the meeting finally ended at about 11 p.m. So much for my dinner at home. The agreed text[14] was released the next day and started new rounds of controversy.

POST-CONFERENCE REVISIONISM

Although for the next several weeks I was at Harvard, I followed this controversy as closely as I could. The two main areas of substantive contention were the dropping of the section guaranteeing Aboriginal rights (now section 35 of the 1982 Act) and the subjection of section 28 to the notwithstanding clause. Section 35 had been inserted in the resolution during the proceedings of the Special Joint Committee the previous January. British Columbia and several other provinces were opposed to its inclusion. Generally there was concern that there was no complete definition of Aboriginal rights and the section could have very unpredictable effects. As I have noted earlier, federal officials had warned their ministers to the same effect. It was also noted that after the section had been added to the Joint Resolution, both the National Indian Brotherhood (status Indians) and the Native Council of Canada (non-status Indians and Métis) had rejected the section. In fact, the National Indian Brotherhood had commenced legal proceedings in the English courts to block the whole patriation process by insisting that the British Parliament still had the responsibility for Aboriginal affairs in Canada.[15] According to the Prime Minister in reporting to Cabinet on conference discussions, he had pressed for the inclusion of section 35 but when the Premiers did not agree he proposed the provision guaranteeing another constitutional conference within a year, to which Aboriginal representatives would be invited, for the purpose of identifying and defining Aboriginal rights.[16] He had found it difficult to insist on inclusion of section 35 because two of the three native groups originally supporting that section had withdrawn their support for it.

However, the abandonment of an Aboriginal rights guarantee immediately evoked strong criticisms of the November 5 Accord. Federal ministers were assailed not only by Native critics but also by many non-native groups and individuals. Within two weeks the New Democratic Party federal cau-

cus withdrew its support from the whole package because of this omission, as it had earlier made such a guarantee a condition of it supporting the government's constitutional package. (That caucus also took exception to section 28 having been made subject to the notwithstanding clause). At least one province, Saskatchewan, was in favour of the restoration of the Aboriginal rights guarantee. In the meantime there was extensive lobbying and demonstrations by Aboriginal groups demanding the restoration of section 35, including by groups that had rejected it only a few months previously and had gone to England to lobby and litigate against the adoption by Westminster of a measure that was expected to contain such a provision! The federal government stood ready at all times to see section 35 restored, and Cabinet confirmed that position on November 19.[17] As a result of many negotiations, mostly by telephone, it was agreed among the ten signatories to the Accord that section 35 be restored, but (at the insistence of Premier Lougheed) with the addition of one word, "existing."[18] The restored section would then read in part "35. (1) The existing aboriginal and treaty rights of the aboriginal peoples of Canada are hereby recognized and confirmed." The apparent purpose of this, in the opinion of at least one Premier, was to exclude from the guarantee Aboriginal rights that had already been lawfully extinguished. With this restoration, the NDP caucus returned to its support of the resolution.

The other, and perhaps more controversial, change that the Accord had made to the resolution as originally approved by the Special Joint Committee of Parliament was the application of the override clause to section 28. The opposition to this was quick and articulate. The National Advisory Council on the Status of Women and several feminist organizations conducted a well-organized campaign to press First Ministers to restore section 28 as it had been approved by the Special Joint Committee. Premier Blakeney had at least a legalistic reason for supporting the change that had been made on November 5: he argued that if section 28 was not made subject to the override clause, it could block desirable affirmative action that might be designed to benefit women more than men.[19] No one seems to have been convinced by this. Demonstrations were held in Ottawa and several provincial capitals. As early as November 9, the Deputy Minister of Justice, Roger Tassé, started contacting provincial officials to request the removal of the phrase "except section 33" from the text of section 28 agreed to by officials on November 5. After several days it was agreed

by all provinces that signed the Accord to revert to the original language of section 28 as approved by the Special Joint Committee of Parliament.

THE JOINT RESOLUTION GOES TO LONDON

After much national angst, Jean Chrétien was able to announce to the House of Commons on November 23 that all the provinces who had signed the November 5 Accord had agreed to the restoration of section 35 as amended, and the removal of the words "except section 33" from section 28. So there was a revised, agreed-upon text of a joint resolution for an Address to the Queen ready for debate in the Parliament of Canada. The debate proceeded quickly, with House of Commons approval on December 2. There, 246 Members of Parliament, including 71 from Quebec, voted for the resolution; 24 voted against—17 Progressive Conservatives, 5 Liberals (including 2 from Quebec), and 2 NDPs. In each case those who opposed voted contrary to their party's policy. There was one NDP abstention.[20]

On December 8, late in the afternoon, the resolution was approved by the Senate by a vote of 59–23.[21] At 6 p.m. Cabinet, sitting as the Governor in Council, met to

> pass a Minute noting the actions taken by the Canadian Parliament and informing the Queen of the request and consent of Canada to the enactment of the Canada Act by the British Parliament. Secondly,...the Prime Minster, would at the same time sign an Instrument of Advice recommending that the Governor General transmit the Minute of Council to Her Majesty.
>
> The Prime Minster read aloud and signed the two documents.[22]

There is an arcane explanation for the requirement of a Minute of a "request and consent" to the legislation, stemming from the terms of the *Statute of Westminster, 1931*,[23] a subtlety dear to the heart of a constitutional lawyer. I had discovered this some years before in giving advice in 1971 on the patriation of the constitution through the then anticipated adoption of the Victoria Charter. The *Statute of Westminster* was designed to give the Dominions legislative autonomy and to restrict UK legislative jurisdiction

over them. Thus section 4 declared that no future Act of the Parliament of the United Kingdom should apply to a Dominion unless it was declared in that Act that "that Dominion has requested, and consented to, the enactment thereof." However, section 7 of the *Statute* said that nothing in it should apply to "the repeal, amendment or alteration of the British North America Acts...." The convention before 1931 had been that those amendments were made at the request of the "Senate and Commons of Canada in Parliament assembled," and by implication pursuant to section 7 of the *Statute* that procedure was to continue for amendments to the *BNA Acts*. Thus, both before and after 1931, UK enactments of amendments to the *BNA Acts* commenced with a preamble: "Whereas the Senate and Commons of Canada in Parliament assembled have submitted an address to Her [His] Majesty praying that Her [His] Majesty may graciously be pleased to cause a Bill to be laid before the Parliament of the United Kingdom for the enactment of the provisions hereinafter set forth: ...." However, in cases under section 4 of the *Statute* where the UK Parliament might, at the request and consent of a Dominion, legislate for it, the British government apparently expected such request and consent to be expressed by the national executive government of that Dominion.[24]

In my researches in 1971 I had noted that the *British North America (No. 1) Act, 1949*,[25] approving the Terms of Union with Newfoundland, recited in its preamble both the request and consent of Canada (as referred to in section 4 of the *Statute of Westminster, 1931*) as well as the address of the Senate and Commons of Canada (as contemplated by section 7 of the *Statute*). I realized that this was because the Terms of Union had not only amended the *BNA Acts*, thus requiring a resolution of the Canadian Parliament as contemplated in section 7 of the *Statute of Westminster, 1931*, but had also amended other laws applicable to Canada, for example the *Statute of Westminster*, thus bringing it within section 4 of the Statute.

A patriation package would similarly require amendments or repeals by the UK of various Imperial Orders-in-Council and legislation including the *Statute of Westminster*, apart from amendments of the *BNA Acts*. Accordingly, I had advised since 1971 that both recitations should appear in the UK legislation effecting patriation. For that reason the Governor in Council on December 8, 1981, adopted this Minute confirming a "request and consent" by Canada, to be transmitted to London along with the Joint Resolution of our Parliament requesting the enactment of the *Constitution*

Act, 1982. Accordingly, when the *Canada Act, 1982*[26] was finally enacted at Westminster, its preamble referred both to the request and consent of Canada for the enactment, as well as the address of the Senate and House of Commons requesting that the measure be put before the UK Parliament.

In a brief ceremony at Rideau Hall on the evening of December 8, 1981, the Speakers of the Senate and of the House of Commons presented the Joint Resolution to the Governor General for transmission to Buckingham Palace. The Prime Minister presented the Minute of Request and Consent adopted an hour earlier by the Governor in Council along with his Instrument of Advice to the Governor General asking him to transmit the Minute to the Queen. The documents were carried personally on a flight to London that night by Esmond Butler, Secretary to the Governor General, and Jean Chrétien, Minister of Justice.

QUEBEC'S COUNTER-OFFENSIVE

While the adoption of the joint resolution in Ottawa proceeded apace, the Government of Quebec was developing a strategy to halt the process. First, the Quebec cabinet on November 25, 1981, issued an Order-in-Council formally expressing Quebec's "veto" of the joint resolution.[27] In a letter of the same date, Premier Lévesque sent to Prime Minister Trudeau a copy of this Order, and he asked Trudeau to table it in both federal Houses. He also asked Trudeau to stop the process of patriation and the adoption of the other amendments because of Quebec's veto. He asked the Prime Minister to do what he had done in 1971, namely halting the adoption of the Victoria Charter, to which all other governments had agreed, because Quebec had opposed it. Lévesque was in an awkward position to insist on a Quebec veto this time since he had been a member of the Gang of Eight that had, only the previous April 16, agreed to an amending formula that did not give any province a veto over most amendments and that was vaunted as vindicating the principle of the equality of the provinces in which none would have any more rights than any other to block amendments. Lévesque, recognizing this apparent inconsistency, said that Quebec had historically always insisted that for patriation and the adoption of an amending formula (whatever the contents of that formula for future application), Quebec's assent would be required. In his view the April Accord to which he had agreed, and that contained no Quebec veto over future amendments, was irrelevant to the entirely different matter of

Quebec's asserted veto over the adoption of the amending formula itself: hence the issue of the veto in the enclosed provincial Order-in-Council.

Trudeau replied to Lévesque in a letter of December 1, carefully meeting all the Premier's arguments. He relied on the Supreme Court decision in the *Patriation Reference* (a proceeding in part instituted by Quebec) as authority that no province in law or by convention had a veto over constitutional amendments including amendments to adopt an amending formula: at most, the Court said that by convention a "substantial measure of provincial consent" was required, but it expressly rejected a unanimity requirement. That reference had been all about the consent required for patriation and the adoption of an amending formula, the matters currently in issue and over which Lévesque now asserted a special veto for Quebec. He then went on to argue that it was Lévesque, not he, who had abandoned the idea of a Quebec veto. Trudeau pointed out that ever since the Victoria Conference in 1971, down to the submission to Parliament of the joint resolution in October 1980, and to the opening of the First Ministers' Conference on November 2, 1981, (one month before this letter) he had advocated the Victoria Formula that provided regional vetoes, with Ontario and Quebec each having a veto in perpetuity regardless of future relative changes in provincial populations. It was Lévesque who had abandoned the exceptionalist doctrine of a Quebec veto by adhering to the April 16, 1981, Accord of the Gang of Eight calling for an amending formula based on the equality of provinces and not of regions, in which no province was given a special veto. Their formula allowed general amendments where there was agreement of two-thirds of the provinces containing at least 50 per cent of the national population. He closed his letter by saying, "This, then, my dear Premier, is my understanding of the constitutional law and history respecting the claim for a provincial veto. Whether we are talking of patriation or of the amending formula, it is hard to understand how—by Order in Council or otherwise—you can maintain that a Quebec veto exists by law or custom."

Lévesque replied on December 2 saying that "C'est avec regret, mais sans surprise, que j'ai pris connaissance de votre lettre..."[28] He asked in effect why, if Ottawa had abandoned several earlier attempts at patriation because of Quebec's objections, it was not willing to do so now? He referred to the "nombreuses inexactitudes" in Trudeau's letter, to which he had no intention of replying. Instead, he informed the Prime Minister

that his government was going to take a reference to the Quebec Court of Appeal as to the existence of the Quebec veto and would adopt any legislation necessary so that the Quebec Court of Appeal decision could be appealed to the Supreme Court.[29] Finally, he asked Trudeau to cease any further steps in the patriation process until the Supreme Court had rendered a decision on this new reference concerning the province's veto, just as had been done the previous April in contemplation of the Supreme Court hearing and deciding the *Patriation Reference*. He enclosed a copy of the order of reference adopted by his cabinet on November 25, 1981[30]; in it the Court of Appeal was asked whether Quebec's consent was necessary for any constitutional amendment that would affect its legislative powers or the status of its government or legislature within the Canadian federation.[31]

On December 4 Trudeau replied to Lévesque's December 2 letter, which had been sent to him by telex (this was before email was common for intergovernmental correspondence!). He reiterated that it was Lévesque, not he, who had abandoned the quest for a Quebec veto to be provided in the constitution. He reasserted that the Supreme Court had already determined that no province had a veto by law or convention and that therefore a further reference was pointless. The proceedings to achieve patriation would thus not be suspended. He ended with this flourish: "Finally, I note that you have declined in your telex of December 2, 1981, to respond to the numerous points set forth in my letter of December 1, 1981, while alleging that my letter contains numerous 'inexactitudes.' You must admit that that is a pretty quick judgment! Until you have explained what you mean by 'inexactitudes,' I will continue to believe my letter to be an accurate reflection of the historic, political and legal developments during the past thirteen years."

Having failed to block the process through political means in Canada, Mr Lévesque, like a good colonial, appealed to the Mother Country. On December 19, 1981, he wrote to Prime Minister Margaret Thatcher asking her to postpone action in the British Parliament in respect of the joint address, which had been received in London on December 9, until after the decision of the Supreme Court in the new reference recently launched by his government on the question of the alleged Quebec veto. Mrs Thatcher replied courteously on January 13, 1982, saying that the British government would act "according to established procedures" and submit the

bill for determination by Parliament as requested by the Government and Parliament of Canada. With respect to further decisions in the Canadian courts, the matter in her view had been decided by the Supreme Court of Canada in the *Patriation Reference*. Any further legal proceeding in Canada "is entirely a Canadian matter."

The reference taken by the Lévesque government continued to wind its way through the courts during and after British action to adopt the *Canada Act, 1982*. It was argued in the Quebec Court of Appeal from March 15 to 17, 1982, just two weeks before the *Canada Act, 1982* received royal assent in London. On April 7, 1982, the Quebec Court of Appeal decided[32] that there was no conventional rule requiring unanimous consent of the provinces for constitutional amendments to be made, relying on the decision of the Supreme Court in the *Patriation Reference*. Nor did it find that Quebec had established a convention to the effect that its consent was required for any such amendment, based on the alleged principle of "duality" (i.e., that Canada is a union of two founding nations, English and French, and that Quebec represents the French in any decision affecting that union). The Court observed that in fact the province's two grounds asserted for the claimed veto were mutually contradictory: a requirement of unanimous provincial consent is necessarily predicated on the equality of provinces, whereas "duality" is based on an asymmetrical view of Canada in which Quebec is superior to any other single province because only it represents a founding nation all by itself. The appeal to the Supreme Court of Canada was argued there on June 14 and 15, 1982. A judgement[33] was issued on December 6, 1982, that essentially agreed with the Court of Appeal. The Supreme Court rejected the respondent Attorney General of Canada's argument that it should decline to decide because of mootness, the measure in question having by that time already been in force for eight months, adopted by a process that the Court had already declared legal in the *Patriation Reference*. Once again the Court preferred its didactic role, even if redundant.

INTERIM CHARTER ACTIVITIES

As it became clearer that constitutional change was indeed going to happen, my branch intensified its activities in preparation for the coming into force of the *Charter*. I have already mentioned the planning we had done for the arm's length development of a book on the *Charter* and an

educational program for judges and lawyers. I had also for some time been pressing for a different approach of the Department of Justice to litigation where it acted for the government and where *Charter* issues were raised. In the years I had spent in the Department I had criticized the way our litigation people dealt with cases involving the *Canadian Bill of Rights, 1960*.[34] It seemed to me that wherever the *Bill of Rights* was invoked to limit government activity in some way or to seek an interpretation of federal laws in a way that would enhance human rights, federal counsel did what any traditional counsel would do—try to defend their client's immediate interests. This usually meant arguing that the *Bill of Rights* should not be interpreted so as to impede what government had done or wanted to do. I believed this had contributed in an important way to the limited impact given to the *Bill* by the courts. Be that as it may, I felt that the *Charter* would represent values and principles to which our client, the Government of Canada, had strongly subscribed, and that we should consider it an important part of government policy to vindicate *Charter* principles in our litigation. Of course, that would not mean acquiescing in irrelevant or frivolous invocation of the *Charter*. But when the *Charter* was invoked in the future against the government or federal legislation we should first consider whether there were principles involved which we should respect rather than oppose such arguments in a knee-jerk reaction. I suggested at least two initiatives: we should have a program within the Department to educate our lawyers, particularly, about the *Charter* that they would soon be encountering in court, and we should broaden the decision-making process within the Department regarding litigation strategy.

In pursuit of the first initiative, my colleagues, during my absence at Harvard and well before the adoption of the *Charter*, put together a large manual on it for departmental lawyers. They also organized regional seminars for hundreds of departmental lawyers where various salient issues could be discussed. I came back to Ottawa from Cambridge to participate in one of these seminars.

In pursuit of the second initiative we started to plan, although this did not come to fruition until the *Charter* was in operation, a Charter Litigation Committee that included representatives from the Litigation Branch as well as my Public Law Branch and, when available, the Deputy Minister. There we discussed current litigation raising *Charter* issues, primarily that involving the federal government directly, but sometimes

other cases where the Attorney General of Canada had simply received notice of a *Charter* question to be argued. In the first group we would discuss what position to take with close regard to what interpretation of the *Charter* would be optimal, not just which would be more convenient for the Crown. Of course, this sometimes involved discussions with client departments who might prefer a hardline approach to further the pursuit of their policies, and we would try to demonstrate that the *Charter* also represented government legal policy that they should take into account. In respect of other cases where the federal government was not a party but where we had received a notice of a *Charter* issue to be raised, we would decide whether the Attorney General should intervene and if so what position should be taken. This committee as planned was already in place and functioning when I returned from Harvard in June 1982.

Also during this interval, in late 1981, I found myself still dabbling at Harvard in the Canadian patriation debate. The University Consortium on North American Research, of which I was a Visiting Scholar, had organized a seminar on the recent Canadian Constitutional Accord signed by the Prime Minister and all Premiers except Quebec's on November 5, 1981. The guest speaker was to be Claude Morin, Quebec's Minister of Intergovernmental Affairs and chief architect of Quebec's constitutional strategy. When he arrived he was, I think, surprised to find me at the table. We had been on the opposite side of most issues for about 12 years, having first met when he was the Deputy Minister of Intergovernmental Affairs in the Bourassa government. I suspect my presence caused him to restrain himself a bit in his account of Quebec's grievances arising out of the so-called "night of the long knives" ("nuit des longues couteaux") when the federal government and other provinces made a deal that became the November 5 Accord. During the discussion period I said: "I have worked on this project for many years. Ever since the Victoria Conference in 1971 I have defended the Victoria Formula which would have given Quebec a veto. I have defended that position in many places, including with my friends from the west who thought it unfair. Now last April you agreed with the Gang of Eight to give it up. Don't you think that was a strategic error?" Claude put on his familiar little half-grin and said, "Well maybe you should have fought harder!"—a non-response worthy of a legislative Question Period.

When the time came, the British government acted with alacrity. The joint resolution arrived in London on December 9, 1981. On December 22 the *Canada Act* was given first reading in the House of Commons, and second reading on February 17, 1982. The bill went into Committee of the whole on February 23 for clause-by-clause study. Although the long title of the bill was "An Act to give effect to a request by the Senate and House of Commons of Canada," a formula we had been told should preclude amendments at Westminster, in fact the Speaker had ruled that amendments could be considered. The Thatcher government was in agreement with us that in accordance with the *Statute of Westminster, 1931* and established practice, the UK Parliament was only at liberty to legislate for Canada as requested by Canada: this principle would preclude any amendments introduced by British parliamentarians. Humphrey Atkins, Lord Privy Seal, who presented the bill on behalf of the British government at second reading, made this position clear notwithstanding the Speaker's ruling, and said the government would oppose any amendments on this basis.[35] Nevertheless, the Chair of Committee of the Whole accepted motions for 26 amendments for debate. Only two of these were ever voted on, the first to remove the word "existing" from section 35, the word added at the insistence of Premier Lougheed to modify the words "aboriginal and treaty rights of the aboriginal peoples of Canada...." This amendment was defeated. Another amendment that would have made any changes to the constitution affecting Native rights subject to approval by Aboriginal organizations was voted on and also defeated. The bill passed from committee and was given third reading in the Commons on March 8, 1982. The bill was then read the first time in the House of Lords on March 9 and received second reading on March 18. Committee of the Whole study was completed by March 23, and the bill received third reading on March 25.[36] Royal assent was given to the *Canada Act, 1982* on March 29, 1982, which was, precisely, the 115th anniversary of Queen Victoria's royal assent to the *British North America Act, 1867.*

The second reading debate[37] in the Commons was windy and at times ill-informed. There was some resentment exhibited for Prime Minister Trudeau's assumption that Westminster should act as a rubber stamp. Those supporting the bill generally articulated the constitutional proprieties with which Westminster should act upon receipt of a proper request

from Canada. There were some assertions, gratifying to Canadians, of respect for Canada and its role in the world. Detractors generally sought delay, to await further court decisions. One of those decisions was in the pending reference taken by Quebec in respect of its veto (the Supreme Court of Canada decision in that case was not in fact rendered until the following December) and the other involved the *Manuel* case brought in London by an Indian group for a declaration that the UK Parliament still had a legislative responsibility for Aboriginal peoples in Canada. The English Court of Appeal had rejected that claim on January 28,[38] a few weeks before the debate. Yet there were some members who were not satisfied with that decision and thought they should await its appeal to the Law Lords in the House of Lords, the highest appellate court in Britain. In fact, no such appeal was heard.

A few interventions in the debate are of interest. Enoch Powell, an independent-minded former Conservative minister who was then sitting as an Ulster Unionist, expressed most eloquently a criticism that many MPs had voiced. He found it paradoxical that Canada should be asking Westminster to abdicate its power over our constitution and also at the same time to legislate major constitutional change for us. Instead, he said, once Westminster had terminated the authority continued by the *Statute of Westminster, 1931* Canadians should enter into an "internal compact" similar to that embodied in the United States constitution "which has no knowledge of a sovereign Parliament" (i.e., Westminster).[39] (Mr Powell voted against the measure on second reading.) The frank answer to this criticism would have to have been along these lines: "We have not gone through a revolution against established order as did the Americans. In the present circumstances of the continuity of our institutions we have reached our compact before coming to London for its validation in the only way our existing laws will recognize."

Other MPs voiced concerns about the proper respect for Aboriginal rights, many of these concerns no doubt the product of intense lobbying in London by the National Indian Brotherhood and some provincial Indian organizations.

But there were lighter moments. Some MPs voluntarily declared the hospitality they had received from various Canadian bodies. For example, Mr Kevin McNamara (Kingston upon Hull, Central) said: "I declare the hospitality that I have received from organisations and institutions in the

federation of Canada. I have had two meals at the High Commission, one at Simpsons, lunch with the Secretary-Agent [*sic*] for Quebec, three days in Quebec as a guest of the Quebec Government, one meal from Nova Scotia *and a Christmas card from Saskatchewan*. I was privileged to visit Canada at an historic time [*sic*] the Constitutional Conference" (emphasis added).[40] Mr McNamara, who had been a vociferous critic of the federal initiative as a member of the Kershaw Committee and also as a participant in the Oxford seminar I attended, nevertheless voted for the bill.

A characterization of the debate was offered by Jonathan Aitken (Thanet East), who reminded the House of his Canadian connections. (His father was born in Canada and his great-uncle was Canadian-born press baron Lord Beaverbrook.)

> As we repeal [*sic*] the British North America Act and enact the Bill, we are walking a constitutional and diplomatic tightrope of particular delicacy. *As we walk it we must beware of being blown off by legalistic or imperialistic hot air, a few breaths of which have been felt in the Chamber this afternoon.* Although in theory we are legislators in the true sense of that word on this or any other Bill in practice on all matters affecting the constitution of Canada convention shows that we should limit ourselves to being ratifiers and implementors of any constitutionally proper request from the Government of Canada. (Emphasis added)[41]

He shared with some other members concern that "the treaty rights of the aboriginal peoples are not protected." Happily this fear, which might have been dispelled by his reading of section 35 of the *Constitution Act, 1982*, has proved ill-founded in light of the jurisprudence that has ensued under that section. Mr Aitken also voted for the measure.

THE FINALE

The *Canada Act, 1982* came into effect upon royal assent on March 29 of that year. While it gave the force of law in Canada to its Schedule B, which was the *Constitution Act, 1982*, it said in section 2 that the latter Act "shall come into force as provided in that Act." Section 58 of the *Constitution Act, 1982* provided that "this Act shall come into force on a day to be fixed by

proclamation by the Queen or the Governor General under the Great Seal of Canada." Prime Minister Trudeau wanted to launch our new constitutional arrangements in the most prestigious fashion, evoking continuity with our past, and for this he sought the participation of the Queen. It was possible to arrange for Her Majesty to be present in Ottawa for a ceremony for this purpose on April 17, less than three weeks after royal assent had been given to the *Canada Act, 1982* in London.

Eleanor and I received various invitations to attend the associated events and I flew to Ottawa for the occasion. On the evening before the signing of the proclamation, there was a dinner at the Chateau Laurier for numerous ministers and officials who had participated in the long and wearying process that had brought Canada to this point. After that dinner Eleanor and I joined Roy McMurtry and Roy Romanow, attorneys-general of Ontario and Saskatchewan respectively, in a piano bar at the Chateau. Roy Romanow and his party (the NDP) were then in the midst of an election campaign, the vote being set for April 26, only ten days later. Roy thought the campaign was going badly for the NDP. We all said, in effect, "Roy, you're a pessimist! You'll win!" Well, he was right. On April 26 his party lost the vote and power, and Roy lost his own constituency. He did not regain power until 1991 when he was sworn in as Premier of Saskatchewan.

The proclamation was to be signed on Parliament Hill the morning of April 17. April is an unreliable month in Ottawa and this was no exception. It was cool and cloudy and rain seemed imminent as we took our assigned seats on the lawn in front of the Centre Block. I was seated with some senior officials from the British High Commission and near other worthies such as the Secretary-General of the Commonwealth and the provincial Premiers. The speaker's platform was sheltered by a canopy and had a large table for the signing ceremony. The platform party had not yet arrived. As we awaited the Queen, a British official said she must be near as she had spotted the Queen's standard flying from the Peace Tower (she explained to me, though I had already guessed) that this was the standard that flew at "Buck House," that is Buckingham Palace. Soon the platform party arrived including Her Majesty, Prime Minister Trudeau, two federal ministers, and two federal officials. As the speeches began so did the rain. Soon the Queen signed the Proclamation, bringing the *Constitution Act, 1982* into force, and we all retired from the Hill with our umbrellas.

Later Eleanor and I attended a reception in Premier Hatfield's hotel suite and then an evening reception at the National Arts Centre where the Queen was present.

So ended for me some 22 years of intermittent work on patriation and the *Charter*.

EPILOGUE

About two months later in Ottawa, we came home one afternoon to find that our house had been robbed in a bold daytime break-in. Several valuables were missing including some paintings. When the police came and we were discussing it with the detectives, one of them said, "Well, there's probably not much we can do. It used to be before this Charter thing that we'd round up a few of the likely suspects and take 'em down to the station. We usually got results."

PART II

POLITICAL AND PRAGMATIC ORIGINS OF THE *CHARTER*

10

FRANK SCOTT, PIERRE TRUDEAU, AND THE CHARTER IDEA

INTRODUCTION

The *Canadian Charter of Rights and Freedoms* was the single most important constitutional or legislative instrument adopted for Canada in the 20th century. It ignited a legal revolution and has changed our society in important ways. So great has been its impact that some analysts, including certain members of the judiciary, ascribe to it almost mystical powers. They see it permeated with principles undreamed of by its originators.

Many Canadians, if asked why we have the *Canadian Charter of Rights and Freedoms*, would simply attribute it to Pierre Trudeau. If pressed further about its contents, they would say that the provisions of the *Charter* represent the philosophical mindset of this same Prime Minister. No doubt his persistence in striving for a Charter was founded in a strong intellectual commitment to the idea of protection of the rights of individuals. But it was tempered by pragmatism.

Although the *Charter* is mainly premised on liberalism and individual rights, Pierre Trudeau as an adolescent did not demonstrate much interest in those values. A book[1] recently written by Max and Monique Nemni, with his consent, co-operation, and access to his apparently meticulous adolescent files, shows his acceptance in the 1930s as a young adult at Collège Jean-de-Brébeuf in Montreal of the mainly illiberal views of the dominant clergy of the Catholic Church in Quebec during the 1930s and 1940s. They were seemingly not much concerned about the growth of totalitarianism in Europe. After all, the Vatican had entered into the Lateran Treaty with

Mussolini in 1929 and the Concordat with Hitler in 1933. (To this day there is a painting of Benito Mussolini mounted on a horse on the ceiling of a Catholic Church in Montreal, Madonna della Difesa!). Trudeau's mentors and his intellectual circle admired Pétain and his Vichy regime that made peace with Hitler and collaborated with the Nazis. Many Quebecers were impressed with Pétain's slogan "Travail, Patrie, Famille," invoking the values of pre-revolutionary France, welcomed in Quebec as superior to the dangerous slogan of the revolution—"Liberté, Égalité, Fraternité." They were also favourably disposed to corporatism as practised by Mussolini and Franco.[2] Trudeau seems to have been indifferent to the war except for his strong opposition to conscription in Canada.[3]

It was apparently not until he left the tutelage of the Jesuits in about 1940 that Trudeau began to open his mind to other points of view. For one who loved to quote Jean Jacques Rousseau in later life, we find that he did not read *Du contrat social* until 1942 when he was in his 22nd year. And before undertaking this venture he first sought the permission of the Church! While a first-year law student at the University of Montreal in 1941, he sent a letter to Church authorities to seek permission to read the following four books on the Index librorum prohibitorum (books Catholics were not permitted to read without permission): *Le Prince* by Machiavelli; *L'esprit des lois* by Montesquieu; *Du contrat social* by Rousseau; and *Das Kapital* by Marx.[4] (It is interesting to note that while Marx's work was on the prohibitory Index, Hitler's *Mein Kampf* was not.[5]) It was in this same period in his early twenties that he read philosophers such as Henri Bergson (*Les deux sources de la morale et de la réligion*, published in 1935), which found a religious basis for the universal brotherhood of man and respect for all individuals.[6] This was also the period when he first read Jacques Maritain (*Humanisme integral*, published in 1936), who linked respect for the individual to Christianity, finding a basis for liberalism and individual rights in the philosophy of Saint Thomas Aquinas. Maritain defended liberalism and the rights of the individual.[7] Maritain was also known for his denunciation of the Vichy régime, and he later helped draft the Universal Declaration of Human Rights for the United Nations. Over time these views must have had an important influence on Trudeau. From Rousseau he obviously drew inspiration for popular sovereignty that, as we have seen, surfaced in the latter years of the struggle for patriation.

But, according to the Nemnis in their second volume, covering Trudeau's intellectual development from 1944 to 1965, it was not until he left Quebec for studies abroad that his world view changed radically, leaving him with a profound set of beliefs that seem to have stayed with him for the rest of his life and are still familiar to those who worked with him.[8] He spent 1944 to 1946 at Harvard where he studied political economy and government, taking an MA. He then spent a year in Paris studying politics and law. Leaving there in 1947, he spent a year at the London School of Economics where he studied under Harold Laski and other leading academics. At all of these institutions he read extensively and deeply, as his analytical summaries show. He made considerable efforts to meet and learn from some of the greatest thinkers of the times. As a result his opinions changed dramatically. During this period he came to believe in the separation of church and state. He developed his antipathy to nationalism: he saw no need for every "nation" to have a state and he came to believe that strong nationalism suppressed individual rights. He became aware of the horrors of the recent war and finally recognized that the war carried on by the Allies had been justified. He learned about and rejected fascism and Nazism, but remained convinced that the conscription imposed by the Canadian government was wrong because the politicians deceived the people. At Harvard he embraced the importance of "constitutionalism," meaning essentially liberal democracy. In Paris he read further in the philosophy of "personalism," a means of reconciling the individual with his society. He preferred the views of Jacques Maritain and Nikolai Berdyaev, who stressed the primacy of the person over the collectivity, and that nationalism is inconsistent with Christianity. Particularly under the influence of Laski, he became convinced that in a large, diverse state federalism was the best device for reconciling special ethnic or local preferences with the interests common to most or all members of the state. Through living in postwar Britain, where the Labour Government was building a welfare state, and through his association with Harold Laski who was an officer of the Labour Party, he came to have a great deal of respect for social democrats, all the while firmly rejecting Marxism. All of these influences made him receptive to the idea of special legal protection against the state or collectivity for individual rights. As a result he had abandoned most of the beliefs of his adolescence and young adulthood, except for his profound and abiding belief in Christianity.

An associate of Trudeau's during his last term as Prime Minister, André Burelle, has written that Trudeau was in fact inconsistent during his career in respect of individual rights. As an intellectual, particularly in his days as editor of *Cité Libre*, he accepted community-oriented or group rights. In some of his constitutional initiatives he was prepared to recognize these, but, according to Burrell, in Trudeau's last term of office in the final struggles for the *Charter* he had become an individualist libertarian. His antipathy to community rights led him even after retirement to continue to oppose community rights such as the declaration of Quebec as a "distinct society" in the abortive Meech Lake Accord.[9] But it seems to me that this is to ascribe to the *Charter* an intellectual consistency it does not possess. In fact, the *Charter* recognizes that certain values pertaining to groups or communities must also be respected. Section 1 confirms that limitations on individual rights may be justifiable in a "free and democratic society." In one of the early leading cases on this section, the Supreme Court of Canada observed that "[t]he rights and freedoms guaranteed by the *Charter* are not, however, absolute. It may become necessary to limit rights and freedoms in circumstances where their exercise would be *inimical to the realization of collective goals of fundamental importance*" (emphasis added).[10] Some other rights are conditioned on the existence of a community: for example, the rights to government services in the official minority language (section 20) or official minority language education at public expense (section 23) depend on the numbers of the minority language community being sufficient to warrant such services. Sections 25 and 27 require respect for Aboriginal and ethnic values in the application of the *Charter*. Section 33, which allows that laws impinging on fundamental freedoms and legal rights may be valid if declared by the enacting legislature that they shall operate notwithstanding sections 2 and 7–15 of the *Charter*, creates a large potential for the interests of the community to trump those of the individual. And, just outside the *Charter* in the same legislative instrument, section 35 of the *Constitution Act, 1982* is a sweeping guarantee of the communal rights of Aboriginal peoples. Trudeau accepted all these qualifications to individual rights, and initiated some of them, usually for the pragmatic reason of getting a settlement. He never rejected in principle all community-based rights: he only rejected the "two founding nations" as a basis for building a constitution.

It is not within the scope of this book nor my competence to follow and analyze more fully the evolution of Trudeau's philosophy. I have entitled this Part "Political and Pragmatic Origins of the *Charter*" because it is these aspects that in my view truly explain how and what the *Charter* came to be.

It is my conclusion that Trudeau came to his belief in Canadian constitutional guarantees of human rights gradually, observing the problems of Canadian society and absorbing the views of his seniors, many of them left-of-centre politicians and academics. He also came to it pragmatically as his own contrarian response to the widespread assumption that the constitution required major changes in the distribution of powers. This assumption of the need for changes in powers was variously shared both by centralizers (most of them left of centre) and advocates of greater provincial autonomy (including Trudeau's fellow Quebecers who argued for some kind of special status for that province). It was Trudeau's view, typically swimming against the tide of conventional wisdom, that if individual rights were adequately protected against intrusions of either level of government, then improvements in the distribution of powers (on which Canadians could never likely agree) were of secondary importance. In particular, it was his idea that pan-Canadian rights to the equal use of both official languages, guaranteed by the constitution, would be a better protection for the French language and culture in a united Canada than any form of francophone haven confined to fortress Quebec, dependent solely on a specially empowered legislature and government of that province, state, nation, or whatever it might be called.

Of his early constitutional mentors who were politically engaged, the most influential was F.R. Scott. Frank Scott was, of course, the renowned constitutional law professor and sometime Dean of the McGill Law School. He was also a much-admired man of Canadian letters as poet, essayist, satirist, and literary translator. But, like Trudeau, he was also a man of political action, and at a time and in a manner that required real sacrifice. Frank was one of the founders of the Co-operative Commonwealth Federation in 1933 and later served for some years as its national president: this at a time when democratic socialists were regarded as part of the Bolshevik threat to ordered society—and in no place more so than among the Anglo Establishment that governed McGill University, his employer. The Catholic hierarchy shared this view: on October 5, 1933, the archbishops and bishops

of all Canada, meeting in Quebec City, condemned the CCF. They warned that "Liberalism is [its] father, Socialism...and Bolshevism is its heir."[11]

Frank shared the view of most socialists of his era, that effective economic and social planning—the desiderata of most socialists—required a central government with more powers. He and many of the leading English-Canadian constitutional scholars, when I was a law student and young lawyer, deplored much of the jurisprudence of the Judicial Committee of the Privy Council (our final court of appeal in constitutional matters until 1950), which had ignored many of the centralizing features of our constitution (the *British North America Act, 1867*) and had extended provincial jurisdiction through some violence to that text. In this the Committee followed the US Supreme Court that in the early days of the Roosevelt New Deal struck down fundamental social reforms that we would today take as minimum conditions for a just society. The Court did this in the name of substantive due process, liberty, and the sanctity of private contracts. With respect to both tribunals, these gratuitous manipulations of constitutional texts in defence of the economic status quo were regarded by liberals everywhere as examples of the evils of judicial activism. In Canada this led many liberals to assume the necessity for flexible constitutional amendment procedures to cure the problems created by the excessive decentralization carried out by the Judicial Committee of the Privy Council and its faithful follower, the Supreme Court of Canada. Frank and those of similar views were therefore skeptical about enhanced judicial powers, but to this he made one exception: the protection of individual liberties.

As previously noted, in the few years after Pierre Trudeau left Collège Jean-de-Brébeuf he read more widely in history and philosophy. In later years he often cited Aquinas, Locke, Rousseau, and Jefferson. He pointed to the American Declaration of Independence of 1776 and the Declaration of the Rights of Man of 1789 in France as victories for the natural and inalienable rights of man. But by his own confirmation years afterward, little constitutional law was taught at the University of Montreal when he was a law student there in the early 1940s and it was only from his later contacts with Frank "that I absorbed much of my constitutional thinking."[12] His background and interests and genius came to lie in the great principles of constitutionalism, federalism, and the relationship between the individual and the state and not in the dry positivism of the

British North America Act, 1867 or the minutiae of Judicial Committee of the Privy Council jurisprudence. He would have been much more at ease in discussing the writings of Rousseau than the judgements of Viscount Haldane. As I said on more than one occasion to federal colleagues at constitutional conferences, "Our leader has one of the best legal minds of the 18th century."

I attended my first constitutional conference in 1960 and my last in 1983. In that time I had the good fortune to know and to work with these remarkable men, both separately and together. My career first connected with them in academe, then later in my constitutional advisory work for the Government of Saskatchewan and the Government of Canada. That experience allowed me to see many of the strands that went into the knitting of the *Charter*, and I cast a few of the stitches myself.

HUMAN RIGHTS IDEAS IN CANADA
AND THE UNITED NATIONS

It would be wrong to imply that Scott and Trudeau were the sole advocates for legal protections of human rights in Canada. I will describe the evolution of their thoughts on the subject and will demonstrate that in my view it was the democratic socialists who contributed the most to the constitutional protection of those rights. But there were other efforts to attain some form of legal protections prior to the adoption of the *Charter*.[13] The Canadian Civil Liberties Association was established in 1947 and it pressed for a bill of rights—apparently a statutory, not a constitutional, bill.[14] Much of the interest in the subject at this time was created by efforts at the United Nations to draft the Universal Declaration of Human Rights. A joint parliamentary committee on human rights and fundamental freedoms was established in 1947 and in 1948 and it studied the draft Universal Declaration. There was at this time general agreement among politicians of all parties that Canada must proceed with caution in respect of any such international obligations for at least two reasons. Firstly, it would be contrary to the principles of parliamentary supremacy for the Government of Canada to undertake any binding obligations to take or refrain from legislative action in deference to human rights guarantees. There was a particularly strong feeling against endorsing social and economic rights that would require legislation and expenditures to be made meaningful. The draft Universal Declaration had many of these,

including the right to work, to an adequate standard of living, and an education. Secondly, neither the Government nor Parliament of Canada could commit the provinces in this regard in respect of matters within their jurisdiction. The federal Department of Justice was particularly adamant on these points.[15] The parliamentary committee approved the draft of the Universal Declaration only on the assumption that it was just a statement of goals. At the United Nations, Canada, along with the Soviet bloc and the white government of South Africa, abstained from voting for the Declaration in the Third Committee. However, on December 10, 1948, Lester Pearson cast the Canadian vote for the Declaration in the General Assembly with the reservation that Canada would not "invade other rights" to give effect to rights in the Declaration.[16] Nevertheless, the existence of the Declaration raised the profile of the human rights debate in Canada. There was a growing movement in Canada from 1948 through 1952 among ethnic and feminist groups, as well as trade unions, for anti-discriminatory measures and for guarantees of social and economic rights.[17] In 1950 a committee of the Senate favoured a constitutional bill of rights in principle but concluded one could not be adopted until we had a Canadian amending formula.[18] The 1950s saw a growth in anti-discrimination legislation, particularly at the provincial level. Much of the national debate in the late 1950s came to be focussed on Prime Minister Diefenbaker's proposal for a *Canadian Bill of Rights* after he was returned to office in 1958 with, at the time, a record majority. While that instrument was adopted by Parliament in 1960,[19] it was the object of much criticism. Various critics lamented that it applied only to the federal government, not the provinces; it contained no entitlements (social and economic rights); and that it was statutory only and thus subject to change by Parliament. It was not a constitutional guarantee that would invalidate laws of Parliament inconsistent with it. Even the Liberal party in Opposition (although—when in government—it had consistently opposed putting individual rights in the constitution) for the first time advocated a constitutional bill of rights![20] While we now know that the legal impact of the *Canadian Bill of Rights* was limited and disappointing, it certainly focussed attention on the possibilities and problems of establishing human rights guarantees.

In the 1950s and 1960s, meanwhile, work was underway at the United Nations to draft the International Covenant on Civil and Political Rights (ICCPR) and the International Covenant on Economic, Social and Cultural

Rights (ICESCR). Drafting was completed in 1966 and the texts were thrown open for accession by member states. As I have discussed in chapter 4, Canada acceded to both Covenants in 1976, the year they came into operation, and this required us to do an examination of all federal and provincial laws so that we could report to the UN Human Rights Committee as to the state of compliance in Canada with the ICCPR, another exercise in consciousness-raising with respect to human rights. In fact, we later drew on parts of the ICCPR in the drafting of the *Canadian Charter of Rights and Freedoms.*

DEMOCRATIC SOCIALISM
AND INDIVIDUAL RIGHTS

It may be thought by some to be anomalous that much of the initiative for constitutional guarantees of individual rights in Canada came from the Canadian socialist movement. After all, those who believe in the importance of the collectivity and the use of the state to further the good of society as a whole are generally thought to attach a subordinate value to individual rights where they conflict with the welfare of the many. When I was a dedicated public servant in the CCF government of Saskatchewan, we often recited the cliché: "You can't make an omelette without breaking eggs." I suppose I helped break a few myself. (For example, I have earlier described my modest role as "legal co-ordinator" of a committee assisting the provincial cabinet in dealing with a traumatic general doctors' strike in Saskatchewan commenced on July 1, 1962, upon the coming into force of the first state-operated medical care insurance scheme in North America. Considered revolutionary at the time by its critics, within a few years such schemes were adopted by every province and partially funded by the federal government.)

Perhaps ironically, it was as a reaction to the efforts of elected governments in Canada to save our country from the tyranny of Bolshevism that Canadian socialists became advocates of individual rights. During the Winnipeg General Strike of 1919, the Government of Canada apparently became so apprehensive that a second Bolshevik Revolution was underway (only two years after the first one) that it rushed through Parliament the infamous amendment that became section 98 of the *Criminal Code.* It declared as an "unlawful association" any organization whose objects were to bring about "governmental, industrial or economic change" by force or

violence. The section then made it an offence to be a member of such an organization, to attend any of its meetings, speak in its favour, distribute its literature, or wear its badge. Penalties of up to 20 years were provided.

One of the early antagonists of this law was Rev. J.S. Woodsworth, a former Methodist minister in Winnipeg who had become a Fabian socialist and social activist as well as a pacifist. During the General Strike in Winnipeg in 1919, at about the time section 98 was being debated in Parliament, he was arrested for seditious libel for writings supporting the strikers. One of his offences involved quoting two verses from the biblical book of Isaiah! He was never tried, but the experience obviously left an impression on him. In 1921 he was elected to Parliament as a member of the Manitoba Independent Labour Party. He was soon advocating the repeal of section 98.[21] He had become acquainted with Canon Scott, a liberally minded Anglican Quebec clergyman and the father of Frank Scott. Frank, then a young professor at McGill, came to know and admire Woodsworth. By 1932 Scott was writing articles advocating freedom of speech and association and deploring section 98 and its uses.[22]

In that same year was formed the League for Social Reconstruction (LSR), a group founded along Fabian Socialist lines to provide intellectual analysis for social reform. Frank Scott was a member of its first provisional executive and became much involved with its work. He and other LSR members participated in the drafting of the Regina Manifesto adopted at the founding convention of the CCF in July 1933. At one public meeting there, from a platform shared with J.S. Woodsworth and M.J. Coldwell (later to become, respectively, the first and second national leaders of the party), Scott assured[23] the audience that the CCF would not interfere with constitutional guarantees of minority rights. Indeed, the Manifesto, though replete with socialist rhetoric, specifically assured the protection of individual rights. It stated:

> The new social order at which we aim is not one in
> which individuality will be crushed out by a system of
> regimentation. Nor shall we interfere with cultural rights
> of racial or religious minorities. What we seek is a proper
> collective organization of our economic resources such as
> will make possible a much greater degree of leisure and a
> much richer individual life for every citizen.

In restoring to the community its natural resources and in taking over industrial enterprises from private into public control we do not propose any policy of outright confiscation.

Among the policies stated in the Manifesto[24] was the following: "FREEDOM: Freedom of speech and assembly for all; repeal of Section 98 of the *Criminal Code*; amendment of the Immigration Act to prevent the present inhuman policy of deportation; equal treatment before the law of all Canadians irrespective of race, nationality or religious or political beliefs." Among those who attended part of this founding convention was Tommy Douglas, then a young Baptist preacher in southern Saskatchewan who had already become active in the organization of the Independent Labour Party of Weyburn. As will be seen later, he continued thereafter to have a strong commitment to the legal protection of individual rights, sometimes in spite of the views of others in his party.

The years that followed the founding of the CCF showed a continuing concern, by Scott and by many members of the party, with rights issues. Frank continued to speak out and write against section 98 until it was repealed by Parliament in 1936. In 1935, in an essay in the LSR publication *Social Planning for Canada*, he advocated a constitutional bill of rights. Not long after that, and largely because of the repeal of section 98, a new *cause célèbre* arose for Frank to embrace. In 1937 the government of Quebec Premier Maurice Duplessis adopted the infamous "Padlock Act"[25]: this Act authorized the Attorney General to lock up any building, including dwellings, that he believed to be used "to propagate communism or bolshevism." Scott attacked the Act not just for its threat to freedom of speech and association, but also because he considered it beyond the power of a province. After all, the Parliament of Canada had only recently repealed section 98, which dealt with much of the same subject matter. (In this view he was ultimately vindicated by the Supreme Court of Canada: in the fifties, Frank was brought in as counsel in the case of *Switzman v Elbling*[26] in which the statute was ultimately struck down as ultra vires of the Quebec legislature). The existence of such legislation, and the efforts of the Quebec government to suppress the Jehovah's Witnesses in that province, further reinforced his support for the constitutional protection of human rights.

During World War II the CCF found itself somewhat divided on the issue of the treatment of Japanese-Canadians. After Pearl Harbor some Canadian politicians were energized by the panic in California over the presence of persons of Japanese ancestry on the US west coast. Americans there somehow imagined that the Japanese would one day invade, assisted by a fifth column of local persons of Japanese descent. The excited Canadian politicians, mostly from British Columbia, demanded draconian treatment for Japanese-Canadians equal to that insisted upon by United States politicians for Japanese-Americans. The federal government, yielding to the blandishments of these statesmen, interned those of Japanese descent whether they were aliens, naturalized British subjects (this preceded the Canadian *Citizenship Act*), or British subjects by virtue of birth in Canada. At the end of the war the government embarked on a program of dispersing such people across the country or persuading them to move to Japan. The minor children of those who "consented" to go would, by virtue of an Order-in-Council adopted in December 1945, be compelled as well to go to Japan—a country devastated by war where they (and sometimes even their parents) had almost certainly never been. There were some CCF politicians in BC and elsewhere who joined in the patriotic fervour to control, or rid the country of, people who were with very few exceptions loyal to Canada, many of them anxious to serve in the Canadian forces though not allowed to until late in the war. The official CCF position appears to have been largely one of acquiescence in these repressive measures, though some Members of Parliament spoke out in favour of Japanese-Canadians. Tommy Douglas, who became the first head of a CCF government when he became Premier of Saskatchewan in 1944, had remained on the sidelines of this issue.[27] However, his government did intervene in support of the Co-operative Committee on Japanese Canadians in a reference taken to the Supreme Court of Canada in early 1946. The Committee and the Attorney General of Saskatchewan were unsuccessful in their attack on the validity of the December 1945 Order-in-Council, in both the Supreme Court and on appeal in the Judicial Committee of the Privy Council[28] in London. It is worth noting that Mr F.A. (Andy) Brewin acted as counsel for both these parties. Mr Brewin was a well-known supporter of the CCF who wrote articles on the constitutional protection of individual rights and later served as a New Democratic Party Member of Parliament.

Tommy Douglas further affirmed his personal commitment to human rights by bringing about the adoption of the first comprehensive human rights law in Canada, *The Saskatchewan Bill of Rights Act*, in 1947.[29] This was not a mere anti-discrimination law (although it did contain such provisions): it also declared fundamental political and religious freedoms. While this law was always somewhat defective in practice (enforcement had to be by prosecutions), it was an inspiration and a symbol at a time when few governments concerned themselves with such matters.

Federally, the CCF began to advocate the amendment of the constitution to entrench certain individual rights, this being one of the policies adopted in the Regina Manifesto. In 1945 Alistair Stewart, a CCF MP, introduced a motion calling for such an amendment to embrace political, egalitarian, and legal rights. On February 7, 1955, the CCF leader introduced a similar proposal in Parliament.

Meanwhile, through intergovernmental discussions the Government of Saskatchewan was staking out a position for such a constitutional change. The passage by Westminster of the *British North America (No. 2) Act, 1949*[30] at the sole request of federal authorities had stirred up considerable controversy. This amendment added a new head 1 to section 91 of the original Act, thereby giving (or so it was generally believed at that time) extensive powers to Parliament to amend the Constitution save for certain specified exceptions. Many provinces were concerned by this and wanted to discuss the whole question of establishing a comprehensive Canadian procedure for amending the constitution that would adequately protect provincial interests. In preparation for a Constitutional Conference called for January 1950 in Quebec to discuss this subject, the Government of Saskatchewan retained two outside consultants: Dean F.C. Cronkite of the College of Law, University of Saskatchewan, and Professor Frank Scott of McGill.

Frank had been a frequent adviser to Douglas as Premier, both formally and informally. He once described to me with enthusiasm, as he and I ascended the front steps at the main entrance to the Saskatchewan Legislative Building in 1960, how he had been there on July 1944, entering the building with Tommy Douglas and his new ministers as they arrived to "take over." Most, he said, did not even know where their departments were.

It is apparent that when called upon to help prepare for the Conference of 1950, Frank urged the Premier to call for a constitutional bill of rights.

This Douglas did in his opening statement to the Conference in Quebec,[31] but without apparently marshalling any support for the idea. It is of interest to note that among the federal staff present at that Conference was one Pierre Elliott Trudeau, at that time employed in the Privy Council Office. As is usually the fate of staff, history does not record his views on the subject matter of the Conference! However in later years he said that he was particularly impressed with the work of Frank Scott at that Conference as a member of the Saskatchewan delegation.[32] He was also apparently influenced by Frank's suggestion, even though stated only tentatively, that if a constitutional bill of rights were adopted it might be possible to consider the abolition of the federal power to disallow provincial laws. I will return to this issue later.

The January 1950 Conference did have some discussion of a possible amending formula, the main bone of contention being how much of the constitution would have to be entrenched (that is, changeable only by unanimous agreement of the provinces as well as of the central government). There were follow-up meetings of the Attorneys-General on this subject and the disagreements were brought back to a further First Ministers' Conference in Quebec in September 1950.

By this time, however, there were many other preoccupations for the governments that met at Quebec, including the Korean War that had started in June. The constitutional differences were not resolved there, nor at subsequent meetings of Attorneys-General, and the whole project died. No further meetings of First Ministers were held on the subject of constitutional reform until some 18 years later. The subject did however arise briefly at a First Ministers' Conference in July 1960, held shortly after the election of the Liberal Party of Jean Lesage in Quebec. There was some discussion, during an otherwise busy agenda, on the possibility of constitutional reform. The *Canadian Bill of Rights* was scheduled to come into force at the beginning of the following month. Lesage himself suggested in his opening remarks that there should be a constitutional bill of rights, and Tommy Douglas speaking after him ad libbed an endorsement of the idea.[33] At the conclusion of the Conference it was agreed that there should be a meeting of the Attorneys-General to examine the possibility of agreement on a Canadian amending formula that would permit the "repatriation" of the constitution, the amendment of which still remained largely within the powers of the United Kingdom Parliament.

Prime Minister Diefenbaker called on his Minister of Justice, Hon. E. Davie Fulton, to chair such a conference, and Mr Fulton convened the first session on October 6 and 7, 1960. There were subsequently three other sessions in the ensuing 12 months. I have described in chapter 2 how I came to attend these sessions as Secretary of the Saskatchewan delegation, how we advocated unsuccessfully the inclusion of a bill of rights in the constitution, and how the resulting Fulton Formula for amendment failed to get unanimous endorsement.

These conferences have significance for the origins of the *Charter* because they demonstrated the democratic socialist commitment to a constitutional bill of rights, and its perception of the interplay with questions of redistributing powers, all in the pre-Trudeau era of constitutional negotiation. In our opening statement (which I drafted), Saskatchewan's Attorney General R.A. Walker first stated the position for a flexible amending formula. He then went on to say, "because we believe in a large measure of flexibility for much of this constitution, we also believe in the inclusion of an entrenched Bill of Rights. A comprehensive Bill of Rights would guarantee those fundamentals which should not be tampered with except by universal agreement, and at the same time permit a flexibility in much of the remaining constitution."[34] As will be seen later, this was a position not unlike that which Pierre Trudeau enunciated in the 1960s and that later became part of federal policy: namely, that the distribution of powers is not so important if basic rights and liberties are protected from intrusion by either level of government. There was little interest shown by any other government in our 1960 call for a bill of rights, however, not even by the Quebec delegation whose Premier had initiated the subject in the First Ministers' Conference some three months previously. No doubt other delegations felt that the discussion of such a bill of rights was not within the mandate of this conference, which was to find an amending formula, although we had tried to demonstrate that some provincial powers pertaining to cultural and language matters would not have to be entrenched if the constitution itself guaranteed these rights. As the meetings proceeded without reference to the rights issue, Saskatchewan shifted its attention to trying to achieve some flexibility in the amending process, suggesting fairly easy delegation of powers between levels of government. Delegation achieved limited support and found its way into the final text. This came to be known as the "Fulton Formula" that was never approved

by all governments. After the shift to a federal Liberal government, that formula was renegotiated into the Fulton-Favreau Formula which, as we have seen, also failed to get unanimous approval.

As for further NDP advocacy of a constitutional bill of rights, few opportunities presented themselves in the ensuing years until Trudeau took over the initiative in 1968. It is important to note, however, that Tommy Douglas remained dedicated to the protection of individual rights and their entrenchment in the constitution. I remember, for example, during the October Crisis of 1970 being in the gallery of the House of Commons the morning of October 16. The *War Measures Act* had been proclaimed in force by the Cabinet in the middle of the night, together with regulations outlawing an organization and providing to the police extraordinary powers of search and arrest without warrant. These measures were of course directed against the Front de Libération du Québec (FLQ) and were occasioned by the political kidnappings recently carried out by the FLQ in Montreal. Having proclaimed the Act and regulations in force during the night, the government tabled these measures for debate in Parliament as soon as possible, as required by law. Of the speakers that morning, only Douglas spoke against these measures on the grounds that they were dangerously oppressive and so far the government had provided no adequate justification for them. This was a brave step to take and one for which he was widely condemned in the press and by much of the public, including many members of his own party. At that time he could invoke no constitutional guarantees to justify his criticism, but he insisted that such powers of search and arrest were unconscionable in the circumstances. In the event he was partly vindicated as the "apprehended insurrection" cited by the government had little substance and the powers so granted to the police were in fact abused.[35]

In later years when Tommy was no longer leader and no longer in Parliament, he continued to support the constitutionalization of rights. As we have seen, in 1980 after the last failure of federal-provincial discussions on a charter, patriation, and other constitutional changes, Trudeau's government took steps to proceed unilaterally, if necessary, to obtain such a package from the UK Parliament. Though the government hoped to get the support of as many provinces as possible, including that of the Blakeney NDP government of Saskatchewan, only Ontario and New Brunswick (two Progressive Conservative governments) came forward. In the lengthy

discussions before the breakdown, Blakeney had raised a series of objections to the *Charter*, much of it based on a reluctance to submit, as he saw it, policy decisions of elected representatives to review and modification or invalidation by non-elected judges. He also had a variety of concerns about other elements of the package, including the possible entrenchment of a role for the unelected Senate in a future constitutional amendment process. As I have described in chapter 8, Ed Broadbent, the NDP leader in the House of Commons, in principle wanted to support the *Charter* as a goal that the CCF and the NDP had long sought. He made the support of his caucus in the House conditional on certain substantive changes being made in the constitutional package which would strengthen provincial control over the marketing of natural resource products. These were changes that Saskatchewan had sought, and Ed hoped to make the package acceptable to his NDP colleagues in that province. There ensued a good deal of debate and growing animosity between the provincial and federal NDP leadership on this issue,[36] and in the event Saskatchewan never did support the adoption of the *Charter* until the eleventh-hour compromise in November 1981. Throughout all this debate Tommy Douglas firmly supported Broadbent and the federal caucus against the Blakeney objections: he kept his eye on the main prize, a constitutional bill of rights the need for which had been well demonstrated to him in his lifetime.

My last conversation with Tommy occurred in November 1983, the occasion being the funeral in Ottawa of Graham Spry who had been Saskatchewan's Agent-General in London for some 20 years and who had been one of the founders of the League for Social Reconstruction. At the ensuing reception my daughter Alison and I chatted with Tommy. He recounted for her some of my early career in his civil service in Saskatchewan, and referred to my work in developing the *Charter*. He ended by saying that the adoption of the *Charter* had given him great satisfaction.

PIERRE TRUDEAU AND THE CONCEPT OF A CHARTER

Pierre graduated in law and was admitted to the Quebec bar in 1943. It would be wrong to think that he entered the profession with a burning commitment to a constitutional bill of rights. There is little to suggest that at that time he instinctively endorsed a constitutional foundation for individual rights and freedoms of Canadians. But he started to come under

the influence of Frank Scott. In 1942 and 1943 he read *Social Planning for Canada*,[37] the work of the League for Social Reconstruction of which Frank was an editor. He attended a lecture on constitutional law given by Frank at the University of Montreal in 1943, and started attending CCF meetings in Montreal where he continued to encounter Frank.[38] He of course readily shared Frank's views on the suppression of freedoms in Quebec by the Duplessis regime, and this was no doubt conducive to an interest in constitutional guarantees that would curb such governmental intrusions. He also came to understand, if perhaps not wholly to accept, Frank's views on the need for constitutional arrangements to support effective state action in regard to matters outside the protected areas of individual rights.[39] During a trip he made with Frank down the Mackenzie River in the summer of 1956, he apparently became firmly convinced, at last, of the need to repatriate the constitution and to include in it a bill of rights.[40]

It must also be remembered that in the decade preceding this trip, Pierre had been active in the Quebec CCF, campaigning for various of their candidates. Indeed, the provincial leader, Thérèse Casgrain, saw him as her potential successor.[41] No doubt during this period Pierre must have been attracted by much of the party platform, in particular its belief in social engineering and using the power of the state to promote social justice. As a contrarian, however, it appears (as I will demonstrate) that he was not impressed with some of the dominant constitutional views within the party. Outside of Quebec, at least, the majority view in the party was that most of this social engineering could be carried out more effectively by the central government, with its greater resources and countrywide jurisdiction. Big government was also required to deal with big business. Pierre took a much more pragmatic view of the distribution of powers. He also disagreed with the conventional wisdom of most fellow Quebecers that their government and legislature required more powers before they could properly protect and promote the interests of French Canadians: in his view what was required was the effective use of existing powers that he believed successive governments of that province had neglected because of their narrow view of the role of the state.[42] In these matters he and Frank Scott would have disagreed, as Frank instinctively preferred a strong central government. Frank felt the Judicial Committee of the Privy Council had wrongly decentralized the country and this resulted in a need for amendments to restore effective central government.

Incidentally, Trudeau's writings of the 1960s belie the common belief, nurtured by opposition politicians and a superficial press, that he was an incurable centralizer. A careful examination of his policies while in office shows, here too, a pragmatic and functional approach, as advocated in his writings. While he did on occasion instigate large federal intrusions into the economy where he was convinced the national economic interest required it, particularly in the petroleum sector (in the face of international manipulation of prices) and in fighting inflation, he did in 1977 reduce Ottawa's conditions attached to much of federal-provincial cost-sharing programs.[43] Also provincial-municipal expenditures grew more rapidly in comparison with federal expenditures during his time in government, which one would not expect in a centralizing state.[44] In its style of governance, his administration was deeply committed to consultation with the provinces in most matters affecting their interests. Those of us in the public service knew that we could not propose such initiatives without a firm plan of consultation in hand.

In one rather arcane area of the assignment of powers in the constitution, Pierre and Frank in my experience did share a common understanding. This pertained to the powers of disallowance and reservation of legislation. By sections 56, 57, and 90 of the *BNA Act, 1867*,[45] the Imperial government was granted power to disallow otherwise valid Acts of the Parliament of Canada and the federal cabinet has power to disallow otherwise valid laws adopted by provincial legislatures. Similarly, the Governor General can withhold royal assent to a federal bill, notwithstanding the advice of his or her Canadian ministers, and refer the matter to the United Kingdom government for decision; and the Lieutenant-Governors can reserve assent to a provincial bill and refer it to the federal cabinet for consideration. While the power of the UK government to intervene in Canadian legislation has long been regarded as a dead letter, both Frank and Pierre regarded these federal powers over provincial legislation to be for the purpose of invalidating conspicuously unjust provincial laws. In other words, they believed the federal government was rightly or wrongly given a supervisory power to protect Canadians from laws that were too intrusive of individual rights and freedoms. There is, however, little in the history or use of these powers to support such an interpretation. In respect of the supervisory powers of the United Kingdom government over federal laws, this was simply a continuation of a system that existed in the

Empire, whereby the Imperial authorities could stop or annul colonial laws that might interfere with the execution of Imperial policy in areas such as trade, defence, and foreign affairs. Among the founding fathers of the Canadian constitution, the dominant view was that there should be a strong central government (to avoid the chaos that had recently reigned in the United States leading up to the Civil War). It thus seemed natural to most to put the new central government in Ottawa in the same position vis-à-vis provincial laws that the Imperial government then enjoyed vis-à-vis the component units of the Empire. It was the policy of the Minister of Justice, from shortly after Confederation, to review provincial laws to see whether they would conflict with "the interest of the whole Dominion" or with federal laws, or were unconstitutional insofar as they were beyond provincial powers. In fact, most of the exercises of the federal power of disallowance involved commercial matters, including the protection of the monopoly of the Canadian Pacific Railway or protecting the financial institutions of Central Canada against the efforts of provinces to protect local creditors or institutions. Some did involve striking down discriminatory laws, although this was usually in the name of protecting good relations with friendly countries whose citizens or former citizens would be prejudiced as such by local laws.[46]

In any event the power of disallowance has not been used since 1943. As for the power of Lieutenant-Governors to reserve royal assent, while they were told soon after Confederation that they should only do this after receiving instructions from the Governor in Council, this stricture was observed more in the breach than the observance. Their use of this power tended to be idiosyncratic and often to the embarrassment of the federal government, and it would be hard to discern a meaningful pattern as to the proper scope of the power. When Frank and Pierre ruminated on this subject in the 1950s, the power of reservation was seemingly moribund, not having been used since 1937. Curiously, the power was used once more and probably for the last time when in 1961 a rather officious Lieutenant-Governor of Saskatchewan decided without any instructions from Ottawa to use it to prevent the coming into force of a bill that would have affected mineral rights leased by a large corporation. An embarrassed Prime Minister Diefenbaker and his cabinet quickly gave the assent that had been withheld by the Queen's representative in Regina. (It was my privilege to write an opinion for the Attorney General of Saskatchewan

immediately following the Lieutenant-Governor's reservation of the bill in 1961—perhaps one of the last legal opinions ever written in Canada on the exercise of that power! In it I predicted that this would create far more of a problem for Ottawa than Regina, and this proved to be the case.)

Notwithstanding these facts, both Frank Scott and Pierre Trudeau saw the disallowance power as a national instrument for the protection of individual rights. It was their prescription for its future that differed because of their contrasting views on federal power. As early as the 1950 federal-provincial conference in Quebec City, Frank was advising that even if there were a constitutional bill of rights, the federal power should be retained because of his reluctance to see a weakening of federal instruments of governance. This was a view not shared by his principal client, Tommy Douglas, who as a provincial Premier saw the power as a means for Ottawa to come to the rescue of the capitalist system in any showdown with provincial governments that wanted to protect their citizens from oppression.[47] Nor did Trudeau accept this approach. On several occasions in the next few years he submitted that if there were to be a constitutional bill of rights (a step that he seems not to have been advocating strongly at that time), then the powers of disallowance and reservation should go. For example, in 1955, in a submission to Quebec's Tremblay Commission on the Constitution, he said, "The Province could well declare herself ready to accept the incorporation of a declaration of human rights in the constitution on the condition that the rights of disallowance and reservation be done away with."[48] This thought was repeated in an essay he contributed to *Social Purpose for Canada*,[49] a 1961 book that aspired to be a modern version of the League for Social Reconstruction's work of 1935: *Social Planning for Canada*. The Trudeau essay is of particular interest because he reveals his disagreement, as mentioned earlier, with the widespread assumption among socialists that effective social and economic reform would require more federal jurisdiction. He dissociated himself from the view that "had the trend of Privy Council decisions favouring provincial autonomy been different, the fate of the Canadian people would have been immeasurably improved in the past." Instead, he argued that much could be accomplished by federal-provincial co-operation on a functional, pragmatic basis. He also urged the value of experimentation by individual provinces in social reforms, where that which was found to be workable in a provincial "laboratory" could be emulated by other provinces or the

federal government. (Indeed, a prime example of this was soon to follow: Saskatchewan, using its existing powers, had in 1962 put in force a full publicly funded universal medical insurance program and by 1970 the Parliament of Canada, through the use of the spending power, had brought all provinces into a similar nationwide scheme. Curiously, Trudeau did not seem too happy with this result when it happened: I recall a particularly petulant Premier Robarts of Ontario complaining of this federal "intrusion" at a federal-provincial conference after Trudeau became Prime Minister, and Trudeau's final riposte was "There'll be no more medicares!") On the subject of a constitutional bill of rights he said in his 1961 essay, consistently with what he had said to the Tremblay Commission, "[f]or example again, when socialists advocate a constitutional amendment enacting a bill of rights for all Canadians and all governments in Canada, they might simultaneously advocate the abolition of the federal right to disallow and to reserve provincial laws, *since such safeguards would then be obsolete*" (emphasis added).[50] He reiterated the same thought in 1965 while there actually advocating a constitutional bill of rights which, "... in addition to protecting traditional political and social rights...would specifically put the French and English languages on an equal basis before the law." If there were such protection for basic rights, "there would be no danger in reducing the central government's predominance in certain areas (for example, by abolishing the right of reservation and disallowance)."[51]

That this linkage was firmly fixed in Trudeau's mind was illustrated at the Victoria Conference in 1971 where we almost achieved agreement on a package of patriation, an amending formula, the method of appointments to the Supreme Court, and a limited range of guarantees of political, egalitarian, and language rights. When it appeared on the last day of the Conference that there would be agreement on the so-called Victoria Charter, the Prime Minister instructed us to prepare a draft to abolish the powers of reservation and disallowance. Because this issue had never been a federal preoccupation (other than, apparently, that of the Prime Minister) during the discussions leading up to Victoria, we had never prepared such a draft. Our principal drafters at Victoria at that time, Jean Beetz for the French version and Gérard La Forest for the English version, quickly prepared the necessary changes to repeal sections 56 and 57 and part of section 90 of the *BNA Act, 1867*. I then took the drafts into the conference room (the BC legislative chamber), squatted by the Prime Minister as he

chaired the meeting, and explained to him the proposed changes. They found their way into the Schedule to the Victoria Charter, but all in vain. Because Premier Bourassa was not prepared to assent finally to the Victoria Charter that day, it was agreed that each First Minister would consult his cabinet and indicate within some 12 days whether his government would recommend it to his legislature. Bourassa, facing criticism from elements of the Quebec press and intelligentsia, and from nationalists both within and outside of his government, indicated that Quebec would not accede to the Victoria Charter. So when the Constitution was finally patriated in 1982, it came complete with the powers of reservation and disallowance, notwithstanding that fundamental rights and liberties had finally been entrenched! Forgotten was the trade-off between the guarantee of rights and the federal power of disallowance so long insisted upon by Pierre Trudeau.

During the 1960s, apart from the references to a bill of rights as discussed above, Trudeau advocated such a measure in the columns of *Cité Libre*, the Montreal periodical that he edited. He was becoming more specific regarding the role of a bill of rights in dealing with the Quebec issue. Writing in *Maclean's* magazine in 1964, after making the case that the redistribution of powers should not be considered until all governments attempted to identify and fulfill their goals on an ad hoc basis under the existing distribution, he said, "what is more important in the present context, a constitutionally entrenched bill of rights seems to be the best tool for breaking the ever-recurring deadlock between Quebec and the rest of the country. If certain language and educational rights were written into the constitution, along with other basic liberties, in such a way that no government—federal or provincial—could legislate against them, French Canadians would cease to feel confined to their Quebec ghetto, and the Spirit of Separatism would be laid [to rest] forever."[52] Trudeau also expanded on his views of constitutional reform and the working of federalism. One of the most brilliant analyses was his paper delivered in Charlottetown in June 1964. The Learned Societies were meeting there on the occasion of the 100th anniversary of the Charlottetown Conference, where delegates from the British North American colonies first met to discuss the possibility of Confederation. Naturally, many of the themes addressed by the social scientists had some relationship to these historic events. Trudeau, then a law professor at the University of Montreal, delivered a

paper to a joint session of the Canadian Political Science Association and the Association of Canadian Law Teachers. I was there as a member of the latter organization and it was the first time I had met Trudeau or heard him speak. His paper, entitled "Federalism, Nationalism, and Reason,"[53] foretold much of his political future. Nationalism he viewed as basically irrational and no longer necessary for building and maintaining a state. Federalism he viewed as "a product of reason in politics" or "functionalism in politics." In his analysis the Fathers of Confederation had adopted a reasonable compromise in 1867, but the workings of federalism had not always been satisfactory in practice. Centralizing trends had set in, and nationalism in the Imperial, or later pan-Canadian, context had incited Quebec nationalism as a reaction. These developments had weakened federalism, and he called for a return to rationalism in politics. It is clear that he was not calling for extensive formal constitutional amendments, but rather a better use of existing powers on rational, functional lines.

These perspectives naturally led the way to his position, oft stated once he was a federal office-holder, that reshuffling the distribution of powers was a low priority and should only follow the adoption of a constitutional bill of rights. It will be seen that these positions were taken on pragmatic, functional grounds and with a view to countering the then-strong political currents of Quebec nationalism.

While distancing himself from Frank Scott's views on centralization, Pierre never departed from their shared commitment to a constitutional bill of rights nor from his admiration for Frank as a scholar and activist. My wife and I attended a dinner at the McGill Faculty Club in 1969 in honour of Frank's 70th birthday. There were distinguished guests from his many fields of endeavour: two national leaders of the CCF/NDP—M.J. Coldwell and David Lewis; Thérèse Casgrain, former leader of the CCF in Quebec; three members of the League for Social Reconstruction—Graham Spry, King Gordon, and Frank Underhill; noted authors Hugh MacLennan and Leon Edel; poet A.J.M. Smith, Frank's collaborator and fellow anthologist; Jean-Louis Gagnon, fellow commissioner of the Royal Commission on Bilingualism and Biculturalism; A.L. Stein, his co-counsel in *Roncarelli v Duplessis*,[54] with whom Eleanor and I shared a table; Bora Laskin, a future Chief Justice of Canada, and Jean Beetz, another future judge of the Supreme Court; his close friend and frequent collaborator Carl Goldenberg;

and several friends from the academic world, including Percy Corbett, the former Dean of Law at McGill, who had first hired Frank as a professor in the 1920s. Pierre Trudeau, by then Prime Minister, proposed the toast to Frank, commencing his remarks with the exclamation, "Great Scott!" He ended by paying tribute "to the total man, to the poet, to the fighter for civil liberties, to the lawyer we admire, to the teacher from whom we have all learned, to the lover of life with whom we have all enjoyed many days of our own lives, and above all to the great human being." Frank in reply thanked Pierre "for being the first Canadian Prime Minister who's never been dull."[55]

Frank remained an advocate of the *Charter* in the 13 years that followed, and on April 17, 1982—the day it was proclaimed in effect by the Queen on Parliament Hill—Frank and his artist wife Marian hosted a party at their Clarke Avenue home in Montreal to celebrate.

11

PIERRE TRUDEAU ENTERS
THE CORRIDORS OF POWER

In 1963 Pierre was still an outsider to government. In the federal election of that year he campaigned for an NDP candidate in Montreal. Pierre's candidate lost, not surprisingly, and Lester Pearson formed a minority government. Hoping to improve that to a majority government, he called a further election in the autumn of 1965. In the face of growing Quebec nationalism and the election that summer of a more militant Union Nationale government there, Pearson wanted to enrich his Quebec caucus and to bring in high-profile people who would visibly strengthen Quebecers' role in the governance of Canada. He approached Jean Marchand and Gérard Pelletier who said they would not come without Trudeau. Thus Trudeau became the last of the so-called Three Wise Men chosen to run for the Liberals in Quebec.

While his better-known colleagues soon became ministers in Ottawa, Pierre was appointed Parliamentary Secretary to Prime Minister Pearson. He first entered the Cabinet in May 1967 as Minister of Justice, and it was then that my association with him began. As mentioned before, in the winter of 1966–1967 Marc Lalonde, then a Special Adviser in the Prime Minister's Office, phoned me in Saskatoon where I was teaching law and asked if I would consider coming to Ottawa to work on the constitution. I said I could not come during the academic year 1967–1968, but as a start I could come for the summer of 1967. I subsequently worked out the details with Jean Beetz, then on leave from the University of Montreal and serving as Assistant Secretary to Cabinet for Federal-Provincial Relations, to work in the Privy Council Office that summer. But before I arrived on

June 1, Pierre Trudeau had become Minister of Justice with responsibility for the constitutional file. I agreed to work with him instead.

Shortly after I arrived I helped prepare a memorandum for the Minister to submit to Cabinet outlining the nature of a possible constitutional bill of rights and proposing that it be discussed with the provinces.[1] The memorandum sought to describe the main features of a constitutional bill including: the nature of constitutional guarantees and how they would differ in effect from legislative bills; the distribution of powers in the constitution pertaining to human rights; the kinds of rights or freedoms that might be considered for protection (political, legal, egalitarian, and linguistic) and those that should not be included (economic). The need for entrenchment was discussed, as well as the implications for judicial review and parliamentary sovereignty. Cabinet agreed that the Prime Minister should meet with the provincial Premiers on July 5 and that he should propose to them a federal-provincial conference for later in the year, with one of its subjects for discussion being a constitutional bill of rights binding on the federal and provincial governments. Prime Minister Pearson did raise the matter with the Premiers on July 5 and told them he would be sending an invitation for such a conference later in the year. At a Cabinet Committee meeting I attended with Pierre Trudeau in early August, the Prime Minister reported this to Cabinet that then agreed on certain preparatory steps.[2] A major theme of discussion was that the federal government must take and retain the leadership in this exercise of rebuilding the nation. In response to the Robarts initiative, there was a firm conviction that provinces do not and should not convoke federal-provincial conferences. (In the event, Ottawa sent only observers to the Confederation of Tomorrow Conference.) In particular, it was agreed by the Cabinet Committee that for the government to retain the initiative, a fairly detailed working paper should be prepared on a constitutional bill of rights for distribution to the provinces prior to the meeting.

I was asked to draft such a paper and I set to work at once. This was not the occasion, nor was there time, for presenting a text of a preferred bill. Once the policy was established, this would have to be worked out in discussions with the provinces. Time did not permit an extensive analysis of all human rights instruments in the world to evaluate their structure and contents; nor were there excruciating analyses of philosophical concepts such as *equality* or *liberty*. I was acutely aware of two things: the limitations

of time and the necessity to outline a bill of rights that had some chance of acceptance by provincial governments. I had few instructions from the Minister: his one requirement was that such a bill contain language rights, although he surely assumed it would also protect the rights and freedoms familiar to Canadian law. First, I adopted Bora Laskin's well-known categorization of rights or freedoms[3]—political, legal, egalitarian, and economic. With the advice and assistance of Hilton McIntosh of the Legislation Section of the Department of Justice, I gathered together all Canadian legislation protecting any or all of these rights. I reviewed carefully the *Canadian Bill of Rights*. I had in mind that we should not omit from constitutional guarantees any rights or freedoms that were potentially applicable throughout Canada if they were already protected somewhere in statutory form. In particular, I knew that we could not leave out the kinds of rights protected in the *Canadian Bill of Rights*,[4] Mr Diefenbaker's 1960 statute that applied only as an interpretive aid to federal laws. I knew that if we did, there would be an outcry—first and foremost from the venerable Leader of the Opposition (soon to be replaced as Leader in September of that year). Among the principal non-Canadian instruments examined were the *United States Bill of Rights*, the *Universal Declaration of Human Rights*, the *European Convention on Human Rights*, and the two 1966 UN instruments, the *International Covenant on Civil and Political Rights* and the *International Covenant on Economic, Social and Cultural Rights*. These latter documents had not yet been acceded to by Canada.

I worked with the guidance of Carl Goldenberg and the advice and assistance of others. In late June Pierre Trudeau had announced the appointment of several advisers to him on the constitution. These included Gerald Le Dain, Mark MacGuigan, Gérard La Forest, Jean Beetz, and myself. I was of course working full-time at that point. As described in chapter 3, these advisers, and often the Minister, came to our board room in the Justice Annex to discuss progress and to make suggestions. I frequently had other opportunities at lunch or in his office to discuss with the Minister this work in progress.

On two or three occasions Frank Scott was also present in Pierre's office making his own contribution. He was still at that time a member of the Royal Commission on Bilingualism and Biculturalism and as such he did not want to have any formal role as an adviser to the government. This did not prevent him from dropping in on his old friend Pierre Trudeau

for a chat and a word of encouragement on this project so close to Frank's heart. One evening that summer my wife had invited Frank to dinner with our family. We were spending Centennial summer at a rambling old cottage on Lake Kingsmere in the Gatineau Hills. The cottage belonged to Graham and Irene Spry whom we had come to know in London when I was doing graduate work at Oxford. They were in the process that summer of returning to Canada, Graham having just retired from his post of Agent-General for Saskatchewan in the United Kingdom, and Irene was about to resume a very distinguished career as a professor of economics, most of it spent at the University of Ottawa. It was a long sunny summer evening, and after we had dined with Frank, our children Alison, Jonathan, and Colin, and I took him for a walk to the estate of former Prime Minister Mackenzie King that was just across the road. Alison and Jonathan showed him where they were taking a summer art class in one of Mr King's outbuildings. I showed Frank Mr King's artificial ruins (bits of stonework from demolished buildings, including some fragments from the Houses of Parliament in London made available for removal by the Luftwaffe and obtained from British wartime authorities by a somewhat embarrassed Canadian diplomat in London, future Prime Minster Lester B. Pearson, on the instructions of Prime Minister King[5]). Frank looked around and exclaimed, "Isn't that remarkable! I've written poetry about these ruins but this is the first time I've ever seen them!" I assume he referred to his epitaph for "W.L.M.K." which began

> How shall we speak of Canada,
> Mackenzie King dead?
> The Mother's boy in the lonely room
> With his dog, his medium and his ruins?

The briefing paper developed that summer followed closely the outline of contents and issues as previously provided to Cabinet. But it included some additional issues that, as then foreseen, have turned out to be contentious. It explained the significance of a constitutional bill of rights as opposed to a statutory bill, applying as it would to all governments and limiting the powers of all legislative and executive bodies—provincial and federal—regardless of normal distribution of powers under the federal system. It outlined possible contents including political rights, legal rights,

egalitarian rights, and linguistic rights, all of which were recommended for inclusion. Economic rights were discussed but rejected on the grounds that they mainly required legislation to implement them instead of merely limiting state action. The paper warned of difficult issues: for example, should the scope of some rights and freedoms be subject to limitations for specific named purposes, as found in the *European Convention on Human Rights* and the *International Covenant on Civil and Political Rights*; should freedom of religion be enlarged to freedom of conscience, and if the latter (the paper foretold, accurately as it turned out), the invalidity of the *Lord's Day Act*; the difficulties in the expression "due process" based on the US experience and the undesirability of entrenching substantive due process; the grounds of discrimination to be prohibited; the possible need to delay coming into force of egalitarian rights provisions; and the possible need for permitting limitations on certain rights in case of emergencies.

We had essentially completed this working paper by the time I had to leave Ottawa at the end of August to return to my teaching duties in Saskatoon. The only significant addition made by others later was a short section on linguistic rights that could not be drafted until the Royal Commission on Bilingualism and Biculturalism made its interim report in late 1967. By this time plans were settled for a Constitutional Conference of First Ministers to be held in Ottawa, February 5–7, 1968. In preparation for distribution and publication, the working paper was rounded out with a number of appendices consisting of the *BNA Act, 1867*, the *Canadian Bill of Rights, 1960*, the leading international covenants and declarations on human rights, and the *United States Bill of Rights* as found in the amendments to its constitution. It was graced with the title *A Canadian Charter of Human Rights*,[6] bound in a black, red, and white cover and published over the name of the Minister of Justice, Pierre Elliott Trudeau. It was tabled in Parliament on February 1, 1968, and distributed to the provinces before the Constitutional Conference commenced on February 5 under the chairmanship of Prime Minister Pearson. It soon became apparent, during and after that Conference, that Pierre Trudeau was a candidate for the leadership of the Liberal Party. As a member of the federal delegation, I marvelled at his lively, sometimes acerbic, debate with Premier Daniel Johnson of Quebec on the merits of a national guarantee of fundamental rights, including language rights, as opposed to special powers for Quebec based on its self-proclaimed role as defender of French

language and culture throughout Canada. The debate became so heated that Prime Minister Pearson, ever the diplomat, suddenly adjourned the conference for a coffee break. This exchange, on national television, was a major boost to the Trudeau candidacy, as was his advocacy of a constitutional Charter during his campaign. Obviously, the working paper became a useful instrument in advancing his cause. Through my lack of foresight or, perhaps, naïveté, I had not anticipated this use of what had started out as an intergovernmental working paper.

The day before I left Ottawa to return to the University of Saskatchewan at the end of August 1967, I called on the Minister to take my leave. He had earlier indicated that he would like me to come back for a year after the end of the next academic term in the spring of 1968. We discussed that briefly and then I said I was about to leave for Saskatoon. (Pierre at this point had not yet experienced cross-country campaigning for the leadership of the party.) He said cheerfully, "Well, if I get to Alberta I'll look you up." "Better try Saskatchewan, Pierre," I said as I edged toward the door.

12

SHAPING THE *CHARTER*

It is not the purpose of this book to detail the years of drafting and negotiations that went into the final adoption of the *Charter*. Suffice it to say this was an ongoing process of politics and pragmatism, just as was its conception. Broader guarantees were narrowed or dropped in the face of the objections of various provincial Premiers. The federal strategy was to get unanimous agreement on the contents of a charter and we were sometimes willing to make trade-offs in other areas of negotiation such as to abandon our goal of properly guaranteeing free trade within Canada or to relinquish some exclusive federal authority over trade in natural resources products. I have described in chapters 3 and 6 how, after years of intermittent discussions, mostly during the years 1968 to 1971 and 1978 to 1980, discussions finally broke down at the September 1980 First Minister's Conference on the Constitution. There were at best only indications of support from Ontario and New Brunswick on the federal proposal for a charter and an amendment formula for patriation. In preparation for this contingency we had drafted legislation for Westminster covering patriation and the *Charter* and a few uncontroversial matters. The draft of the *Charter* then proposed was not everything we would have preferred, but it was crafted, we thought, in a way that many if not most provinces could support or at least tolerate. Within days after the failed conference, along with three other federal officials, I was on a plane to London to discuss the draft with British officials in anticipation of a formal request by the Parliament of Canada to Westminster to enact this one last measure for Canada. That being done, the "unilateral package" was announced. Predictably, those who could not agree on anything else agreed to reject this proposal. But the nature and degree of public support for the *Charter* became apparent during the work of the Special Joint Committee of the Senate and House

of Commons on the Constitution (earlier referred to as the Special Joint Committee) studying the proposed resolution for an address to the Queen containing the legislation for patriation and the *Charter*. Arrangements were made for its meetings to be televised nationally "from gavel to gavel." Hundreds of written submissions were received, and dozens of organizations were heard. With only one exception, the oral submissions called for broader or stronger guarantees. As a result we were able to strengthen the *Charter*, often along the lines we had originally preferred but could not sell to the provinces. Thus the *Charter* took its final form more through the dynamics of politics and public opinion than through philosophical imperatives. A few examples will illustrate.

SECTION 1

Section 1 of the *Charter*, as finally adopted, states that the *Charter* "guarantees the rights and freedoms set out in it subject only to such reasonable limits prescribed by law as can be demonstrably justified in a free and democratic society." This section had a long evolution. In the working paper, referred to above, that I had drafted in 1967, and that later formed the basis for Pierre Trudeau's 1968 publication *A Canadian Charter of Human Rights*,[1] I had identified the issue of the possible need for limitations on guaranteed rights in special situations. I suggested three possibilities: a permitted legislative limitation in times of emergencies (as was permitted in the *Canadian Bill of Rights*, section 6); possible detailed grounds for limitation of particular rights (as is provided for in the *European Convention on Human Rights* and the *International Covenant on Civil and Political Rights*); or leaving it to the courts where they might deem it appropriate to read possible limitations into some otherwise unqualified rights (as has been done by the Supreme Court of the United States in certain cases). The basic rationale for any such method of limitation was a recognition that individual rights could not always be realized absolutely without regard to the rights of others or the needs of society. The first option identified would allow governments unilaterally and without any judicial review to declare emergencies: this would in effect allow the government, by adopting restrictive measures, to suspend various individual rights. The second option—that of specifying criteria for permissible abridgments of individual rights that would have constrained to varying degree (depending on how the criteria were defined) the occasions upon which limitations could

be imposed—would probably have required the approval of legislatures to impose the limits, and would have subjected such limits to judicial review. The third option would be based on the fiction that rights are absolute and rely on the courts to find necessary limits on them in special circumstances, such as Justice Holmes did when he said that freedom of speech does not give anyone the right to shout "Fire!" in a crowded theatre.

One of the first federal attempts to articulate a general limitation clause was in Bill C-60[2] tabled by the government in Parliament in 1978 for the purpose of study and debate. Bill C-60 was an attempt to consolidate and reformulate the constitution with important reforms including a charter of rights. The chief draftsman was Donald Thorson. As I have related in chapter 5, when he was in the course of drafting he asked me to outline for him what I thought should be the contents of an ideal charter. There had been many policy papers written on this subject but no definitive draft. It was early summer and I was at our cottage. I sat down at the kitchen table and made my list. Much of it survived the drafting process. I believe it was my suggestion that there be a general remedies section that survived ultimately in the form of subsection 24(1) of the present *Charter*. I also suggested a limitations section; as presented in Bill C-60, the proposed Charter included clause 25 which provided the following: "Nothing in this Charter shall be held to prevent such limitations on the exercise or enjoyment of any of the individual rights or freedoms declared by this Charter as are justifiable in a free and democratic society in the interests of public safety or health, the interests of the peace and security of the public, or the interests of the rights and freedoms of others, whether such limitations are imposed by law or by virtue of the construction or application of any law." This very broad language was an amalgam of limitations permitted of particular rights in various of the international human rights instruments. It would have done much to preserve the legislative supremacy so ardently guarded by most provinces.

As recounted in chapter 5, C-60 sparked a vigorous debate with the provinces, most of which saw it as a sinister attempt to diminish their legislative powers and property rights, as well as being an assault on the monarchy. There ensued a series of federal-provincial discussions on constitutional reform throughout 1978 and 1979, ranging over many topics, from freedoms to fisheries. Discussions on a possible charter were characterized by a lack of provincial interest accompanied by steady provincial resistance to any

effective constraints on the jurisdiction of legislatures. As a result, at an October 1979 meeting of the federal-provincial Continuing Committee of Ministers on the Constitution (known as the CCMC, as noted earlier) in Halifax (during the Clark government) we presented a new federal draft that, on the one hand, restricted the power of limitation of rights and freedoms to two areas, Fundamental Freedoms and Legal Rights, but on the other hand broadened the grounds for those limitations to include the protection of morals or to deal with emergencies officially proclaimed.[3]

In the following year, as described in chapter 6, after the Quebec referendum, strenuous efforts were renewed to reach a constitutional consensus, and the federal government presented a new draft Charter on July 4, 1980 for discussion at a meeting of the CCMC. In a further effort to attract provincial support, this draft went farther than the Halifax draft in extending the possible areas for rights and freedoms to be limited by legislatures.[4] It followed the pattern of the *European Convention* and the *International Covenant on Civil and Political Rights* in having separate derogation clauses for various categories of rights and allowing derogations on broad grounds such as public safety, order, morality, et cetera. This draft was released to the public and attracted strong criticism from civil libertarians. *Le Devoir*, in a scathing editorial, argued that most of the potential benefits of such a charter would be swallowed up in the many exceptions to its rights and freedoms that legislatures would be allowed to make. As a result, a further federal draft was presented to the CCMC on August 22, 1980.[5] For the first time a single limitation clause was placed at the beginning, applying to all rights and freedoms guaranteed by the *Charter*. It stated: "1. The *Canadian Charter of Rights and Freedoms* recognizes the following rights and freedoms subject only to such reasonable limits as are generally accepted in a free and democratic society." The provinces were still not induced to agree to the principle of having a charter but at the same meeting they tabled a draft Charter dated August 29, 1980, headed "In the Event that there is Going to be Entrenchment" of a Charter.[6] That draft in section 1 replaced the words in the federal draft "in a free and democratic society" with the words "in a free society living under a parliamentary democracy." In their view, presumably, in such democracies there is parliamentary supremacy.

That meeting of the CCMC of course failed to reach consensus on this or much of anything else, and it was followed by a First Ministers' Meeting in September 1980 that broke up in disaccord. It was at this point that the

federal government decided—agreement with the provinces appearing impossible—to follow its backup plan and proceed unilaterally if necessary with a Joint Resolution by the Parliament of Canada to the Queen, requesting, one last time, amendments to our constitution by the UK Parliament. The package of amendments would include an amending formula for the constitution, thus achieving patriation of the constitution by having a domestic amendment procedure for the future. It would also include a charter. Although the government was prepared to proceed without any provincial support if necessary, it wanted very much to have support from as many provinces as possible. With that in mind, the text submitted to Parliament for approval was designed to reflect many of the provincial concerns expressed during past years of negotiation. Therefore, in the proposed section 1 of the *Charter*, the rights and freedoms of the *Charter* would be subject to such reasonable limits "as are generally accepted in a free and democratic society with a parliamentary system of government."[7] The inclusion of the reference to a parliamentary system of government was specifically designed to gain provincial support since these words had appeared in the provincial draft of August 28 referred to above.

The proposed Joint Resolution with the attached text of the amendments to be sought from Westminster was placed before the Special Joint Committee. When Minister of Justice Jean Chrétien and his officials, of which I was one, appeared before that committee to explain and defend the proposal, we were soon put on the defensive about section 1. The committee had already received critical submissions from human rights groups[8] and there had been comments in the press criticizing in particular the reference to the phrase "a parliamentary system of government," which we had adopted from the provincial draft of August 1980. The essential complaint was that this would justify any limitation of rights or freedoms if it was adopted by a duly elected legislative body. So well had the critics made their complaint that many members of the committee (particularly government members) pressed for change. On December 11, 1980, Cabinet agreed[9] to a more exigent test for a valid limitation: we dropped the reference to a "parliamentary system of government." We further strengthened rights by requiring that any limit be "prescribed by law" and that it be "demonstrably justified in a free and democratic society," thus putting a reverse onus on governments or officials who defended such legal limitations. Undoubtedly, the net result was a much better limitation clause,

less menacing to the rights and freedoms guaranteed by the *Charter*, but how we got to that result had much to do with politics and pragmatism.

SECTION 7

Another salient example of pragmatic evolution was that of the development of section 7. It now provides: "7. Everyone has the right to life, liberty and security of the person and the right not to be deprived thereof except in accordance with the principles of fundamental justice." This kind of general guarantee was inspired by the Fifth Amendment to the Constitution of the United States, which states that no person shall "be deprived of life, liberty, or property without due process of law; nor shall private property be taken for public use, without just compensation." The statutory *Canadian Bill of Rights* adopted by Parliament in 1960 asserted "the right of the individual to life, liberty, security of the person and enjoyment of property, and the right not to be deprived thereof except by due process of law."[10] In the early days of the summer of 1967, in sketching out a proposal for a charter, I recognized that a constitutional bill of rights that did not contain some such general provision would be quickly subject to attack, but I drew to Pierre Trudeau's attention the potential difficulties lying particularly in the references to "property" and "due process." These problems were discussed in Trudeau's subsequent publication *A Canadian Charter of Human Rights*.[11] Reference was made to the American experience with the Fifth Amendment, as follows:

> The words "due process of law" have been given a double interpretation in the United States. The first of these is as a guarantee of procedural fairness. In this respect similar words used in the Canadian Bill of Rights are intended to guarantee the specific requirements of fair procedure. The words "due process" have, in addition, been given a substantive interpretation in the United States' courts with the result that the words have been employed as a standard by which the propriety of all legislation is judged. At one time the words used in this latter sense resulted in the judicial invalidation of minimum wage legislation, laws against child labour, and hours-of-work statutes. They were also used as a basis for courts to review public utility rates

set by legislatures or regulatory agencies in order to ensure that the rates were, in the view of the courts, adequately compensatory. While more recently the substantive effect given to "due process" has diminished considerably in the United States, the demonstrated potential of this phrase could create some uncertainty in Canada unless its meaning was clearly recited.

In examining American experience with "due process" it appears that the guarantee as applied to protection of "life" and personal "liberty" has been generally satisfactory, whereas substantive due process as applied to "liberty" of contract and to "property" has created the most controversy. It might therefore be possible to apply the due process guarantee only to "life," personal "liberty" and "security of the person." The specific guarantees of procedural fairness set out elsewhere in the bill would continue to apply to any interference with contracts or property. In this fashion the possibility of any substantive "due process" problems would be avoided.

In the alternative, if "due process" is to remain applicable to "liberty" of contract and to "property," there should be spelled out in some detail what is involved. The European Convention and some modern constitutions use this technique with respect to each of the guarantees of life, liberty and property.[12]

This really set the tone for successive federal proposals: namely that economic rights should not be guaranteed in a substantive sense. Several drafts spoke of "liberty" in the context of personal integrity (i.e., always in association with "life" and "security of the person" and these values were to be protected by "due process." On the other hand such guarantees as there were to be of "property" were stated separately and subject only to the guarantee of not being removed "except in accordance with law" (or similar phraseology), thus avoiding the potentially ambiguous term *due process*.[13]

As apprehensive as the federal government was from 1968 onward about creating a possibility for judicial imposition of substantive due process, provincial governments were even more worried about this. Many provinces (some of them with conservative regimes) were also particularly adamant that there should not be any "property" guarantee because this would threaten their jurisdiction over land ownership, town planning, expropriation for public purposes, environmental management, et cetera. They were also opposed to any use of the term *due process* because of the substantive interpretation it had been given in the United States. Thus as a counter-offer at the August 1980 meeting of the CCMC, the federal delegation submitted a new draft in which there was no mention of property rights, although the words "due process" still appeared.[14] This was still not sufficient to attract provincial support to the idea of an entrenched Charter. That draft failed to get approval of the CCMC or of the First Ministers' Meeting that followed in September. When the federal government next presented a draft[15] of the proposed Joint Resolution to Parliament on October 6, 1980, section 7 (as it had now become) for the first time substituted the words "in accordance with the principles of fundamental justice" in place of "by due process of law." It was hoped that this change would yet attract support from some provinces because it appeared to avoid the universally rejected notion of substantive due process.[16] We obviously underestimated the potential for judicial innovation.

When the text of the proposed section 7 was before the Special Joint Committee, questions were raised regarding the meaning of "principles of fundamental justice." As Assistant Deputy Minister of Justice, I testified as follows: "Mr Chairman, it was our belief that the words 'fundamental justice' would cover the same thing as what is called procedural due process, that is the meaning of due process in relation to requiring fair procedure. However, it in our view does not cover the concept of what is called substantive due process, which would impose substantive requirements as to policy of the law in question."[17] The Deputy Minister, Roger Tassé, testified to similar effect, saying that we assumed that the courts would regard fundamental justice as having a "meaning somewhat like natural justice or inherent fairness." The Minister of Justice, Jean Chrétien, confirmed this understanding and said that it would not matter a great deal if the term "natural justice" (a clearly procedural concept) were substituted for

fundamental justice. (We had avoided the term *natural justice* because at that time, before the more generous common law requirement of "fairness" had been developed fully, the procedural protections afforded by "natural justice" had been generally confined to a more narrow range of decision makers. We hoped to rid ourselves of that baggage by employing a different term.) When the meaning of "principles of fundamental justice" was argued before the Supreme Court of Canada in *Reference re Section 94(2) of the Motor Vehicle Act*,[18] the province of British Columbia relied on, among other things, these quotations to show that this phrase was not intended to provide for substantive due process. But the Supreme Court airily dismissed Roger's and my evidence as follows: "Moreover, the simple fact remains that the Charter is not the product of a few individual public servants, however distinguished, but of a multiplicity of individuals who played major roles in the negotiating, drafting and adoption of the Charter. How can one say with any confidence that within this enormous multiplicity of actors, without forgetting the role of the provinces, the comments of a few federal civil servants can in any way be determinative."[19] With respect, the Court missed the whole point of the evidence. It was not put in, I suggest, to show that the Court should accept our opinions because we were so clever. Instead, I believe it was put before the Court to show the common understanding among governments that they did not want to entrench substantive due process: it was the information the Special Committee had before it with respect to the intended meaning of the words *fundamental justice*—the same meaning that Parliament and nine provincial governments had when they subsequently endorsed the joint resolution based on this understanding. The Supreme Court in the same case reaffirmed the view that constitutional interpretation should be "purposive."[20] It also piously reminded its readers that "the decision to entrench the *Charter*...was taken not by the courts but by the elected representatives of the people of Canada." In other words, "the Devil makes us do this." One might be forgiven for assuming that if the Court was trying to follow the directives of the elected representatives in its application of the *Charter*, it might have paid heed to the best information available as to what the elected representatives of the people thought they were endorsing with the words "fundamental justice." Admittedly, those words bear some ambiguity and in such case most courts would seek better

evidence of the *purpose* of the provision (that is, to achieve a *purposive* interpretation), which was readily available here. The Court shared with us this vague guide to the meaning it would give to the term "fundamental justice": "the principles of fundamental justice are to be found in the basic tenets and principles, not only of our judicial process, but also of the other components of our legal system."[21] Try as I might, I have not been able to find a basic tenet of our legal system that in 1985 nurtured the idea that courts should second-guess legislatures on matters of wisdom or policy of legislation.[22] Yet that is what the Court was doing in this case by interpreting "fundamental justice" as a guarantee of substantive due process.

So while the Special Committee sought from us background information that addressed the source and intention of various provisions in the draft resolution, and presumably voted on that basis, this was to be much less significant than the ex post facto views of the Supreme Court about what the legislators thought they were doing. Nor was it a case where a long period of time had elapsed and changing social values had emerged so as to justify a revisiting of the proper ambit of section 7. Only three years had passed since the "elected representatives of the people" (Parliament and nine provincial governments) had adopted this language in the belief it meant "procedural fairness." As I said, perhaps irreverently, at a legal conference 20 years ago: "If the Supreme Court believes that the nine Premiers who signed the 1981 accord thought they were endorsing substantive due process, the Court is dreaming in Technicolor." What the Court in effect decided was that this is what the "elected representatives" *should* have wanted to do. This is not a mere quibble, a passing whim of the Court that has had no long-term consequences. Instead, the Court has taken itself quite seriously on this point, and has thereby obliged all Canadian courts to pass judgement on the wisdom of legislative dispositions. I have discussed this elsewhere,[23] but perhaps one case well illustrates the point. In *Chaoulli v Quebec*[24] three out of a majority of four of the Supreme Court held that a provincial law prohibiting the sale or purchase of medical insurance from private sources (the purpose being to protect the universal coverage of the public medical insurance plan) was contrary to fundamental justice because the Court was not satisfied the law would have its desired effect. This was an issue over which politicians and commissions of study had disagreed for years.

SECTION 15

This section provides:

15. (1) Every individual is equal before and under the law and has the right to the equal protection and equal benefit of the law without discrimination and, in particular, without discrimination based on race, national or ethnic origin, colour, religion, sex, age or mental or physical disability.

(2) Subsection (1) does not preclude any law, program or activity that has as its object the amelioration of conditions of disadvantaged individuals or groups including those that are disadvantaged because of race, national or ethnic origin, colour, religion, sex, age or mental or physical disability.

It is apparent from the history of thought in Canada in support of legal prohibitions against discrimination that there were a few core areas of concern. Abroad we had seen peoples displaced or destroyed because of their race, national origin, colour, or religion. At home we had seen official persecution, through laws and administration, of people because of their religion (e.g., the Jehovah's Witnesses in Quebec, or quotas limiting the number of Jews admitted to public universities), their race and national origin (e.g., the Japanese-Canadians during World War II through internment and expulsion, or persons of Chinese or Japanese origin in matters of employment in provinces such as British Columbia and Saskatchewan), and sex (e.g., earlier restraints on women from voting, holding office, or holding public employment if their spouse had government employment). It was no doubt this type of blatant, intentional type of governmental discrimination that people like Frank Scott and Pierre Trudeau had in mind when they advocated a constitutional bill of rights. In Isaiah Berlin's analysis,[25] the right not to be discriminated against is a "negative right" that deserves legal protection to prevent the state from actively harming certain classes of persons. That is what we originally thought we were trying to do with section 15.[26] In the Berlin analysis, "positive rights" involve entitlements that require the state to act in favour of particular individuals or groups. We did not think we were creating these in the sense of

imposing judicially enforceable obligations on the state to spend money on entitlements defined by the courts.

The leading international instruments that served as inspirations for, first, the *Canadian Bill of Rights* of 1960, and, later, the *Canadian Charter of Rights and Freedoms*, were the *Universal Declaration of Human Rights* adopted by the United Nations in 1948 and the *European Convention on Human Rights* adopted by the Council of Europe in 1950. The *Charter* was also influenced by the *International Covenant on Civil and Political Rights* that was adopted by the UN in 1966 after the *Canadian Bill of Rights* had been adopted but before the *Charter* had been developed. Canada acceded to the Covenant in 1976, which gave it additional cogency in this country. All three international instruments, as well as the *Bill of Rights*, treated discrimination in the same way: they did not create an independent and general right not to be discriminated against, but rather gave everyone a right to enjoy without discrimination the other specific rights set out in the instrument (e.g., the right to a fair trial, the right not to be tortured, the right to life, liberty, and security of the person, etc.). The *Universal Declaration* and the *International Covenant*, apart from this, have a provision guaranteeing everyone equality before the law and equal protection of the law. In the context of those texts this guarantee appears to be concerned with how the legal system itself treats those who come before it. The *International Covenant* also obliged all signatories to adopt laws within their jurisdiction to prohibit discrimination generally and to provide effective remedies for the victims of discrimination. The prohibited grounds of discrimination common to all these instruments are race, colour, sex, language, religion, political or other opinion, national or social origin, property, birth, or other status. To these the *European Convention* adds "association with a national minority."

The *Canadian Bill of Rights* generally adopted the approach, though not all the details, of these anti-discrimination provisions in the international instruments. It declared that the rights it wanted to protect, such as the right to "equality before the law and equal protection of the law," as well as freedom of religion, of speech, assembly and association, and of the press, "shall continue to exist without discrimination by reason of race, national origin, colour, religion or sex." Thus it did not pick up all the criteria of discrimination prohibited in the international instruments such as "language...political or other opinion...social origin, property, birth

or other status." But like the *Universal Declaration* and the *International Covenant* it did assert, beyond the prohibition against discrimination in the enjoyment of rights otherwise stated in the instrument, the independent guarantee of "equality before the law and the protection of the law."

In first addressing the contents of a possible constitutional guarantee against discrimination in the 1968 publication *A Canadian Charter of Human Rights*,[27] we raised questions as to what should be the prohibited grounds of discrimination. We assumed that the grounds cited in the *Canadian Bill of Rights* should form the core, to which we suggested adding "ethnic origin." We also discussed in what fields of governmental activity discriminatory acts should be prohibited. Obviously, at that time we did not envisage a completely open-ended provision. Subsequently, in the years of constitutional negotiation, the federal proposals for what we had labelled "Egalitarian Rights" went through several iterations. Bill C-60 in 1978 had a structure in this respect similar to the *Canadian Bill of Rights*, but it included two additional prohibited grounds: age and language (the latter never to be seen again in a federal draft). The draft presented to the CCMC in Halifax during the Clark government, in a vain attempt to get provincial support, contained no equality provision. The draft presented to the CCMC on July 4, 1980, did have such a provision, prohibiting denials of equal protection "without distinction or restriction" but adding "other than any distinction or restriction provided by law that is fair and reasonable having regard to the object of the law." Because not even this was a sufficient attenuation of egalitarian rights to attract provincial support, and because this draft, once released to the public, attracted much criticism, a new federal draft was presented on August 22, 1980. For the first time egalitarian rights started to take on a structure similar to what is now in subsection 15(1). It stated as follows: "17. (1) Everyone has the right to equality before the law and to equal protection of the law without discrimination because of race, national or ethnic origin, colour, religion, age or sex."[28] In response, the provincial proposal for the contents of a Charter "(In the Event That There is Going to be Entrenchment)" contained no egalitarian rights at all.

The ensuing impasse at the First Ministers' Meeting in September led to the tabling in Parliament on October 6, 1980, of the proposed Joint Resolution for constitutional amendment including a draft Charter. The egalitarian right section, 15 as it had then become, had a subsection (1)

in terms identical to those in the August 22 draft quoted above. This proposal went, of course, before the Special Joint Committee where we had to defend it.

Section 15 attracted more submissions from the public than any other section. While the great majority of these favoured the principle, only one endorsed the actual text of the draft section. The most comprehensive criticism came from feminist groups, in particular the Advisory Council on the Status of Women.[29] Their concerns largely grew out of the jurisprudence under the equal protection provision of the *Canadian Bill of Rights*. This had been interpreted so as to permit more stringent requirements for unemployment insurance benefits for pregnant women than for other unemployed (discrimination said to be based on the condition of pregnancy and not on "sex")[30] and not to interfere with the loss of Indian status by Indian women, but not Indian men, who married non-Indians.[31] (This was adjudged by the Supreme Court not to deny equality "before the law," which was generally regarded as only protecting equality in legal proceedings.) In respect of this concern, women's interest groups pressed for, and achieved, the addition of another preposition ("under" the law) and another noun modified by "equal," namely "benefit." Another range of concerns voiced by these groups reflected the apparent willingness of the Government and the intention of the Special Joint Committee to broaden the enumerated grounds of prohibited discrimination to include "age" and "mental or physical disability." While the feminist groups did not, of course, object to better protection against discrimination on these grounds, they were concerned that the inclusion of such grounds would attenuate the effect of the *Charter* as a protection against discrimination based on "sex." They could foresee that differential treatment based on these other grounds might well be justifiable in many instances (e.g., denial of drivers' licenses to 12-year-olds or blind persons) and that this would promote a loose jurisprudence that would come to find justifications for all manner of inequality. The Advisory Council thus proposed a significantly new approach to the section, calling for a general prohibition against discrimination and then a more specific enumeration of grounds that it hoped would suggest more strict enforcement by the courts. Thus was born the language of section 15: "Every individual is equal...without discrimination and, *in particular*, without discrimination based on race... sex..." et cetera. It remained a matter of concern that age and disability were

still grouped with the other enumerated grounds.[32] The addition of the words "in particular" was thought to make the grounds of discrimination open-ended: it left open the possibility that non-enumerated grounds could also be found by the courts in the future, such as sexual orientation and matters on which there was no consensus in 1981.[33]

This section illustrates very well the pragmatic approach to Charter-drafting. When the Charter project was first launched by Pierre Trudeau in 1968 we were preoccupied, insofar as equality rights were concerned, with preventing the kind of blatant state racism and sexism with which we were familiar in the 20th century up to that point. Our approach was also much influenced by the terms of the statutory *Canadian Bill of Rights* and contemporary anti-discrimination laws, mostly at that time at the provincial level. The political forces at play in constitutional negotiations, up to the time our refined proposals reached the Special Joint Committee in 1980, had been largely shaped by the provinces that resisted the idea of a charter and consequently sought to narrow it. (As previously mentioned, the provincial proposal of August 1980, referred to above, contained no equality rights). After the federal draft went before the Committee, however, new pressures for its strengthening came from rights-minded parliamentarians, interest groups, and members of the public. The resulting changes in section 15 were profound. The enumerated grounds were enlarged. An open-ended prohibition against discrimination was also incorporated for the first time by the use of the words *in particular*, signalling to the courts that they were not limited to striking down discrimination just on the enumerated grounds.

And, I believe, the addition of the term *equal benefit* has had and will have a profound effect on jurisprudence, far more than I think the parliamentarians of the day intended. It amounted to the entrenchment of a positive right. After all, the idea of equality of benefit had, in effect (if not in this precise context) been examined and rejected throughout the federal-provincial dialogue on the *Charter* over the course of 12 years. A guarantee of equality of benefit was inspired in part by the *International Covenant on Economic and Social Rights* of 1966, which had been seen by decision makers in Canada as a statement of aspirations and not of legal entitlements. The idea of including "equal benefit" emerged before the Special Joint Committee largely as an ad hoc reaction to one Supreme Court decision, *Bliss v A.G. of Canada*.[34] But the effect of its inclusion has been

to engage the courts in measuring, for example, social security benefits as between one group and another to see if there are real differences that justify real distinctions. The determination of appropriate levels of publicly provided benefits for different categories of persons is not a task for which the courts are well equipped and is the proper function of legislators. It was not part of the original concept of the Charter.

SECTION 33

One further example of pragmatic, as opposed to ideological, constitution-making can be found in section 33 of the *Charter* that provides:

33. (1) Parliament or the legislature of a province may expressly declare in an Act of Parliament or of the legislature, as the case may be, that the Act or a provision thereof shall operate notwithstanding a provision included in section 2 or sections 7 to 15 of this Charter.

(2) An Act or a provision of an Act in respect of which a declaration made under this section is in effect shall have such operation as it would have but for the provision of this Charter referred to in the declaration.

(3) A declaration made under subsection (1) shall cease to have effect five years after it comes into force or on such earlier date as may be specified in the declaration.

(4) Parliament or the legislature of a province may re-enact a declaration made under subsection (1).

(5) Subsection (3) applies in respect of a re-enactment made under subsection (4).

As I have described in chapter 9, this was a vital element in the compromise among 10 of the 11 First Ministers that made possible the Accord they signed on November 5, 1981. On that same day (much later in the evening) federal and provincial officials approved the actual text that became, with a few politically charged changes before its enactment by

Westminster, the *Constitution Act, 1982*. Section 33 has come to be called "the notwithstanding clause." There have been several claims to authorship of the concept as a last-minute tiebreaker. In fact the idea was not new and had been canvassed from time to time. Again, it did not flow from some ideological preconception of what a charter should contain: certainly it was anathema to the *Charter*'s principal champion—Pierre Trudeau. It was the product, pure and simple, of a political deal, a trade-off in order to have any sort of a charter.

Perhaps the historical roots for a notwithstanding clause were predominantly to be found in the *Canadian Bill of Rights* of 1960.[35] Section 2 of the *Bill* allowed Parliament to declare in any statute that it was to apply notwithstanding the *Canadian Bill of Rights*. By section 6 of the *Bill*, the *War Measures Act* was amended to provide that while a proclamation by the Governor in Council of a state of war, invasion, or insurrection, real or apprehended, was in existence, emergency measures taken under that Act would be deemed not to infringe the *Canadian Bill of Rights*. Here we see the basic concept enunciated: that at certain times public interests must trump private rights. Section 6 was a particularly draconian implementation of that principle. It only required the fiat of the Governor in Council to suspend the protection of the *Canadian Bill of Rights* in respect of anything done under the *War Measures Act*. It was such a fiat that the federal cabinet issued in the early hours of October 16, 1970 (during the FLQ crisis in Quebec), invoking the *War Measures Act* and providing for guilt by association, arrest without warrant, and the holding of people without charges being laid: and all this without fear of interference from the *Canadian Bill of Rights* because of its section 6.

In the policy paper I helped prepare that was published in 1968, *A Canadian Charter of Human Rights*,[36] we had identified as an issue the possibility of some forms of limitations on rights, as discussed earlier in connection with what later became section 1 of the *Charter*. The possibility of a provision like section 6 of the *Canadian Bill of Rights* was identified as one possibility, although not advocated. I do not believe it attracted any serious discussion until a First Ministers' Meeting in February 1979, when Premier Lougheed of Alberta referred to a notwithstanding clause as one possible means of making the Charter less unpalatable to some provinces. The matter was not pursued at that time by First Ministers.

During the summer of 1980, in the course of intensive federal-provincial

discussions of the Continuing Committee of Ministers on the Constitution (CCMC) and its supporting committees of officials, the subcommittee of officials on the Charter were exploring a possible basis on which there could be some agreement in principle. On August 29 this subcommittee submitted a report that, it was made clear, was "without prejudice to any province's position on the principle of entrenchment itself." The report included the following.

LEGISLATIVE OVERRIDE CLAUSE

9. Some consideration was given to the possible inclusion in an entrenched Charter of an override clause whereby a legislative body could expressly provide that a law would operate notwithstanding a Charter right. While some doubt was voiced about the desirability of including such a provision, there was general agreement that further consideration should be given to this matter.

10. One mechanism that was discussed, in the event it is decided that an override clause is necessary (and this could depend on the ultimate scope and wording of an entrenched Charter), is a requirement that any law enacted under an override provision be adopted by a 60% majority of the legislative body and that any such law would expire after a specified time period, e.g. five years unless repealed earlier. There was no discussion of the particular categories of rights to which any override clause might apply.[37]

The fact that an override provision was being discussed seriously reflected the acute need felt by federal officials to explore the elements of a possible consensus upon which the adoption of a Charter could be based. But my colleagues and I also suggested that if there were to be such a clause (which we did not concede at that point), its use and its effect should be limited in terms of the majority required to exercise it, the duration for which it would be effective, and the portions of the Charter to which it could be applied.

As the CCMC was unable to resolve the basic issue of entrenchment, the matter came before the First Ministers' Meeting two weeks later, in September 1980. The discussion was desultory and inconclusive. The only attention given to the idea of a notwithstanding clause was by Premier Blakeney of Saskatchewan, who suggested that Saskatchewan and perhaps some other provinces might be able to accept entrenchment if the Charter contained such a clause.[38] The matter received no further attention at that time and the First Ministers' Meeting failed to reach any agreement. It did not resurface for further discussion for another year. In the meantime the federal government had launched its initiative to ask Westminster for the necessary amendments to the Constitution for an amending formula and a Charter, litigation in three provincial courts of appeal had been decided and appealed, and the Supreme Court had rendered its decision in the *Patriation Reference*.[39] As described in chapter 9, this in turn led to the convoking of another First Ministers' Meeting set for early November 1981 for the purpose of determining whether an agreement with a substantial number of provinces could be reached as admonished by a majority of the Supreme Court.

In preparation for this meeting we certainly discussed within the federal government the possibility of such a clause as part of a compromise package. It received little enthusiasm from the Prime Minister, who saw it as antithetical to the supremacy of the rights of man. But in informal discussions among federal and provincial officials it became apparent that some provinces also saw the notwithstanding clause as a possible part of a solution to the impasse. The story of how, on the eve of the final day of the Conference, negotiations proceeded among those provinces interested in finding a solution (i.e., all but Quebec) and a compromise emerged that included the provinces' preferred amending formula and a charter with a notwithstanding clause applying to certain sections, has been told elsewhere.[40] On this basis, the Constitutional Accord of 1981 was signed by ten First Ministers on November 5, 1981, and the way was paved for the ultimate adoption of the *Constitution Act, 1982*. Thus section 33, the notwithstanding section in that Act, was the product of another compromise. While it was offensive to the basic concept of a charter that contemplates rights trumping ordinary legislation, its potential harm was very greatly attenuated by the conditions we were able to attach to it: it only provided an override for section 2 (Fundamental Freedoms) and

sections 7–15 (Legal Rights and Equality Rights) and, at the insistence of the Prime Minister, the duration of any declaration of override was limited to five years.[41] We assumed, and this has largely been proven correct, that the political cost to a government of putting such legislation through its legislative body would deter any casual use of the power, and the need to repeat the process after five years would discourage any indefinite extensions of an override. (Only in the National Assembly of Quebec did this prediction prove untrue for a time). I think, however, that the very existence of section 33 was an enduring source of regret for Pierre Trudeau.

13

A SOCIAL DEMOCRAT
IN THE COURT OF THE
PHILOSOPHER KING

Pierre Trudeau was sometimes referred to as a philosopher king, usually by his detractors, implying that he was (perhaps) a wise man given to rule us, by (perhaps) undemocratic means. It is said that the young Trudeau himself in his dalliance with corporatism saw the ideal head of such a state as an autocratic but wise figure.[1]

When I came to Ottawa to work on constitutional reform, I had a certain public policy orientation based on my years as an official in the Douglas and Lloyd governments and later as an active supporter of the New Democratic Party. In the latter role I had served as chair of the legal policy committee of the Saskatchewan NDP and we had made recommendations on civil liberty issues such as the establishment of a Human Rights Commission and of an Ombudsman office. (Both measures were adopted after the NDP returned to power in 1971.) I brought with me traditional CCF and NDP views on the desirability of constitutional safeguards for human rights. But I also remained convinced that social policy decisions should be made by elected representatives and that constitutional safeguards of individual rights should not be framed in such a way as to encourage judges to set the social agenda. I and my liberal contemporaries were too familiar with what the US Supreme Court had done to the Roosevelt New Deal and what the Judicial Committee of the Privy Council had done to Prime Minister Bennett's belated efforts to follow the path of Roosevelt. In this I was closer to Frank Scott than to Pierre Trudeau.

What attracted me to Trudeau was his rational approach to public policy, and in particular to constitutional reform. For any proposed course of

action he wanted the logical consequences to be considered. I had already become somewhat cynical of the superficiality and disingenuousness of much of what passes for public policy debate in Canada. Trudeau, particularly in his earlier years in power, challenged his colleagues and staff to go beyond that. I was always skeptical about the Liberal Party, its history and some of the interests it seemed to represent. But I never had any doubts about my duty as a public servant to contribute to and implement government policy in my field.

Pierre was undoubtedly committed to the better protection of human rights, although I think that, apart from language rights, he was focussed on combatting the sort of suppressions of freedom of speech and religion that he had known in Quebec, and on stopping deliberate governmental discrimination based on the familiar grounds of race, religion, gender, and colour. These were the evils of which we were conscious, and we all shared an intention to proscribe them. Pierre was more ambivalent on the relationship between political and judicial power: he was not nearly so critical of the Privy Council because he felt that it had often protected genuine provincial rights. He rejected the tendency among social democrats to assume that major social policies should be implemented by the federal government and not the provinces. Yet in the final analysis he assumed an important role for governments generally in improving the lives of Canadians. He merely thought that many of these initiatives should come from the provinces.[2] As he demonstrated later, he believed in the positive state, a concept that had been anathema in the Quebec where he was raised. So we shared the goals of better protection for human rights and preserving the role of governments to set social policy.

Pierre Trudeau obviously had absorbed the fact of my earlier activities in the NDP. During our first summer of collaboration, he would on occasion ask me how I thought that party would react to one proposal or another. (I was hardly in a position to say.) One day that summer I met in Pierre's office Jean Marchand, one of the "Three Wise Men" from Quebec and a minister also. Pierre had obviously spoken to him about me. Marchand, who was a former trade unionist with at least some philosophical kinship with the NDP, shook my hand warmly and said, "You're the kind of guy I can work with." In later years when the "unilateral package" was announced, I was the official sent to brief the NDP caucus. Later, as Trudeau was trying to get Ed Broadbent and his caucus on side by amending the package to

Author sworn in as member of the Federal Court by Chief Justice Thurlow, August 1983.

enhance provincial powers over trade in natural resource commodities, I was on the team negotiating with him as well as with Saskatchewan officials of the Blakeney government.

One instance of this thought association by the Prime Minister stands out vividly in my memory and the memory of some of my colleagues who were there. It was during the failing First Ministers' Conference of September 1980 that was of course being broadcast live on national television. The subject was possible revision of constitutional provisions concerning the judiciary. Saskatchewan's NDP Premier, Allan Blakeney, was criticizing the constitutional provision that empowers the federal government to appoint judges of provincial superior courts. The following exchange occurred:

> HON. ALLAN BLAKENEY: ...Our party has been an effective voice in Saskatchewan politics for 40 years....Now, in all of that time, in the dozens and dozens of judicial appointments that have been made...to courts of appeal and Queen's Bench and district court, I am unable to recall one single judge who has ever been of the persuasion of our party except last year when a Family Court judge with some links to our party was appointed.

13: *A Social Democrat in the Court of the Philosopher King*   273

THE CHAIRMAN: [Trudeau] I can make him a judge [pointing to me].

HON. ALLAN BLAKENEY: Fair enough, make him a judge but no one has made him a judge.

HON. WILLIAM DAVIS: He could pass an Order in Council to do it.

THE CHAIRMAN: We want more western voices.

HON. ALLAN BLAKENEY: I want to be awfully clear that I am not critical of our judges—do I get a fee, Barry?[3]

Some of my colleagues from the federal delegation went out to get a congratulatory card, which they inscribed "To the first judge to be appointed on national television," which card was signed by many present, including Trudeau and Blakeney. I of course took none of this seriously at the time.

Some three months later I encountered Premier Blakeney in Ottawa, where he was appearing before the Joint Parliamentary Committee to make submissions on the joint resolution. When he saw me he said, "I thought you were supposed to be a judge by now!" I said, "Oh, you know the Prime Minister—he said he was going to double-track the CNR and he hasn't done that either!" Three years later, however, I was appointed to the Federal Court by Pierre Trudeau's government.

PART III

CONCLUSION

14

SUMMING UP

Was it all worth it? I think it was. I believe that as a result of this constitutional revolution Canada is a more mature nation, not dependent on any other country for its most fundamental legislation: the amendment of the constitution. It is a more profoundly and irreversibly pluralistic society, where respect for individual differences is underwritten by the *Charter*, comprehensive legislation, and national commitments to international human rights norms. And it is a country where the rights of our Aboriginal peoples are better guaranteed by law: not that these rights are yet always respected, but they are no longer fundamentally disputed and they are coming to be interpreted in a more generous manner, all as directed by the constitution.

This is not to say that either the politics of patriation, or judicial review under the *Charter*, have unfolded in an entirely foreseen, foreseeable, or satisfactory manner. I will enlarge on this subject in respect of the major elements of the revolution.[1]

PATRIATION

This was an undoubted legal success in that the authority of the United Kingdom Parliament over our constitution was terminated and we now have an established domestic procedure for constitutional amendments. It must be said, however, that the formula agreed upon is unsatisfactory in that it allows provinces who do not support amendments with national impact, and who do not support changes that at least seven provinces representing 50 per cent of the population have approved, to refuse to have the amendment apply to them. If such amendments are nevertheless made, the result could be a checkerboard of jurisdictions with the constitution meaning one thing in one province and something else in

another. Perhaps more cogent is the likelihood that, faced with such a prospect, Ottawa will veto such amendments, which it can always do if it appears some provinces will opt out.

But the greater disappointment is that patriation has not resulted in a country universally proud of the completion of its national sovereignty. There is an abiding conviction among Quebec nationalists and their sympathizers, both within and outside of that province, that patriation was illegitimate because the separatist government of Quebec refused to sign the November 1981 Accord to which the Prime Minister and nine provincial Premiers adhered. It was this Accord that enabled Parliament to approve a Joint Address to the Queen requesting the patriation legislation. Those who reject the legitimacy of that measure are fond of saying that Quebec was "humiliated" in the process, and the more extreme view among many is that the *Constitution Act, 1982* does not apply in Quebec because its provincial government in 1981 did not agree with it.

But, I still ask, how was Quebec wronged by a process whose propriety was confirmed twice by the Supreme Court of Canada in legal proceedings to which Quebec was a party and whose judgement on the matter was deliberately sought by the Government of Quebec? That Government twice passed legislation to ensure that the decisions of the Quebec Court of Appeal in references it took to that Court on the requirements for provincial consent (and in particular Quebec's consent) to the patriation package would be appealable to the Supreme Court of Canada.[2] And though the subsequent steps taken for patriation were accepted by nine provinces, the Parliament of Canada, and the Parliament of the United Kingdom, as having the "substantial measure" of provincial support that the Supreme Court said was what the constitutional conventions required, there is a certain body of opinion in Quebec and among some well-meaning federalists elsewhere, that somehow the *Constitution Act, 1982* does not apply in Quebec. The Supreme Court judgements, that the Government of Quebec itself sought, are treated as irrelevant or invalid as they did not produce the answer Quebec wanted.

Was Quebec "humiliated" by this process? Well, no doubt Mr Lévesque, his Minister of Intergovernmental Affairs, Claude Morin, their colleagues of the Parti Québécois, and some other provincial politicians were humiliated. No doubt many other nationalists in Quebec felt humiliated. But that is not the whole picture either then nor now. At the time, 71 out of 75 of

the democratically elected Members of Parliament from Quebec voted for patriation and the *Charter*. A public opinion poll taken in May 1982, the month after the proclamation of the *Constitution Act, 1982*, showed that 49% of the people in Quebec approved of the patriation measure, while only 16% opposed it. In British Columbia, *whose government had signed the Accord*, only 50% were in favour—only 1% more than in Quebec—but 17% opposed it (1% more than Quebecers).[3] More recently, in a national poll taken in 2007 on public attitudes to the *Charter*, residents of Quebec showed the highest degree of satisfaction with the *Charter*—61%—of any province.[4] Now if the patriation package was such a felt humiliation, how can this many Quebecers have positive thoughts about the *Charter*, a major feature of that package? Indeed, if because of this felt "humiliation" or an abiding belief that a constitutional amendment without the consent of Quebec is invalid, how can they harbour such support for a nullity? Obviously, they think the *Charter* applies to them and they support it.

The fact is that Mr Lévesque and his supporters were humiliated because he made fundamental strategic errors. He was hoist by his own petard. He was so determined to block Trudeau's initiative and thus to humiliate Trudeau that he agreed with five other provinces in 1980 to take a reference to his Court of Appeal on whether the federal initiative was legal and in accord with constitutional conventions, and this was done in full anticipation that the issues would ultimately be decided by the Supreme Court. He thus became a hostage of fortune to the unpredictable views of the Supreme Court. Then he entered into a pact[5] with the Gang of Eight in April 1981 to present the Prime Minister with an ultimatum: Trudeau would either have to accept their preferred amending formula without a charter, or there would be no patriation. This bound Lévesque to an amending formula that he would never have agreed to otherwise: it contained no veto for Quebec over amendments derogating from provincial powers or property. But he was prepared to sign on because he was sure Trudeau would never accept it, because the formula also required federal compensation to any province opting out of an amendment equal to the per capita costs of federal programs adopted pursuant to the amendments in the provinces accepting the amendment. He trusted in the assurances of an indissoluble united front with his seven allies, without regard to what pressures some of the other Premiers would come under from their voters to achieve an agreement and a Charter. But then Lévesque himself abandoned this bloc

when, at the September 1981 "Last Chance" Conference, he briefly agreed on holding a national referendum to decide on the amending formula and the Charter.[6] The other Premiers, abhorring referenda and already looking for a compromise with Trudeau, saw this as a justification to abandon Lévesque and the all-or-nothing pact of the previous April.

I am satisfied that if, after the May 1980 referendum, in which a majority of Quebecers told their government they wanted to remain part of Canada, that government had participated in a genuine effort to reach agreement, there could have been one. Trudeau did until the last minute try to establish a veto for Quebec under an amending formula.[7] While Lévesque vehemently opposed the *Charter*, the idea of guarantees of individual rights by law was clearly acceptable to him: Quebec had for some time had its own legislated *Québec Charter of Human Rights and Freedoms*.[8] About the only specific objection Quebec took to the contents of the federal proposal for a Charter was in the area of language rights: while Quebec law at that time only guaranteed English-language education in that province for the children of parents who had been educated in English *in Quebec*, the federal proposal would extend that right to the children of any parent educated in English *in Canada*. The only rationale Quebec offered by way of objection was that such decisions should only be made by the National Assembly of Quebec. Ignored was the fact that for the first time in Canadian history French minority language education was to be guaranteed throughout the rest of Canada, and nine other provinces were prepared to, and did, accept limitations on the powers of their legislatures in order to guarantee minority French-language education in their jurisdictions.

There is no tangible evidence that either the federal government or the other nine provinces wanted to isolate Quebec. But a Quebec representative had intimated that whatever the Supreme Court decided, or whatever action was finally taken by Ottawa and the other provinces—or Westminster even—without Quebec's consent, it would be a "win" for Quebec, presumably in political terms.[9] By this and by the nature of their participation in countless sessions, it was apparent that they had no motivation to achieve an agreement. The Prime Minister and the Premiers were well aware that public opinion across the country, even in Quebec, wanted to see agreement on patriation and a Charter.[10] They were not, of course, indifferent to the possible negative reactions in Quebec and elsewhere,

but they had to make decisions having regard to public opinion across Canada including Quebec. Using a procedure that the Supreme Court had said would be legal as well as in accordance with the conventions of the Constitution, they made the difficult decision to proceed. And although without the support of Quebec, the Prime Minister kept trying to preserve the veto for Quebec that he had first proposed in the Victoria Formula in 1971. Even after the signing of the Accord without Quebec's participation on November 5, 1981, Trudeau continued to seek successfully some changes in the *Constitution Act, 1982* to Quebec's advantages, in matters of financial compensation for any province opting out of amendments concerning education or culture, and in making minority language education for the children of English speakers in Quebec (but not educated in English in Canada) subject to approval by the National Assembly of that province.

Nevertheless, the "humiliation" of Quebec in 1981 and 1982 has become part of our national mythology and it is never far from the surface of Canadian politics. It is manifested every so often in bursts of nationalist fervour in Quebec, such as during the 1995 referendum, or flourishes of goodwill such as the resolution passed in Parliament on November 27, 2006, declaring that the "Québécois" form a "nation." One can only hope that time will heal these wounds. It may be a long time. After all, it took a century after the American Civil War before the Republican Party—the party of Lincoln and of the oppressive Reconstruction in the South after that war—to become a potent political force again in the states of the former Confederacy!

THE *CHARTER*

Although not without creating problems, which I shall address below, the *Charter* has made a profound change in this country and its legal system. In general it has legally underpinned the pluralism in fact of contemporary Canadian society through its strictures against discrimination. And it has made us a society far more respectful of individual rights and freedoms, even for those belonging to powerless minorities. Much of this impact has been direct and through the legal system, but it has also been indirect through the promotion of a human rights culture. The *Charter* has, as I think Pierre Trudeau foresaw, seriously enhanced national unity. It has brought Canadians of all provinces, territories, and languages to recognize that we share the same core values protected by the *Charter*. And it has

immeasurably enhanced the role of the Supreme Court of Canada as a national institution respected by most Canadians *a mari usque ad mare*: more so—it might be ventured to suggest—than certain other national institutions based in Ottawa.

From this the creators of the *Charter* may take much satisfaction. But that satisfaction is tainted in my view by a judicial activism that was not foreseen by the drafters and the politicians who approved it. As I have demonstrated previously in chapters 6 to 9, there was strong provincial opposition to a charter, mostly because they feared the possibility of important issues of social policy being decided by the courts rather than by governments or legislatures. The federal government was also very conscious of the American precedents, where the tests of substantive "due process" had been used to strike down socially progressive legislation and we had avoided that language.

I suppose during the drafting and negotiations leading to the *Charter* I had a mindset that in Canada we would not be turning over to the courts the right to make social policy. This was based on my own research and writings. My book on constitutional judicial review, first published in the very different days of 1968,[11] had sought to define the proper role of the judiciary in constitutional cases. In the third edition, published in 1988 after the advent of the *Charter* and by way of a reconciliation of *Charter*-based judicial review with parliamentary democracy, I wrote:

> The danger of legislative power being "transferred to the judiciary" has been much exaggerated. Even in its most activist form, judicial review is interstitial, sporadic, and fortuitous. The judges can only "legislate" in those matters which happen to be brought before them. These are specific cases, not categories of social or economic problems, and the courts' decisions immediately apply only to the actual parties before them. Moreover, unlike legislation, judicial decisions before being finalized are normally subject to repeated reconsideration and refinement through the system of appeals.[12]

Even when this was written it was probably too optimistic, and in light of what has followed it seems hopelessly naive. What has instead ensued is

that the Supreme Court does not confine itself to the issues brought before it as those issues were pleaded and dealt with in the courts below. It is not uncommon for the Court, which can itself state the constitutional issue to be determined by it, to go well beyond the case raised by the parties at trial and turn what was a specific issue involving only the parties into a general question whose answer will apply to a whole class of people. It feels free to admit a wide range of interveners who most often never appeared in the lower courts, and while they are not parties and should not be able to introduce new issues at this late stage, it is obvious that they engage the Court's attention in matters never addressed in the courts below and help shape the factors that go into the Court's final decision. Thus my reassurance that judicial decisions "are normally subjected to repeated reconsideration and refinement" does not represent the reality of current constitutional adjudication in the Supreme Court. I was naively referring to what I had always understood to be the function of a final court of appeal: to ask the question, "Was the court below wrong?" Often the inarticulate question that seems to be asked by the Supreme Court now is "How can we fix this problem of social policy?" This approach is combined with the receipt in appellate factums of new "facts" (so-called "legislative facts") that were never produced before the trial or intermediate appellate court.

Further, judicial remedies have come to include legislating in effect. The courts are no longer content to declare a particular regime invalid (most probably because it denies "equal benefit "of the law, with reasons as to why it is invalid) but are willing to dictate what the legislation must be taken to prescribe: the so-called "reading-in" of desirable provisions in legislation as if they had always been there.

Combined with these judicial acts of self-empowerment is the bold claim to be able to second-guess legislatures on the wisdom or fairness of the policy of legislation, flowing from the 1985 decision of the Supreme Court[13] which held that the rights to life, liberty, and security of the person and the right "not to be deprived thereof except in accordance with the principles of fundamental justice" enabled the courts to determine whether the law depriving one of such rights was itself fair and just. In other words, "fundamental justice" was turned into the Canadian version of "substantive due process" found south of the border. This has given rise to judicial encroachment on the legislative role never foreseen by those who drafted and approved the *Charter*.[14]

Conventional wisdom among today's liberally minded lawyers, political scientists, and many journalists is for the most part in favour of this judicial adventurism. To them I say, "Be careful what you wish for." Past experience in Canada and the United States shows that judicial activism can just as easily be used to promote an illiberal agenda. Today one can see the same trend reappearing in the US Supreme Court where a conservative majority renders regressive decisions. Further, activism subjects courts to political criticism because they have no mandate in our system of separation of functions to make public policy. Nor are they well equipped to do so. They normally see only a fragment of a social policy issue and they are reliant for their information base, for the most part, on what the parties and interveners choose to provide them. Interveners are self-selected and do not necessarily represent every valid point of view bearing on the problem.

It is my hope that the Supreme Court and those who must apply its jurisprudence come to have a more modest view of its abilities, and its mandate, to direct social policy.

HUMAN RIGHTS LEGISLATION AND INTERNATIONAL HUMAN RIGHTS REGIMES

Developments in these areas in the last four decades, of which I have written in chapter 4, have had an important influence and impact complementary to the legal effects of the *Charter*. There has been interaction among all these elements: for example, international instruments are sometimes looked to by the courts for inspiration in the interpretation of the *Charter*, and the *Charter* has forced the broadening of the scope of human rights legislation.[15] All have contributed to a human rights culture, which generally marks a profound social difference in Canadian society of the early 21st century from that which prevailed in the mid-20th.

ABORIGINAL RIGHTS

Not part of the *Charter*, but an important part of the *Constitution Act, 1982*, is section 35, which recognizes and affirms the Aboriginal and treaty rights of the "Indian, Inuit, and Métis peoples of Canada." In chapters 8 and 9 I have written of the political origins of this provision and the apprehension about the unknown that I and some of my colleagues felt at the time of its adoption. Our apprehension stemmed from such uncertainties as the following. What all would come to be embraced within "Aboriginal rights"?

We were familiar with rights to land usage, and to fishing and hunting, but not with other rights that might be asserted. Would they include the right to self-government? Would "recognition" in the constitution entrench them against legislative intrusions? Although not part of the *Charter*, would they be subject to some legislative limitations similar to those permitted under section 1 and section 33 of the *Charter* in respect of the rights in that document? How would "Métis" be defined? While these were unknowns in 1982, the Supreme Court has given answers to most of these questions and in a generally just way. (So far we have no definitive answers as to the existence and scope of the alleged right of self-government).[16] This constitutional change has put the existence of Aboriginal rights beyond dispute and beyond legislative or administrative destruction. In this it has been a milestone in the reconciliation of the interests of Aboriginal peoples with the non-indigenous population, even though there is yet much distance to be travelled.

ONE JUDGE'S PERSPECTIVE

As I have mentioned before in passing, I was appointed a judge of the Federal Court Trial Division in 1983 and later of the Federal Court of Appeal in 1994. In that latter year I was also given an extra part-time responsibility as Chief Justice of the Court Martial Appeal Court of Canada.

In these various judicial posts I had occasion to interpret many of the instruments in whose drafting or implementation I had had a part. Often I was to learn through my judgements being appealed that I had not understood what they meant. Nevertheless, I enjoyed the challenge of being faced with issues never before litigated and of having to find an answer.

In my first year as a judge I was invited to strike down a section of the *Parole Act* providing for automatic cancellation of earned remission of an inmate where his parole is revoked, on the basis that this violated section 7 of the *Charter*, which in its term "fundamental justice" guaranteed that the law be fair or just—i.e., it is equivalent to "substantive due process." As far as I was aware, it was the first time this kind of argument had been made. As I had testified three years earlier before Parliament, that section 7 does not guarantee substantive due process, and as counsel produced no arguments to persuade me otherwise, I held that the guarantee of "fundamental justice" was procedural only.[17] I obviously misspoke myself because one year later, in 1985, the Supreme Court held that "fundamental justice"

requires that the laws themselves be, in the opinion of the court, fair and just (i.e., it *is* a guarantee of substantive due process).[18]

As it happened, for most of my judicial career I was not again faced with a situation where section 7 was invoked because of some alleged substantive unfairness in the law, and I was not obliged to apply the Supreme Court's interpretation of section 7 as pronounced in 1985. Ironically, it was in one of the last cases of my judicial career where I was compelled to do so. Some time after I retired from the Federal Court of Appeal, I was asked by the Chief Justice of the Federal Court (the renamed former Trial Division of the Federal Court where I had started my judicial career) to serve from time to time as a Deputy Judge of his Court. The *Federal Courts Act* authorizes the Chief Justice to invite any former judge of a superior court to act as a Deputy Judge, an ad hoc arrangement that allows him to make use of experienced judges to handle specific cases, usually to reduce backlogs.[19] In late 2007 I was asked to preside over a judicial review involving an attack on the validity of federal regulations controlling access to marijuana for medical purposes. In several previous cases, provincial courts, including provincial courts of appeal, had determined that persons with certain terminal diseases, and others with such conditions as epilepsy, had a right to access to marijuana for palliative purposes. Unreasonable denial of access by the federal government was a violation of their section 7 rights: of their liberty, because of the underlying risk of imprisonment if they had to obtain marijuana illicitly; and of the security of their person, because of the denial of a pain-relieving substance. In effect the courts had pronounced marijuana to have therapeutic effects that outweighed any of the negative consequences of its use that society had generally thought to justify its prohibition. These courts had held that existing restrictions on access violated section 7 because they did not have any reasonably justifiable purpose in legitimate protection of the state's interests. I felt uncomfortable with this jurisprudence. While I had every sympathy with the felt needs for marijuana of this class of persons, I was uneasy about the courts in effect pronouncing on the therapeutic benefits of marijuana, which was not a drug authorized by our elaborate system of approval for therapeutic drugs sold to the public. Faced with evidence similar to that before the provincial courts, I felt obliged by the pronouncements of the Supreme Court on section 7, and the findings of several previous courts (applying the Supreme Court jurisprudence to these facts) to strike down

the most recent regulations as invalid because they were unreasonable restraints on access to medical marijuana. As one of my last judicial pronouncements it was perhaps fitting that I could say this:

> I have some misgivings about the Court prescribing therapeutic substances which are not drugs approved under the elaborate and scientific processes of the *Food and Drug Act*, and on which there is far from a scientific consensus as to their benefits. But matters have moved well beyond that issue. The courts would not find themselves in the business of prescribing medical treatment were it not for the decision over 20 years ago that section 7 authorizes them, (see *Re BC Motor Vehicle Act* [1985] 2 SCR 486), in the determination of what is contrary to the principles of fundamental justice, to pass judgment not only on the procedural fairness but also on the substantive correctness of the law. But we must apply the constitution as the Supreme Court of Canada has found it to be.[20]

I privately wondered how long it would be before someone came to court with some experts to argue that under section 7 of the *Charter* he has a right to a drug necessary for his health but for which Health Canada had refused to issue a Notice of Compliance permitting its distribution.

I heard one of the earliest cases under section 15 in autumn, 1985, the same year that section had come into effect on April 17. This was an action by a multinational pharmaceutical company and its inventors attacking the constitutionality of the *Patent Act* provisions that at that time compelled a pharmaceutical patent-holder to grant a license to a generic company permitting it to produce drugs covered by the patent. The compensation for this compulsory license was to be fixed by the Commissioner of Patents, and patent-holders regarded the compensation normally allowed as woefully inadequate and non-compensatory for the originator company and inventor. It was argued that the plaintiffs suffered from discrimination because, unlike other patent-holders and inventors, medical patentees and inventors were forced to share patents with generics at a remuneration that was so low as to be confiscatory, whereas other originators were not so obliged. Subsection 15(1), it will be

recalled, provides: "15(1) Every individual is equal before and under the law and has the right to the equal protection and equal benefit of the law without discrimination and, in particular, without discrimination based on race, national or ethnic origin, religion, sex, age or mental or physical disability." First I determined that the corporate plaintiffs could not invoke section 15 because it applies only to "every *individual*," but I found that the non-corporate plaintiffs who were the inventors of the drug in question could rely on the section. The discrimination they alleged was based on the difference between the inventor of a medicinal patent and the inventor of anything else. While it was clear, from the use in section 15 of the words "and in particular..." that the enumerated categories of discrimination were not intended to be exhaustive, how did one determine what other kinds of legislative distinctions between individuals were to be prohibited? After all, it is a normal part of governance to treat people differently for different purposes. Was this all to be prohibited? This was the first case I could find where a plaintiff was relying on a non-enumerated ground of discrimination. Reading deeply in academic analyses and *Canadian Bill of Rights* jurisprudence, I came up with an approach that would require stricter construction of acts of discrimination involving the enumerated grounds, and less strict in respect of non-enumerated grounds. If the alleged prejudicial treatment engaged any of the enumerated grounds, there was a presumption of discrimination and the government's only defence would be a justification under section 1. If such treatment was not in relation to a prescribed ground, it could be justified if it had a rational purpose and the means were reasonable.[21] The degree of difficulty I had with this case of first impression is shown by the length of my judgement—some 85 pages of typescript and the longest one I ever wrote in my judicial career. It contained numerous other issues apart from section 15 of the *Charter*. By the time the case reached the Federal Court of Appeal, there had been some six or seven decisions in appellate courts in Ontario and British Columbia taking a different approach, all decided after my judgement. Hugessen, JA, of the Federal Court of Appeal graciously pointed this out in preferring their approach to mine in respect of unenumerated grounds. He concluded that where grounds are alleged other than those enumerated, they should be accepted on the same footing as the enumerated grounds if they are "analogous" to the enumerated grounds.[22] This of course became the established approach to

unenumerated grounds. Incidentally, the Federal Court of Appeal upheld the result in my judgement that included a myriad of issues.

I also had an early and important case on judicial remedies under the *Charter* in *Schacter v Canada*.[23] The plaintiff was a male spouse who had applied for "paternity benefits" under the *Unemployment Insurance Act* to enable him to stay home from work with their new-born child so that his wife could return to work. The *Act* of course provided 15 weeks of maternity benefits for the biological mother in such circumstances and he was told that he was not entitled to these as the father. The *Act* however also provided 15 weeks of child care benefits for an adoptive couple, and they could choose which one would stay home with the newly arrived adopted child and receive the benefits. Mr Schacter also applied unsuccessfully for these benefits. He said he was being discriminated against because he and his wife did not have the same options as would adoptive parents. I found that there was discrimination based on sex—the stereotyping of roles that parents should play, with the woman bearing the child and the man, as breadwinner, going out to work. I found that it was not sufficient that a natural mother would get 15 weeks of maternity benefits, the same period for which adoptive parents received child care benefits. I held that the two kinds of benefits could not be equated: the natural mother required maternity benefits to cope with the natural preparation for, giving of, and recovery from, childbirth. Counsel provided me ample evidence to support this conclusion. Child care benefits, though very important, served a different purpose and would be equally relevant to the natural parents of a child newly arrived in their home. I was thus faced with a problem of first impression: assuming the court finds a violation of subsection 15(1) because of a denial of equal benefits under the law, what should the court do about it? It would cure the inequality if one struck down the whole scheme, leaving natural parents and adoptive parents without any benefits. Or it would perhaps be a vindication of equal benefits to strike down child care benefits for adoptive parents, thus leaving both categories of parents without child care benefits (on the basis that maternity benefits are different from child care benefits and can properly be limited to those who experience maternity). But instead I made a declaration that any scheme that would not provide child care benefits for natural parents equal to the entitlements of adoptive parents (as long as those entitlements were provided by law) would not provide equal benefit under the law as required by

section 15 of the *Charter*. I tried to respect the proper roles of Parliament and the Courts. I made it clear that I was giving Parliament the opportunity to determine the most desirable scheme while working within these principles. As was permitted under the *Federal Court Rules* I suspended my judgement pending appeal and made it clear this would give Parliament time to equalize the scheme by either raising the benefits for natural parents or lowering those for adoptive parents, or some combination of the two. In doing so I was working with the instruments available to me. (Only later did the Supreme Court invent the device of prospective overruling that was to have the same effect as a stay pending appeal in giving Parliament the time to correct the matter in its own preferred way.) But, at the time, my judgement was considered an affront to parliamentary democracy. Members of the government thought I had ordered Parliament to spend the money to provide a system of child care benefits for natural parents: some estimated that my order would cost the Treasury some $2 billion a year. Meanwhile, the government conceded the correctness of my finding that there was denial of equal benefits and amended the *Unemployment Insurance Act* accordingly. In its appeal of my judgement it did not challenge my findings of inequality of benefits. The government simply argued in the Federal Court of Appeal that I had applied the wrong remedy. I had contented myself with a declaration under subsection 24(1) of the *Charter* that the scheme as enacted denied equal benefit. Subsection 24(1) provides as follows: "Anyone whose rights or freedoms, as guaranteed by this Charter, have been infringed or denied may apply to a court of competent jurisdiction to obtain such remedy as the court considers appropriate and just in the circumstances." I concluded that it would not be "appropriate and just" in the circumstances to strike down the provisions under which benefits were already being paid to adoptive parents. But the government argued I should have struck down the existing scheme under section 52, the remedy being the appropriate one for statutes inconsistent with the Constitution. A majority of the Federal Court of Appeal agreed with my approach, but when the matter reached the Supreme Court it was the occasion for many pages of turgid prose. By this time the legislation had already been amended in a manner consistent with my declaration. The Court, however, said that I should have struck down the offending provisions under section 52 (the section that says that laws inconsistent with the constitution must be treated as invalid). It then entered into a discursive

Author invested as an Officer of the Order of Canada, April 7, 2010, by Her Excellency Michaëlle Jean, Governor General of Canada. The citation referred to the author's work on the development of the *Charter*.

analysis of the remedy of "reading-in" which proved to be *obiter dicta* as the Court did not feel this to be an appropriate case to read-in the provisions that would make the statute consistent with the *Charter*. It concluded (at last) by the 92nd paragraph of its judgement[24] that in a situation of under-inclusiveness as was evident in this case, it would be inappropriate to strike down the existing provisions immediately (I did not do that) because this would deny benefits to present beneficiaries. Instead, there should be a declaration of invalidity that should "be suspended to allow Parliament time to bring the provision into line with constitutional requirements" (this is precisely what I did with the easiest instrument available to me, a stay pending judgement). Seemingly, neither counsel nor the Court read my judgement carefully enough to see that is what I had done.

These are a few examples of the "teething problems" of the new *Charter* in which courts had to seek approaches that would stand the test of time. It was not apparent to anyone, even those such as me who had contributed to the drafting of this great instrument, what would be its consequences in a myriad of new and largely unforeseen situations. And that is how it happens with any revolution: there are unintended consequences.

NOTES

PREFACE

1. 22 Geo V, c 4 (UK).
2. 30&31 Vict, c 3 (UK).
3. Cited in the Official Law Reports as *AG Ont v Israel Winner* [1954] AC 541.
4. *Supra* note 2.
5. See AV Dicey, *Introduction to the Study of the Law of the Constitution* (Macmillan, 10th ed, 1965) at 43.
6. *Judicial Review of Legislation in Canada* (Toronto: University of Toronto Press, 1968); later republished in the second (1983) and third (1988) editions by Butterworths under the title *The Canadian Constitution and the Courts: The Function and Scope of Judicial Review*.

INTRODUCTION

1. Schedule B to the *Canada Act 1982* (UK), 1982, c 11.
2. *Ibid* Part 1.
3. *Ibid* s 35.

1 ORIGINS OF THE PROBLEM

1. 30&31 Vict, c 3 (UK).
2. I have described this relationship between Imperial laws and colonial laws in Barry L Strayer, *The Canadian Constitution and the Courts: The Function and Scope of Judicial Review*, 3d ed (Toronto: Butterworths, 1988) at 5–7.
3. 14 Geo II, c 83 (UK).
4. (1774), 1 Cowp 204, 98 ER 1045 (KB).
5. Schedule B to the *Canada Act 1982* (UK) 1982, c 11. See e.g., *Reference re Resolution to Amend the Constitution* (commonly referred to as the *Patriation Reference*) [1981] 1 SCR 753; *Manuel v AG* [1982] 3 All ER 822 (CA).
6. 28&29 Vict c 63, s 2, 3 (UK).
7. *Supra* note 5. This occurred because the new description of the Constitution of Canada in subsection 52(2) did not include the *Colonial*

Laws Validity Act, 1865. Also, subsection 7(1) of the *Statute of Westminster, 1931* that had continued the paramountcy of the *BNA Acts* over Canadian laws was repealed by the 1982 Act.

8. *Commonwealth of Australia Constitution Act*, 63&64 Vict, c 12 (UK). In 1857 New Zealand had been given a very limited authority to amend its constitution: see *New Zealand Constitution Amendment Act, 1857*, 20&21 Vict, c 53.

9. *Supra* note 1. I have set out at more length the practices of constitutional amendment in this period in "The Patriation and Legitimacy of the Canadian Constitution," Cronkite Lectures, delivered at the University of Saskatchewan, 1982 at 3–6 to 3–8.

10. I have described this and further attempts up to 1965 to reach agreement on an amending formula in Barry L Strayer, "Saskatchewan and the Amendment of the Canadian Constitution" (1967) 12 McGill L J 443. See also, Cronkite Lectures *ibid* at 3–8 to 3–10; James Ross Hurley, *Amending Canada's Constitution: History, Processes, Problems and Prospects* (Ottawa: Minister of Supply and Services Canada, 1996) at 23–67.

11. *Summary of Proceedings of the Imperial Conference, London, 1926* (Ottawa: King's Printer, 1926) at 12.

12. 22 Geo V, c 4 (UK).

13. See John E Read, "Problems of an External Affairs Legal Adviser," (1966–1967) 22 Int'l J, 376–94.

14. *Supra* note 6.

15. *Supra* note 10. See also Guy Favreau, *The Amendment of the Constitution of Canada* (Ottawa: Queen's Printer, 1965) *passim*.

2   MY INTRODUCTION TO CONSTITUTIONAL REFORM

1. (Toronto: University of Toronto Press, 1950).

2. Barry L Strayer, *Judicial Review of Legislation in Canada* (Toronto: University of Toronto Press, 1968).

3. See generally Barry L Strayer, "Saskatchewan and the Amendment of the Canadian Constitution" (1967) 12 McGill L J 443.

4. *Globe and Mail* (4 November 1960) 2.

5. See generally William Tetley, *The October Crisis, 1970: An Insider's View* (Montreal: McGill-Queens University Press, 2007). While that crisis also involved matters of life and death, and the provincial government was widely opposed by many intellectuals and unionists, it was supported by major media, much of the business community, and by the governments of Canada and of the City of Montreal. Interestingly, concurrently with this political and public order crisis there was a strike of medical specialists opposing the introduction of medicare then occurring in Quebec. The

provincial government legislated them back to work the day before the imposition of the *War Measures Act* by Ottawa. The Government of Saskatchewan would never have dared do that in 1962! In the heated atmosphere in Quebec of that day, however, few noticed the plight of the doctors.

6. This formula was explained and defended in Guy Favreau, *The Amendment of the Constitution of Canada* (Ottawa: Queen's Printer, 1965).

3   THE CENTENNIAL INITIATIVE

1. Montreal: Éd. renaissance, 1965.
2. *The Constitutional Review: Secretary's Report 1968–1971* (Ottawa: 1972) at 3–6.
3. Ottawa: Queen's Printer, 1968.
4. *House of Commons Debates*, (8 February 1968) at 6489.
5. Ottawa: Information Canada, 1971.
6. Ottawa: Information Canada, 1974.
7. See e.g., Peter H Russell, *Constitutional Odyssey: Can Canadians Become a Sovereign People?* 3d ed (Toronto: University of Toronto Press, 2004) at 10.
8. See e.g., Janet Ajzenstat, *The Canadian Founding: John Locke and Parliament* (Montreal: McGill-Queen's University Press, 2007) ch 1.
9. *Secretary's Report, supra* note 2 at 386–88.
10. *General Theory of Law and State* (Cambridge, MA: Harvard University Press, 1945) at 115–23; and see my discussion of Kelsen and the application of his theories in Commonwealth countries in Barry L Strayer, *The Patriation and Legitimacy of the Canadian Constitution* (Cronkite Lectures, University of Saskatchewan, 1982) at 3-2 to 3-4.
11. See e.g., SA de Smith, "Constitutional Lawyers in Revolutionary Situations" (1968) 7 West Ont L Rev 93.
12. See e.g., Norman Rogers, "The Compact Theory of Confederation" (1931) 9 Can B Rev 395; "The New Nationality: The Climate of Opinion in 1867" in Frank K Underhill, ed, *The Image of Confederation* (1964) CBC Massey Lectures 3d Series; Desmond Morton, *The Critical Years: The Union of British North America 1857–1873* (1964), esp. ch 11; and see Russell, *supra* note 7 at 33–50.
13. See Janet Ajzenstat, *supra* note 8 at 6–9, 24–27.
14. These laws and their effect are discussed in chapter 1, *supra*.
15. *Senate Reference* [1980] 1 SCR 54; *Patriation Reference* [1981] 1 SCR 753.
16. See TO Elias, "The Commonwealth in Africa" (1968) 31 Mod L Rev 284.
17. 5 December 1968.
18. See e.g., SA de Smith, *The New Commonwealth and its Constitutions* (London, UK: Stevens & Sons, 1964) and his article cited *supra* note 11.
19. *Secretary's Report, supra* note 2 at 410–12.
20. (UK) 1982, c 11.

21. "Prime Minister: Premier Ministre," *The New Yorker* (5 July 1969) at 36. As far as I can determine, she never published an article on the Victoria Conference.

22. See *supra* note 2, at 485–58.

23. Quoted in note 19, *supra*, and accompanying text.

24. *Secretary's Report, ibid* at 487–88.

25. This text may be found in Anne F Bayefsky, *Canada's Constitution Act 1982 and Amendments: A Documentary History*, vol 1 (Whitby: McGraw-Hill Ryerson, 1989) at 214.

4 A NON-CONSTITUTIONAL INTERLUDE

1. *Newfoundland Act*, 12-13 Geo VI, c 22 (UK), Schedule B.

2. It was not until 1987, some 16 years later, that the Pentecostal Assemblies were specifically included in the constitutional guarantees of public funding: *Constitution Amendment, 1987* (Newfoundland Act). But after further broadening of the denominational school system in 1997, by the *Constitution Amendment, 1997* (Newfoundland Act), the whole system was secularized in 1998: *Constitution Amendment, 1998* (Newfoundland Act).

3. Reproduced in RSC 1985, Appendices at 1.

4. The Crown was represented by Imperial authorities in what is now Canada until Confederation, except in the old Province of Canada, which was given this responsibility in 1844.

5. *Constitution Act, 1867* 30&31 Vict, c 3 (UK) Section 91, head 24.

6. See e.g., *R v Sikyea* [1964] SCR 642; *R v White and Bob* (1965), 52 DLR (2d) 481.

7. Ottawa: Indian Affairs Branch, 1966–1967.

8. Canada, Department of Indian Affairs and Northern Development (Ottawa: Queen's Printer, 1969).

9. See e.g., his speech given 8 August 1969, in Vancouver, reproduced in Peter A Cumming & Neil H Mickenberg, *Native Rights in Canada*, 2d ed (Toronto: The Indian-Eskimo Association of Canada and General Publishing, 1972) at 331.

10. *Calder v British Columbia* [1973] SCR 313. The Nisga'a claim was not finally settled until 2000 when an agreement among the Nisga'a, the federal government, and the government of British Columbia came into effect containing many unique features such as self-government and extensive law-making powers for the Nisga'a people: see Tom Molloy, *The World is our Witness: The Historic Journey of the Nisga'a into Canada* (Calgary: Fifth House, 2000).

11. The history of the development and impact of this paper has been best told by Gérard V La Forest himself: see "Reminiscences of Aboriginal Rights at the time of the *Calder* case and its Aftermath" published in Hamar Foster, Heather Raven, & Jeremy Webber, eds, *Let Right Be Done: Aboriginal Title,*

the *Calder Case, and the Future of Aboriginal Rights* (Vancouver: University of British Columbia Press, 2007) 54 (proceedings of a conference on the 30th anniversary of the *Calder* case held in Victoria, 13–15 November 2003).

12. This understanding was based on considerable jurisprudence, the leading authority being the decision of the Judicial Committee of the Privy Council in *St. Catherine's Milling and Lumber Co v The Queen* (1888) 14 AC 46. Since the adoption of section 35 of the *Constitution Act, 1982*, the Supreme Court has held that Aboriginal title is not limited to the traditional uses made of the land by the occupants' ancestors but "encompasses the right to exclusive use and occupation of the land held pursuant to that title for a variety of purposes, which need not be aspects of those aboriginal practices...." *Delgamuukw v British Columbia* [1997] 3 SCR 1010 at para 117.

13. SC 1898, c 3.

14. SC 1912, c 45.

15. Schedule B to the *Canada Act, 1982* (UK) 1982, c 11.

16. 1972 (PEI) c 40, s 1, amending section 3 of the *Real Property Act*, RSPEI 1951, c 138.

17. Stat. Sask. 1973–74, c 98.

18. *Federal-Provincial Committee on Foreign Ownership of Land: Report to the First Ministers* (Ottawa: Information Canada, 1975).

19. *Supra* note 5.

20. RSC 1970, c C-19.

21. A decision upholding the PEI law notwithstanding the provisions of the *Citizenship Act* had already been decided in the province's favour by the Supreme Court of PEI and later, after our report, this was confirmed on appeal by the Supreme Court of Canada in *Morgan v P.E.I.* [1976] 2 SCR 349. The Court held that the provincial law was not in relation to aliens, as it treated non-residents—Canadian and foreign—alike and this was all that s 24 of the *Citizenship Act* required. The provincial law was held to be in pith and substance a law in relation to property and civil rights.

22. SC 1976–77, c 33.

23. *The Saskatchewan Bill of Rights Act, 1947*, SS 1947, c 35.

24. *The Canadian Bill of Rights*, 2d rev ed (Toronto: McClelland & Stewart, 1975).

25. *International Labour Organization's Constitution of June 28th 1919*, concluded in Versailles and entered into force 10 January 1920.

26. ILO *Convention no (100) Concerning Equal Remuneration for Men and Women Workers for Work of Equal Value*, adopted by the General Conference of the International Labour Organization, called in Geneva by the Administration Council of the International Labour Office for its 34th session, 29 June 1951.

27. *Supra* note 22.

28. *Canadian Human Rights Commission v Canadian Liberty Net et al* [1996] 1

FC 787.

29. [1998] 1 SCR 626.
30. *Supra* note 5.
31. RSC 1970, c I-6.
32. SC 2008, c 30, s 1.
33. [1985] 1 FC 856.
34. I have discussed this in Barry L Strayer, "In the Beginning...The Origins of Section 15 of the Charter" (2006) 5 JL & Equality 13 at 18; and see *infra* chapter 10, notes 15, 16.
35. Strayer, *ibid.*
36. Part I of the *Constitution Act, 1982, supra* note 15.
37. SC 1985, c 27.
38. See *Twinn v Canada* [1987] 3 FC 227 (TD); *Sawridge Band v Canada* [1997] 3 FC 580 (CA).
39. *Corbiere et al v HM the Queen et al* [1994] 1 FC 394.

5 CONSTITUTIONAL DIALOGUE BEFORE THE QUEBEC REFERENDUM

1. See its *Final Report* (Ottawa: Queen's Printer, 1972).
2. *Ibid*, ch 3.
3. Enacted as Schedule B to the *Canada Act, 1982* (UK), c 11.
4. *Supra* note 1 at 21.
5. *Ibid* at 19.
6. First so held in *Reference re Section 94(2) of the Motor Vehicle Act* [1985] 2 SCR 486.
7. The following history of events is drawn from a federal Memorandum to Cabinet No. 584–76 dated 7 December 1976.
8. The full text may be found in Anne F Bayefsky, *Canada's Constitution Act 1982 and Amendments: A Documentary History*, vol 1 (Whitby: McGraw-Hill Ryerson, 1989) at 331.
9. *A Future Together* (Ottawa: Information Canada, 1979). Its recommendations are reproduced in Bayefsky, *ibid* vol 2 at 530.
10. *A Time for Action: Toward the Renewal of the Canadian Federation* (Ottawa: Minister of Supply and Services Canada, 1978) at 1. Reproduced in Bayefsky, *supra* note 8, vol 1 at 437.
11. *Ibid* at 8.
12. *Ibid* at 2–3.
13. *An Act to amend the Constitution of Canada....*Third Session, Thirtieth Parliament, 26–27 Eliz II, 1977–78; given First Reading on 20 June 1978. (Reproduced in Bayefsky, *supra* note 8, vol 1 at 340).
14. *Supra* note 3.
15. Cab. Doc. 28–78 CBM, at 6.

16. Eugene Forsey, *The Royal Power of Dissolution of Parliament in the British Commonwealth* (first published 1945; reprinted by Oxford University Press, Canadian Branch, 1968).

17. *Supra* note 13, para 53(2)(b).

18. *Reference re Legislative Authority of the Parliament of Canada in Relation to the Upper House* [1980] 1 SCR 54 (*Senate Reference*).

19. Guy Favreau, *The Amendment of the Constitution of Canada* (Ottawa: Queen's Printer, 1965) at 15.

20. I have analyzed this decision elsewhere: see Barry L Strayer, *The Patriation and Legitimacy of the Canadian Constitution* (Cronkite Lectures, University of Saskatchewan, 1982) at 3–10 to 3–12; Barry L Strayer, "Ken Lysyk and the Patriation Reference" (2005) 38 UBC L Rev 423 at 428–9.

21. Reproduced in Bayefsky, *supra* note 8, vol 1 at 514.

22. *Ibid* at 516.

23. *Supra* note 3.

24. See respectively *Canadian Industrial Gas & Oil Ltd v Government of Saskatchewan* [1978] 2 SCR 545; and *Central Canada Potash Co v Saskatchewan* [1979] 1 SCR 42. Saskatchewan's complaint about these decisions and the federal interventions in these cases may be seen in a letter from Premier Blakeney to Prime Minister Trudeau dated 10 October 1978, reproduced in Bayefsky, *supra* note 8, vol 1 at 519.

25. See e.g., Allan Blakeney, *An Honourable Calling: Political Memoirs* (Toronto: University of Toronto Press, 2008) at 127–56.

26. *Reference re Seabed and Subsoil of the Continental Shelf Offshore Newfoundland* [1984] 1 SCR 86.

27. SC 1960, c 44.

28. Ottawa: Queen's Printer, 1968, at 30.

6   POST-REFERENDUM NEGOTIATIONS

1. Which it generally was not.

2. Cab. Doc. 63–80 CBM.

3. Cab. Doc. 453–80 RD.

4. Reproduced in Anne F Bayefsky *Canada's Constitution Act, 1982 and Amendments: A Documentary History*, vol 2 (Whitby: McGraw-Hill Ryerson, 1989) at 742.

5. Enacted as Schedule B to the *Canada Act, 1982* (UK) 1982, c 11. The amending procedure forms Part VI of the *Constitution Act, 1982*.

6. Reproduced in Bayefsky, *op. cit. supra* note 4, vol 2 at 678.

7. Ottawa: Minister of Supply and Services Canada, 1980.

8. It is noteworthy that the measures for which we strove in 1980 are even more necessary today. There is a patent need for effective federal regulation of securities transactions and financial markets. In spite of mild provincial gestures to the contrary, provincial protectionism remains rife. As our

1980 paper pointed out, there was freer trade among the sovereign states of Europe than there was among our provinces. This hindered—and continues to hinder—the movement of persons and capital as well as of goods. The persistence of provincial government procurement policies that give preference to local suppliers made it impossible to prohibit such protectionism in the North American Free Trade Agreement; the lack of such a prohibition has more recently been felt by Canadians as states and cities in the US adopt "Buy American" policies in connection with vast works of infrastructure.

9. Minutes of Cabinet 5 September 1980, Cab. Doc. 73–80 CBM.

10. Barry L Strayer, "The Flexibility of the BNA Act" in T Lloyd & J McLeod, eds, *Agenda 1970* (Toronto: University of Toronto Press, 1968) at 197.

11. See the *Constitution Act, 1867* s 92A as amended by the *Constitution Act, 1982, supra* note 5, ss 50, 51.

12. Barry L Strayer, "Amendment of the Canadian Constitution: Why the Fulton-Favreau Formula?" (1966) 1 Ca Legal Stud 119.

13. See his Introduction to Guy Favreau, *The Amendment of the Canadian Constitution* (Ottawa: Queen's Printer, 1965) at viii.

14. Report to the Cabinet on Constitutional Discussions, Summer 1980, and the Outlook for the First Ministers' Conference and Beyond (30 August 1980).

15. *Ibid* at 60. It has been suggested that he misquoted Machiavelli: instead of ending with "than initiating changes in a state's constitution," the original passage in *The Prince* is said to end with "than to take the lead in the introduction of a new order of things." See Robert Sheppard & Michael Valpy, *The National Deal: The Fight for a Canadian Constitution* (Toronto: Macmillan, 1982) at 55. But variations may be due to the fact that there are numerous translations into English of *The Prince*.

16. According to a report in the *Globe and Mail* of 21 September 1981, a year later, after extensive investigations into the leaking of the document, the RCMP's primary suspect was a senior official in the Department of External Affairs. No charges were laid but he ultimately resigned.

17. *Supra* note 14 at 49–50.

18. *Ibid* at 53.

19. See e.g., Barry L Strayer, *The Canadian Constitution and the Courts: The Function and Scope of Judicial Review*, 3d ed (Toronto: Butterworths, 1988) at 216–36.

20. *Supra* note 14 at 51.

21. *Ibid.*

22. *Ibid.*

23. *Macbeth*, Act I, Scene VII.

24. First Ministers' Conference Document 800–14/085 (Ottawa: Canadian Intergovernmental Conference Secretariat).

25. See Sheppard & Valpy, *supra* note 15 at 62. The Chateau Consensus does not appear to be included in the official record of the Conference but the full text may be seen in James Ross Hurley, *Amending Canada's Constitution: History, Processes, Problems and Prospects* (Ottawa: Minister of Supply and Services Canada, 1996) at 207–14.

26. Peter H Russell, *Constitutional Odyssey: Can Canadians Become a Sovereign People?* 3d ed (Toronto: University of Toronto Press, 2004) at 110–11.

27. *First Ministers' Conferences 1906–2004*, (Ottawa, Canadian Intergovernmental Conference Secretariat, 2004) at 72.

28. Conference Proceedings, 1045.

29. *Ibid* 1074–87.

30. *Ibid* 1087–89.

31. *Ibid* at 1022.

32. *Ibid* at 1045.

33. *Ibid* at 1068.

34. Published as, *Fatal Tilt: Speaking about Sovereignty—Point of View* (Toronto: Harper Collins, 1991) at 2–3; also published simultaneously in (1991) 41 UTLJ 3.

7 PREPARING THE PATRIATION PACKAGE

1. Robert Sheppard & Michael Valpy, *The National Deal: The Fight for a Canadian Constitution* (Toronto: Fleet Books, 1982) at 52, 201.

2. 22 Geo V, c 4 (UK).

3. I had in mind what the Court had implied in the *Senate Reference* [1980] 1 SCR 54.

4. See Sheppard & Valpy, *supra* note 1 at 65–77.

5. See Peter H Russell, *Constitutional Odyssey: Can Canadians become a sovereign people?* 3d ed (Toronto: University of Toronto Press, 2004) at 111.

6. Cab. Doc. 76–80 CBM, minutes of meeting of 2 October 1980.

7. See Sheppard & Valpy, *supra* note 1 at 98–100, 112–14.

8. The full text is set out in Anne F Bayefsky, *Canada's Constitution Act 1982 and Amendments: A Documentary History*, vol 2 (Whitby: McGraw-Hill Ryerson, 1989) at 765.

9. Sheppard & Valpy, *supra* note 1 at 116–17.

8 A YEAR OF CONFLICT

1. See e.g., Robert Sheppard & Michael Valpy, *The National Deal: The Fight for a Canadian Constitution* (Toronto: Fleet Books, 1982); Roy Romanow, John Whyte, & Howard Leeson, *Canada...Notwithstanding: The Making of the Constitution 1976–1982* (Toronto: Carswell/Methuen, 1984) at 106–87; Ron Graham, *The Last Act: Pierre Trudeau, the Gang of Eight, and the Fight for Canada* (Toronto: Allen Lane, 2011), *passim*.

2. See minutes of Cabinet for 3 June 1980 Cab. Doc. 63–80 CBM.

3. See Sheppard & Valpy, *supra* note 1 at 138–40.

4. *Minutes of Proceedings and Evidence of the Special Joint Committee of the Senate and the House of Commons on the Constitution of Canada*, 32d Parliament, 1st Session, at 57.

5. [1985] 2 SCR 486.

6. See *Committee Proceedings, supra* note 4, 27 January 1981, at 46:32–4.

7. I have discussed the problems we envisaged, and some of the subsequent judicial solutions, in Barry L Strayer, "The Constitution Act, *1982*: The Foreseen and Unforeseen," (2007) 16 Const Forum Const 51 at 52–60.

8. The earlier discussion of this issue in the federal-provincial negotiations of 1978–1979 is described in chapter 5.

9. [1978] 2 SCR 545.

10. [1979] 1 SCR 42.

11. The details of political efforts to get the support of Saskatchewan for the joint resolution are set out in Sheppard & Valpy, *supra* note 1 at 126–33; Graham, *supra* note 1 at 170–80.

12. Cab. Doc. 15–81 CBM at 19.

13. 28&29 Vict, c 63 (UK).

14. See Barry L Strayer, *The Canadian Constitution and the Courts: The Function and Scope of Judicial Review*, 3d ed (Toronto: Butterworths, 1988) at 6–8, 32–33.

15. See e.g., *R v Big M Drug Mart Ltd* [1985] 1 SCR 295 at 312–13, 315–16.

16. *Reference re Secession of Québec* [1998] 2 SCR 217, para 72.

17. I have discussed this phenomenon elsewhere: see e.g., Barry L Strayer, "Ken Lysyk and the Patriation Reference" (2005) 38 UBC L Rev 423 at 445–46; *Singh v AG of Canada et al* [2000] 3 FC 185 at paras 14–17.

18. Minutes *supra* note 11 at 5.

19. *The British North America Acts: The Role of Parliament*, House of Commons, First Report of Foreign Affairs Committee, 1980–81, 30 January 1981 (London: Her Majesty's Stationery Office, 1981).

20. Montreal: Wilson and Lafleur, 1982.

21. See Sheppard & Valpy, *supra* note 1 at 177.

22. See Bryan Schwartz & John D Whyte, "The Patriation References and the Idea of Canada" (1982–83) 8 Queen's LJ 158 at 159.

23. [1981] 1 SCR 753 at 768.

24. See for example the decision of the Judicial Committee of the Privy Council in *Madzimbamuto v Lardner-Burke* [1969] 1 AC 645 at 723.

25. See Barry L Strayer, *The Canadian Constitution and the Courts: The Function and Scope of Judicial Review*, 3d ed (Toronto: Butterworths, 1988) at 330.

26. SQ 1980 c 24, s 1. The legislation was framed in such a way as specifically to authorize an appeal from the Court of Appeal to the Supreme Court from

any decision of the Court of Appeal on a reference on any joint resolution presented in the Parliament of Canada for an address to the Queen in respect of any constitutional amendment. Thus it showed the clearest intention that this matter should ultimately be decided by the Supreme Court. It was also broad enough to cover a further reference that Quebec took to its Court of Appeal regarding the existence of a Quebec veto over constitutional amendments. This was also decided against Quebec by the Supreme Court: see *Reference re Amendment of the Canadian Constitution* [1982] 2 SCR 793.

27. 117 DLR (3d) 1.
28. 120 DLR (3d) 385.
29. 118 DLR (3d) 1.
30. Sheppard & Valpy, *supra* note 1 at 224–25.
31. Barry L Strayer, *Judicial Review of Legislation in Canada* (Toronto: University of Toronto Press, 1968).
32. [1981] 1 SCR 753 at 806.
33. See Barry L Strayer, "Ken Lysyk and the Patriation Reference" (2005) 18 UBC L Rev 423 at 438–49; Barry L Strayer, Book Review of *The Court and the Constitution: Comments on the Supreme Court Reference on Constitutional Amendment*, [1983] 15 Ottawa L Rev 231; Barry L Strayer, *The Timlin Lecture* (University of Saskatchewan, 2007) at 17–24.
34. See Sheppard & Valpy, *supra* note 1 at 252–55.
35. See Romanow, Whyte, & Leeson, *supra* note 1 at 134.
36. The path of her rise and fall is well described in "Margaret Thatcher, l'inflexible," *Le Monde* 2 May 2009, at 55, especially at 59–60 concerning the 1980–1982 period.
37. See Sheppard & Valpy, *supra* note 1 at 52, 201.
38. *Ibid* at 202–03.
39. *Ibid* at 343.
40. *Ibid* at 209–10.
41. *Ibid* at 212.
42. Sheppard & Valpy, *supra* note 1 at 187.
43. *Op. cit. supra* note 19.
44. *Ibid* para 57.
45. *Ibid* para 14(10).
46. Jean Chrétien, *The Role of the United Kingdom in the Amendment of the Canadian Constitution* (Ottawa: Publications Canada, 1981) at para 82.
47. *Madden and AGBC v Nelson and Fort Sheppard Railway Company and AG of Canada* [1899] AC 626.

9 THE DENOUEMENT

1. From a speech by Martin Luther King Jr, made at the Lincoln Memorial in Washington on 28 August 1963.

2. Reported in: "Debaters decide new constitution not what we need," *Ottawa Citizen* (8 September 1981) 3. "L'étude de l'avenir constitutionnel canadien se déplace à New York," *Le Devoir* (8 September 1981) 6.

3. Robert Sheppard & Michael Valpy, *The National Deal: The Fight for a Canadian Constitution* (Toronto: Fleet Books, 1982) at 254.

4. Cabinet Minutes, 13 October 1981, Cab. Doc. 33-81 CBM at 204-07.

5. Sheppard & Valpy, *supra* note 3 at 257-58.

6. Ron Graham, *The Last Act: Pierre Trudeau, the Gang of Eight, and the Fight for Canada* (Toronto: Allen Lane, 2011) at 136. According to this source, the polling showed 90 per cent in every province in favour of patriation, and over 80 per cent in favour of the *Charter*.

7. See e.g., Sheppard & Valpy, *ibid* at 263-302; Roy Romanow, John Whyte, & Howard Leeson, *Canada...Notwithstanding: The Making of the Constitution, 1976-1982* (Toronto: Carswell/Methuen, 1984) at 188-212; Howard Leeson, *The Patriation Minutes* (Edmonton: Centre for Constitutional Studies, University of Alberta, 2011); Graham, *ibid*.

8. Cabinet Minutes, 3 November 1981, Cab. Doc. 37(B)-81 CBM.

9. Romanow et al, *supra* note 7 at 208.

10. Enacted as Schedule B to the *Canada Act, 1982* (UK) 1982, c 11.

11. Reproduced in Anne F Bayefsky, *Canada's Constitution Act 1982 and Amendments: A Documentary History*, vol 2 (Whitby: McGraw-Hill Ryerson, 1989) at 904.

12. Romanow et al, *supra* note 7 at 213.

13. Cabinet Minutes, 12 November 1981, Cab. Doc. 40-81 CBM at 5.

14. Reproduced in Bayefsky, *supra* note 11, vol 2 at 906.

15. They ultimately lost this action by a decision of the English Court of Appeal on 28 January 1982: *Manuel v AG* [1982] 3 All ER 822 (CA). Barbara Reed, a very able lawyer from my branch, spent considerable time in London during the winter of 1981-1982 assisting our English counsel in this case.

16. Cabinet Minutes, 6 November 1981, Cab. Doc. 39-81 CBM at 5.

17. Cabinet Minutes, 19 November 1981, Cab. Doc. 43-81 CBM at 7-8.

18. Romanow et al, *supra* note 6 at 213-14.

19. Allan Blakeney, *An Honourable Calling: Political Memoirs* (Toronto: University of Toronto Press, 2008) at 191-95.

20. Sheppard & Valpy, *supra* note 3 at 310-11.

21. *Ibid* at 311.

22. Cabinet Minutes, 8 December 1981, Cab. Doc. 46-81 CBM at 3-4.

23. 22&23 Geo V, c 4 (UK).

24. For example, when King Edward VIII signed an Instrument of Abdication

on December 10, 1936, having no heirs, it became necessary for the UK Parliament to pass legislation providing for the throne to pass to his brother Albert (the future George VI). As this would have the effect of changing the head of state of the Commonwealth countries identified in the *Statute of Westminster, 1931*, it was necessary by section 4 of that *Statute* to obtain the request and consent of each of those countries for the change in succession. All Dominions were contacted on December 10. Canada's Privy Council confirmed its request and consent that night, and this information was conveyed by telephone early in the morning of December 11. Westminster legislated that day confirming the abdication, declaring a demise of the Crown and thus clearing the way for George VI's succession: see *His Majesty's Declaration of Abdication Act, 1936* (UK) 1 Edw VIII and 1 Geo VI, c 3.

25. 12–13 Geo VI, c 22 (UK).
26. *Supra* note 10.
27. Décret 3214–81.
28. There seems to be no English version of this letter.
29. In fact, it appears to me that the National Assembly had already passed legislation in respect of the *Patriation Reference* that was broad enough to cover an appeal to the Supreme Court on this reference as well: see SQ 1980, c 24, s 1. However, a new Act was passed to ensure that the Quebec veto reference could be appealed to the Supreme Court: SQ 1981, c 17.
30. Décret 3215–81.
31. The Supreme Court ultimately answered these questions in the negative: *Reference re Amendment of the Canadian Constitution* [1982] 2 SCR 793.
32. (1982) 134 DLR (3d) 719.
33. *Supra* note 31.
34. SC 1960, c 44.
35. *House of Commons Debates* (17 February 1982) at 294, 297–98.
36. Bayefsky, *supra* note 11, vol 2 at 940.
37. *Supra* note 35 at 292–374.
38. *Supra* note 15.
39. *Supra* note 35 at 320–21.
40. *Ibid* at 324.
41. *Ibid* at 343.

10   FRANK SCOTT, PIERRE TRUDEAU, AND THE CHARTER IDEA

1. Max Nemni & Monique Nemni, *Young Trudeau: Son of Quebec, Father of Canada, 1919–1944* (Toronto: McClelland & Stewart, 2006).
2. *Ibid* at 134–51, 176–82, 196.
3. *Ibid* at 171.

4. *Ibid* at 52.
5. *Ibid* at 178.
6. *Ibid* at 160–64.
7. *Ibid* at 239–43.
8. Max Nemni & Monique Nemni, *Trudeau Transformed: The Shaping of a Statesman 1944–1965* (Toronto: McClelland & Stewart, 2011) chapters 1, 2, and 3.
9. André Burelle, *Pierre Elliott Trudeau: L'intellectuel et la politique* (Éditions Fides, 2005), at 1–14, 45–51.
10. *R v Oakes* [1986] 1 SCR 103 at para 65.
11. Nemni & Nemni, *supra* note 1 at 130.
12. Sandra Djwa, *The Politics of the Imagination: A Life of F.R. Scott* (Toronto: McClelland & Stewart, 1987) at 326.
13. See generally Christopher MacLennan, *Toward the Charter: Canadians and the Demand for a National Bill of Rights, 1929–1960* (Montreal: McGill-Queen's University Press, 2003) *passim*; Walter Surma Tarnopolsky, *The Canadian Bill of Rights*, 2d rev ed (Toronto: McClelland & Stewart, 1975) at 3–14.
14. MacLennan, *ibid* at 47–48.
15. *Ibid* at 56–57.
16. *Ibid* at 72–74.
17. *Ibid* at 90–99.
18. Tarnopolsky, *supra* note 13 at 12–13.
19. 8–9 Eliz II, c 44.
20. McLennan, *supra* note 13 at 115–45.
21. Djwa, *supra* note 12 at 109; Kenneth McNaught, *A Prophet in Politics* (Toronto: University of Toronto Press, 1959) at 168–71.
22. See "The trial of the Toronto Communists" (1932) 39 Queen's Quarterly 512; *Freedom of Speech in Canada*, Canadian Political Science Association, *Papers and Proceedings* 1933, at 168 (both reproduced in FR Scott, *Essays on the Constitution: Aspects of Canadian Law and Politics* (Toronto: University of Toronto Press, 1977) at 49, 60.
23. Djwa, *supra* note 12 at 144.
24. The entire Manifesto is reproduced in McNaught, *supra* note 21 at 321–30.
25. *An Act respecting Communistic Propaganda*, SQ 1937, c 11.
26. [1957] SCR 285.
27. Thomas H McLeod & Ian McLeod, *Tommy Douglas: The Road to Jerusalem* (Hurtig, 1987) at 93–95.
28. *Co-operative Committee on Japanese Canadians v AG for Canada* [1947] AC 87.
29. Stat. Sask. 1947, c 35.
30. 13 Geo VI, c 81 (UK).
31. *Proceedings of the Constitutional Conference of Federal and Provincial*

Governments, January 10–12, 1950 (Ottawa, 1950) at 32–40.

32. Djwa, *supra* note 12 at 266.

33. TC Douglas to FC Cronkite, 8 August 1960 (my personal files).

34. Personal files.

35. See McLeod & McLeod, *supra* note 27 at 263–67. It is fair to note, however, that one insider, William Tetley, who was at the time a member of the Quebec cabinet, has said that much of Douglas's criticisms were incorrect or exaggerated: William Tetley, *The October Crisis, 1970: An Insider's View* (Montreal: McGill-Queen's University Press, 2007) at 108. Part of Douglas's complaint was that the federal government had not provided Parliament with enough information about what was actually going on.

36. At a national NDP Convention in Vancouver in July 1981, there was a harsh debate over Broadbent's support for Trudeau's Charter. Tommy Douglas spoke in support of Broadbent, as did Stanley Knowles. In a vote, 63 per cent supported Broadbent. See Robert Sheppard & Michael Valpy, *The National Deal: The Fight for a Canadian Constitution* (Toronto: Macmillan of Canada, 1982) at 133–34.

37. (Toronto: Thomas Nelson & Sons, 1935).

38. Djwa, *supra* note 12 at 319.

39. *Ibid.*

40. *Ibid* at 318–37.

41. In 1970 as Prime Minister, he appointed her to that most un-CCF institution, the Canadian Senate.

42. See *infra* note 49.

43. *Fiscal Arrangements and Established Programs Act*, 1976–77 SC c 10.

44. See e.g., *Report of the Royal Commission on the Economic Union and Development Prospects for Canada* (Ottawa: Minister of Supply and Services, 1985) at 25, where it is reported that since World War II there has been a steady decline in the share of federal, as compared with provincial-municipal, expenditures: federal expenditures were 51.9% in 1950, and only 38.8% in 1980, while provincial-municipal expenditures grew in the same period from 48.1% to 59.1%; and at 223, the federal share of government revenues dropped from 67.1% in 1955 to 43.3% in 1983, while the provincial-municipal share rose in the same period from 32.9% to 56.7%. See also John English, *Just Watch Me: The Life of Pierre Elliot Trudeau, 1968–2000* (Knopf, 2009) at 362–63.

45. 30&31 Vict, c 3 (UK), now named the *Constitution Act, 1867*.

46. See generally Gérard V La Forest, *Disallowance and Reservation of Provincial Legislation* (Ottawa: Department of Justice, 1955) *passim*.

47. See Djwa, *supra* note 12 at 266–67.

48. Quoted in Pierre Elliot Trudeau, *Federalism and the French Canadians* (Toronto: Macmillan, 1968) at 53.

49. Michael Oliver, ed, (Toronto: University of Toronto Press, 1961).

50. The essay entitled "The Practice and Theory of Federalism" is reproduced in Trudeau, *supra* note 48 at 124. For the passages referred to here, see 148–54.

51. In a brief entitled *Quebec and the Constitutional Problem* that was intended for, but never submitted to, the Constitution Committee of the Quebec Legislative Assembly; reproduced in Trudeau, *supra* note 48 at 3. See especially 44–45.

52. Reproduced in Pierre Trudeau, *Against the Current: Selected Writings* (Gérard Pelletier, ed) (Toronto: McClelland & Stewart, 1996) at 215–16.

53. Reproduced in Trudeau, *supra* note 48 at 182.

54. [1959] SCR 121.

55. Personal files.

11 PIERRE TRUDEAU ENTERS
THE CORRIDORS OF POWER

1. Memorandum to Cabinet, 23 June 1967, Cab. Doc. 383/67.

2. Memorandum to Cabinet, 1 August 1967, Cab. Doc. 470/67.

3. "An Inquiry into the Diefenbaker Bill of Rights" (1959) 37 Can Bar Rev 77.

4. 8–9 Eliz II, c 44.

5. *Mike: The Memoirs of the Rt. Hon. Lester B. Pearson*, vol 1 (Toronto: University of Toronto Press, 1972) at 187–88.

6. Ottawa: Queen's Printer, 1968. Also reproduced in Anne F Bayefsky, *Canada's Constitution Act 1982 and Amendments: A Documentary History*, vol 1 (Whitby: McGraw-Hill Ryerson, 1989) at 51. I do not recall any prior suggestion of the term *Charter*. I assume this was a Gallic preference of the Minister related to a more felicitous rendering in French in place of *Bill of Rights*. Or perhaps it was chosen to distinguish better the proposed instrument from Mr Diefenbaker's rather ineffective statutory measure of 1960.

12 SHAPING THE *CHARTER*

1. Ottawa: Queen's Printer, 1968; also reproduced in Anne F Bayefsky, *Canada's Constitution Act 1982 and Amendments: A Documentary History*, vol 1 (Whitby: McGraw-Hill Ryerson, 1989) at 51.

2. *An Act to amend the Constitution of Canada*, Third Session, Thirtieth Parliament, 26–27 Eliz II, 1977–78; given First Reading on 20 June 1978. Reproduced in Bayefsky, *ibid* vol 1 at 340.

3. Bayefsky, *op. cit. supra* note 1 vol 2 at 574.

4. *Ibid* vol 2 at 599.

5. *Ibid* vol 2 at 669.

6. *Ibid* vol 2 at 678.

7. *Ibid* vol 2 at 745.

8. The Canadian Civil Liberties Association, represented by Professor Walter Tarnopolsky, had been particularly critical of this phraseology: *Minutes of Proceedings and Evidence of the Special Joint Committee of the Senate and House of Commons on the Constitution of Canada, 1980–81* at 7:9.

9. Minutes of Cabinet, 11 December 1980, 86–80 CBM.

10. SC 8–9 Eliz II, c 44, para 1(a).

11. *Supra* note 1.

12. *Ibid* at 19–20 of the Trudeau paper, reproduced in Bayefsky, vol 1 at 56.

13. E.g., Pierre Trudeau, *The Constitution and the People of Canada* (Ottawa: Queen's Printer, 1969) at 52; Bill C-60, *supra* note 2; federal draft of July 4, 1980, presented to the CCMC, *supra* note 4.

14. *Supra* note 5.

15. *Supra* note 7.

16. The term "fundamental justice," as it had appeared in the *Canadian Bill of Rights*, had been interpreted by the Supreme Court in *Duke v the Queen* [1972] SCR 917 as guaranteeing procedural rights.

17. *Minutes, supra* note 8 at 46:32–34.

18. [1985] SCR 486.

19. *Ibid* para 50.

20. *Ibid* para 21.

21. *Ibid* para 62.

22. See my analysis in "*The Constitution Act, 1982:* The Foreseen and the Unforeseen," (2007) 16 Const Forum Const 2, 51 at 56.

23. Barry L Strayer, *Patriation of the Constitution and the Charter: 25 Years After*. The Timlin Lecture, University of Saskatchewan, 2007, at 18–24.

24. [2005] 1 SCR 791. See also AG *Canada v* PHS *Community Services Society et al* 2011 SCC 44 paras 126–35, where the Court found the refusal by the Minister of National Health to issue to a Vancouver needle clinic a discretionary exemption under the *Controlled Drugs and Substances Act* was a violation of fundamental justice for the staff and clientele, thus determining that the provision of a safe environment for illegal drug users was in effect underwritten by the *Charter*.

25. *Four Essays on Liberty* (Oxford University Press, 1969) at 118.

26. I have discussed this at more length elsewhere. See Barry L Strayer, "In the Beginning...The Origins of Section 15 of the Charter," 2006 5 JL & Equality 13 at 17–19; Timlin Lectures, *supra* note 23 at 18–19.

27. *Supra* note 1.

28. Reproduced in Bayefsky, *op cit supra* note 1, vol 2 at 670.

29. See e.g., *Minutes supra* note 8 at 9:125–28.

30. *Bliss v* AG *Canada* [1979] 1 SCR 183.

31. *Lavell v* AG *Canada* [1974] SCR 1349.

32. For a discussion of these developments see, e.g., Dale Gibson, *The Law of the Charter: Equality Rights* (Toronto: Carswell, 1990) at 42–43; Roy Romanow, John Whyte, & Howard Leeson, *Canada...Notwithstanding: The Making of the Constitution, 1976–1982* (Toronto: Carswell/Methuen, 1984) at 253–56.

33. I have related elsewhere how certain groups were apprehensive about this declaration of equality for all and managed to get some recognition of their particularity in other sections of the *Charter*: the status Indian leadership who obtained section 25; ethnic minorities who obtained section 27; and the Catholic hierarchy of Newfoundland who obtained section 29. One group, the monarchists, who feared that section 15 would abolish the Canadian monarchy by requiring the Crown to descend equally through male and female lines (which it does not) and eliminate the requirement that the head of state be a Protestant (as still specified in the *Act of Settlement, 1701*). We managed to reassure them and no change was made to meet their concerns. See "In the Beginning...The Origins of Section 15 of the Charter," *supra* note 26 at 21–23.

34. *Supra* note 30.

35. *Supra* note 10.

36. *Supra* note 1 and accompanying text.

37. Reproduced in Bayefsky, *op cit supra* note 1, vol 2 at 681.

38. See Romanow et al, *supra* note 32 at 241–42.

39. [1981] 1 SCR 753.

40. See e.g., Romanow et al, *supra* note 32 at 207–12; Robert Sheppard & Michael Valpy, *The National Deal: The Fight for a Canadian Constitution* (Toronto: Macmillan of Canada, 1982) at 263–302; Ron Graham, *The Last Act: Pierre Trudeau, the Gang of Eight, and the Fight for Canada* (Toronto: Allen Lane, 2011), Parts 1, 2, and 3; Howard Leeson, *The Patriation Minutes* (Edmonton: Centre for Constitutional Studies, University of Alberta, 2011) *passim*; J Peter Meekison, ed, *Constitutional Patriation: The Lougheed-Lévesque Correspondence* (Institute of Intergovernmental Relations, Queen's University/Canada West Foundation, 1999) at 15–30.

41. Leeson, *ibid* at 70.

13   A SOCIAL DEMOCRAT IN THE COURT
OF THE PHILOSPHER KING

1. Max Nemni & Monique Nemni, *Young Trudeau: Son of Quebec, Father of Canada, 1919–1944* (Toronto: McClelland & Stewart, 2006) at 217–25.

2. See e.g., *The Practice and Theory of Federalism* (originally published as an essay) in Michael Oliver, ed, *Social Purpose for Canada* (Toronto: University of Toronto Press, 1961), reproduced in Pierre Elliot Trudeau, *Federalism and the French Canadians* (Toronto: Macmillan, 1968) at 124.

3. Record of Federal-Provincial Conference of First Ministers on the Constitution, Ottawa, morning session 11 September 1980.

14 SUMMING UP

1. I have written more extensively on these themes in Barry L Strayer, *Patriation and the Charter: 25 Years After* (Timlin Lecture, University of Saskatchewan, 2007), and Barry L Strayer *"The Constitution Act, 1982*: The Foreseen and the Unforeseen" (2007) 16 Const Forum Const 51.
2. I have described these events in chapters 8 and 9.
3. "Close to one third of Canadians unsure if new constitution good," *Ottawa Citizen* (19 June 1982) 4.
4. Kirk Makin, "Two Thirds Back Electing Judges: Twenty-Five Years Later, poll shows strong support for Charter," *Globe and Mail* (9 April 2007) A5.
5. Reproduced in Anne F Bayefsky, *Canada's Constitution Act 1982 and Amendments: A Documentary History*, vol 2 (Whitby: McGraw-Hill Ryerson, 1989) at 805.
6. See chapter 9.
7. Howard Leeson, *The Patriation Minutes* (Edmonton: Centre for Constitutional Studies, University of Alberta, 2011) at 28, 49; Ron Graham, *The Last Act: Pierre Trudeau, the Gang of Eight, and the Fight for Canada* (Toronto: Allen Lane, 2011) at 78.
8. RSQ c C-12.
9. J Peter Meekison, ed, *Constitutional Patriation: The Lougheed-Lévesque Correspondence* (Institute of Intergovernmental Relations, Queen's University/Canada West Foundation, 1999) at 7.
10. Graham, *supra* note 7 at 88, 136; Leeson, *supra* note 7 at 50, 58.
11. Barry L Strayer, *Judicial Review of Legislation in Canada* (Toronto: University of Toronto Press, 1968).
12. Barry L Strayer, *The Canadian Constitution and the Courts: The Function and Scope of Judicial Review*, 3d ed (Toronto: Butterworths, 1968).
13. *Reference re s 94(2) of the Motor Vehicle Act*, RSBC 1979 [1985] 2 SCR 486.
14. I have dealt with these subjects in more detail in the materials cited in note 1, *supra*. See Timlin Lecture at 14 Const Forum Const article at 54–57.
15. See e.g., *Haig v Canada* (1992), 9 OR (3d) 495 (OCA); *Vriend v Alberta* [1998] 1 SCR 493.
16. I have written on this at greater length in the *Constitutional Forum* article cited in note 1 at 57–60.
17. *Latham v Canada* [1984] 2 FC 734 (TD).
18. *Supra* note 13.
19. It has recently been held that the *Act* does not authorize the use of Deputy Judges who are 75 or older: *Felipa v Canada* 2011 FCA 272.
20. *Sfetkopoulos v Canada* [2008] 3 FCR 399; *aff'd* [2008] FCJ No 1472; *leave to appeal refused* [2008] SCCA No 531.

21. *Smith Kline & French v Canada* [1986] 1 FC 274 (TD).
22. [1987] 2 FC 359.
23. [1988] 3 FC 515 (TD).
24. [1992] 2 SCR 679.

INDEX

Hatfield, Richard, 137, 146, 215–16
Hawthorn Report, 54
Hayes, Harry, 153
Hnatyshyn, Ray, 17–18, 156
Hogg, Peter, 131
Hong Kong, constitutional reform, 42–43, 83–85
House of Commons, reform of, 94, 100
Howe, C.D., 190
Howe, Sir Geoffrey, 42
Hugessen, J.A., 288
human rights
    constitutional conference (1960–61), 232–33
    criticism of patriation package (1980), 148–49
    democratic socialism and, 225, 227–35, 271
    historical background, 64–65, 225–27
    human rights culture, 80, 86, 277, 281, 284
    joint committee on UN Declaration (1947–48), 225–26
    positive and negative rights, 77, 86, 261–62, 265
    See also bill of rights; *Canadian Charter of Rights and Freedoms; Canadian Human Rights Act; International Covenant on Civil and Political Rights* and *Optional Protocol, UN; Universal Declaration of Human Rights, UN*
Human Rights Institute, University of Ottawa, 166–67
Hunt, Douglas, 171

ICCPR. See *International Covenant on Civil and Political Rights* and *Optional Protocol, UN*
ICESCR. See *International Covenant on Economic, Social and Cultural Rights, UN*

Independent Labour Party, 229
India, sovereignty, 35, 180
Indian Act
    CHRA not to affect, 73
    status of Indian women, 79–80, 264
    UN Human Rights Committee complaints, 79–80
Indians. *See* Aboriginal peoples
International Covenant on Civil and Political Rights and *Optional Protocol, UN*
    BLS's role in Canada, 77–83
    BLS's role in Hong Kong, 83–85
    Canada as member on UN Human Rights Committee, 78–79
    coming into effect, 79, 247
    complaints by individuals, 78, 79–80
    compliance report from Canada, 80–83, 227
    equality of benefits, 265–66
    equality rights, 262–63
    impact of, 80, 226–27, 247, 284
    legal obligations for rights, 78
    limitations in, 249, 252, 254
    self-determination (Art 1, s 1), 78, 82–83
International Covenant on Economic, Social and Cultural Rights, UN
    BLS's role in, 77–78, 83–86
    human rights culture, 284
    impact of, 226–27, 247
Inuit peoples, rights, 159
    See also Aboriginal peoples
Ireland, sovereignty, 34–35

Jackson, Michael, 188
James Bay land claims, 60–61
Japanese-Canadians, internment of, 230
Jean, Michaëlle, *291*
Johnson, A.W., 7, 13

Nehru, Jawaharlal, xii
Neill, Patrick, 187
Nemni, Max and Monique, 219, 221
Nepal, constitutional reform, 85–86
New Brunswick, constitutional
   reform, 137, 146, 177
New Democratic Party
   for Aboriginal rights, 157–58,
      202–03
   BLS as member, 17, 20, 31, 148,
      272–73
   BLS's role in legal policies of,
      65–66, 271
   for constitutional bill of rights, 159,
      235
   for Saskatchewan positions on
      resources and taxation, 160–61
   See also democratic socialism
New Zealand, sovereignty, 3, 294n8
Newfoundland, constitutional reform
   conference (1980), 136–37
   fisheries (s 91, head 12), 127
   Labrador's status, 52–53
   offshore natural resources, 112–13
   patriation reference, 168–73
   Patriation Reference, 170, 172–79
   religious school funding, 50–52, 162
   trade re hydroelectricity (1981),
      171–72
Nisga'a land claims, 56–57
notwithstanding clause. See Canadian
   Charter of Rights and Freedoms,
   by section, notwithstanding
   clause (s 33)
Nova Scotia, constitutional reform, 33,
   137, 159

October Crisis (1970), 234, 294n5
offshore resources, constitutional
   reform, 112–13, 115
Ontario, constitutional reform
   compact theory of Confederation,
      139, 176

conference (1967), 23–24, 245–46
conferences and discussions, 9,
   124, 137
patriation preparations (1980), 146
Patriation Reference, 177
Task Force on Canadian Unity
   (1977), 90
O'Sullivan, Joseph F., 169
Oxford University, BLS at, 5–6, 6, 19,
   39, 187–89, 248

Parliament of Canada committees
   joint committee on human rights
      (1947–48), 225–26
   See also entries beginning with
      Special Joint Committee
Parliament of United Kingdom. See
   United Kingdom Parliament
Parole Act, 285–86
Parti Québécois, 89–90
Patent Act, 287–89
patriation and amending (1980 Oct
   to 1982)
   Aboriginal rights, 157–58
   BLS's views on, 277–81
   conference (Nov 1981), 195–202, 198
   Kershaw Report, 166, 183–85,
      188–89, 194
   patriation references in provincial
      courts of appeal (1980–81), 168–72
   public hearings, 153–54
   public opinion, 195, 280–81
   submissions and consultations, 153
   terminology, 4
   time frame for patriation process,
      151–52, 153, 165, 173–74
   See also Canada Act, 1982 (United
      Kingdom); Patriation Reference;
      Special Joint Committee on
      the Constitution (1980 Oct to
      1981 Feb); United Kingdom
      Parliament, patriation process
      and entries beginning with

legislation on request from
  Canada, 3–4
negotiations for patriation process,
  38–43
opposition in UK to, 182–83
patriation difficulties (1981–82),
  179–80
patriation framework (1971), 37–38,
  45–48
preparation for (1980–81), 141–49,
  180–91
"request and consent" Minute,
  204–06
Thatcher's support for, 194–95
time frame for patriation process
  (1981), 151–52, 153, 165, 173–74
See also Canada Act, 1982 (United
  Kingdom)
United Nations international
  covenants, See entries beginning
  with International Covenant
United Nations Universal Declaration
  of Human Rights. See Universal
  Declaration of Human Rights, UN
United States
  influence on medicare in
    Saskatchewan, 12, 13
  influence on treatment of
    Japanese-Canadians, 230
United States Bill of Rights, 247
United States Constitution
  due process (Fifth Amendment),
    155, 249, 256–58, 282
  full faith and credit (Article IV),
    127
  Kelsen's theory of constitutional
    legitimacy, 32
United States Supreme Court
  BLS on judicial activism, 224, 271,
    284
  due process, 155, 249, 282
  freedom of speech restraints, 71

Universal Declaration of Human
  Rights, UN
  equality rights, 262–63
  impact of, 225–26, 247, 284
  positive and negative rights, 77
University Consortium on North
  American Research, 193, 211
University of Saskatchewan
  BLS as professor, xvi, 5–6, 11, 17,
    19–20, 27, 28, 65–66, 142, 250
  BLS as student, x, xiv–xv, 67, 156

Victoria Conference (1971)
  issues, 44, 47
  media coverage, 44
  powers of disallowance and
    reservation, 47, 240–41
  preparations for, 30–31, 35–38,
    44–45
  Quebec's issues, 31, 44–45, 48–49,
    211, 241
  two-stage amending process, 35–36
Victoria Charter, 37–38, 40–43,
  240–41
Victoria Charter (UK Enactment),
  45–46
Victoria Charter, failure of, 48–49,
  87
Victoria Formula, 31, 110, 147, 184,
  196, 207, 211, 281

Waddell, Ian, 158
Wadds, Jean, 145
Walker, Robert A., 7, 233
War Measures Act, 234, 267, 295n5
Wells, Clyde, 170–72, 175
Westminster. See United Kingdom
  Parliament, patriation process
Whyte, John, 148, 159, 201
Winnipeg General Strike of 1919,
  227–28
"W.L.M.K." (Scott), 248

Other Titles from
The University of Alberta Press

RETIRING THE CROW RATE
A Narrative of Political Management

Arthur Kroeger; John Fraser, Afterword

280 pages • 20 B&W photographs, map, charts, notes,
bibliography, index
Political Science/Agriculture/Memoir
978-0-88864-513-5 | $34.95 (T) paper

FORGING ALBERTA'S
CONSTITUTIONAL FRAMEWORK

Richard Connors & John M. Law, Editors

576 pages • Notes, bibliography, index
Canadian History/Law
978-0-88864-457-2 | $65.00 (S) cloth
978-0-88864-458-9 | $49.95 (S) paper

THE ALBERTA SUPREME COURT
AT 100
History and Authority

Jonathan Swainger, Editor

392 pages • B&W photos, index
Copublished with The Osgoode Society for Canadian
Legal History
Canadian History
978-0-88864-493-0 | $45.00 (S) cloth

CPSIA information can be obtained at www.ICGtesting.com
Printed in the USA
LVOW130144171212

311920LV00005BA/12/P